The Battle over Spanish between 1800 and 2000

This book examines the ways in which a group of key Spanish and Latin American intellectuals of the nineteenth and twentieth centuries discussed the concept of Spanish as a language, and how these discussions related to the construction of national identities and the idea of a Hispanic culture.

Among the many historical processes that have characterized the life of Spain and Latin American nations over the past two hundred years, two are particularly relevant for this book: Spain's modernization, and the postcolonial construction of the Hispanic community. Also dealt with is a phenomenon closely associated with these processes – the discussion of language matters in various spheres of public life.

Key issues include:

- The political character of the debate over what Spanish is, what it represents, and who has the authority to settle linguistic disputes.
- The specific form these discussions have taken in the context of the lives of Hispanic nations during the nineteenth and twentieth centuries.
- The role of institutions such as the Spanish Royal Academy and the Instituto Cervantes.
- The role of leading intellectuals such as Andrés Bello, Domingo Faustino Sarmiento, Juan Valera, Rufino José Cuervo, Miguel de Unamuno, Ramón Menéndez Pidal, José Ortega y Gasset and José María Arguedas.

This book will be essential reading for sociolinguists, scholars of the Spanish language, historians of Hispanic culture, and all those with an interest in the relationship between language and culture.

José del Valle teaches Spanish language and linguistics at Fordham University. He has published articles on linguistics and Hispanic cultural history in journals such as *Bulletin of Hispanic Studies*, *Hispanic Review*, *Language and Communication*, and *Quimera*. He is author of *El trueque s/x en español antiguo: aproximaciones teóricas* (Tübingen, 1996).

Luis Gabriel-Stheeman teaches Spanish language and literature at The College of New Jersey. He has published articles on Spanish and Latin American contemporary narrative in journals such as *Inti* and *Estudios orteguianos* and more recently, *Función retórica del recurso etimológico en la obra de José Ortega y Gasset* (Coruña, 2000).

Routledge Studies in the History of Linguistics
Series Editor: Talbot Taylor

1 Linguistics and the Third Reich
Mother-tongue fascism, race and the science of language
Christopher M. Hutton

2 Women, Language and Linguistics
Three American stories from the first half of the twentieth century
Julia S. Falk

3 Ethnocentrism and the English Dictionary
Phil Benson

4 The Battle Over Spanish Between 1800 and 2000
Language ideologies and Hispanic intellectuals
Edited by José del Valle and Luis Gabriel-Stheeman

The Battle over Spanish between 1800 and 2000

Language ideologies and Hispanic intellectuals

Edited by José del Valle and
Luis Gabriel-Stheeman

London and New York

First published 2002 by Routledge
2 Park Square, Milton Park, Abingdon, Oxon OX14 4RN
Simultaneously published in the USA and Canada
by Routledge
711 Third Ave, New York, NY 10017

Routledge is an imprint of the Taylor & Francis Group

First issued in paperback 2012

© 2002 Editorial material and selection, Jose del Valle and
Luis Gabriel-Stheeman, individual chapters, the authors

Typeset in Baskerville by BC Typesetting, Bristol

All rights reserved. No part of this book may be reprinted or
reproduced or utilised in any form or by any electronic, mechanical,
or other means, now known or hereafter invented, including
photocopying and recording, or in any information storage or
retrieval system, without permission in writing from the publishers.

British Library Cataloguing in Publication Data
A catalogue record for this book is available from the British Library

Library of Congress Cataloguing in Publication Data
The battle over Spanish between 1800 and 2000: language ideologies
and hispanic intellectuals/edited by José del Valle and Luis Gabriel-
Stheeman.
   p.   cm.
  Includes bibliographical references and index.
    1. Spanish language–Political apsects. 2. Spanish language–
Social aspects. 3. Spain–Intellectual life–19th century.
4. Spain–Intellectual life–20th century. 5. Latin America–
Intellectual life–19th century 6. Latin America–Intellectual
life–20th century. I. Valle, José del. II. Gabriel-Stheeman,
Luis, 1962–

PC4074.73.B38 2001
460′.9′09034–dc21   2001019653

ISBN13: 978-0-415-25256-0 (HBK)
ISBN13: 978-0-415-62978-2 (PBK)

Contents

Contributors   viii
Biographical notes   ix
Preface   xii
Acknowledgments   xiv

1 Nationalism, *hispanismo*, and monoglossic culture   1
JOSÉ DEL VALLE AND LUIS GABRIEL-STHEEMAN

Introduction 1
The two phases of nationalism 1
Spanish nationalism and its challenges 4
The persistence of the cultural empire 6
The acceptance of language as a national symbol 7
The language battle 9
Monoglossic culture and the dogma of homogeneism *10*
Linguistic reasoning and legitimacy 12
Notes 13

2 Linguistic anti-academicism and Hispanic community: Sarmiento and Unamuno   14
BARRY L. VELLEMAN

Sarmiento, the Generation of 1837, and Spain 14
Sarmiento and the Spanish Royal Academy 18
Sarmiento and orthographic reform 20
Sarmiento's conception of the norm 24
Sarmiento and Unamuno: spiritual twins 25
Language and society 27
Sarmiento, Unamuno, and the RAE 28
Linguistic and social regeneration 30
The fragmentation polemic 31

vi   *Contents*

> *Unamuno's view of Latin America* 34
> *Conclusion* 35
> *Notes* 36

3 **The ideological construction of an empirical base: selection and elaboration in Andrés Bello's grammar**   42
   BELFORD MORÉ

> *Preserving unity, producing unity* 42
> *Selection and grammatical knowledge* 43
> *Selection criteria* 44
> *Notes* 60

4 **Historical linguistics and cultural history: the polemic between Rufino José Cuervo and Juan Valera**   64
   JOSÉ DEL VALLE

> *The polemic* 65
> *The linguistic-cultural context: Valera* 68
> *The linguistic-cultural context: Cuervo* 71
> *Notes* 75

5 **Menéndez Pidal, national regeneration and the linguistic utopia**   78
   JOSÉ DEL VALLE

> *Pidal and the turn-of-the-century crisis* 78
> *Pidal and the language battle* 80
> *Regaining hegemony* 81
> *Holding the* skeptron 82
> *Spreading the word* 85
> *Unity and uniformity: the academic texts* 86
> *Unity and uniformity: the popularizing texts* 89
> *Laws of linguistic gravity* 91
> *"We"* 93
> *Erasing dissent* 96
> *Spanish: a* modern *language* 98
> *Notes* 100

6 **"For their own good": the Spanish identity and its Great Inquisitor, Miguel de Unamuno**   106
   JOAN RAMON RESINA

> *Notes* 128

7 A nobleman grabs the broom: Ortega y Gasset's verbal hygiene 134
LUIS GABRIEL-STHEEMAN

Ortega as a language maven 134
On understanding Ortega's verbal hygiene 137
Ortega's linguistic reasoning 140
The social dimension 147
The Spanish dimension: society 150
The Spanish dimension: geography 153
The rhetorical factor 156
The question of authority 160
Notes 161

8 José María Arguedas: Peruvian Spanish as subversive assimilation 167
JOHN C. LANDREAU

Introduction 167
Spanish and the unification of Peru: 1880–1930 168
Arguedas and the assimilationist position 172
Transculturation and Peruvian Spanish 176
Spanish as translation: the utopia of language 180
Conclusion 185
Notes 185

9 "Codo con codo": Hispanic community and the language spectacle 193
JOSÉ DEL VALLE AND LUIS GABRIEL-STHEEMAN

So . . . ? 193
Language grandeur*: Spanish on three battlefronts 195*
The fragility of language: the need for a linguistic elite 199
The language pyramid, ignorance and disloyalty 200
Cultural unity and the language spectacle 204
His master's voice 206
Disruption and discipline 207
The language monarchy 210
Notes 212

References 217
Index 231

Contributors

José del Valle teaches Spanish language and linguistics at Fordham University. He has published articles on linguistics and Hispanic cultural history in journals such as *Bulletin of Hispanic Studies*, *Hispanic Review*, *Language and Communication*, and *Quimera*. He is the author of *El trueque s/x en español antiguo: aproximaciones teóricas* (Tübingen, 1996).

Luis Gabriel-Stheeman teaches Spanish language and literature at The College of New Jersey. He has published articles on Spanish and Latin American contemporary narrative in journals such as *Inti* and *Estudios orteguianos* and, more recently, *Función retórica del recurso etimológico en la obra de José Ortega y Gasset* (Coruña, 2000).

John C. Landreau is Associate Professor of Spanish at The College of New Jersey. He is currently finishing a book manuscript on the work of José María Arguedas. His articles on Andean language and literature have appeared in journals such as *Revista Iberoamericana* and *Latin American Essays*.

Belford Moré teaches Latin American literature at the Universidad de Los Andes. His research focuses on Venezuelan and Latin American literary criticism and history. He has published articles in journals such as *Estudios* and *Voz y escritura*.

Joan Ramon Resina is Professor of Romance Studies and Comparative Literature at Cornell University. His research is divided between literary and visual studies of the city and the critique of academic disciplines. He is the author of several books including most recently *El cadáver en la cocina. La novela policíaca en la cultura del desencanto* (Barcelona, 1997). He has edited four volumes and is the editor of *Diacritics*.

Barry L. Velleman is Professor of Spanish at Marquette University. He is currently researching topics in the cultural and linguistic history of Latin America and Spain. His publications include *Andrés Bello y sus libros* (Caracas, 1995). His book *My Dear Sir: Mary Mann's Letters to Sarmiento: 1865–1881* is scheduled to appear in 2001.

Biographical notes

Andrés Bello (Venezuela, 1781–Chile, 1865) was the foremost Latin American humanist of the nineteenth century. During the decades he spent in London (1810-1829), Bello investigated literary, cultural and scientific topics and published a number of poetic works and short studies in the journals which he founded (*Repertorio americano*, *Biblioteca americana*). Bello's most active period was in Chile (1829-1865), where he founded the University of Chile (1843), serving as its President until his death, and wrote Chile's *Civil Code* (1856), a *Cosmography* (1848), and numerous studies on Roman and International Law, science, literary criticism, philosophy and education. His *Semantic Analysis of the Spanish Tenses* (1841) and *Spanish Grammar* (1847) place him among the most astute and influential language scholars in the history of Hispanic letters.

Domingo Faustino Sarmiento (b. Argentina, 1811; d. Asunción, Paraguay, 1888). He studied educational systems in North America and Europe, contributed to the creation of a pedagogical literature in Latin America, and established schools in Argentina and Chile. In 1842 he was named Rector of the newly-founded Escuela Normal in Santiago. In politics, he was an influential figure and one of the major ideologues of Argentina's transition from a Spanish colony to a modern independent state. He was President of Argentina from 1868 to 1874.

Juan Valera (Spain, 1824–1905). Born and raised in Andalucia, don Juan moved to Madrid as a young adult and pursued a political career, becoming a member of parliament for the Liberal Party. He held important posts in the diplomatic corps, including an ambassadorship to the United States. Valera distinguished himself among his contemporaries as a writer (his best-known novel being *Pepita Jiménez*), but mostly as a true man of letters, an impressive intellectual, and a sharp literary critic. He was a member of the Spanish Royal Academy (one of its most progressive members). He took great interest in "Spanish-American" literature and was instrumental in introducing Ruben Dario's poetry in Spain. Refined diplomat, casual polititian, idealist writer, and enthusiastic polemicist, the Andalucian's oeuvre – which included literary, journalistic and epistolary

x   *Biographical notes*

pieces as well as essays – is a most valuable resource for interpreting nineteenth-century Spain.

Rufino José Cuervo (b. Bogotá, Colombia, 1844; d. Paris, France, 1911). Cuervo is considered to be the greatest Hispanic philologist of the nineteenth century. His classic works include the *Apuntaciones críticas sobre el lenguaje bogotano*, an edition of Bello's *Gramática*, and the *Diccionario de construcción y régimen de la lengua castellana*. He did not pursue an academic career, and only held, early in his life, a few teaching jobs in Bogotá. He made a living running, with his brother, a beer-brewing company. In 1882, the Cuervo brothers sold the factory and moved to Paris, where Rufino José would give his heart and soul to the study of philology until his death.

Miguel de Unamuno (b. Bilbao, Spanish Basque Country, 29 September 1864; d. Salamanca, 12 December 1936). He was a poet, novelist and essayist with a late romantic cast of mind and a tortured obsession with death and the need for certainty about a personal afterlife. A polemical figure who enjoyed and promoted debate, his personality often takes center stage in the expression of his opinions, which often take the form of convictions and are persistently colored by a strong individualism. As a consequence of this subjectivism, he often swapped his social and political views in contradictory ways. From his platform as Rector of the University of Salamanca, he took part in public life through intense writing for the press and eventually came to see himself as a prophetic figure and a moral leader of Spain. A substantial part of his thought helped to give form to the discourse of Spanish nationalism and an expansive Transatlantic Hispanism based on the substitution of linguistic and cultural hegemony of Castile's "spiritual blood" for Spain's lost imperial dominions. His better known works include the essays *En torno al casticismo* (Barcelona 1902), *Del sentimiento trágico de la vida* (Madrid 1913), *L'agonie du christianisme* (Paris 1925; first Spanish edition: Madrid 1931), and the novels *Niebla* (Madrid 1914), *Abel Sánchez* (Madrid, 1917), and *San Manuel Bueno, mártir* (Madrid 1933).

Ramón Menéndez Pidal (Spain, 1869–1968). A titanic intellectual. His oeuvre includes works in historiography, linguistics, philology, literary history and paleography. His outstanding intelligence, selfless dedication and powerful family connections brought him to positions of great responsibility within Spain's cultural and political establishment. His power within the cultural institutions of the state (he was Head of the Center for Historical Studies and Director of the Spanish Royal Academy) enabled him to create a prolific and wide-ranging school of thought deeply committed to the regeneration of Spain through intellectual and cultural development. His biographers often associate him with the members of the Generation of 98.

José Ortega y Gasset (1883–1955) is Spain's most important philosopher, and one of the very few Spanish thinkers ever to achieve wide international recognition. Educated in Spain and Germany, in 1910 he became Professor of Metaphysics at the University of Madrid. A person of great insight, perspicuity and charisma, Ortega soon became a leading intellectual figure, an advocate of Spain's Europeanization and a passionate, exemplary contributor to his country's cultural and scientific revival. He was a true erudite, a voracious reader and a prolific writer; one versed in a broad range of disciplines that included, besides his philosophical interests, art criticism, history, sociology and linguistics. He founded several journals and magazines, including the influential *Revista de Occidente*, a forum through which he introduced to the public a high number of foreign cultural luminaries. Ortega's commitment to Spain's recovery also led him to participate in the political arena, both as an assiduous commentator and as a member of the parliament that elaborated the republican constitution. He is best known for *The Revolt of the Masses* (1930), a clever and controversial analysis of the crisis of modern civilization. His most important works include *The Modern Theme* (1923), *The Dehumanization of Art* (1925) and *Man and People* (1950).

José María Arguedas (Peru, 1911–1969) is one of the most influential twentieth-century Peruvian intellectuals. His prolific writings are almost singularly focused on the place of Andeans, and Andean culture, within Peruvian society. His works include narrative fiction, ethnographies, articles on Andean folklore, as well as numerous collections and translations of songs, stories, legends and myths from Quechua oral tradition. He is perhaps best known for his narrative fiction: his most well-regarded novel is *Los ríos profundos* (1959). One of the most original features of Arguedas's fiction is that it actively incorporates aspects of Quechua orality into written Spanish. This is important because Arguedas viewed the hybrid form and language of his novels as a kind of model in miniature of an ideal Peruvian nation in which social inequality would be eliminated, and the world-view of Quechua-speakers would be foundational.

Preface

Among the many historical processes that have characterized the life of Spain and Latin American nations in the past two hundred years, two are particularly relevant for the present book: Spain's modernization, including the delicate administrative articulation of the state, and the post-colonial construction of the Hispanic community, including Spain's renewed presence in Latin American economies. While we recognize the complexity and multi-dimensionality of these processes – their cultural, economic, political and social repercussions – our project deals more directly with one phenomenon closely associated with them: the discussion of language matters in various spheres of public life. In particular, the present book examines the political essence of the debate over what Spanish is, what it represents, and who has the authority to settle linguistic disputes and dilemmas. The public debate about linguistic topics is in no way new. However, the chapters that follow explore the specific form these discussions have taken in the context of the lives of Hispanic nations during the nineteenth and twentieth centuries.

Since this project revolves around a well-defined aspect of the interface between language and politics, it cannot afford to and is not meant to be comprehensive. For excellent surveys of the politics of language in the Spanish-speaking world, we refer the reader to Miranda Stewart (1999) and Clare Mar-Molinero (2000). These texts offer concise and insightful discussions of the broad spectrum of language debates surrounding Spanish.

The – at times latent – linguistic debates that constitute the thematic core of this book are far from settled (as chapter 9 will show). Numerous examples of the existing controversies can still be found in Spain's daily press and in popular as well as academic publications: Angel López García's award winning *El rumor de los desarraigados* (1985), Gregorio Salvador's *Lengua española y lenguas de España* (1987), Fernando Lázaro Carreter's *El dardo en la palabra* (1997), Juan M. Lope Blanch's *La lengua española y sus problemas* (1997), Alex Grijelmo's *Defensa apasionada del idioma español* (1998), Juan Ramón Lodares' *El paraíso políglota* (2000), etc. The publication of these essays and the commercial success of most of them attest to the currency of the issue and underscore the need to produce critical approaches to such influential texts.

To date, in the Hispanic intellectual context there has been a remarkable absence of in-depth critical studies of the ideological/political foundations and implications of linguistic standardization. While there is a continuing tradition of works calling for the maintenance of a unitary *and* uniform linguistic standard across the Spanish-speaking world, there have been few attempts to study the inevitably hierarchical structures that result from such efforts.

With this book we hope to spark among Spanish and Latin American intellectuals, as well as among Hispanists everywhere, a discussion that will lead to a useful critical analysis of the public debate about language. There is no question that we are presenting our readers with a piece of sociopolitically engaged scholarship. Given the political twist of our academic undertaking – its provocative character – we can only hope that our ideological or intellectual adversaries respond to our texts not with anger or disdain, but with alternative analyses and with careful critiques of their own.

Acknowledgments

We would like to express our gratitude to the people who helped us proofread the final version of the text. Our thanks to Joe Goebel, Susan Martin-Márquez, Peggy Van Kirk and Barry Velleman; very special thanks to Regina Morin. We would also like to acknowledge Tim Connelly's assistance with the translation of chapter 4 from its original Spanish version.

We thank The College of New Jersey's FIRSL Committee for granting Luis Gabriel-Stheeman a course reduction for the completion of this project.

We are grateful to our contributors for accepting our challenge and agreeing to collaborate in our project. Their diligence and willingness to maintain a constant dialogue with us have allowed us to produce a well-focused and cohesive text. We are especially grateful to Barry Velleman for his invaluable help with bibliographic matters.

This book would have not been possible without the guidance and support of Routledge's editorial and production teams. Special thanks go to Joe Whiting, Annabel Watson and Tom Chandler. We are particularly indebted to Tolly Taylor. His willingness to listen to our ideas, his confidence in the viability of our project and his generous, expert advice were essential to successfully launch this work.

A slightly abbreviated Spanish version of chapter 4 appeared in R. Blake, D. Ranson, and R. Wright (eds.), *Essays in Hispanic Linguistics Dedicated to Paul M. Lloyd*, Delaware: Juan de la Cuesta, 1999. Thanks to Tom Lathrop and Juan de la Cuesta for permission to translate and reprint this article. Chapter 6 was originally presented at the conference "De nuevo el 98" held at UCLA on 29–31 October 1998. It has been previously published in J. Torrecilla (ed.), *La Generación del 98 frente al nuevo fin de siglo* (Amsterdam: Rodopi, 2000), 235–67. Thanks to Fred van der Zee and Rodopi for granting us permission to reprint it.

1 Nationalism, *hispanismo*, and monoglossic culture

José del Valle and Luis Gabriel-Stheeman

Introduction

In the history of Hispanic culture, the first few decades of the nineteenth century were marked by the independence movements that led to the birth of most Latin American nations (Cuba and Puerto Rico would remain Spanish until the fateful year, 1898). The movement toward independence of Spanish colonies was not an exclusively political phenomenon; it was accompanied by various projects of cultural emancipation, by a cultural schism. Latin American liberalism was surely influenced by a number of Spanish intellectuals (C. M. Rama 1982: 67–102), but the failure of the Spanish liberal project – evidenced by Spain's submission to Napoleon (1808–14) and the subsequent setback under Ferdinand VII (1814–33) – caused the intellectual leaders of the independence movement to shift their attention from the former metropolis to the French and Anglo-Saxon world. While these nations represented progress and modernity, functioning as beacons for the young Latin American nations, Spain continued to be identified by many with the Inquisition and the reactionary structures of traditional societies.

Naturally, in Latin America, independence created the urgent need to construct the administrative structures and cultural contents through which nations materialize. In Spain, despite the existence of the political infrastructures and cultural prestige of one of the old national states, liberal politicians and intellectuals also confronted the challenge of creating a *modern* nation that would serve the interest of what was becoming the new dominant social class, the bourgeoisie.

The two phases of nationalism

In contrast with the ideas spread by the creators of nationalist mythology, many contemporary scholars have emphasized the modern character of the nation. Contrary to its conception as a natural and eternal entity, endowed with an objective existence, many historians define it as a construct, or, to use Benedict Anderson's well-known term, as an *imagined community* (1983).

After the Age of Revolutions, the power of the state was displaced from the monarchy, the aristocracy, and the interests they represented, to the bourgeoisie; this change in the source of power entailed a parallel displacement of sovereignty from God to the people. It was at this point that the state, the nation and the people became equated and that the material and ideological creation of the nation occurred. According to Hobsbawm, the nineteenth century witnessed the unfolding of the first phase of nationalism, favored by the liberal bourgeoisie and closely connected with the development of capitalism. In this period, the great national states – many of which had emerged during the Renaissance – completed their construction. The correlation between capitalism and national development had a clear corollary: only those territories in which economic growth was possible could be considered nations. This is what Hobsbawm refers to as the *threshold principle*, which he illustrates with the following statements made in the nineteenth century by the German liberal economist Friedrich List:

> A large population and an extensive territory endowed with manifold national resources, are essential requirements of the normal nationality . . . A nation restricted in the number of its population and in territory, especially if it has a separate language, can only possess a crippled literature, crippled institutions for promoting art and science. A small state can never bring to complete perfection within its territory the various branches of production.
> (quoted in Hobsbawm 1992: 30–1)

For Hobsbawm, three other criteria, in addition to the threshold principle, were established to determine whether a territory could constitute a national entity: "Historic association with a state, . . . a long-established cultural elite, *possessing a written national literary and administrative vernacular*, . . . and a proven capacity for conquest" (37–8, emphasis added). As we can see, one of these criteria makes reference to language. However, according to Hobsbawm, in the discourse of nineteenth-century liberal nationalism, the connection between language and nation was stated much less emphatically than it would be after 1880, the onset of the second phase of nationalism. The existence of a national language was certainly considered a defining criterion, but it was taken for granted that all citizens would adopt it as a model of linguistic behavior in view of the obvious material advantages that could be derived from its knowledge and use. With this attitude, the presence of other languages – minority languages as well as dialectal usage – was not perceived as a threat, but as a natural situation that, in an equally natural fashion, would be progressively modified according to the dictates of the laws of progress.

After 1880, however, a new type of nationalism started to emerge. Ignoring the threshold principle, this new nationalism based its discourse mainly on linguistic and ethnic criteria. Several reasons have been proposed as reasons for this new development. Among them, two are particularly useful for understanding the attitude of philology and modern linguistics towards language (Hobsbawm 1992: 109–11). The first one is the democratization of politics, which reduced, at least on the surface, the distance between the common citizen and the institutions of power. The capitalist bourgeoisie, in order to ground its power in the sovereign *people*, had to create mechanisms that allowed the citizens to intervene – or at least appear to intervene – in matters of the state. At the same time, the defenders of the capitalist national state had to create more or less subtle control mechanisms that guaranteed the loyalty of the individual to the dominant system. Thus the modern state infiltrated the daily life of all its citizens, through the school, the army, the police, the postal system, the census, the telegraph and the railway system. This complex administrative network facilitated the spread of ideas from the top down, but it also allowed for the rapid diffusion of ideas that were contrary to the established order. Towards the end of the nineteenth century, the *new* highly popular nationalisms competed with the national state for the loyalty of the citizens. Consequently, the great nations would have to use the full power of the ideological state apparatus in order to spread their idea of nation and integrate all citizens, persuading them of their membership in a national, cultural and *linguistic* whole.

A second reason for the appearance of the new nationalism was the great population movements. Migrations brought into contact peoples who spoke different dialects and mutually unintelligible languages and increased the linguistic, cultural and social diversity of urban centers. The growth and greater protagonism of non-traditional social groups, due to the mobility of capitalist liberal society, seemed to weaken the political, cultural and linguistic order that in the first phase of nationalism had remained unquestioned. Next to the urban bourgeoisie and its cultural elite, new groups of population were growing, and their linguistic usage – as well as many other patterns of behavior – displayed a disconcerting distance from the standard language. The emergence of these centrifugal elements triggered the intensification of a homogenizing centripetal activity. These trends, as González Stephan has indicated, often manifested themselves in the elaboration of *disciplinary texts* ["escrituras disciplinarias"], that is, texts that civilize subjectivity: constitutions, grammars and etiquette handbooks:

> El proyecto de nación y ciudadanía fue un imaginario de minorías pero . . . se postuló como expansivo, y que efectivamente tuvo la capacidad de englobar-domesticar a comunidades diferenciales que ofrecían resistencia a costa de no fáciles negociaciones.[1]
> (González Stephan 1995: 25)

In sum, the emergence of language-based peripheral nationalisms and the protagonism of marginal social groups forced the defenders of liberal nationalism to react by intensifying the production of discourses that would secure the loyalty of citizens as well as their faith in the indivisible unity of the national state.

Spanish nationalism and its challenges

From this perspective, it seems reasonable to suggest that nineteenth-century Spain was an ideal candidate for the construction of one of the great European national states. Its size practically guaranteed compliance with the threshold principle; its historical association with a state apparatus was unquestionable; its capacity for conquest could still be dreamed of, thanks to its imperial past, the actual remains of the empire, and more recent expansionist adventures:

> The capture of Tetuan evoked a nation-wide apotheosis of the army with the queen as the heiress of the Great Isabella. The war brought no territorial gains . . . but vindicated Spain's mission against the infidel and slaked the thirst for national regeneration . . . this was a proof that national patriotism could still subsume regional loyalties in the sixties.
>
> (Carr 1982: 261)

Finally, the existence of a cultural elite loyal to the administrative and literary standard was the obvious legacy of a long tradition that could be traced back to the *alfonsí* court and Renaissance humanism, that had culminated in 1713 with the creation of the Spanish Royal Academy, that would be continued in the twentieth century in the form of a prestigious school of philological and linguistic studies (cf. chapter 5), and that will be maintained, it seems, in the twenty-first century by highly publicized, state and corporately funded, cultural-linguistic institutions (cf. chapter 9).

Throughout the nineteenth century, Spain slowly engaged in the project of articulating the territory of the state as a modern nation: the railway, the extension of the postal network, the creation of national banks, the expansion of the school system and the opening of government offices in all provinces, are some of the accomplishments associated with modernization and national construction. According to García de Cortázar and González Vesga, the 1812 Constitution had already established the bases for a national unification:

> Hasta el más mínimo detalle es regulado por la Constitución de 1812, cuyo diseño de Estado unitario imponía los derechos de los *españoles* por encima de los históricos de cada *reino*. La igualdad de los ciudadanos reclamaba una burocracia centralizada, una fiscalidad común, un ejército nacional y un mercado liberado de la rémora de aduanas interiores. Sobre estos cimientos, la burguesía construirá, a través de los

resortes de la administración, la *nación española*, cuya idea venía siendo perfilada desde el siglo anterior.²

(García de Cortázar and González Vesga 1999: 431)

The process of national construction was not easy, and had to face internal and external challenges. Industrialization was slow, in spite of the promising prospects which, according to Pierre Vilar (1985: 73–5), the demographic and economic progress of the eighteenth century had anticipated. In addition, throughout the century, the pressure generated by the Latin American secessionist movements was intensified by the specter of secessionism in Spain's own periphery. *Carlismo*, a movement associated with traditional ideologies and with the maintenance of the privileges of the *Ancien Régime*, demanded the preservation of the Basque Country's legal and fiscal dispensations. In the late 1860s, the growing power of federalists within the democratic party caused the defection of those (*unitarios*) who felt Spain's unity to be in jeopardy. Towards the end of the century, the vigor of centrifugal forces was intensified as echoes of the new nationalism reached Spain; the emergence of peripheral nationalism – in Catalonia, the Basque Country and Galicia – presented a challenge to the political articulation and cultural definition of Spain. Spanish history, due in part to the absence of a coherent natural system of communications, had generated a level of economic, cultural and linguistic diversity that had only become more complex with industrialization and urban growth.

From a nationalist perspective, this diversity had to be overcome, not only materially but also ideologically. The intervention of the state's ideological apparatus thus became necessary, its mission being the configuration of a homogeneous space that guaranteed the linguistic, cultural and national unity of Spain: "The identification of the state with one nation ... implied a homogenization and standardization of its inhabitants, essentially, by means of a written 'national language'" (Hobsbawm 1992: 93).

Slow industrialization and internal dissent produced a sense of crisis that was reflected in the intellectual polemics that revolved around the "problem of Spain," that is to say, the nation's cultural stagnation and scientific backwardness with respect to the European neighbors. The "polémica de la ciencia española" and the debate over religious intolerance and the Inquisition, revealed the concerns that haunted turn-of-the-century intellectuals: doubts about the dignity of Spain's past and desolation in view of the "intellectual wasteland" that characterized their time (cf. Pérez Villanueva 1991: 82–5; Varela 1999).

The feeling of national insecurity, caused by economic and political instability, by the danger of disintegration, by the crisis of cultural identity, and by general apathy, reached unprecedented levels after Spain's infamous 1898 defeat by the United States and the subsequent loss of the final remains of the old empire. The outcome of the Spanish–American war (immortalized as the "Desastre") has been chosen by Spanish historiography to represent the general feeling of crisis with which intellectuals entered the twentieth century.

The persistence of the cultural empire

Despite the irreversibility of the process of Latin American independence, throughout the nineteenth century, Spanish governments persevered in their attempts to regain control over the former colonies, both by military means (cf. Pike 1971: 3; Fogelquist 1968: 15–16) and by way of cultural diplomacy. The organization of different conferences and symposia, as well as the publication of journals such as *La Ilustración Ibérica*, *La Revista Española de Ambos Mundos* and *La Ilustración Española y Americana*, was meant to create a climate of harmony that, on the one hand, would foster the subsequent establishment of commercial links, and on the other, preserve the image of a truly Hispanic civilization rooted in Spain and spread over the Americas. One of the first journals espousing this ideology was *La Revista Española de Ambos Mundos*, which in its first issue stated:

> Destinada a España y América, pondremos particular esmero en estrechar sus relaciones. La Providencia no une a los pueblos con los lazos de un mismo origen, religión, costumbres e idioma para que se miren con desvío y se vuelvan las espaldas así en la próspera como en la adversa fortuna. Felizmente han desaparecido las causas que nos llevaron a la arena del combate, y hoy el pueblo americano y el ibero no son, ni deben ser, más que miembros de una misma familia; *la gran familia española, que Dios arrojó del otro lado del océano para que, con la sangre de sus venas, con su valor e inteligencia, conquistase a la civilización un nuevo mundo.*[3]
> (quoted in Fogelquist 1968: 13–14; emphasis added)

The movement inspiring these initiatives of cultural diplomacy began soon after the independence of the Latin American republics in the 1820s and is variously known as *hispanismo*, *hispanoamericanismo* and *panhispanismo*. While difficult to define in precise terms, *hispanismo* can be said to consist of at least the following ideas: The existence of a unique Spanish culture, lifestyle, characteristics, traditions and values, *all of them embodied in its language*; the idea that Spanish American culture is nothing but Spanish culture transplanted to the New World; and the notion that Hispanic culture has an internal hierarchy in which Spain occupies a hegemonic position (cf. Pike 1971).

From the perspective of Spain's state of crisis, *hispanismo* can be interpreted in two different but complementary lights. First, in order to present itself on a par with the United States and the European powers – which best represented the expansionist character of the modern nation – Spain needed to demonstrate some sort of preeminence over its former colonies, especially in view of the United States' increasingly interventionist policies in those territories. Since economic and military hegemony were largely out of the question, the cultural solution implicit in *hispanismo* – the persistence of the cultural empire – became the essential instrument to reach the expected level of international prestige. Second, as we have already mentioned, Spain underwent a sustained identity crisis throughout the nineteenth century, a crisis that culminated with the questioning of the nation's integrity by the development of nationalist movements in the peripheral areas of the Peninsula. In this context, the notions proposed by *hispanismo* provided the much-needed signs of identity which Spain could display in front of those who questioned its integrity and viability as a modern nation.

The acceptance of language as a national symbol

In view of the developmental parameters of nationalism, Spain needed to define itself, not only as an effective unit of political action, but also as a social and cultural unit (cf. Haugen 1972: 244). As Hobsbawm indicated (1992: 93), the process of unification that nation-building entails requires homogenization, that is, the minimization of internal differences; individual and local idiosyncrasies must be subordinated – even sacrificed – for the sake of the nation's identity. Since, as we have seen, language is conceived of in the romantic and post-romantic era as the embodiment of the *Volksgeist*, and, therefore, as one of the essential components of any specific culture, it became imperative for any supralocal community to achieve the desired unity by exercising a strict control over language. Selected individuals and institutions would thus be assigned the task of determining the legitimate forms of speech and of developing mechanisms that influence people's linguistic behavior and attitudes. In other words, language unity is attempted through the designing of language planning mechanisms.

Language planning (henceforth LP) has been defined in a variety of ways. For Robert Kaplan and Richard Baldauf, who provided an insightful and detailed definition, LP consists of

> [i]deas, laws and regulations (language policy), change rules, beliefs and practices intended to achieve a planned change (or to stop change from happening) in the language use in one or more communities. To put it differently, language planning involves *deliberate*, although not always overt, *future oriented* change in systems of language code and/or speaking in a societal context. (1997: 3)

One of the most important processes in which language planners become involved is *standardization*. Following Haugen (1972: 237–54), this process is normally considered to consist of four stages: *selection, codification, elaboration* and *acceptance*. Selection entails the identification of an existing vernacular that will serve as a model for the targeted standard. Codification constitutes the development of the form of a language, i.e. its phonology, grammar, lexicon and orthography. Elaboration is the expansion of the standard so that it may perform a maximal number of functions, that is, so that it is usable in every possible context. Finally, in the acceptance stage, language planners must earn the consent of the people and persuade them to learn and use the standard. These stages do not always occur in a strict sequence, and in fact, often coincide in time (cf. chapter 3).

Standard languages function in a variety of ways. They perform an *instrumental* function when used within the community for administrative convenience; they perform a *communicative* function when they serve as a common linguistic system for everyday social interactions; and finally, but most importantly for our purposes, they also function *symbolically*, as they allegedly embody the spirit of the nation and/or represent national unity. Investing the language with this symbolic power is often what poses the biggest problem for language planners:

> I would dare to suggest that the most frequent single problem in installing a national language has nothing to do with vocabulary expansion, spelling or grammar standardization, the adequacy of the educational system or the presence of an ensconced colonial language. *The biggest problem is that there often simply is no language that a sufficiently large majority of the citizens will accept as a symbol of national identity.*
> (Fasold 1988: 185, emphasis added)

It can be argued then that people's reluctance to accept the standard as the national language *is* a language problem. Therefore, LP agencies as well as individuals and institutions that support them have the responsibility of confronting it.

We must keep in mind that LP is a goal-oriented activity intended to influence people's linguistic behavior and attitudes. Often, LP may include strategies of *coercion*: a civil servant, for example, may have to demonstrate a certain level of proficiency in a given language in order to have access to certain jobs; or a journal publisher may have to commit to using a certain language or a certain variety of a language in order to receive public funding. However, strategies of *persuasion* are likely to be more effective than openly coercive measures: "The linguist with his grammar and lexicon may propose what he will, if the methods that could assure acceptance are missing . . . In the end the decisions are made by the users of language" (Haugen 1972: 178). Successful LP efforts, therefore, will persuade people that speaking a certain way and holding certain linguistic beliefs are in their best interest, or even better, natural. In other words, the goal of these strategies is to naturalize and legitimize the behavior and attitudes that the LP agencies are trying to promote.

The language battle

We may now understand the importance of LP for the processes of nation-building undertaken by the newly created Latin American nations and for the *hispanismo* movement, so closely associated with the modernization of Spain. For Latin American intellectuals who were involved in the process of building their own nations, gaining control over language – over its selection, codification, elaboration, and acceptance – was a natural consequence of independence. For intellectuals involved in the creation of a modern Spain, retaining control over those same processes became a necessity to demonstrate Spain's viability as a nation. As the reader will recall, being one of the old European national states, Spain needed to boost its international image and demonstrate the loyalty of its former colonies. The clash between the discourses that verbalized these two conflicting projects constitutes what Carlos Rama has referred to as *the language battle* ["la batalla del idioma"] (1982: 115–59).

While in both discourses, the variable nature of language is a prominent and highly symbolic issue, the treatment of change varies according to each author, as they hold different views on the extent to which linguistic evolution can be channeled and the direction in which it can be channeled. Would change inevitably cause the fragmentation of the Spanish language or could unity be preserved? In such a case, who should be in charge of channeling change in order to preserve this unity? These are the questions that seem to underlie the language battle. Some authors such as Domingo Faustino Sarmiento (cf. chapter 2) welcomed the fragmentation of Spanish as a step towards the consummation of the cultural autonomy of the new Latin American nations. Others, such as Rufino José Cuervo, saw fragmentation as the unfortunate but inevitable outcome of language change (cf. chapter 4). However, many others – Bello, Valera, Palma – believed that language unity could be maintained in spite of evolution (cf. chapters 3, 4 and 5).[4] The preservation of this unity would of course require well-coordinated and widely accepted LP strategies. But where did the legitimacy of language planners reside in the post-colonial Hispanic community? Again, the different views postulated in this regard revealed underlying tensions that seriously hampered the achievement of any consensus regarding LP.

In the previous section, we pointed out that the symbolic function of languages often has more social relevance than the merely instrumental and communicative. In fact, as this book will attempt to demonstrate, the language battle has been in reality a manifestation of the power struggles associated with the modern elaboration of the cultural and political map of the Hispanic community.

Monoglossic culture and the *dogma of homogeneism*

As we indicated above, the identification between language and nation became particularly intense towards the end of the nineteenth century, when the old national states where challenged by the emerging culture-based nationalisms. At this time, the nation-states intensified the cultural component of their nationalist discourse in order to secure the loyalty of their citizens for which they now had to compete with aspiring national entities. This was precisely the case in Spain, where the emergence of Catalan, Basque and Galician regionalist movements disrupted the process of construction of the modern nation. The equation language = nation on which these battling nationalist movements (Basque, Catalan, Galician and Spanish) rest is a synthetic formulation of the dominant linguistic culture of modern times: the linguistic culture of monoglossia (cf. del Valle 2000).

The term *linguistic culture* – as we are using it in this book – is taken from a theoretical framework developed by Harold Schiffman in *Linguistic Culture and Language Policy* (1996). Linguistic culture refers to a relatively abstract and supposedly universal set of beliefs about general concepts such as language, speech, speech community, literacy, etc. In heteroglossic cultures, for example, several linguistic norms coexist, and the verbal behavior of individuals is best represented as a series of vectors that point in the directions of the multiple norms available to them. While each linguistic norm may be associated with a different culture, their coexistence and complex interaction are considered natural and may in themselves constitute a source of identity. As Ana Celia Zentella has shown (1997), New York City Hispanics use multiple varieties of English and Spanish both to communicate for practical purposes and to express their complex identity. Their linguistic behavior, as Zentella indicates, should be represented as a constant process of choosing from a wide linguistic repertoire and not as the simple interaction of two grammars.

In Western societies, however, heteroglossic cultures have been for the most part either ignored or stigmatized. As we noted above, the dominant nationalist ideology was constructed on a very different conceptualization of the relationship between language and identity: the linguistic culture of monoglossia, which, as del Valle defined it (2000), consists of two principles. The *principle of focalization* reflects the idea that speaking always entails using a grammar, understood as a well-defined and minimally variable system; unfocused or highly variable linguistic behaviors are thus stigmatized in linguistic communities where monoglossic culture is dominant. The *principle of convergence*, which is the diachronic counterpart of focalization, assumes that the verbal behavior of the members of a community tends to become more and more homogeneous with time. Multilingualism is assumed to slowly disappear as people acquire the dominant language, and dialectal variation is believed to decrease as the educational system spreads the dominant variety.

The culture of monoglossia is consistent with the conceptualization of human communities as naturally homogeneous, an idea referred to by Blommaert and Verschueren (1991, 1998) as the *dogma of homogeneism*:

> [A] view of society in which differences are seen as dangerous and centrifugal and in which the "best" society is suggested to be one without inter-group differences . . . Nationalism, interpreted as the struggle to keep groups as "pure" and homogeneous as possible, is considered to be a positive attitude within the dogma of homogeneism. Pluriethnic or plurilingual societies are seen as problem-prone, because they require forms of state organization that run counter to the "natural" characteristics of groupings of people. (1998: 195)

It is precisely the convergence of the linguistic culture of monoglossia and the dogma of homogeneism that produces the philosophical foundations of cultural nationalism. National communities are imagined as culturally and linguistically homogeneous (or as moving towards the ideal homogeneity), and this uniformity justifies the political claim for self-government.

While nationalist ideology is always grounded in monoglossic culture, each nationalist movement produces its own *language ideologies*. In this book, we consider a language ideology to include a vision of the linguistic configuration of a specific community, as well as the reasoning that first, produces that vision, and second, justifies its value. Through our use of the term *language ideologies*, we explicitly recognize our association with a growing school of thought that explores the cultural, economic, political and social foundations and implications of language and discourse on language (cf. Joseph and Taylor 1990; Kroskrity 2000; Schieffelin, Woolard and Kroskrity 1998).

As the reader will hopefully recognize, the language ideologies produced by the authors analyzed in this book are all grounded in the linguistic culture of monoglossia. In one way or another, they all revolve around the maintenance or development of a national language, that is, a well-defined linguistic system in which the verbal behavior of all members of the community must converge. In keeping with the monoglossic basis of their ideologies, language becomes instrumental for our authors' conceptualizations of either the national or the *super*national community. Since their at times contradictory language ideologies are grounded in the very same linguistic culture, and since they often pursue similar goals, in an apparent paradox, all the authors resort to ultimately equivalent strategies of argumentation and self-legitimization.

Linguistic reasoning and legitimacy

The reasons for nationalism's obsession with homogeneity can be explained using Bertrand Russell's views on the origin of the nation (1972). For Russell, the nation emerges in the context of the romantic movement's conflict between the belief in the absolute freedom of the individual and the undeniable need for that individual to live in community. The conflict is resolved, Russell claims, by projecting the individual ego onto the community: by inventing the nation. This projection, we may add, is made possible by the logical transgression between the argument of *quality* and the argument of *quantity*. Since in quantitative terms, the addition of five units equals the multiplication of one unit by five, the nationalist mind erroneously assumes that the multiplication of an ideal citizen by the total number of individuals in a given community equals the addition of all its members; the fallacy of this argument resides in the fact that, for the previous equation to be true, qualitative differences among individuals must be erased.

Erasure is in fact one of several types of rhetorical reasoning commonly used in language debates. Irvine and Gal have defined it as "the process in which ideology, in simplifying the sociolinguistic field, renders some persons or activities (or sociolinguistic phenomena) invisible. Facts that are inconsistent with the ideological scheme either go unnoticed or get explained away" (2000: 38). Another strategy used in the process of legitimizing language ideologies is *iconization*. According to Irvine and Gal, this process

> involves the transformation of the sign relationship between linguistic features (or varieties) and the social images with which they are linked. Linguistic features that index social groups or activities appear to be iconic representations of them, as if a linguistic feature somehow depicted or displayed a social group's inherent nature or essence. (37)

As we will emphasize throughout the book, the intellectuals studied here have often attempted to establish the hegemony of their language ideologies by using erasure, that is, by ignoring or explaining away problematic phenomena or alternative ideologies. We will also see how the Spanish language, a certain variety of it, its orthography, or its history, have often became iconized, that is, they have been discursively associated with features that supposedly reflect the spirit of the community.

In the chapters that follow, it will also become apparent that this type of rhetorical reasoning often goes hand in hand with an urge to use the legitimizing power of language science. Linguistics emerged as an independent academic discipline in the nineteenth century, associated from birth with the methods and conceptual frameworks of the natural sciences – the dominant scientific paradigm of the time. Many of our authors took full advantage of their association with the prestigious discipline of linguistics to intervene in a deeply political debate such as the Hispanic language battle. This association invested these intellectuals with a degree of legitimacy that empowered them in the process of presenting their language ideologies as *natural*, surrounding them with a halo of scientific truth. As we anticipated above, this naturalization is essential for earning the consent of the people, a consent that implies not only sharing the vision but also recognizing the legitimacy of the visionary.

Notes

1 "The project of nation and citizenship was imagined by minorities, but it was presented as expansive; furthermore, through difficult negotiations, they were able to integrate-civilize those different communities that offered resistance."
2 "Even the most minute detail is regulated by the 1812 Constitution, whose unitary-state design places the rights of *Spaniards* above the historical rights of each *kingdom*. Equality among citizens demanded a centralized bureaucracy, a common fiscal system, a national army and a market free from the burden of internal levies. On this basis, the bourgeoisie would construct, through the resources of the administration, the *Spanish Nation*, an idea whose conception had begun in the previous century."
3 "Since the journal is meant for both Spain and Latin America, we will pay special attention to strengthening their relations. Providence does not unite peoples with bonds such as the same origin, religion, customs and language so that later they look at each other with suspicion and turn their backs on each other whether in prosperous or adverse times. Fortunately, the causes that brought us to the battlefield have disappeared, and today, the Iberian and Latin American peoples are, and should not be anything but, members of the same family; *the great Spanish family, that God sent across the ocean so that, with its blood, with its courage and intelligence, they would conquer a new world for civilization*" (emphasis added).
4 Peruvian writer Ricardo Palma (1833–1919) was perhaps one of the most distinguished Latin American defenders of hispanismo. He was also the most prominent member of his country's language academy. While most nineteenth-century Latin American writers refused to collaborate with the Spanish Royal Academy, the Peruvian institution was more willing to cooperate. Between 1892 and 1893, Palma visited Spain and presented the Spanish *académicos* with a number of words commonly used in American Spanish. After his first few proposals were rejected, he simply gave up on the possibility of reaching a linguistic consensus (cf. C. M. Rama 1982: 140–4).

2 Linguistic anti-academicism and Hispanic community
Sarmiento and Unamuno
Barry L. Velleman

> Toda la actividad política y cultural del siglo XIX hispanoamericano está relacionada con el proyecto de construcción de las naciones, y el planteamiento de la cuestión de la lengua (dimensión simbólica de su uso, normas orales o escritas, representación gráfica, etc.) es inseparable de la problemática de la identidad nacional.[1]
>
> (Arnoux and Lois 1996: 1)

Sarmiento, the Generation of 1837, and Spain

The writers known as Argentina's Generation of 1837 have been called "perhaps the most articulate and self-conscious group of Latin American intellectuals" of their century (Katra 1996: 7). Juan Bautista Alberdi, Esteban Echeverría, Juan María Gutiérrez, and Domingo F. Sarmiento, all born during the period 1805–11, were the children of Argentina's independence from Spain (1810–16) and witnesses to the struggles of their country's troubled post-colonial era. As Argentina attempted to become a modern nation, its intellectual and political leaders were divided on various political and cultural matters. There were, for example, conflicts between the Unitarians, who favored the centralization of cultural and political hegemony in Buenos Aires, and the Federalists, who argued for a broad sociopolitical base in which the interior provinces played a stronger role. Also, defenders of traditional Hispanic values struggled against those who attempted to impose liberal European ideals, especially those of France. For Sarmiento, the revolution had served to bring about yet another confrontation, in this case between two opposing elements which were already present in pre-independence Argentine society: barbarism and civilization.

> Habia ántes de 1810 en la República Arjentina dos sociedades distintas, rivales e incompatibles; dos civilizaciones diversas; la una española europea culta, i la otra bárbara, americana, casi indíjena; i la revolución de las ciudades solo iba a servir de causa, de móvil, para que estas dos maneras distintas de ser de un pueblo se pusiesen en presencia una de

otra, se acometiesen, i despues de largos años de lucha, la una absorviese a la otra.[2]

(Sarmiento 1961: 63)[3]

The leader of the Generation was Esteban Echeverría (1805–51), who had absorbed the influence of Saintsimonian Socialism and the linguistic nationalism of Herder during his visit to Europe (1826–30).[4] Echeverría's return to Argentina marked the beginning of the romantic movement there. During the 1830s, the young idealists of 1837 found themselves increasingly in conflict with the government of Juan Manuel de Rosas (1793–1877), whose authoritarian rule represented, in the view of several among them, the victory of barbarism over civilization. As a result, the Generation of 1837 also came to be known as the Generation of Exiles: between 1839 and 1841, they had fled Rosas' Argentina for Montevideo, Uruguay (Alberdi, Gutiérrez, Echeverría) or Santiago, Chile (Vicente Fidel López, Sarmiento).

While the members of this group were hardly in accord on every detail of their social and political agendas, they shared a central core of beliefs. As Katra has pointed out, they tended to view social progress as integral: "the condition of any one institution generally reflected the stage or level of development of the society in its totality" (1996: 88). Therefore, in their view, political independence had to lead to an analogous liberation of the intelligence and, indeed, of all cultural phenomena. This meant, of course, breaking with the Spanish intellectual tradition, one which they saw as stagnant (Katra 1996: 88). Alberdi, in his 1838 essay "Reacción contra el españolismo," attributed to Spain every characteristic of his culture which he deemed regressive:

> Es evidente que aun conservamos infinitos restos del régimen colonial . . . ya que los españoles nos habían dado el despotismo en sus costumbres obscuras y miserables. . . . no tenemos hoy una idea, una habitud, una tendencia retrógrada que no sea de origen español.[5]
> (Alberdi quoted in Costa Álvarez 1922: 31)

In particular, these writers considered literary and linguistic autonomy from Spain to be the natural consequence of political independence. Echeverría wrote: "We believe that it is ridiculous for us to be Spanish in literature and American in politics . . . The Argentine language is not the Spanish language" (quoted in Rosenblat 1960: 558). Even though Echeverría would proclaim the Spanish language as the only legacy from the mother country which Latin Americans would willingly accept, he also stated that they could only accept it "on the condition of its improvement, of its progressive transformation, that is, of its emancipation" (Echeverría 1951: 511). Rosenblat offers the following summary of the linguistic ideas of this group of intellectuals:

> Todos ellos coinciden en un anti-españolismo cultural y lingüístico, que a veces llega a la hispanofobia; en un entusiasmo ferviente y neófito por la literatura y el pensamiento francés; en la devoción por el pueblo y la tierra; en la afirmación de la inspiración americana . . .; en la exaltación de las ideas y el menosprecio de las palabras; en el rechazo de toda tutela académica o academicista; en la afirmación de la libertad de la lengua, para que pueda progresar con las ideas nuevas. *Sarmiento, Alberdi y Juan María Gutiérrez llegaban a proclamar la soberanía popular en materia de lenguaje.*[6]
>
> (1960: 557, emphasis added)

It is in the work of Domingo Faustino Sarmiento (1811–88) that the cultural and linguistic conflicts associated with nation-building in the Latin American post-colonial era appear in their most dramatic form (Rosenblat 1960: 558). As indicated above, Sarmiento fled Argentina; he lived in exile in Chile several times between 1831 and 1855. It was precisely during his exile in Santiago in the 1840s that he wrote his most important work, *Facundo* (1845; cf. Sarmiento 1961), and participated intensely in the famous intellectual and linguistic battles waged in the Chilean press (cf. Jaksić 1994). Sarmiento's interest in language was a result of the convergence of his pedagogical and political concerns; this relationship between politics and pedagogy was immediate in the context of the above-mentioned notion of integral social progress, shared by the members of the Generation of 1837.

In Sarmiento's view, Spain, through the errors of its despots – especially the Inquisition – had produced an inert civilization that Latin America had of course inherited. In his view, even the barbarism of Rosas' Argentina was a reflection of its Spanish heritage: "Rosas is the personalization of the political Inquisition of old Spain . . . despotic, cruel, and an enemy of everything that is not national, that is, barbaric, Spanish" (Sarmiento 1843e: 73–4). Through the mid-1840s Sarmiento still saw Spanish influence as diametrically opposed to the needs of the independent Latin American states. He decried the new Spanish publication *El Observador de Ultramar* for treating what he called "colonial interests" from the perspective of the metropolis: "the submission to the authority of the mother country, the preaching of all the doctrines that promote the continuation of colonial stagnation, the shameful trafficking of Negro slaves, and all the methods of prolonging colonial subordination" (1843/44: 105).

For Sarmiento, Spanish, the tongue of an inert culture, was necessarily a dead language, incapable of expressing modern ideas. He wrote in 1843: "Spain does not have a single writer who can teach us, nor books that are useful to us" (Sarmiento 1843c: 38). In 1867 Sarmiento wrote to President Mitre of Argentina:

> ¡Estamos hablando un idioma muerto! Las colonias no se emanciparán, sino abandonándolo, o traduciendo entero otro. Esto último será obra

de varón. Lo otro sucederá por la lenta acción de otras razas, que poblarán nuestro suelo, sirviendo nosotros de abono a la tierra.[7] (1911: 370)

Echoing Larra, Sarmiento found Spanish to be merely a language of translation, a "beggar" dependent on the languages of modern civilization such as French and especially English, the language of free institutions, business, and government (cf. Cassullo 1962).

In Sarmiento's view, the plethora of French books in Latin America had produced positive results compensating for the lack of works written in Spanish. However, in spite of accepting them, he expressed surprising reservations about the possible ill effects of neologisms on Spanish:

> En América, entre las personas que cultivan la inteligencia, circulan con más abundancia que las españolas las obras de los autores franceses en historia, bellas letras y política. Esta necesaria transformación, y aquella desviación de las antiguas tradiciones nacionales, trae, sin embargo, un inconveniente, y es la inevitable adulteración de las formas del idioma, si al mismo tiempo que se beben las ideas de otras naciones más avanzadas no se cuida de depurarlas de todo limo extraño, por el estudio de las peculiaridades de la lengua castellana.[8] (1849: 331)[9]

In 1849, Sarmiento welcomed the publication in Madrid of the first volumes of Rivadeneyra's *Biblioteca de autores españoles*, a series of editions of Peninsular literary works. In a passage surprisingly conciliatory and reminiscent of Bello, Sarmiento expressed his belief that Peninsular literary models would reduce language divergence in America through the propagation of prestige Peninsular norms, "as an indispensable corrective for the language errors which could be caused by the work of time, distance, and that lack of community of interests and political life that American independence has brought about" (Sarmiento 1849). However, the benefits had to be mutual, since American writers deserving of wider recognition in Spain would also have to be included in the series, "as very distinguished members of the intelligent family of Spain" (1849: 332–3).

Apparently, then, Sarmiento's belief in the sterility of the Spanish culture of his time coexisted with his acknowledgement of a cultural bond between Latin America and Spain ("la familia intelijente de la España") and of the need for a prestige norm ("correctivo indispensable"). Already in 1842 he had pointed out the usefulness of "studying the most frequent errors of popular speech and indicating the corrective" (1842c: 227). Sarmiento's writings from later in the decade show a more conciliatory tone toward the Hispanic literary tradition. As Verdevoye has suggested, this transformation may have been the result of the influence of Andrés Bello's more moderate linguistic ideas, or to Sarmiento's retreat from excessively zealous earlier positions (Verdevoye 1981: 106–7). There are other factors, however, which may account for the general softening in Sarmiento's tone. On the one hand, Jaksić (1994: 45–6) has pointed out the importance of Sarmiento's 1842 article "Diálogo entre el editor y el escritor" (1842f: 323–9), in which an unnamed editor, presumably the Spaniard Manuel Rivadeneyra (1805–72), advises an unnamed writer (Sarmiento) to exercise patience and restraint in his polemical writings in the face of the latter's growing sense of isolation and frustration with the Chilean press. One must not forget this was also a period of codification and institutionalization. The newly-founded University of Chile necessarily attempted to appease both conservatives and liberals, reflecting the concept of what has been called a *mission civilisatrice* – in which culture serves as "an assimilative agent that underpins linguistic, political, and administrative homogeneity," overriding political divisions (cf. Neave and Rhoades 1987: 225; Serrano 1994: 65; Silvert and Reissman 1976: 113–18). On the other hand, the official restoration of relations between Chile and Spain in 1844 may have also played a role in Sarmiento's rhetorical softening. The same year, the Argentine exiles in Chile were obliged to step back from extreme positions after they had been accused of supporting Francisco Bilbao (1823–65), who was convicted of blasphemy and immorality for his anti-Catholic, anti-Spanish article "Sociabilidad chilena." Especially after the Bilbao affair, Sarmiento was "careful . . . to assail barbarism and not the Spanish heritage as the primary cause of the political chaos of the present" (Kristal 1993: 67–8).

Sarmiento's toning down, therefore, could be interpreted more as a rhetorical strategy than as a radical change of mind. Given the low esteem in which the Argentinean held Spanish men of letters, one should not ignore the undeniable irony that underlies his later statements of 1867. While representing Argentina as Minister to the United States, Sarmiento claimed that his earlier rhetoric had been misinterpreted: in reality, he had urged the translation of foreign books "fearful that the language of Cervantes would someday be lost in America" (1867: 319).

Sarmiento and the Spanish Royal Academy

If the stagnation of Spanish culture was a consequence of the Inquisition and stifling, autocratic rule, its principal linguistic representative was the *Real Academia Española* (RAE). The role of a legislative body in linguistic matters was one of the issues debated in a polemic carried out in the Chilean press in 1842. On 27 April of that year, Pedro Fernández Garfias (1805–64), a professor at the Instituto Nacional in Santiago, published in *El Mercurio* the first part of a manual entitled *Ejercicios populares de lengua castellana*. This text, essentially a list of lexical archaisms to be avoided, with a parallel enumeration of "correct" forms, was based on a meticulous study of the RAE's Dictionary (Salas Lavaqui 1876: 459). The list was preceded by a brief commentary by Sarmiento, in which the Argentinean expressed his support of prescriptive works of this kind, even if their influence is limited due to the uncontrollable nature of linguistic change:

> La soberanía del pueblo tiene todo su valor y su predominio en el idioma; l[o]s gramátic[o]s son como el senado conservador, creado para resistir a los embates populares, para conservar la rutina y las tradiciones. Son a nuestro juicio, si nos perdonan la mala palabra, el partido retrógrado, estacionario, de la sociedad habladora; pero, como los de su clase en política, su derecho está reducido a gritar y desternillarse contra la corrupción, contra los abusos, contra las innovaciones. El torrente los empuja y hoy admiten una palabra nueva, mañana un extranjerismo vivito, al otro día una vulgaridad chocante; pero ¿qué se ha de hacer? todos han dado en usarla, todos la escriben y la hablan, fuerza es agregarla al diccionario y quieran que no, enojados y mohinos, la agregan, y que no hay remedio, y el pueblo triunfa y lo corrompe y lo adultera todo.[10] (1842c: 226)

The populist leanings of Sarmiento's rhetoric contrast markedly with Andrés Bello's faith in a linguistic elite. Bello (1781–1865), the moderate Venezuelan who had come to Chile in 1829, published a response to Sarmiento in *El Mercurio* on 12 May 1842 under the pseudonym "Un Quidam." In his reply, Bello contended that linguistic institutions did not have to be as conservative and therefore as inoperative as Sarmiento claimed: "Popular new words and idioms have never been and will never be excluded from corrected usage if they are expressive and do not glaringly violate the analogies and characteristics of our language" (Bello 1842a: 241). However, it is not the common people, he claimed, who introduce foreign words, but rather the intellectuals, "[t]hose who are familiar with foreign languages and, with no knowledge of the admirable models of our rich [Spanish] literature, begin writing following the version which they have read the most" (1842a: 241). Bello claims that it is appropriate for grammarians to oppose these writers, "not as preservers of tradition and routine . . . but as philosophers and guardians whom society charges, by useful convention, with establishing the words used by educated people" and to condemn "exotic expressions, phrases which conflict with the genius of our language, and those coarse vulgarities and idioms of the masses" (1842a: 242). Thus, for Bello, in language as in politics,

> es indispensable que haya un cuerpo de sabios, que así dicte las leyes convenientes a sus necesidades; como las del habla en que ha de expresarlas; y no sería menos ridículo confiar al pueblo la decisión de sus leyes, que autorizarle en la formación del idioma.[11] (1842a: 242)

In contrast with this view, Sarmiento restated that "cuerpos de sabios" such as the RAE should not legislate but merely document common usage:

> [. . .] si hay en España una academia que reúna en un diccionario las palabras que el uso general del pueblo ya tiene sancionadas, no es porque ella autorice su uso, ni forme el lenguaje con sus decisiones, sino porque recoge como en un armario las palabras cuyo uso está autorizado unánimemente por el pueblo mismo y por los poetas.[12]
> (Sarmiento 1842e: 252)[13]

In his writings from 1843, Sarmiento emphasizes what he sees as a lack of legitimacy in the RAE, even in Spain. Its members are derivative thinkers: "Despite being Spain's the most notable writers, they are second-rank, common thinkers who import ideas from neighboring nations to their own, or like Hermosilla and some other poor devils, who fight tooth and nail to maintain the past" (1843c: 6). This lack of legitimacy and therefore authority justifies, in Sarmiento's view, the cultural separatism from that country which lies at the very heart of American nationhood:

> [E]l estarnos esperando que una academia impotente, sin autoridad en España mismo, sin prestigio y aletargada por la conciencia de su propia nulidad, nos dé reglas, que no nos vendrán bien después de todo, es abyección indigna de naciones que han asumido el rango de tales.[14]
> (1843c: 29)

Thus, the RAE is "powerless, dethroned, royal, and foreign" (1843c: 23). It has no interest in Sarmiento's principal objectives: teaching children to read and developing the common man intellectually.

According to the Argentinean, since the RAE's orthography is founded partially on etymological grounds, and partially on the conventions of a literary standard which is inadequate, it may be useful for professional men of letters, but not for the public at large. The Academy's recommendations are even less relevant in America, where certain sounds have been lost, "precisely those whose graphic representations give us most difficulty," that is, *c, z, b* and *v* (1843f: 60). Sarmiento writes: "It is ridiculous to be using the orthography of a nation which pronounces words differently from us" (1843c: 3). As unenlightened as this observation may seem, the point is the fact that the nation in question is Spain.[15]

Sarmiento and orthographic reform

Sarmiento's demands for orthographic reform were consistent with the integrative conception of cultural progress that the members of his generation espoused. Just as he had argued with respect to language change, orthographic reform was only natural in the new post-colonial process: "When Spain, sirs, had no government in [18]10, we took ourselves nicely out of the noose which it had around our necks: why wouldn't we do the same in orthography?" (1843c: 36). For the Argentinean, it could not be claimed that a spelling reform would betray the cultural tradition of Latin America: "Castilian orthography is today open to any reform; because since it does not have a literature of its own, there are no precedents to destroy" (1843c: 33). He insisted that an American orthography was a necessity (see below on his pedagogical arguments), and that the new nations had to take advantage of "this moment of anarchy" to reconstruct it according to pronunciation.

Soon after his arrival in Chile in 1840, with a view toward improving elementary education, Sarmiento proposed the establishment of a Normal School, the first in the Southern Hemisphere (Contreras 1993: 31). In January 1842, Manuel Montt, Minister of Public Instruction, decreed the creation of the school, naming Sarmiento as Director, and assigning him the task of assessing the methods used to teach reading in the country. The result was Sarmiento's *Análisis de las cartillas, silabarios i otros métodos de lectura conocidos i practicados en Chile* (1842a).[16] Sarmiento saw that the efficient teaching of reading was hindered by an orthographic system which did not accurately reflect the pronunciation of the learners.

On 19 November 1842, the plan to establish the University of Chile was approved, with Andrés Bello as President and Sarmiento as a founding member. One of the charges of the new university was the supervision of elementary education. Bello, who had written a number of articles on orthographic reform, encouraged Sarmiento to investigate that question further. On 17 October 1843, exactly one month after the inauguration of the university, Sarmiento presented his "Memoria sobre ortografía americana" (1843c). His suggested orthographic reforms were based principally on earlier proposals of García del Río and Bello (1823), but went further in calling for a strictly Latin American orthography. Moreover, Sarmiento's text reflected a strongly anti-Spanish stance:

> Eso es lo que diferencia fundamentalmente su sistema del de Bello, el cual veía con alarma todo signo de escisión lingüística, de fraccionamiento de la amplia comunidad hispánica. Sarmiento en cambio se dejaba llevar por el violento anti-españolismo que en las generaciones jóvenes había seguido a la guerra de la Independencia.[17]
>
> (Rosenblat 1981: cvii)

In the "Memoria" Sarmiento argued that there was an obvious lack of orthographic uniformity in Latin America, which reflected the cultural void of the post-revolutionary period. In turn, this cultural void stemmed from the dearth of acceptable literary models in Spain, a nation which had for centuries turned its back on the progress of modern civilization (Sarmiento 1843c: 9–11).

Sarmiento rejected two of the three traditional orthographic criteria. On the one hand, he maintained that *constant use* hardly existed in the Hispanic nations, given the lack of eminent writers who might serve as models. On the other, *etymology* was deemed unpractical, since it was beyond the understanding of the common man. Consequently, *pronunciation* remained the only viable criterion for orthographic reform (Sarmiento 1843c: 12–13). He agreed that Bello and García del Río's 1823 proposals were important innovations, but pointed out that they had not been implemented consistently, not even by the authors themselves.

Sarmiento's conclusions can be summarized as follows: there is no orthographic system of Spanish based on constant use; the system proposed by the RAE is inappropriate for most Latin Americans, in that it presupposes that to write a letter correctly one must study Latin first; the spoken language of America differs from that of Spain, and therefore, in a system based on pronunciation, the symbols used to represent the different sounds must also differ; the adoption of a simple, perfect system is within Latin America's reach; European publishers will adopt it willingly; finally, any schism between Spanish and Latin American orthographies will have no ill effects for either Spaniards or Latin Americans (Sarmiento 1843c: 47). Sarmiento believed that his proposed orthography, which would represent the final stage of independence from Spain, would be a model for all of Latin America: "Twenty million Americans will salute us as those who help them to become free of the last claw that Spain still has in us" (Sarmiento 1843c: 48).

After Sarmiento had presented his "Memoria," Bello named a committee to review it, and supported its publication. But Sarmiento, impatient to bring the matter into the arena of public debate, published it on his own, beginning months of discussion in the popular press. Only days after the appearance of the "Memoria," Rafael Minvielle (1800–87) published an attack on the document in *El Progreso* of Santiago (cf. Contreras 1993: 37–40). Minvielle, a Spaniard who was a founding member of the University of Chile, believed that the "Memoria" unfairly dismissed the literary tradition of Spain, represented a cruel attack on the Spanish people, and, in calling for a specifically Spanish American orthography, would create a cultural schism between the mother country and its former colonies. Sarmiento was quick to respond, publishing eight open letters on the subject in *La Gaceta del Comercio* in October and November. He repeated his assertion that a Spanish American orthography, based on pronunciation, was pedagogically desirable; and that its discrepancies from Peninsular models would be insignificant, "because Spain does not have books" (1843f: 60). Sarmiento further refuted the claims that he had been unfair to the Spanish people:

> Cuando digo España en materia de letras, incluyo a la América . . . La España, como pueblo que trabaja por salir de la nulidad a que la han condenado los errores de sus antiguos déspotas, es la nación más digna de respeto. (1843f: 61)

> Los españoles de ahora, los españoles ilustrados como nosotros, combaten gloriosamente por dejar de ser españoles y hacerse europeos, es

decir, franceses en sus ideas y en sus costumbres, ingleses en su forma de gobierno.[18] (1843e: 75)[19]

On 18 November 1843 *El Mercurio* published another article criticizing Sarmiento's "Memoria."[20] The article posed the question of why Chile needed an orthographic reform, when "países cultos" such as England and France had no such movement. Sarmiento replied that the cultural position of the American republics – their "pequeñez de insectos" – was simply not comparable to that of "colosos" such as England and France. Reform is inevitable in the context of a cultural void:

> nosotros reformamos porque podemos, y aquellas naciones no lo hacen porque no pueden; de la misma manera que hemos adoptado el gobierno republicano porque podíamos adoptarlo sin inconveniente, y aquellas no lo adoptan por las resistencias con que tienen que luchar.[21]
> (Sarmiento 1843a: 90)

On 21 November 1843, an anonymous "Professor of Spanish and French Grammar," writing in *El Progreso*, repeated Minvielle's earlier fear that a Spanish American orthography would lead to the fragmentation of the Spanish language (cf. Contreras 1993: 58–61). Sarmiento began his response with the charge that his interlocutor was hiding behind the title of Professor, a title which "only he knows to what extent it suits him." Sarmiento asked for clarification of the Professor's claim that he knew many Americans who pronounced the *z*, in the Argentinean's view an asystematic, affected mannerism appropriate to a small number of social contexts:

> Sé muy bien que hay diez o doce jóvenes que se han ejercitado en imitar, en *singer* el habla de los castellanos; usted será uno de ellos y yo también soy otro; pero todos esos no hablan habitualmente; leen cuando más así, o cuando hablan ex-catedra; tienen, o más bien diré, tenemos dos idiomas, uno de parada, otro para el uso común.[22]
> (Sarmiento 1843b: 107; cf. Rosenblat 1940: 52–3)

In sum, he simply dismissed Minvielle's criticism on the basis of the fragmentation argument.

Although Sarmiento was certainly aware of the general and immediate opposition to his orthographic reforms,[23] he was careful to point out that the first individuals to attack them in public all served Spanish interests: Minvielle and the Professor of Grammar were both Spaniards, and *El Mercurio de Valparaíso* was published by Santos Tornero, also a native of the Peninsula. Even if most of the writers for *El Mercurio* were Latin Americans, they were pro-Spain because "they are serving other interests." With this argument Sarmiento isolated his detractors, avoided mention of the reaction of the University of Chile, and emphasized the appropriateness of the title of his "Memoria" "since it is taking on a purely *American* character" (1843d: 115, emphasis in the original).

On 25 April 1844, the School of Humanities of the University of Chile issued its decision on the question of orthographic reform. Sarmiento's proposals had gone too far, and would isolate Chile from the other Spanish-speaking nations.[24] In spite of the rejection, this reform proposal paved the way for the temporary adoption of Bello's more conservative system. More importantly, it served to establish a context for the discussion of the broader issues of Hispanic cultural continuity in America.

Sarmiento's conception of the norm

Sarmiento's integral concept of sociocultural advancement implied that cultural progress would eventually and necessarily lead to perfectibility: "We believe in progress, that is, we believe that man, society, languages, nature itself, are on their way toward perfectibility" (1842d: 306). With respect to language, perfectibility was seen as a reflection of intellectual development expressed in a broad and stable lexicon:

> Un idioma es tanto más perfecto cuanto más usado ha sido para expresar mayor número de ideas, cuanto más fijo está el significado de las palabras, cuanto más elaborado está el pensamiento del pueblo que lo usa, cuantos más progresos ha hecho la inteligencia que de él se sirve para desenvolverse.[25] (1843d: 127)

Thus, Sarmiento conceived language as a depository of the ideas of a culture. This conception – which differed markedly from Humboldt's more abstract view of the relationship between the spirit of speakers of a language and its internal form (Di Tullio 1988: 20) – justified his rejection of a Peninsular Spanish linguistic model on the basis of the latter's alleged intellectual inferiority.

Sarmiento's intensely pragmatic conception of language and the specific circumstances of the new Latin American nations prevented him from granting too much value to the preservation of a well-established norm. Not surprisingly, *El Mercurio*, in the above-mentioned article, accused Sarmiento of possibly promulgating errors by not adequately criticizing substandard forms. Sarmiento's reply of 23 November was a discussion of what an error really is, of its implications for language variation, and of the function of linguistic prescriptivism – themes further developed in nine important articles published in *El Progreso* between 24 November and 7 December. For the Argentinean, the key to correctness was general acceptability throughout all levels of society:

> Cuando una parte de la sociedad, la plebe solamente, dice *quero*, *sordao*, *benío*, *truje*, etc., pueden considerarse estos defectos como verdaderos

vicios; pero cuando todos los hombres que hablan un idioma lo dicen, eso no es vicio, sino trasformación, y entra a figurar en el lenguaje correcto.[26] (1843a: 93)

For example, Bello had believed American *seseo* to be an improper feature, although an uncorrectable one. In Sarmiento's view, Bello, having been "educated by Spanish authors," naturally considered *seseo* to be substandard simply because it diverged from prestige Peninsular norms (cf. Moré's chapter 3). Bello's prescriptivism was misguided in that American *seseo* is a fact: "It matters little that the observer considers it to be an error or not" (1843b: 106).

Finally, in the same pragmatic vein, the inevitability of language change implies that the possible fragmentation of Spanish would be a function of social and historical factors which lie beyond the control of learned individuals and associations. The common people are "the great modifier, the corrupter, if you will, of languages, but a corrupter that no one can contain" (Sarmiento 1843d: 122). Dialectal divergence will occur under the conditions of language contact resulting from colonization, migration, and influence in the areas of religion and customs (Sarmiento 1843a: 95). Under this interpretation, language maintenance in Latin America depends on its continuing contact with Peninsular cultural practices and institutions, a situation which Sarmiento sees as impossible. In order for Spanish to be preserved in America as it is spoken in Spain,

> preciso es que sus libros anden en manos de todos, y que sus leyes, sus costumbres y aun su forma de gobierno imperen aquí como en la península misma. Que esto no sucede y que no sucederá jamás, es lo que he querido probar en la segunda parte de mi *Memoria*.[27]
>
> (Sarmiento 1843d: 123)[28]

Sarmiento and Unamuno: spiritual twins

More than half a century after Sarmiento's polemics in Chile, Miguel de Unamuno, in Spain, would return to many of the same questions. It is revealing that the first proper name we find in Bunkley's biography of Sarmiento is that of Unamuno (Bunkley 1966: 3). Bunkley relates that on one occasion the Spanish writer read parts of a book to a blind friend without identifying its author. The friend, poet Cándido Rodríguez Pinilla, believed that the author was typically Spanish for having criticized Spain "as only a Spaniard can." The book in question was Sarmiento's *Facundo*.

Unamuno called himself a "devout reader and very enthusiastic panegyrist" of Sarmiento, and at one point he entertained the notion of writing a book about the Argentinean (Holguín 1964: 155; Unamuno 1997: 34). Unamuno called Sarmiento his favorite Spanish writer of the nineteenth century, one who was "more Spanish than the Spaniards," despite – more precisely, because of – his attacks on Spain (Unamuno 1905a: 903). If Sarmiento was striving to "erase Spanish tradition from his country," he was also maintaining the more important tradition: "The intimate tradition, the one that lies beneath history, radical and deep, the one that is tied to the blood, to customs, and above all to language, that is the one which he maintained like no one else" (Unamuno 1905a: 905). Sarmiento was for Unamuno "perhaps the most Spanish of all the South American writers and thinkers" (Cúneo 1963: 175), a "Hispanophobe so profoundly and radically Spanish" (Unamuno 1908a: 588). In Sarmiento's work Unamuno found the continuity of what he saw as fundamentally Spanish. In his study *Sarmiento y Unamuno*, Cúneo wonders whether Sarmiento might be the American precursor of the Spanish criticism of the Generation of 98: "He raged, in 1846, in Spain, just as half a century later Unamuno would rage. A rage in the Spanish style" (Cúneo 1963: 173–4). Unamuno himself seemed to have thought the same, as he wrote in a 1907 letter to Agustín Klappenbach:

> [Sarmiento] fué un precursor de nuestros censores indígenas propios. Su alma era un alma castiza y honradamente española, y su lengua, con sus negligencias y descuidos todos, me suena más a cosa nuestra que la lengua artificiosamente depurada de los juristas.[29]
> (Unamuno quoted in Maurín Navarro 1952: n.p.)

Unamuno's background appears to have little in common with that of Sarmiento: between the two writers there were great differences of time, place, social situation, and training. Unamuno had a degree in Philology.[30] He was a professor of Greek and the history of the Spanish language, and was familiar with the work of Diez, Hermann Paul, Müller, Sievers, Brücke, Whitney, Humboldt and Menéndez Pidal. Meanwhile, Sarmiento, an autodidact writing more than twenty years before Unamuno's birth, had no university degree and little, if any, contact with the developing historical-comparative movement in linguistics. Nevertheless, he had read widely in social and political history, and knew Herder through his French interpreters (Rosenblat 1960: 557). Despite these differences, Sarmiento's largely intuitive linguistic thought shares striking similarities with that of the Spanish thinker.

The claim that Unamuno found in Sarmiento a spiritual twin (Chaves 1964: 97–9) rests on the evidence of a number of parallelisms of character. Both egotists – Unamuno wrote "I who, like Sarmiento, distinguish myself by my modesty" (1920a: 435) – they shared a tendency toward the asystematic, the seemingly improvised, the practical over the theoretical, the paradoxical. Both rejected purely ornamental literature and empty French cultural finery. Both preferred substance to form; Unamuno adopted Sarmiento's slogan "We have to do things; even if we do them badly, we must do them" (García Blanco 1964: 318). Both shared Unamuno's romantic doctrine of "I want no method other than that of passion" (Unamuno

1906c: 925). Larra was an important force for each of their generations (Cúneo 1963: 145). Both suffered periods of exile. Sarmiento's Rosas corresponds to Unamuno's Primo de Rivera, "whom I will crush as Sarmiento did Rosas" (quoted in Cúneo 1963: 51). Both were teachers who saw education as the basis of the longed-for "regeneración" of their countries. Both writers saw civilization as the reflex of *civitas*, the city.[31] Finally, both were profoundly interested in language in their societies.

Language and society

An examination of Sarmiento's and Unamuno's visions of language reveals that neither writer had great interest in the inquiries of formal linguistics. For our authors, knowledge about language must be humanized to have value. Unamuno once wrote: "For me philology is never more than a pretext, or better a trampoline" (n.d.: 1374). Both writers made an immediate connection between language and social criticism: "[Unamuno's] vision of language and his perplexity over the deep conflicts with his society arose out of the same circumstances . . . His vision of language and his insight into the dysfunctionings of his society are simultaneous" (Lacy 1967: 120, 101). Likewise, as we have seen, for the Argentinean writer, linguistic freedom was, in the context of integral social progress, the basis on which civilization was to be constructed.

Unable to find suitable linguistic and cultural models in the Hispanic tradition, Sarmiento searched for external influences to transform Spanish into the conducting wire of modern ideas (Sarmiento 1899: 241). In contrast, Unamuno sought the eternal popular base of the language within the language itself. Language is not only the conductor of ideas, but also "the blood of the spirit of the race" (1911c: 600). Unamuno's country, then, is any that speaks Spanish: "la unidad de lengua era . . . un determinante suficiente de unidad de espíritu" (Huarte Morton 1954: 106). In his *Rosario de sonetos líricos* Unamuno writes:

> La sangre de mi espíritu es mi lengua
> y mi patria es allí donde resuene
> soberano su verbo, que no amengua
> su voz por mucho que ambos mundos llene.[32] (1910b: 375)

In defining the relationship between language and culture, the views of Sarmiento and Unamuno also differ. We have seen that, for Sarmiento, language is a monument to and a depository of the ideas of a culture: "The language of a people is the most complete historical monument of its diverse epochs and of the ideas that have nourished it" (Sarmiento 1887: 220). Therefore, language is the basis for all cultural progress, since it makes possible the betterment of the individual through book learning (Katra

1996: 168).³³ But Unamuno, reflecting the influence of Humboldt, prefers to identify language with a root rather than with a depository:

> Un idioma de habla es una raíz, más que depósito, de tradiciones, y lleva en sí una visión y una audición del universo mundo, una concepción de la vida y del destino humano, un arte, una filosofía y hasta una religión.³⁴ (1935: 652-3)

In other words, whereas Sarmiento believed that a language's richness was measured by its lexical breadth and stability (Sarmiento 1843d: 127), Unamuno found its richness in its potential for future productivity:

> La riqueza de una lengua no está en el número de vocablos o giros que posee, sino en el que puede poseer: está en su fecundidad, en su facilidad para crear nuevas voces que respondan a nuevas ideas, y en su facilidad para asimilarse voces extrañas.³⁵
>
> (Unamuno 1910a: 390)

Sarmiento, Unamuno, and the RAE

Sarmiento and Unamuno shared a deep skepticism with respect to the usefulness and legitimacy of the Spanish Royal Academy: They were reluctant to accept that "a body of wise men" could play a positive role in the linguistic life of a community; they saw "the people" as the true holders of language legitimacy and insisted on defending a necessarily pragmatic view of language.

For Sarmiento, the Academy was useless for practical matters: "It was not concerned at that time with primary schools, nor with the development of the intelligence of the people" (1843c: 23). Similarly, Unamuno wrote: "Such an Academy is an aristocratic institution that does not work for popular culture" (1907c: 372). Moreover, in their criticisms of the Academy, both authors emphasized the impossibility of stabilizing a living language. Unamuno affirmed the futility of such efforts:

> [D]ejemos a la Real Academia que fije la lengua castellana, haciéndole hipoteca inmueble, y, por nuestra parte, nosotros, los vivos heterodoxos, los que por favor de la naturaleza no somos instituciones ni tiramos a serlo, ya que tenemos que servirnos de esa lengua, procuremos, en la medida de nuestras fuerzas cada uno, movilizarla, aunque para conseguirlo tengamos que ensuciarla algo y quitarle algún esplendor.³⁶ (1903a: 1072)

We have also seen that Sarmiento had opposed Bello's view that in language a body of wise men was necessary to "pass suitable laws," and had defined the appropriate function of the Academy to be that of "collecting, as in a closet, the words authorized by the people and the poets" (Sarmiento 1842e: 252). Unamuno, repeating the words "legislar" and "recoger," states: "It is absurd that there is a legislative Body for language. It is appropriate to compile information on the life of a language, but not to legislate about it" (1917a: 424).[37]

Prevalent among romantic notions of language is the acceptance of popular usage as the chief source of language legitimacy. Alberdi had written: "Languages are not the work of Academies; they are born and formed in the mouth of the people" (quoted in Cambours Ocampo 1983: 34). And Unamuno: "People, not the Academies make language, my dear Sir" (1907c: 369). However, unlike the Latin American writers, Unamuno sees the popular basis of language as a guarantee of the unity of Spanish. He was familiar with the popular speech of Spain, and emphasized its parallels with that of Latin America: "Our common, everyday language is more like the one spoken in Argentina or Peru or Mexico than it is like the one that the Academy wants us to speak" (1911c: 603; cf. Pidal's views presented in chapter 5).

Unamuno's conception of linguistic correctness is similar to Sarmiento's. Just as the Argentinean had considered that an error becomes a transformation when it is characterized by general usage, Unamuno concludes: "When an entire people adopts a way of speaking, it ceases to be pathological and becomes physiologically normal" (1906a: 208). For the Spaniard, the Academy's rejection of forms characteristic of common speech "is equivalent to having the Academy of Natural Science begin to determine which birds or what coleoptera living in Spain are legitimate and which are not" (1911c: 605).

Sarmiento saw the ideal Academy as a body of great writers; therefore, in the alleged absence of worthy Spanish authors, he concluded that the Academy need not be taken into account, especially in Latin America. Unamuno's view was variable on this point: although there are moments when he found an academy of language to be useless regardless of who its members might be (cf. 1917a: 423), at other times he expressed his preference that if Academicians are to exist, they should be linguists, dedicated to the production of "scientific works," rather than "a Pantheon of famous writers . . . who write admirably but don't know a thing about linguistic matters" (quoted in Cabrera Perera 1989: 417–19). Unamuno was therefore pleased with Menéndez Pidal's entrance into the Academy in 1901 (cf. García Blanco 1952: 37; cf. del Valle's reference to this matter in chapter 5), and criticized the controversy which resulted when Commelerán, a "technical linguist," was chosen over Galdós (1899a: 743; 1907c: 370–1).[38] The discrepancy with Sarmiento's conception demonstrates Unamuno's professional stance within a context of a developing "linguistic science" in Spain during the second half of the nineteenth century.

Linguistic and social regeneration

In accordance with Sarmiento's belief in the integral perfectibility of society, social regeneration implies linguistic regeneration, and models from previous epochs are precluded: "It is absurd to look back and seek language models in a past century . . . as if in a time of social regeneration, the language bequeathed by the past could escape innovation and revolution" (Sarmiento 1842d: 307).[39] It seems then that, for Sarmiento, language regeneration is the natural consequence of social progress. Unamuno, however, reverses the terms of the relation: a revolution of ideas is only illusory without a revolution of language, the latter being "the most profound revolution" possible (Unamuno 1901a: 1003). In spite of this most significant difference – which greatly determined these authors' views on language fragmentation – they both based those views on the belief in the existence of a close connection between sociocultural regeneration and linguistic revolution.

Both authors were educators who deplored form for its own sake. Unamuno stated: "Our pedagogy focuses too much on form . . . it is not form but shapeless substance that we need, and with children, it is more necessary to provide them with a good lexicon than teaching them the futile task of learning the declensions and conjugating" (Unamuno 1906b: 158). He attacked pedagogical grammars ("Grammar" was for Sarmiento a sterile science: 1843c: 30) which were compilations of dead categories, reflecting the codifying tradition of languages no longer spoken, and therefore devoid of explanatory value (Unamuno 1906b: 152–3).

Unamuno, coinciding again with Sarmiento, found the "eruditos" – Hellenists, purely decorative poets – not appropriate for the cultural state of his nation. If, as Sarmiento had argued, Bello had been too profound for Latin America's nascent civilization (cf. note 13), Unamuno found the study of Greek philology appropriate only for "un país hecho": "It was not precisely Hellenists that Spain needed" (Salcedo 1964: 71).

Sarmiento claimed that neologisms and lexical borrowings enrich a language because they are a sign of cultural development. Language is ultimately variable and arbitrary:

> El que una voz no sea castellana es para nosotros objeción de poquísima importancia; en ninguna parte hemos encontrado todavía el pacto que ha hecho el hombre con la divinidad ni con la naturaleza, de usar tal o cual combinación de sílabas para entenderse; desde el momento que por mutuo acuerdo una palabra se entiende, ya es buena.[40]
>
> (Sarmiento 1842b: 302–3)

Sarmiento attributes the neologisms of Argentine speakers to language contact among various groups in the "active, intelligent, and progressive Río Plata basin" (cf. Carilla 1964: 71–2). Conversely, the archaism of certain dialects is due to their isolation ("por falta de roce") (1900: 348; Costa Álvarez 1922: 54). The Argentinean believed therefore that the first step toward the creation of a Latin American literary presence would be the development of the popular press: "When the periodical press, the only national literature possible, has developed, when every province has a press and every political party a newspaper, then the babel will be more complete, as it is in all of the democratic countries" (Sarmiento 1842e: 255). For Alberdi as well, language contact would provide the spark of cultural and linguistic regeneration: since languages, like groups sharing a common cultural tradition ("razas"), improve through cross-fertilization, America has a "providential" role to fulfill: "Immense and universal Babel, *rendez-vous* of all the nations of the globe, America has as a providential role, the improvement of cultural groups, institutions, and languages, amalgamating them in the direction of their future and best common destinies" (quoted in Cambours Ocampo 1983: 37). From these moments of anarchy would emerge the revitalized language which would most appropriately support and reflect cultural progress in America.

Similarly, for Unamuno, the necessary adoption of neologisms and foreign loans produces only a momentary linguistic anarchy, which is soon resolved by accommodation ("Anarchy in language is the one to be feared least, since men will strive to understand each other" [1901b: 1006]) and ultimately results in linguistic progress ("our language owes a great part of its progress to the invasion of hideous barbarisms" [1895: 791]).

Near the end of his life, Unamuno described America's providential role as precisely that of a cultural "melting pot," but one in which Spanish, "our common language," would balance transformation with integration, with foreign languages serving as a catalyst in this process (Unamuno 1935: 656). The apparently harmonious coexistence, in Unamuno's discourse, of external influence ("invasión de atroces barbarismos") and the preservation of "nuestro común idioma" bears witness to the precarious balance between centripetal and centrifugal forces that underlies the continuing controversy over the nature and control of the Spanish language.

The fragmentation polemic

The first generation of post-revolutionary Argentina had welcomed political independence, but remained faithful to their cultural and linguistic ancestry (Rosenblat 1960: 556; Morse 1989: 17). In 1835 Florencio Varela (1807–48), a member of that generation, wrote:

> Nada hay en nuestra patria más abandonado que el cultivo de nuestra lengua; de esta lengua, la más rica, sonora y numerosa de todas las vivas, aun en el concepto de los extranjeros sensatos . . . y de la cual, sin embargo, han dicho, poco hace, los diarios de Buenos Aires, que era

pobre e incapaz de competir con los idiomas extranjeros; probando que no saben su habla, ni han leído los buenos libros que hay en ella.[41]

(Varela quoted in Costa Álvarez 1922: 22–3)

However, the Generation of 1837, influenced by Herder's linguistic nationalism, by the ideas of the French and American revolutions, and by Larra's critical pessimism in Spain, reacted against those views. In the controversy over the possible fragmentation of the Spanish language in America, Sarmiento's separatist position held that the immediate progress of society was paramount, even if the continuity of Spanish was a casualty in its wake. In contrast, other Latin American writers, such as Andrés Bello in his *Gramática*, expressed more concern for Hispanic linguistic unity and saw the fragmentation of spoken Latin into the various Romance languages as a dangerous precedent:

Juzgo importante la conservación de la lengua de nuestros padres en su posible pureza, como un medio providencial de comunicación y un vínculo de fraternidad entre las varias naciones de origen español derramadas sobre los dos continentes . . . [L]a avenida de neologismos de construcción, que inunda y enturbia mucha parte de lo que se escribe en América, y alterando la estructura del idioma, tiende a convertirlo en una mulititud de dialectos irregulares, licenciosos, bárbaros; embriones de idiomas futuros, que durante una larga elaboración reproducirían en América lo que fue la Europa en el tenebroso período de la corrupción del latín.[42]

(Bello 1981: 129–30)

The late nineteenth and early twentieth century saw the intensification of the debate concerning the fragmentation issue. The Spanish writer Juan Valera and the Colombian philologist Rufino J. Cuervo had engaged in an acrimonious polemic (cf. chapter 4). Unamuno backed Valera's position, rejecting Cuervo's idea that Spanish would inevitably split into many languages. He also wrote a great deal about the fragmentationist theory of the French writer Luciano Abeille (1860–1949), whose book *Idioma nacional de los argentinos* advanced the idea that for Argentineans to speak Spanish was contrary to "the inherent right of a people to speak its own language" (1900: 5). Abeille believed that "el argentino" would become a separate language because, among other features, it used the passive voice more, whereas Spanish preferred the active voice (176); because it used more articles in its enumerations (169 ff.); and because of *voseo* and some cases of lexical diversity from the Peninsula. Unamuno – who probably had only second-hand knowledge of Abeille's book (Guitarte 1980/1: 173, n. 13) – observed that Abeille understood neither the nature of language change nor, more importantly, the popular speech of Spain (Unamuno 1902a: 1013). No better informed, he maintained, was the source of many of

Abeille's examples, Carlos Pellegrini, who had predicted that within a century Spanish would separate into several languages (Unamuno 1920b: 636). For Unamuno, what in Argentina is called the national language "is nothing more or less than Spanish. And learned Argentineans know perfectly well that almost all of the idioms and expressions popular there, the ones in *Martín Fierro*, for instance, are of Spanish origin" (Unamuno 1920b: 635–6). According to Unamuno, Abeille's insistence on linguistic differentiation arose from his aversion to Spain – just as hatred had fostered regionalist separatism in the Peninsula (Unamuno 1903b: 577). He described Abeille as "biased and lacking scientific rigor, due to his origin" (1903b: 575, note). As Guitarte has pointed out, Unamuno attributed the French writer's anti-Spanish bias to the latter's perceived envy of the Spanish linguistic empire in America, one for which the Spaniard sees world dominance: "[Spain] is envied for its future, it is envied for the imperial extension of its language – it is envied for the audience which its publicists will have, because those seventy million [people scattered throughout twenty nations] will double, will triple, will multiply" (Unamuno 1911b: 1306–7; Guitarte 1980/1: 170–1); "The Hispanic language, today the patrimony of some twenty nations . . . is the language that will one day share with English world dominance" (Unamuno 1911a: 598–9).

Unamuno argued that the situation of Latin during and after the Roman Empire was quite different from that of Spanish in America. In addition to diverse conditions of substrate, and far higher and broader levels of cultural literacy in the latter case, linguistic fragmentation in America would be prevented or retarded by the rise of a working class (resulting from the growth of post-industrialist commercialism) and the advent of technological innovations (such as printing, which perpetuated a conservative written norm [cf. Unamuno 1908b: 591–3]). Instead of the disintegration of spoken Latin, the historical analogue which Unamuno invoked was the integration of Leonese and Aragonese into Castilian during the Reconquest, a process which he saw as continuing in modern times in the cases of Galician and Valencian, and which would ultimately incorporate Catalan (1907b: 523; 1906d: 1302).

As we have seen, Sarmiento believed that the lack of a worthy literature would make a Peninsular model impossible in Latin America; Cuervo's position was similar, in that he thought it unlikely that the Hispanic intellectual community would agree on a common norm (cf. chapter 4). But Unamuno emphasized the centrality of a common language as an intra-historical tradition in creating society: "Society is nothing more than a common language" (1918: 438); "What forms the continuity of a people is not so much the historical tradition of a literature as the intra-historical tradition of a language; even when the former is broken, it is reborn thanks to the latter" (quoted in Betancur 1964: 87). The literary tradition documents "the history of fleeting events," while language is an eternal, permanent testimony to the silent tradition shared by members of the speech community. It is this testimony, language, that represents the substance of progress (Serrano Poncela 1964: 205–6).

In arguing for language maintenance as the source of cultural continuity, rather than its result, Unamuno recognizes the people as the site of legitimacy for language and insists in its practical nature: "Language is primarily and principally for life and not for literature" (1906e: 227). For this reason Spanish will not be lost in Latin America because of the lack of worthy writers in the Peninsula: "If this were the case, it would have disappeared in Spain some time ago . . . If Spanish persists in America, it is not because of our poets or our writers: it is because merchants have to place their orders in Castilian" (Unamuno 1906e: 227–8).

Unamuno finds the source of Hispanic unity in a shared language that he calls "sobrecastellano" or "hispanoamericano" (Unamuno 1911b: 1306). Unamuno identifies "sobrecastellano" as "el viejo romance castellano" enriched by its contact with new ideas and new cultures. "The future Hispanic language cannot and must not be a mere expansion of pure Castilian, but rather an integration of differentiated variants upon its base, respecting its nature, or not respecting it, as the case requires" (1903a: 1065).

The equivocal status of Unamuno's projected respect for the Castilian base within a context of differentiation reflects the tension inherent in his theory of integration – which Guitarte has traced to his early devotion to Spencer, expressed within the Hegelian dialectic (1980/1: 157–9). In this view, Peninsular speakers and writers must relinquish their privileged linguistic position in order to build a future of spiritual (i.e. linguistic) brotherhood with Latin America. The disaster of 1898 can be considered, in this sense, as "the beginning of a new life" for Spain:

> Creo que España, la verdadera España, la España íntima y espiritual, ha ganado mucho con verse reducida al solar de sus abuelos. Tal vez hemos perdido América para mejor ganarla, como deben ganarse los pueblos, mutuamente y comulgando en la cultura.[43]
>
> (Unamuno 1996: 201–2)

Unamuno's view of Latin America

Some of Unamuno's letters to his Latin American friends reflect a highly egalitarian attitude regarding the relationship between Spain and Latin America. He wrote for example to Ricardo Rojas in 1904:

> Cierto también que ahí [i.e. in Buenos Aires] parece han dominado prejuicios anti-españoles, triste correspondencia de los prejuicios anti-americanistas que aquí dominaban y aún dominan. Todo eso se corregirá el día en que nosotros los españoles abandonemos la necia pretensión de seguir siendo, ni en lenguaje, ni en nada, la metrópoli, la

madre patria, la que dirige y da la ley, y cesemos de ver en esas repúblicas hijuelas nuestras.[44]

(quoted in García Blanco 1964: 253)

Similarly, writing in 1906 to the editor of the Buenos Aires journal *La Nación*, Unamuno claimed: "In language there is no metropolis or mother country; it is equally for all who speak it" (1996: 263).

Fiddian, however, has suggested that in his articles written immediately after the crucial events of 1898, Unamuno assessed Latin American literature within a context of recolonization, viewing it as a "proyecto de nostalgia imperial" (Fiddian 1999: 119). Unamuno's correspondence with Spaniards suggests that Fiddian's assessment is accurate. In 1908 he wrote to Menéndez Pidal: "My tribune is *La Nación* of Buenos Aires, in which I promote Spanishness in my way, and, especially, I try to destroy certain additions that were going against what was Spanish there" (quoted in Unamuno 1970: 26).[45]

Unamuno's attitude towards Latin America changed over time. In 1905, Sarmiento's 1846 assessment of the vacuity of Spanish literary and scholarly culture in his *Viajes* (1993: 128) still held true for Unamuno (1996: 207). After 1908, however, there is increasing negative criticism of Sarmiento. By 1911, Unamuno found Sarmiento's conceptualization of Spanish history to be misinformed: this "most profoundly Spanish" writer was now the victim of *afrancesamiento*. Unlike Vicente Fidel López (Argentina; 1815–1903), who studied the history of Spain using original texts, Sarmiento knew little of the subject: "He hardly was familiar with it except through the systematic falsifications of the French writers who forged our slanderous [black] legend" (Unamuno 1911a: 596). During this period Unamuno's writings manifest a decreasing interest in American matters. If in 1899 Unamuno wrote to Darío: "Every day America interests me more" (1996: 71), a 1911 letter to Pedro Jiménez Ilundain rationalized his failed attempt to visit Argentina: "I feel farther and farther away from that. The better I come to know them, the more I recognize the abyss that separates me from their spirit. I'm too Spanish for that. In a sense, they are too Europeanizing" (1996: 372).

Conclusion

Sarmiento's and Unamuno's linguistic ideas bear directly on their conceptions of nationhood, and the feasibility and desirability of Hispanic unity. The Sarmiento of 1842 and 1843 rejected Peninsular models as representative of a decadent culture, and the Spanish language as incapable of expressing the ideas of modern civilization. In particular, the Argentinean found the Spanish Royal Academy powerless to contribute to the formation of a Latin American culture within which social progress could occur. The RAE was for Sarmiento a symbol of the bygone days of "la colonia," of decadent culture. In addition, acceptable contemporary Peninsular literary models were non-existent, and the traditional orthography, anarchistic and archaic, represented an impediment to the pedagogical regeneration which was the foundation of cultural advancement in Latin America. For these reasons, the independent republics would need to look to the cultural models of "wise nations." Sarmiento's travels to Europe and the United States (1846–8) were crucial in this search for cultural (i.e. educational) models. Whatever their source, new ideas would inevitably bring about linguistic changes in Latin America which individuals and Academies would be unable to impede. The unity of the Spanish language might be lost in this process but America's "immediate needs" must be given precedence.

Like Sarmiento, Unamuno wished to break with antiquated linguistic models, exemplified in the RAE and the "monopolismo casticista" of the purists. But while the Argentinean believed that linguistic uniformity would necessarily erode as the result of the discontinuity of cultural practices and institutions brought about by independence and Spain's impoverished cultural *milieu*, Unamuno took this existing uniformity to be the "spiritual" basis of past, present and future ties among Spanish-speaking nations.

Notes

1 "All political and cultural activity in nineteenth-century Spanish America is related to the project of nation-building, and the language issue (the symbolic dimension of usage, written or spoken norms, graphic representation, etc.) is inseparable from the problem of national identity."
2 "Prior to 1810 there were in Argentina two different, rival, incompatible societies: one learned, Spanish, European, and the other barbaric, American, almost indigenous; and the revolution of the cities only served as a cause, as an impetus, for these two ways of life to come into the presence of each other, to oppose each other, and after many years of struggle, for one to absorb the other."
3 In this study, citations appear in the orthography of the quoted document.
4 "Socialism," used in this sense, was a brand of "utopian" thought defined by Sarmiento as "the need for science, art, and politics to join together with the sole goal of improving the plight of a people, favoring liberal tendencies, combatting retrograde concerns, and rehabilitating the common people, the mulatto, and all those who suffer" (quoted in Katra 1996: 90).
5 "It is clear that we still maintain countless remnants of the Colonial regime ... since the Spaniards had given us despotism with its backward, wretched customs ... today we do not have a single retrograde idea, habit, or tendency that is not of Spanish origin."
6 "They all have in common a cultural and linguistic aversion to Spain, which at times reaches Hispanophobia; a fervent neophyte's enthusiasm for French literature and thought; the love of the people and of the earth; the affirmation of an American inspiration ...; the exaltation of ideas and the disdain for words; the rejection of all Academic teaching; the affirmation of freedom in language, so that it can keep pace with new ideas. Sarmiento, Alberdi, and Juan María Gutiérrez called for popular sovereignty in the area of language."
7 "We are speaking a dead language! The colonies can be emancipated only by abandoning it, or translating another language whole. This last will be a man's job. The other will take place through the slow action of other races, who will populate our land, with us serving as fertilizer for the earth."

8 "In America, among those people who cultivate intelligence, the works of French authors circulate more abundantly than Spanish ones in History, literature, and politics. This necessary transformation, and that separation from former national traditions brings with it, however, a difficulty, and that is the inevitable adulteration of language forms, if as the ideas of more advanced nations are absorbed there is not an effort to remove from them the foreign sludge, through the study of the characteristics of the Castilian language."

9 Alberdi, in 1871, expressed similar views, but with less reservation about the adulteration of Spanish: "Menos inconvenientes, en efecto, tiene el que la lengua española se bastardece por su roce con lenguas sabias, como el francés, el inglés, el alemán, el italiano, que los tenía por su mezcla con las lenguas bárbaras de los indígenas, cuyo peligro no inquietó nunca a la Academia. Esas lenguas compensan al idioma castellano, que habla Sudamérica, en nutrición y sustancia, lo que le quitan en pureza" (Alberdi quoted in Cambours Ocampo 1983: 37; "Indeed, it is less objectionable that the Spanish language be bastardized by contact with learned languages such as French, English, German, and Italian, than by its mixing with the barbarous indigenous languages, the danger of which never troubled the Academy. For Spanish, the former languages, in their nutrition and substance, make up for what they take away in purity.")

10 "The sovereignty of the people has all of its value and importance in language; grammarians are like the conservative Senate, created to repel popular uprisings, to preserve routine and tradition. In our view, they are, pardon the expression, the retrograde, stationary party of speaking society; but, like those of their class in politics, they can only scream and pull their hair out about the corruption, the abuses, the innovations. The torrent pushes them and today they admit a new word, tomorrow a lively foreign loan, the next day a shocking vulgar form; but what can they do? Everyone has started to use it, everyone writes and says it; it must be put into the dictionary and whether they like it or not, angry and sad, they put it in, and there is no alternative, and the people triumph and corrupt and adulterate everything."

11 "It is necessary that there be a body of wise men to state the laws suitable to the needs [of language and politics]; such as those of the language in which these should be expressed; and it would not be less ludicrous to entrust to the people the determination of their laws, than to authorize them to construct language."

12 "If in Spain there is an academy that compiles in a dictionary the words that the general usage of the people has already sanctioned, it is not because the academy authorizes their use, or forms language with its decisions, but rather because it gathers as in a closet the words whose use is unanimously authorized by the people themselves and by the poets."

13 Sarmiento's response, which appeared on 19 and 22 May, reflects the romantic notion of the perfectibility of social institutions through the progress of the enlightened masses. In a republic, according to the Argentinean, political bodies represent the will of the "pueblo," a term which Bello had misinterpreted in "an aristocratically false sense." Sarmiento wonders whether the Venezuelan's reference to a "cuerpo de sabios" was written "en una república donde el dogma de la soberanía del pueblo es la base de todas las instituciones y de donde emanan las leyes y el gobierno" (1842e: 251). He calls the Venezuelan excessively profound for the immediate needs of Chile's cultural milieu (1842e: 256). For Sarmiento, the cultural level of the Latin American republics was not sufficiently high to support what he considered to be linguistic purism. "¡Mire usted, en países como los americanos, sin literatura, sin ciencias, sin arte, sin cultura, aprendiendo recién los rudimentos del saber, y ya con pretensiones de formarse un estilo castizo y correcto que sólo puede ser la flor de una civilización desarrollada

y completa!" (1842e: 255; "Consider, in countries such as those in America, without literature, without sciences, without art, without culture, just learning the rudiments of knowledge, already with pretensions of forming a pure and correct style that can only be the product of a developed and complete civilization!"). Bello's participation in the polemic ended at this point: "Al hacer de un problema lingüístico una cuestión política, Sarmiento lleva la discusión a un terreno a donde el venezolano no quiere seguirlo" (Verdevoye 1981: 105; "On making a linguistic problem a political matter, Sarmiento takes the discussion to an area where the Venezuelan does not wish to follow him.") The argument was continued by Bello's disciple José María Núñez (1812–54) on May 28 and June 6, to whom Sarmiento also responded (cf. Durán Cerda 1957: 259–80).

14 "It is an abjection unworthy of nations that have assumed the rank of such to be expecting a powerless academy – without authority even in Spain, without prestige and lethargized by its own incompetence – to give us rules."

15 In his later years, Sarmiento believed that the RAE had become less "foreign." It had recognized such American writers as Bello and Baralt (1899: 311) and had offered membership to the Argentineans Juan María Gutiérrez (who rejected the diploma) and Juan B. Alberdi (who accepted it). In 1883 the mature Sarmiento conceded that Bello had been "the Quintilian of letters" ("el Quintiliano de las buenas letras"): "La verdad es que Bello tenía razón y sabía infinitamente más que todos nosotros" (quoted in Carilla 1964: 49; "The truth is that Bello was right and knew infinitely more than any of us").

16 For a summary of the history of orthographic reform prior to this period, see Rosenblat (1981), Contreras (1993).

17 "That is the fundamental difference between his system and Bello's: the latter was alarmed at any sign of linguistic excision, of fragmentation of the broad Hispanic community. Sarmiento, in contrast, let himself be carried away with the violent anti-Spanish feelings that had followed the wars of independence in the younger generations."

18 "When I say Spain in the area of letters, I include America . . . Spain, as a people who are struggling to move beyond the worthlessness to which the errors of its former despots have condemned it, is the nation most worthy of respect." "Today's Spaniards, enlightened Spaniards like us, are fighting gloriously to cease being Spanish and become European, that is, French in their ideas and customs, English in their form of government."

19 Having taken Larra's criticism of Spain as a model ("lloremos y traduzcamos"), Sarmiento asks why Minvielle had not opposed the earlier attacks against Spanish culture by the author of *Artículos de costumbres*, and he finds the answer in Minvielle's discrimination against Latin Americans: "Pero Larra era español, y yo que soy un americano y un paria en Chile, no debo, no puedo decir lo que los españoles dicen" (1843f: 61; "But Larra was a Spaniard, and I, an American and a pariah in Chile must not, cannot say what the Spaniards say.")

20 The author was probably the Argentinean Miguel Piñero, who had replaced Sarmiento as editor of that periodical the previous year (Barrenechea *et al.* 1997: 9). Excerpts from the article appear in Contreras (1993: 205–6).

21 "We reform because we can, and those nations do not because they cannot; in the same way as we have adopted republican government because we could adopt it without difficulty, and they do not adopt it because of the resistance against which they have to fight."

22 "I fully realize that there are ten or twelve young people who have attempted to imitate, to 'ape,' the speech of the Castilians; you may be one of them and I may be another; but all of them do not speak [with this feature] habitually; at most,

they read or speak *ex cathedra* like that; they have, or I should say, we have two languages, one for show and the other for common use."

23 Of his proposed system, he wrote in a letter to Félix Frías in February, 1844: "Ningún literato lo apoya" (Barrenechea *et al.* 1997: 29; "No writers support it.") See also Contreras 1993: 37.

24 In particular, the University rejected those recommendations which reflected the most clearly Americanist of Sarmiento's leanings: *s* for *c* before front vowels, and the elimination of *v* and *z* (Guirao Massif 1957: 109, Barrenechea *et al.* 1997: 55 n. 6). The University report on the orthography question, from 26 April 1844, recommended what was essentially a return to the Bello-García del Río system (1823), with the additional conventions of excluding the graph *h* (except in interjections such as *ah, oh*), simplifying the *qu* digraph to *q*, and using *rr* to represent the alveolar trill, except in word-initial position (Barrenechea *et al.* 1997: 259–65; 55, n. 6; Contreras 1993: 389). There then followed a period of inconsistent application of these conventions in the press and in educational institutions. In 1847 – with Sarmiento out of the country – Bello's periodical *El Araucano* and the *Anales de la Universidad de Chile* stopped using the reformed system, and Sarmiento himself abandoned it in his 1849 book *Educación popular*. In 1851 Andrés Bello recommended the discontinuance of the reform, and the Ministry of Public Education issued a decree to that effect (Contreras 1993: 132–3, Guirao Massif 1957: 56).

25 "A language is correspondingly more perfect as it has been used to express a greater number of ideas, as the meanings of its words are more stable, as the thought of the people who use it is more advanced, as the intelligence that uses it to develop has made greater progress."

26 "When part of a society, just the common people, says *quero, sordao, benío, truje*, etc., these defects can be considered true errors; but when everyone who speaks a language says it, this is not an error, but a transformation, and it becomes part of correct language" (1843a: 93).

27 "It is necessary that its books be in everyone's hands, and that its laws, its customs, and even its form of government reign here as well as on the Peninsula itself. That this is not the case and that it never will be, is what I attempted to prove in the second part of my *Memoria*."

28 Sarmiento expressed the same view with regard to linguistic diversity on the Iberian Peninsula: "Hasta hoy existen en España varios dialectos [*sic*], el vascuence, el portugués, el cántabro, y no es con la ortografía con lo que el idioma castellano los ha de incorporar al fin en su propia masa, sino con la fuerza de sus armas, de sus leyes, de sus libros y de su civilización" (1843d: 122; "Still today there exist in Spain several dialects [*sic*], Basque, Portuguese, Cantabrian, and it is not with orthography that the Castilian language will ultimately incorporate them into itself, but with the force of its arms, its laws, its books, and its civilization.")

29 "[Sarmiento] was a precursor of our own native critics. His soul was a pure and honorably Spanish one, and his language, for all of its carelessness and errors, sounds more to me like something of our own than the artificially purified language of the jurists."

30 On Unamuno's linguistic formation, see Huarte Morton (1954), Blanco Aguinaga (1954), Otero (1970), Jiménez Hernández (1973), Rabanal (1980).

31 Unamuno wrote: "La civilización nació en las ciudades y es ciudadana. . . . Sarmiento tuvo en esto, como en tantas otras cosas, visión penetrante y larga" (1907a: 305; "Civilization was born in the cities and it is civic . . . Sarmiento had in this, as in so many other things, a long-ranging and penetrating vision.")

32 "The blood of my spirit is my language / and my country is wherever its sovereign word resounds, / as its voice is not diminished / no matter how much it may fill both worlds."

33 Sarmiento sees the same purpose in the study of a foreign language: "A foreign language, understood as merely a manifestation of written culture and a reading instrument, was an eminently practical tool that distinguished its user from those who could not read it. In Sarmiento's view, there was nothing worth reading in Spanish anyway" (Altamirano and Sarlo 1994: 162).

34 "A language is a root, more than a depository, of traditions, and it carries with it a vision and an audition of the world-universe, a conception of life and of human destiny, an art, a philosophy, and even a religion."

35 "A language's richness does not reside in the number of words or expressions that it has, but rather in that which it can have: it resides in its fecundity, in its facility for creating new words in response to new ideas, and in its facility for assimilating new words."

36 "Let us allow the Royal Academy to stabilize the Castilian language, making it immobile, and for our part, we, the living heterodox, those who through a favor of nature are not institutions and do not aspire to be, since we have to use that language, let us attempt, the best each of us can, to mobilize it, even if in order to do that we must dirty it a bit and remove some of its splendor."

37 Rabanal (1980: 13) has pointed out the influence of Darwinism during Unamuno's formative period as a source of his anti-Academy stance and his steadfast opposition to attempts to "stabilize" the language. Meanwhile, Sarmiento abandoned his popular, romantic perspective of the 1840s in favor of a scientific evolutionism in his later years (Fontanella de Weinberg 1988: 71).

38 Unamuno's letters to the Peruvian writer Ricardo Palma (1833–1919) make several references to the issue: "El pecado original de la Academia es aspirar a ser una autoridad que define lo que es bueno y lo que es malo, y no una corporación que investigue el lenguaje" (1996: 170; "The Academy's original sin is to aspire to be an authority that defines what is good and what is bad, and not a body that researches language.")

39 "It is absurd to look back and seek language models in a past century . . . as if in a time of social regeneration, the language bequeathed by the past could escape innovation and revolution."

40 "The fact that a word is not Castilian is hardly an important objection to us; nowhere have we ever found the pact that man has made with the divinity or with nature, to use such and such combination of syllables to make himself understood; from the moment that by mutual agreement a word is understood, it is good."

41 "There is nothing more neglected in our country than the cultivation of our language; of this language, the richest, most harmonious and abundant of all living languages, as even sensitive foreigners believe . . . and of which, nevertheless, the newspapers of Buenos Aires said recently that it was poor and incapable of competing with foreign languages; proving that they do not know their language, and that they have not read the good books that have been written in it."

42 "I believe that the preservation of our forefathers' tongue in all possible purity is important, as a providential means of communication and a fraternal link among the various nations of Spanish origin scattered over the two continents . . . [T]he torrent of grammatical neologisms which inundate and render obscure much of what is written in America, and which by altering the structure of the language tend to change it into a multitude of irregular, undisciplined, and barbaric dialects; embryos of future languages which, during a long development, would reproduce in America what happened in Europe during the dark period of the corruption of Latin" (trans. in Bello 1997: 101).

43 "I believe that Spain, the real Spain, the intimate and spiritual Spain, has gained a great deal from having been brought back to its ancestral home. Perhaps we have lost America to win it in a better way, as peoples should be won, mutually and through cultural sharing."
44 "It is also true that there [in Buenos Aires] it appears that anti-Spanish prejudices have prevailed, a sad parallel to the anti-American prejudices that previously prevailed here, and still do. All of that will be corrected the day that we Spaniards abandon the foolish pretension of continuing to be, in language or in anything, the metropolis, the *mother* country, the one that controls and gives the law, and we stop seeing our little daughters in those republics."
45 Unamuno contributed some 400 articles to *La Nación* between 1899 and 1924 (cf. Unamuno 1970, 1994, 1997). While his earliest articles frequently treat Latin American literature and language, and Hispanic cultural (linguistic) relations, by 1911 his interest in these topics had declined substantially. Unamuno had initially sought to use the Argentine journal to promote himself in Europe; however, by 1914 he preferred to present himself to the Continent, and especially to Italy, directly (1996: 420).

3 The ideological construction of an empirical base
Selection and elaboration in Andrés Bello's grammar

Belford Moré

Preserving unity, producing unity

Few Bello scholars would deny that the main concern behind the Venezuelan's extensive production of grammatical texts was the problem of the unity of the language. With unparalleled enthusiasm and determination, Bello assumed the role of *standard-bearer* in the nineteenth-century campaign for the "preservation of the Castilian language" in the newly-born Latin American nations. In an often-quoted passage from the prologue to his *Gramática de la lengua castellana destinada al uso de los americanos* (1847), he explicitly indicated that the main reason for writing this grammar was the danger that Spanish would become "a multitude of irregular, undisciplined and barbaric dialects," which in time would reproduce in America a phenomenon parallel to the corruption of Latin (Bello 1847: 12).

Assuming the defense of unity against fragmentation and formulating the problem of unity are different (though related) issues. If we pay careful attention to how Bello presented the problem, a number of significant details become visible. Bello did not of course present the idea of linguistic fragmentation in positive terms. His intention was not even to make a reasonable prediction about whether fragmentation would occur or not. Instead, he used the idea of fragmentation only as a *potential* danger, thus leaving the door open for the necessary corrections that would channel language development in the direction of unity. However, linguistic unity – which in his argumentation was taken for granted and which functioned as a point of departure – was not as solid and widespread as he desired: Bello was acutely aware of language diversity. On one hand, diversity was manifest in the speech of a majority of Spanish speakers who, in his opinion, did not know how to use "their own language grammatically" (Bello 1823: 71); on the other, it was reflected in the many indigenous languages still in use among large population groups in Latin America. Consequently, unity was not simply a state that must be protected from future threats, but also – and especially – a condition that must be created and expanded through a process that homogenizes language use under the rule of a single code shared, at least, by the dominant and middle sectors of society.

Both objectives – preserving and producing unity – converge in the design and implementation of a series of actions that we may label as language planning, since they constitute an effort to consciously influence speakers (Fasold 1987: 246). One dimension of this type of process is the development of an educational system in which the study of "the language spoken in the country of birth" (Bello 1823: 71) occupies a prominent place. As is well known, Bello actively participated in this process through his role in the organization of Chile's educational system (cf. also chapter 2). Another aspect of language planning is the production of texts required for the formulation of the policy's general guidelines, for its implementation, and for its political and cultural legitimization. With respect to this last process – i.e. the legitimization of language policy – Bello's contribution had great impact throughout Latin America; an impact that, given the reception of his oeuvre, it continues to have in certain areas of cultural power.

In spite of the many different goals and accomplishments of Bello's linguistic work, we can say that, as a whole, it embodies a grammatical knowledge that serves as the basis for language planning. This corpus – his grammatical oeuvre – states the general goals of language policy, establishes the most appropriate lines of action, legitimizes planning from positions of power and, most importantly, organizes a discourse that, on one hand, is said to represent "the language," and on the other, tries to impact and shape people's linguistic behavior. Consequently, the role played by this body of grammatical knowledge within language planning is more than strictly functional. The degree to which power pressures are rationalized and the social authority with which this grammatical knowledge is invested make it a privileged source of legitimacy for language policy and for every linguistic decision. Ultimately, grammar is the discourse that expresses and defines the decisions (what to teach, how to teach, whom to teach, why teach, etc.) which, once translated into actions, will accomplish the immediate objectives of the intervention of power in language use: uniformity of linguistic behavior and unity of the communicative code.

Selection and grammatical knowledge

Homogenization presupposes a hierarchical conceptualization of linguistic diversity which is the result of an operation that consists of establishing which variety is valid and which are not. Such operation is known, in the Sociology of Language, as *selection*.

We might be tempted to consider that, in Bello's writings, selection is only of secondary importance, since even in his most controversial articles, we do not find a systematic effort to persuade his interlocutors of the need to choose a given variety at the expense of others. This may be due to the fact that linguistic selection is seldom openly discussed in the intellectual forum. In Bello's writings, selection tends implicitly to comply with the following principle: the privileged variety is the Spanish spoken by the educated classes; indigenous languages and other varieties of Spanish, especially those used by the members of the lower tiers of the cultural hierarchy, are thus excluded.

From the standard perspective of the Sociology of Language, the previous explanation would be sufficient to account for the process of selection: Bello, like many of his contemporaries, would have selected, from a series of clearly defined varieties, the one that best served the immediate linguistic needs identified by those in power. However, such an approach is in fact insufficient, since, in addition to the general choice of a given variety, language selection includes many specific choices that after all create the standard. The principle that the privileged variety must be the one associated with the educated is also realized in the determination of the specific characteristics of such variety. At this level of the selection process, we must analyze the application of more specific criteria associated with multiple contexts of use. As we will see, these specific criteria often collide with the more general principle of selection.

This forces us to reframe the issue. Rather than the choice of a clearly defined variety, selection consists of the identification of forms that exist in different areas of language use bringing them together to form a supposedly systematic whole: the "specific theory" of the system that is the language (Bello 1847: 6). In this sense, selection does not precede but is simultaneous with the construction of the grammar; both selection and construction are governed by the desire to build the only valid norm on which speakers can base correct usage.

Selection criteria

An examination of Bello's specific choices in the development of his grammatical discourse suggests that, in his case, selection takes place on three general levels: (1) socio-cultural; (2) dialectal; (3) discursive-semiotic. The first is explicitly formulated and the determination of its features is fairly simple. The second and third are latent and tend to be operative rather than explicitly formulated.

Selection at the socio-cultural level

> La GRAMATICA de una lengua es el arte de hablarla correctamente, esto es, conforme al buen uso, que es el de la gente educada.[1]
>
> (Bello 1847: 15)

This statement shows that Bello did not simply define grammar as a system of linguistic units and rules that govern people's linguistic behavior. He also affirmed that grammar is organized with reference to the specific realm of language use. Grammar is not an arbitrary product of the spirit in its imaginative processes (like weak "metaphysical speculations"). Instead, all of its formulations are based on empirical facts. These facts occur at the level of language use, or better, in a space whose borders are clearly perceived: "The use of the educated." Thus, in his definition of grammar, Bello becomes involved in the process of selection, inasmuch as grammar is not the art that brings together and represents a multiplicity of uses; it only refers to one of them, that of the educated, which guarantees, in principle, the uniformity and stability required by language planning.

At this level, the definition of the legitimate variety is not based on strictly linguistic features. It is not considered "good use" because of its semantic, orthological or syntactic peculiarities, or because of its communicative efficiency. Rather, what informs the choice is rather the association of this variety with a human group. The borders of the chosen variety coincide with the borders of the educated group and, in this sense, its configuration as a uniform, constant and separable entity among all linguistic varieties is only possible with a previous separation that has taken place in the realm of the social. First, the educated group is identified, and then the linguistic features associated with it are described.

This means that the selection of a given variety is actually based on the criteria used by the structures of power to represent the social body. Bello's definition clearly shows that these criteria are not strictly economic or political. As indicated by his many criticisms of the speech of those who hold economic or political power, Bello implicitly excludes the possibility of selecting a variety simply because it is the speech of the wealthy or the politically powerful. The selection criterion is often defined in cultural terms. Educated people are identified with those who share patterns of behavior, beliefs, knowledge, etc. that to various degrees have been passed on through a process of formal education and through contact with the educated Western tradition. This distinguishes the members of this social group not only from the majority of the population (the "ínfima plebe" or "ínfimo vulgo," in Bello's own words) but also from members of the hegemonic group that do not possess the same cultural capital and whose activities depend less on the written word.

In contrast with other human groups, the educated class extends well beyond the local level and even reaches a supranational dimension. Due to the technology available to them (writing and printing), the communication networks that articulate these groups do not require the simultaneous presence of their members in time and space, and, therefore, different members of these educated groups may be, and in fact are, located in places very distant from each other. Thus, the group identified as "the educated" is not limited to a particular city, a nation such as Chile, or a group of nations such as those of Latin America. It includes the totality of the Hispanic cultural community whose linguistic bond is preserved and strengthened through language planning.

It is precisely the supralocal character of the legitimate variety that makes it possible to "imagine" linguistic homogeneity in such a large territory. The level at which interaction among the educated takes place provides an instrument of communication that connects the various distant groups over and above the diversity of linguistic codes used in the lower levels of society. For this reason, from Bello's perspective, the educated are the only group capable of providing a linguistic model with the desired degree of uniformity. The goal of language planning is to spread the use of Spanish to the entire continent, and at that level only the educated share a minimally variable and stable linguistic norm. Consequently, the selection of any other variety is discarded:

> Se prefiere este uso porque es el más uniforme en las varias provincias y pueblos que hablan una misma lengua, y por lo tanto el que hace que más fácil y generalmente se entienda lo que se dice; al paso que las palabras y frases propias de la gente ignorante varían mucho de unos pueblos a otros, y no son fácilmente entendidas fuera de aquel recinto en que las usa el vulgo.[2]
>
> (Bello 1847: 15)

Since grammar is written assuming a preexisting uniformity, language planning can be said to aim for the spread of that uniform variety.

The implementation of the socio-cultural criterion, however, reveals certain inconsistencies. In spite of having many elements in common, the linguistic behavior of the educated is not completely homogeneous. Their use varies from one place to another in such a way that, in some cases, the homogenizing goal is seriously challenged. Thus, it is not surprising that Bello at times rejects the usage associated with the educated. When discussing the use of the Imperative, for example, he states:

> *Imperativo.* Nada es más común, aun entre personas de buena educación, que alterar el acento de la segunda persona de singular del imperativo de casi todos lo verbos, diciendo, verbigracia, *mirá, andá, levantáte, sentáte, socegáte* [sic]. Estas palabras y sus análogas no existen, y deben evitarse con el mayor cuidado, porque prueban una ignorancia grosera de la lengua.[3]
>
> (Bello 1833–4: 148)

The shifted stress is present in the speech of educated Chileans (preachers and lawyers are constantly criticized by Bello). However, instead of accepting it as correct – since it is used by those who, according to Bello's criteria, should be held as a model – its validity is flatly denied. Obviously, for Bello, association with the educated is not sufficient to guarantee the validity of a linguistic form.

Selection at the dialectal level

Bello's second selection criterion refers to the hierarchical relationship among dialects. Although its nature is less obvious – Bello never formulated it explicitly – it is still possible to identify its implicit presence and operation, especially when the socio-cultural criterion is inadequate for either questioning or authorizing a given form. One of the many examples in which we see this principle at work is the following:

> Usase en el foro [en Chile], y en el lenguaje ordinario, un verbo *transar*, que creemos no hay en castellano. *Pedro y Juan se transaron, es necesario transar el asunto*, son expresiones que se oyen en bocas de todos, inclusos (sic) los abogados y jueces. Pero ni el *Diccionario* de la Academia trae tal verbo, ni lo hemos visto en las obras de los jurisconsultos españoles, que, según lo hemos podido observar, sólo usan en este sentido el verbo *transigir* neutro. Dícese, pues, *Pedro y Juan transigieron, nadie debe transigir con el honor*.[4]
>
> (Bello 1833–4: 158)

In Chile, the verb "transar" is used in contexts in which educated people (such as lawyers or judges) interact. We would expect this to be enough to validate the word. However, there are two reasons that allow Bello to exclude it from the inventory of the legitimate language. On one hand, the verb is not included in the *Diccionario de la Real Academia de la Lengua*; and on the other (and this is the most relevant reason for our present purposes), *transar* is not used in the Spanish judicial system. This argument rests on a further stratification of the language practices of the educated. According to this stratification, the forms used by people who work in the Spanish judicial system are given a higher value than those used by their Chilean counterparts. In this case, the selection of the correct form does not depend on the socio-cultural position of speakers, since it is equivalent in both cases. The verb *transigir* should replace *transar* not because it is used by members of the law profession, but because it is used by Spaniards.

Bello does not limit the use of this criterion to refer to formal contexts in which educated people interact. In different points in his work, he suggests that, in some regions of Spain we find language varieties that are much closer to the ideal Hispanic linguistic norm. Thus when he responded to those who, in Chile, claimed that daily use is enough to learn the mother tongue and that, consequently, knowledge of grammar is unnecessary, he said:

> Si esto se dijese en Valladolid o en Toledo, todavía se pudiera responder que el caudal de voces y frases que andan en la circulación general no es más que una pequeña parte de las riquezas de la lengua; que su cultivo la uniforma entre todos los pueblos que la hablan, y hace mucho más

lentas las alteraciones que produce el tiempo en esta como en todas las cosas humanas; que . . . disminuye una de las trabas más incómodas a que está sujeto el comercio entre los diferentes pueblos y se facilita asimismo el comercio entre las diferentes edades . . .; que todas las naciones altamente civilizadas han cultivado con esmero particular su propio idioma . . . De este modo pudiera responderse, aun en los países *donde se habla el idioma nacional con pureza*, a los que condenan el estudio como innecesario y estéril.[5]

(Bello 1832: 175–6; emphasis added)

The everyday dialects of Toledo and Valladolid, though insufficient to function as languages regulated by grammar, are more pure than other varieties (especially Latin American varieties). Some of Bello's harshest criticisms of the Spanish spoken by Latin Americans are based on this consideration:

C, Z. No hay hábito más universalmente arraigado en los americanos y más difícil de corregir, que el de dar a la *z* el valor de la *s*, de manera que en su boca no se distinguen *baza* y *basa*, *caza* y *casa*, *cima* y *sima*, *cocer* y *coser*, *lazo* y *laso*, *pozo* y *poso*, *riza* y *risa*, *roza* y *rosa*, etc.

En el mismo inconveniente, caen los que dan a la *s* el sonido de *z*, que es lo que se llama *ceceo*, y los que emplean estos sonidos sin discernimiento, como lo hacen algunos. Es cosa ya desesperada restablecer en América los sonidos castellanos que corresponden respectivamente a la *s*, a la *z*, o a *c* subseguida de una de las vocales *e*, *i*.[6]

(Bello 1835: 22)

These words clearly contradict the interpretation of Bello's grammatical oeuvre as an attempt to construct an "American Spanish."[7] While a good part of his most important works is directed to his Latin American brothers, when he determines the legitimate use of language using geographic criteria, he continues to reinforce the dialectal hierarchies characteristic of the colonial period.

This is confirmed when we consider the way in which Bello includes American contributions to the language. Dialectal hierarchization does not necessarily translate into an *a priori* rejection of the linguistic forms produced by the speakers of the inferior American dialects. In the prologue to *Gramática de la lengua castellana destinada al uso de los americanos* he states:

No se crea que recomendando la conservación del castellano sea mi ánimo tachar de vicioso y espurio todo lo que es peculiar de los americanos. Hay locuciones castizas que en la Península pasan por anticuadas y que subsisten tradicionalmente en Hispano-América ¿por qué proscribirlas? Si según la practica general de los americanos es más analógica la conjugación de algún verbo, ¿por qué razón hemos de preferir la que caprichosamente haya prevalecido en Castilla? Si de raíces castellanas hemos formado vocablos nuevos, según los procederes ordinarios de derivación que el castellano reconoce, y de que se ha servido y se sirve continuamente para aumentar su caudal, ¿qué motivos hay para que nos avergoncemos de usarlos? Chile y Venezuela tienen tanto derecho como Aragón y Andalucía para que se tomen sus accidentales divergencias, cuando las patrocina la costumbre uniforme y auténtica de la gente educada.[8]

(Bello 1847: 13)

The terms in which Bello presents this open attitude reveal, however, its limitations. The phenomena to which he refers do not entail a radical break from the assumptions and levels at which, for Bello, the language is defined. Anachronisms are remnants of previous stages and, in many cases, this gives them a special dignity. Greater regularity in verb conjugation brings language use closer to the ideal system since it renders it more regular and functional than the more arbitrary ("caprichosa") Peninsular conjugation. The new forms comply with the principle that all innovations must be controlled so that they do not run counter to the essential structure of the language. They are, therefore, marginal phenomena of secondary importance; in addition, they are validated by the socio-cultural background of their users.

Bello's presentation of the accentuation rule for Spanish tripthongs illustrates the operation of these criteria:

Todo triptongo es acentuado, y el acento cae siempre sobre su segunda vocal: *cambiáis, fragüéis*. De aquí se sigue que no hay dicción castellana en que se encuentre más de un triptongo.

Esto, sin embargo, parece más un hecho accidental de la lengua, el cual puede variar a consecuencia de nuevas adquisiciones, que no un carácter permanente de ella, fundado en su genio y pronunciación natural; pues no creo se diga que es dura o repugnante a nuestros hábitos la prolación de vocablos en que haya triptongos inacentuados. Y aún más se puede afirmar que existen tales vocablos castellanos; pues lo son verdaderamente los nombres propios de lugares o de regiones en que la lengua nativa es la castellana, y los apelativos de las tribus o razas que moran en ellos, y todos los derivados de unos y otros. El triptongo *guai* es frecuente en los nombres geográficos y nacionales de América, y entre ellos hay varios que, como *guaireño* (natural de la *Guaira*) y *guaiquerí* (raza de indios), forman excepciones a la regla anterior. Tenemos también los nombres propios *Miaulina, Miauregato*, formados caprichosamente, aquel por Cervantes, y éste por el fabulista Samaniego; uno y otro fáciles de pronunciar, y nada desagradables al oído.[9]

(Bello 1835: 66)

We should first point out the contradiction between the contents of both paragraphs. In the first, Bello presents an apparently iron-clad rule and therefore seems to hold a rigorous, normative-representational value. But immediately thereafter he refers to phenomena that cannot be considered exceptions confirming the rule but rather elements that destabilize it. When both lines are brought together, Spanish tripthongs are defined as stressed forms that can also be unstressed. A way of resolving this contradiction would be to create a rule that better suits the characteristics of the language. However, he does not choose this alternative. While the rule that discards unstressed tripthongs is presented as unquestionable, its representational limitations are also indicated.

If we notice the dialogic nature of the relation between both parts of the paragraph, we can understand the contradiction. What characterizes the general rule is that, in its formulation, Spanish American pronunciation and sporadic forms from classics of Spanish literature are not taken into account.[10] The exclusion of the American usage reveals that the rule is based on Peninsular Spanish. Consequently, the contradiction reproduces the tensions generated by the dialectal hierarchy that we have indicated. In the general rule, Peninsular Spanish is endowed with a centrality that erases or marginalizes the Latin American forms.

The second paragraph is an attempt to challenge that centrality problematic, since it reframes the content of the rule by paying attention to words used in Latin American countries whose native language is Spanish. However, the challenge is rather limited and actually reproduces the dialectal hierarchy. Although Bello assumes that both varieties are valid, the first is posited more eloquently than the second, a fact which strengthens its normative power. It also makes clear that the forms to which it refers are not rule-governed phenomena that call into question the essential mechanisms of the system. On the contrary, the legitimacy attributed to them is grounded in the fact that their presence is virtually defined in the genius of the language.

This limited incorporation of the marginal into legitimate linguistic space explains the geo-political status given to American forms. Inasmuch as they emerge and circulate in the margins they cannot go beyond having the same right to be recognized as those from the regions still subjected to the dominant axis of Castile.[11]

Given their centrality, Peninsular dialects constitute one of the most important linguistic repertoires on which the grammar of the prestigious variety is built. They are the basis of a good part of the rules that form the orthology and, in spite of changes in terminology and definition, the verb system. However, at this level, just as at the socio-cultural, there is no automatic selection. Certain linguistic features of the metropolis may be censured due to their distance from the norm, and may even be included in the catalogue of illegitimate provincialisms:

Hay variedad [Bello points out in his *Principios de la ortología y métrica de la lengua castellana*] acerca del valor de la *d* final, pues unos la pronuncian y otros no . . .; y de aquellos que la pronuncian, los unos le dan un sonido que se acerca más o menos al de la *z* (*virtuz, miraz*), y los otros le conservan su natural valor. *Virtú, mirá* es un resabio de pronunciación descuidada y baja, y el valor de la *z* aplicado a la *d* final, aunque propio de algunos pueblos de Castilla, no ha sido ni aun mencionado siquiera en la *Ortografía* de la Real Academia Española; lo que me induce a mirarlo como un provincialismo que no debe imitarse.[12]

(Bello 1835: 23)

This critical attitude shows that the dialectal hierarchy is not the only criterion that operates in Bello's construction of the "correct" variety. Selection may prefer forms associated with a group of culturally, politically or socially prestigious people; or forms associated with the educated groups from a specific place. However, linguistic borders do not strictly coincide with geopolitical borders. Socio-cultural, semiotic and discourse criteria interlace with dialectal criteria and function as pillars that guide the configuration of linguistic legitimacy.

Selection at the semiotic and discourse levels

Bello's application of the semiotic/discourse criteria is even less evident: there is not a single paragraph in his grammatical oeuvre in which they are explicitly present. As we will soon see, a superficial analysis of his work may lead to conclusions that completely ignore them; however, a closer reading discloses not only the presence of these criteria but also their importance. An examination of Bello's determination of what is pertinent for the creation of a body of linguistic knowledge and of the origin of the empirical materials he used reveals that in the selection of the standard there is an unequal relation between alphabetic writing and orality.[13] According to this relation, the semiotic realm of writing and some discourses organized around it constitute the privileged ground on which the grammar is built.

The clarification of this issue leads us to focus on the details of the relation between writing and orality in Bello's work, and to present the characteristics and implications of the inventory of texts to which his grammatical observations refer.

Writing and orality

If we focus on statements made by Bello in his works on orthography, we conclude that for him writing was subordinated to orality. Writing is a system of discrete signs (letters) that constitute the graphic transposition of phonetic phenomena. In his "Indicaciones . . ." he states:

> El mayor grado de perfección de que la escritura es susceptible, y el punto a que por consiguiente deben conspirar todas las reformas, se cifra en una cabal correspondencia entre los sonidos elementales de la lengua y los signos o letras que han de representarlos, por manera que a cada sonido elemental corresponda invariablemente una letra, y a cada letra corresponda con una misma invariabilidad un sonido.[14]
>
> (Bello 1823: 78)

For Bello, thus, the ideal writing system is based on a close correlation between graphic signs and sounds, and the design of an orthographic system must therefore aim for that goal.

The formulation of these principles reflects the conception of writing on which they are based. Writing does not constitute a differentiated semiotic field that operates according to its own dynamics; its function is simply to reproduce orality. It is therefore a secondary system whose structure and operations are determined outside of it, in a more essential component of the language. Language is, above all, oral. Writing presents it to the eyes and creates the possibility of its permanence.

The misleading nature of this conception becomes apparent when we notice the practical problems faced by those who design and promote orthography. The one-to-one correlation between sound and letter is disrupted by an apparently accidental phenomenon: diversity at the phonetic level. This diversity is acknowledged by Bello. In an article published in 1827 he responded in the following manner to the objection that the Chilean orthographic reform would make it difficult to find words in a dictionary:

> Pero ¿no les sucede ahora lo mismo? ¿No les es necesario buscar una palabra con *b* o con *v*; con *z*, con *c* o con *s*; y también con *h* y sin *h*? Oye uno hablar por la primera vez de un árbol cuyo nombre suena *aya*; lo busca probablemente en la *a*; no lo encuentra, y tiene que buscarlo en la *h*. *La verdadera causa de estas dobles investigaciones es a veces la incorrecta pronunciación*, y otras el uso de letras inútiles o el doble valor de las letras. Lo primero no puede evitarse en ningún sistema de ortografía; lo segundo se evitaría completamente por medio de una ortografía racional y sencilla.[15]
>
> (Bello 1827: 105; emphasis added)

Thus, on one hand, pronunciation is not uniform and, on the other, there are different ways of representing the same sequence of sounds. However, this diversity is understood within the framework of a hierarchical relation that separates the "correct" from the "incorrect" pronunciation. We understand then why, while knowing that there are different ways to produce the same sound, the idea that writing is a mere representation of orality is still confidently promoted. The sound–grapheme correlation is only possible inasmuch as the phonetic level has been subjected to a process of selection that has determined the legitimate forms. Thus the establishment of a legitimate pronunciation is a prerequisite for orthographic stability. Grammar organizes a special field, orthology, defined on the basis of this objective: "The goal of Orthology is the correct pronunciation of words" (Bello 1835: 11).

Paradoxical as it may seem, the "correct" pronunciation is determined on the basis of the writing system. What allows its formulation in terms of simplicity and regularity, as in orthology, is the simplicity and regularity of the writing system. This happens, not only because grammatical disciplines require writing to become a legitimate discourse and to circulate in the context of the literate high culture, but also because the concept of language is defined in relation to the experience generated by contact with written texts. This causes writing to become the filter through which orality is conceived, so that instead of writing being subordinated to speech, it is speech that is subordinated to writing. The representation of speech depends to a great extent on the pertinent frame established by writing. Let us look at two examples.

The first comes from the treatment given in the *Principios de la ortología y métrica de la lengua castellana* (1835) to the topic of the "basic sounds" of the language. Bello assumes as a point of departure a strict distinction between the elementary sounds and the graphic signs that represent them. When he refers to the categories *vowel* and *consonant* he states:

> Debe notarse que los términos *vocal* y *consonante* significan no solamente las dos especies de sonidos elementales de que se componen todas las palabras, sino las letras o caracteres que los representan en la escritura. Yo procuraré siempre distinguir estas dos acepciones.[16]
>
> (Bello 1835: 13–14)

This distinction is not rigorously followed throughout the book. Instead of basing his analysis on the phonetic patterns of Spanish, Bello focuses on the letters of the alphabet to establish their respective sounds. Therefore, he gives prominence to certain topics that, from a strictly phonetic point of view, do not deserve it. Thus the letter *h* is discussed pointing out its graphemic value and indicating that it does not represent any sound:

> H. La letra *h* es a veces parte material del carácter o signo complejo *Ch*, y otras veces figura por sí sola. En este segundo caso, se hace sentir a veces en la pronunciación, y a veces es enteramente muda.[17]
>
> (Bello 1835: 23)

This passage reveals one of the ways in which orthography determines phonetic considerations. The analysis of the basic elements of sonority is presented following the patterns of perception imposed by writing. The result is a description that refers, first, to the graphemic dimension and second, to the phonetic dimension of language, of which the former is considered to be a mere transposition. This operation has an additional consequence for the prescriptive terms of the grammar and especially of the orthology. The problem for the grammarian is not so much deciding what sounds will constitute the inventory of correct forms in order to assign to them the appropriate graphic signs; the problem is rather to decide what sounds can be legitimately assigned to a particular letter. Instead of proposing, for example, the use of two letters to represent the two pronunciations of the letter *x*, Bello decides in favor of one of them:

> Si se me permitiera elegir entre esas diferentes opiniones, me decidiría ciertamente por la de aquellos que dan a la *x* en todos los casos el valor de la combinación [gs], no sólo porque este sonido lleva a otro la ventaja de la suavidad, sino porque creo que el uso está más generalmente en favor de esta práctica.[18]

(Bello 1835: 21)

It is not pronunciation that controls orthography. On the contrary, orthography controls pronunciation by establishing that the existence of one sign should determine the production of only one sound.

The other element revealed by the principle that guides the relation between writing and speech is the preeminence of segmental over suprasegmental phenomena in the determination of what is orthographically and orthologically pertinent. As indicated by contemporary studies on grammatology, alphabetic writing is not a mere transposition of speech since graphic representation does not include the whole range of phonetic phenomena.[19] The design of a writing system of this kind is a process of abstraction in which certain phenomena considered irrelevant are excluded. An individual who wants to create or modify an orthography must, therefore, determine what is pertinent and what is not. Bello is in a similar situation and responds to concrete questions related to this. Thus, he refutes García del Pozo's proposal that the *grave* accent must be used in Spanish orthography, since even though he admits that there are words whose stress loses intensity when in contact with others, it would be a completely unnecessary element:

> ¿A qué . . . marcar con una señal peculiar un accidente que los que hablan no pueden menos de ejecutar en el vocablo agudo, sea que la lleve o que no? Los griegos tendrían sus razones particulares para hacerlo así; en nuestra lengua no hallamos ninguna; y si para señalar ese accidente hubiese de introducirse un signo nuevo, ¿por qué no para tantos otros como dependen, ya del sentido, ya de la pasión de que está poseído el que habla?[20]

(Bello 1849: 137)

The economy of resources is the criterion for the determination of what must be registered. An approach that questions this selection principle reveals the complexity underneath its simple appearance. Behind its pragmatism we find several operations that provide the "common sense," an air of naturalness to the ideas presented in the quote.

First, we find the affective elements of the human mind. The sounds of language, with their multiple dimensions, represent the different levels of subjectivity: ideas, emotions, passions, etc. Writing is not expected to provide such detailed representation; in this register, linguistic phenomena related to the expression of ideas will be given preference. In contrast, phonetic phenomena associated with emotions are not deemed important enough to be given a graphic sign. Thus, the mechanism for determining what is pertinent at the graphemic level is based on a hierarchy of mental processes. Inasmuch as rationality is given a first-order role, those aspects of speech associated with it will be given priority.

Second, we find those aspects of speech that depend on meaning. Here we find a hierarchy established in the semantic field. Writing excludes what is linked to the temporary value of signs in daily speech events.

Thus, we can say that selection of linguistic phenomena for graphic "reproduction" privileges those that represent general, stable, and systematic dimensions of the human spirit . This is crucial in the decision as to what is pertinent for the task of the rationalization and control of grammar. Linguistic phenomena closely related to "abstract meaning," such as "basic sounds" or stress, will become the focus of interest. Aspects connected with other dimensions of subjectivity, such as quantity or intonation, will receive secondary attention and will not be the object of a systematization that establishes in detail the norms for their use.[21]

Paradoxically, the distinction between these two components translates into a tolerant attitude towards variation, which differs from the prescriptive rigor applied to the elements of "greatest linguistic importance." This may be illustrated by Bello's description of the "provincial or national accent" in his *Principios de la ortología y métrica de la lengua castellana*. Bello points out the correlation between different intonation patterns and the different geographic origin of speakers. It is evident that Andalucians "sing" the language differently from "all other Spanish provinces" (Bello 1835: 49). This peculiar "singing" is not criticized; it is presented as an inevitable, natural event which leads to a general rule within which its legitimacy is guaranteed:

> Acerca del acento nacional o provincial, puede darse una sola regla, y es que en la modulación de las frases se debe tomar por modelo la costumbre de la gente bien educada, evitando todo resabio de rusticidad o vulgarismo.[22]

(Bello 1835: 49)

While at the segmental level differences must be eliminated in favor of a single pronunciation (for example, the obsession with preserving the *s* vs. *c/z* distinction), differences in intonation are easily accepted, with the only condition that they comply with the principles of socio-cultural selection that, as we have seen, presuppose a certain diversity.

At this point, it is possible to establish the way in which writing's mediation of our conceptualization of speech controls the selection of the dominant variety. Understood in terms of homogeneity and stability – as language planning requires – the correct variety will be composed mainly of the elements that are pertinent in writing and/or those that are conceived through the frames of perception defined by writing. The language to which Bello refers is principally the one that is represented by the alphabet.

The selection of textual models

The consequences of the operations described in the previous section are not limited to the systematization of rules nor to Bello's approach to the representation of orality. At a more concrete level, they are also crucial in the selection of the empirical data on which grammatical knowledge is based. Since the fundamental experience of language is found in alphabetic writing, written texts have a primary importance in the selection of the corpus assumed to be paradigmatic.

This does not mean that all written texts are valued in the same manner as models of "good speech." Although more uniform than the spectrum of speech varieties, the written language also presents a wide range of both diachronic and synchronic variation. For this reason, the definition of the dominant variety is supported by the selection of a limited number of paradigmatic texts that allow for a cleaner selection process that circumvents the problems caused by diversity. It is the only way in which the language can be understood as highly homogeneous.

The selection of materials is based on the value given to them. They are considered to carry textual qualities which constitute the ideal forms and uses of the purest form of language. However, the value of those materials not only depends on their immanent properties. There are also external circumstances that strengthen their importance: their authors have historically recognized prestige; the period in which they were produced has wide resonance in the representation of the cultural past, etc. All these elements are essential for the authority with which, as models, they must be invested; and they clearly reveal the political resonance of their selection.

An analysis of the quotes used by Bello to illustrate and support his statements allows us to approach the origin and, to a certain extent, the hierarchy of the materials that integrate the inventory. For our purposes, it will suffice to examine Bello's essential text: *Gramática de la lengua castellana destinada al uso de los americanos*.

Bello's examples come from three types of sources. The first group includes works from the Golden Age of Spanish literature. There are many references to authors such as Lope de Vega, Calderón, Santa Teresa, Tirso de Molina, Fray Luis de León, and especially, Miguel de Cervantes and Fray Luis de Granada. The second group includes materials that were contemporary to Bello's time, that is, from between the middle of the eighteenth to the middle of the nineteenth centuries. The most important figure of this period is Gaspar de Jovellanos, followed by Francisco Martínez de la Rosa, Leandro Fernández de Moratín and the *Resumen de la historia de Venezuela* by Rafael M. Baralt and Ramón Díaz, the only text in this group written by Spanish Americans. The third group includes texts from the Middle Ages, of which the *Poem of the Cid* is the one of greatest importance (cf. Velleman 1987).

We immediately notice a deep incongruence between this inventory and Bello's principles for language selection: current use. "A grammar must not represent what used to be but what is" (Bello 1832: 181), he stated in his article "Gramática castellana." Giving central authority to texts from the past is clearly at odds with this principle, since linguistic forms of the past would be projected onto present usage.

This contradiction can be explained if we take into account not only what he included but also what he excluded. As we would expect, Bello is not very explicit about the latter. What he considers irrelevant only emerges in his discourse when strictly necessary for the process of argumentation. However, several statements shed light on his process of exclusion. For example, regarding the peculiarities of the speech of educated Spanish Americans, he says:

> En ellas se peca mucho menos contra la pureza y corrección del lenguaje, que en las locuciones afrancesadas, de que no dejan de estar salpicadas hoy en día aun las obras más estimables de los escritores peninsulares.[23]
> (Bello 1847: 13)

Two issues are integrated here. On the one hand, Bello establishes a hierarchy of transgressions against the purity of the language. From this point of view, the forms used by Spanish Americans are less distant from the norms, and are, therefore, more tolerable; the use of Gallicisms constitutes a higher level of transgression and deserves stronger censure. On the other hand, Bello also presents a critical view of the language that characterizes the literary works of important Peninsular writers and also, though implicitly, Spanish American writers. These include forms distant from the linguistic canon, a crucial factor which excludes them from the models and elements that constitute the empirical basis of the grammar. This is what happens for example with Benito Jerónimo Feijoo, an author who, in spite of the high rhetorical-stylistic quality of his writings, could not be proposed as a "model of a *castizo* language" (Bello 1830: 314).

The strong influence of French on Spanish and the appearance of "coarse vulgarities and idioms of the populace" (Bello 1842b: 438) determine the exclusion of a large number of texts from the paradigmatic corpus of the Spanish language, which is "in our days" the same as in Lope de Vega and Cervantes (1842b: 439).[24] We can see at this point the implications of privileging the classics over the contemporary literary productions that, according to the principle of current use, should be taken as models. The paradigmatic status assigned to the "great works and figures" of Spanish literature is associated with one of the main objectives of language policy: the preservation of certain identifying cultural patterns, whose survival is considered essential for the cultural and historical survival of the community. In more precise terms, the classics of Spanish literature function as reference points to which the present use of the language should refer in order to guarantee its historical continuity and, consequently, that of the Hispanic cultural community with which it is closely associated.

However, the authority which Bello grants to the privileged space of writing does not have enough weight to guarantee the validity of its forms automatically. Here, as in the other levels already discussed, selective procedures are used. For example, forms commonly found in Golden Age texts may be contrasted with contemporary educated usage, leading us to exclude the validity of the former:

> El uso moderno del relativo *quien* es algo diferente del que vemos en los escritores castellanos hasta después de la edad de Cervantes y Lope de Vega: "Quiérote mostrar las maravillas que este transparente alcázar solapa, de *quien* yo soy alcaide y guarda valor perpetuo, porque soy el mismo Montesinos de *quien* la cueva toma nombre" (Cervantes). El uso del día autoriza el segundo de estos *quien*, porque se refiere a persona; pero no el primero, porque le falta esa circunstancia.[25]
>
> (Bello 1847: 106)

Writing (and within writing a limited group of texts), the dialect of Castile, and the speech of the educated: these three more or less imprecise frames of linguistic praxis constitute the main sources for the norm and become its empirical basis. They have been detached from the universe of textual production, a universe whose diversity makes it highly resistant to ordering and regulating pressures. However, overall they do not constitute a rigorously homogeneous space. On the contrary, these frames contain internal variation and there exist significant disagreements among them that reveal a threatening diversity.

Diversity poses a serious obstacle for the unifying goals of grammar and language policy. Given the diversity within and among these areas of language use, it is not possible to elaborate a detailed and systematic description of their characteristics which would achieve the required degree of coherence. Since such a description would reveal numerous contradictions and inconsistencies, representation must therefore be partial and will depend on the requirements imposed by the process of argumentation.

Depending on the need to validate one preference or another and to provide empirical evidence for a general rule, Bello appeals either to the use of the educated, the dialect of Castile, or the classics of Spanish literature.[26]

Therefore, the uniformity and coherence that, at least apparently, distinguish the selected variety are not properties of actual language use, but rather the result of procedures developed at a different level. In terms of discourse, that level is grammar. The high level of generality that characterizes its utterances and the totalizing effect that this involves allow the integration of its diversity and divergence into a system that appears to be regular and uniform. Since this system is postulated as "an intellectual vision of reality" (Bello 1841: 7), we can assume that this reality embodies an existing regularity and uniformity. In extradiscursive terms, the level where selection occurs is defined as a culturally structured subjectivity. For the determination of what is legitimate, linguistic forms must be filtered through the grammarian's subjective perspective. This is where the general principles and formulations are articulated, and where the primary selections and exclusions that define uniformity within the reality of diversity operate. It is in this sphere of subjectivity that the fragmentary representations are articulated and where we can resolve the conflicts which occur within each level of usage and those that occur at points of contact between and among differing levels.

The selection and exclusion procedures develop from basic criteria. These constantly participate in the elaboration of grammar, and most of the time operate as subjacencies hiding behind rules and observations. At other times, they appear in the argumentation itself. In either case, they always point toward spheres of subjectivity that, to a great extent, transcend the rational level. Thus, it is common that, when deciding to favor one form over another, Bello refers not only to the location of its use but also to the sensorial and emotional reactions that alternatives of usage generate in the subject, grouped under the concept of "taste." The passage quoted on p. 54 illustrates this point. The preference for [gs] is based, among other reasons, on its "softness." Synesthesia does not refer to an objective quality of the sound but to a sensation that it provokes in the subject, who experiences a feeling equivalent to that produced by the tactile qualities of certain objects. However, the selection process goes well beyond the purely psychological sphere. Following the same sensorial processes, Bello – or any other speaker – might have preferred the "hard" [ks] instead of the "soft" [gs]. This possibility shifts the selection mechanism to what we might call the cultural configuration of subjectivity. At this level we have values that organize hierarchically sensorial processes, and through this, objective phenomena that are considered to be their causes. These scales display a certain level of objectivity: they belong to a group of individuals but not all. Likewise, they shape the subject in a process of internalization that is developed in historically and socially localized institutional frameworks. Therefore, they cannot be attributed to any natural, universal or primary condition of human beings. On the contrary, they are processes grounded in that complex dimension that we call culture.

We can now understand the selection of the linguistic forms and uses that constitute the empirical base of grammar. The subject assumes as legitimate those linguistic phenomena that agree with preferences that correspond, first of all, to a strictly personal dimension. For this reason, the grammar promoted through language policy is primarily defined at the idiolectal level of the grammarian. But these preferences are determined by a cultural configuration that, in spite of being condensed in the individual, integrates elements from a transindividual and semiotic existence. Therefore, they may be imaginarily proposed as decisions congruent with values shared by certain groups within the community – groups that are invested with an unquestioned authority.

This is thus one of the most evidently rhetorical problems faced by Bello in the legitimization of his grammar and of his language policy in general. He must present what in essence is a series of decisions made by him as an individual as if they derived from transindividual and objective values: the use of the educated, the use of Castile, the models of Castilian literature. The problem is resolved by constantly resorting to these three levels which have been invested with authority and that are presented as the empirical basis that controls the design of grammatical representations.

Notes

1 "The GRAMMAR of a language is the art of speaking it correctly, that is, in agreement with proper usage, the way the educated speak."
2 "This variety is preferred because it is the most uniform throughout the provinces and villages that speak the same language, and it is therefore the one that makes communication easier; in contrast, the words and phrases of ignorant people vary notably from one village to the next and are not easily understood outside the area where they are used."
3 "*Imperative*. Nothing is more common, even among well educated people, than shifting the stress in the second person singular of the imperative in most verbs by saying, for example, *mirá, andá, levantáte, sentáte, socegáte* [sic]. These forms do not exist and must be carefully avoided since they are indications of a gross ignorance of language."
4 "People in Chile and in ordinary speech, use the verb *transar*, which we do not think exists in Castilian. *Pedro y Juan se transaron, es necesario transar el asunto* [Pedro y Juan compromised, we need to settle this matter], are expressions that we hear from everybody, lawyers and judges included. But neither the RAE's Dictionary contains that verb, nor have we seen it in the writings of Spanish legal experts who, according to what we have been able to see, only use the intransitive verb *transigir* in that sense. Thus, we must say *Pedro y Juan transigieron, nadie debe transigir con el honor*."
5 "If this was said in Valladolid or in Toledo, we could still answer that the many words and expressions exchanged in everyday life are only a small part of the wealth of language; we could also say that cultivating the language makes it uniform among the different groups of people who speak it, and that it slows down the natural changes produced by time, in this as well as in other human matters;

that . . . it helps overcome one of the most uncomfortable obstacles to communication between the different countries and among peoples of different ages . . .; that all highly civilized nations have cultivated with particular care their own language . . . All this could be answered to those who condemn the study of the language as something unnecessary and sterile, even in those countries *where the national language is spoken in all its purity*" (emphasis added).

6 "C, Z. There is not one single habit more universal among Latin Americans, nor is there one harder to correct, than pronouncing *s* for *z* – not differentiating *baza* and *basa*, *caza* and *casa*, *cima* and *sima*, *cocer* and *coser*, *lazo* and *laso*, *pozo* and *poso*, *riza* and *risa*, *roza* and *rosa*.

It is also a nuisance to pronounce *z* for *s* – a habit called *ceceo* – as well as to use both sounds interchangeably, as some people do. It is by now hopeless to try to reestablish in America the Castilian sounds that correspond respectively to *s*, *z* or *c* followed by the vowels *e* or *i*."

7 As Amado Alonso maintains (1951), in Bello there is no "call for a linguistic independence that would complete political independence" (p. xvi).

8 "My recommendation to maintain the Castilian language should not be taken for a condemnation of everything that is distinctively American. There are still in Spanish America pure, authentic expressions that are deemed old-fashioned by Spaniards – why should we eliminate them? If a particular verb conjugation is more regular in American usage, why should we prefer the one that has heedlessly prevailed in Castile? If we have formed new words based on Castilian roots, following ordinary derivation processes recognized by the Castilian norm – the very same processes through which it continues to increase its wealth – why then should we feel ashamed to use them? Chile and Venezuela have as much right as Aragón and Andalucía to have their unique variants accepted, if they are supported by the uniform and authentic speaking habits of educated people."

9 "Any triphthong is stressed, and the stress always falls on its second vowel: *cambiáis*, *fragüéis*. It follows that there is no Castilian word with more than one triphthong.

This is, however, an accidental fact of language – something which could change as a consequence of new acquisitions – and not a permanent characteristic, one that is consistent with its genius and natural pronunciation. I don't think it could be said that the pronunciation of words with unstressed triphthongs is difficult or contrary to our habits. Even more, it could be argued that such Castilian words do exist, since toponyms from places and regions where the native language is Castilian are truly Castilian, and so are the names for the tribes or races that live there, plus all the derivatives. The triphthong *guai* is common in geographical and national names in America and among them are several that constitute exceptions to the mentioned rule, such as *guaireño* (native from la *Guaira*) and *guaiquerí* (an indigenous race). We also have whimsically formed proper names such as *Miaulina* and *Miauregato*, from the works of Cervantes and Samaniego respectively; both of them are easy to pronounce and not unpleasant to the ear."

10 The exclusion of the latter ones is not really relevant for our purposes since its pertinence is not defined at a geopolitical level.

11 Cf. Ramos (1993). This author identifies the usage referred to by Bello with Latin American spoken dialects. This leads him to declare the irregularity and monstruosity of the dialectal word, a word too close to the realm of emotions, which, at the same time, incarnates the Latin American difference.

12 "There are differences regarding the realization of final *d*, since some people pronounce it and some do not . . .; and among those who do, some make it sound more or less like *z* (*virtuz*, *miraz*) and some keep its original phonetic value. Pronouncing *virtú*, *mirá* is a bad, careless habit; as for the pronunciation of final

    d as *z* – even though it can also be found in some villages in Castile – it has not even been mentioned in the RAE's *Orthography*, which makes me think it is a provincialism that must not be imitated."
13. For purely stylistic reasons I will refer to alphabetic writing without using the adjective. I recognize that writing systems are extremely diverse and that the postulation of alphabetic writing as a "superior" form is deeply ideological and ethnocentric.
14. "The higher degree of perfection that spelling is capable of, and consequently the goal of any reform, is a one to one correspondence between the basic sounds of a language and the signs or letters that must represent them, in such a way that each basic sound should be always represented by one letter and each letter should always represent the same sound."
15. "But is it not what they have to do already? Don't they have to look up a word with *b* or with *v*, with *c* or with *s*, and also with or without *h*? If, for the first time, they hear the name of a tree that sounds like *aya*, they will probably look it up under *a*; if they do not find it, they will look under *h*. *The true cause behind these double searches is sometimes an incorrect pronunciation* and other times the presence of useless letters or even their double value. We cannot avoid the first problem with any orthographic system; the second one could be easily avoided with a rational, simple orthography" (emphasis added).
16. "It should be noted that the terms *vowel* and *consonant* refer not only to the two types of basic sounds, but also to the letters and characters that represent them in writing. I will always try to differentiate between them."
17. "*H*. The letter *h* is sometimes part of the complex character *Ch*; other times it appears on its own. In this second case, sometimes it is pronounced, and sometimes it is completely silent."
18. "If I was asked to choose between these opinions, I would certainly support those that give *x*, on all occasions, the value [gs], not only because this sound is smoother than the other but also because I think it is more widespread."
19. In his classic work *Orality and Literacy: The Technologizing of the Word* (1982),Walter Ong offers a valuable synthesis of the diversity of problems related to this issue and the different ways to approach it.
20. "Why . . . mark with a particular sign a feature that speakers cannot but produce in the word as acute, whether it has it or not? The Greeks must have had their reasons for doing so; we cannot find any justification for doing it in our own language, and if a new sign were to be introduced to indicate this feature, why not do the same thing with so many others that depend either on the intention or the emotional state of the speaker?"
21. This is caused in part by what one could call the epistemological obstacle. We should not forget that the technological resources that permit us to carry out a systematic study of these processes were not available at that time.
22. "Concerning the national or regional accent, one can give only one rule: Take as a model for intonation the usage of the educated, avoiding any vulgar or boorish tendencies."
23. "These constitute a much lesser violation of the purity and proper use of language than those 'French-style' expressions that appear even in the best works of contemporary Peninsular writers."
24. This criticism is meant mostly for the writing circles of Spanish American countries. The fragment that includes the passage just quoted alludes to Argentina's journalistic production: "once we admit the exotic expressions, the turns of phrases that are opposed to the genius of our language, and those coarse idioms and vulgarities spoken by the masses, we would end up falling into darkness and chaos, after which degradation would come, as we can already notice in one

American nation, formerly so illustrious, and in whose newspapers one can see how Castilian degenerates in a Franco-Spanish dialect" (1842b: 438).

25 "The modern use of the relative pronoun *quien* is somewhat different from the one we read in Castilian writers of Cervantes' and Lope de Vega's time: 'Quiérote mostrar las maravillas que este transparente alcázar solapa, de *quien* yo soy alcaide y guarda valor perpetuo, porque soy el mismo Montesinos de *quien* la cueva toma nombre' (Cervantes). Today's usage admits the second *quien* because it refers to a human; but not the first one, which doesn't refer to any human."

26 As this demonstrates, the realm of usage is a ground better suited for Rhetoric than for rigorously scientific discourse. From an epistemological perspective, it does not constitute a reference for empirical correlation but it works rather as a source of authority that legitimizes both the cognitive claims and the normative validity of grammatical discourse.

4 Historical linguistics and cultural history
The polemic between Rufino José Cuervo and Juan Valera

José del Valle

> Toda ciencia o facultad ha tenido y tiene sus orates; pero una de las más peligrosas para los que poseen un cerebro poco firme y un juicio poco sólido y sentado es esta ciencia de la lingüística.[1]
>
> (Valera 1869: 1103)

Linguistics as an autonomous academic discipline emerged in the nineteenth century and since then, linguists – always enthusiastically committed to the scientific character of their work – have faithfully relied on positivist epistemology and the classificatory methods of the natural sciences. If the precursors of modern linguistics (e.g. Humboldt) acknowledged in their works the complexity of language – as both a collective and individual phenomenon and as simultaneously autonomous and heteronomous from human mental activity – the later protagonists of the historical development of the discipline (e.g. Schleicher, Saussure, Chomsky) gave priority to definitions of language that emphasized its conceptualization as a formal system. Linguists' historical predilection for formalism, the premise of objectivity, and the empirical base on which this discipline necessarily rests tend to eclipse the cultural, political and social grounding of language science and, conversely, the impact that it has had and continues to have in other areas of cultural and intellectual life in the West.

In this chapter, I will present and discuss a most transparent episode in the battle over Spanish that this book is analyzing: the famous polemic between Colombian philologist Rufino José Cuervo (1844–1911) and Spanish writer and diplomat Juan Valera (1824–1905). This famous controversy coincided with two turning points in the modern political and intellectual history of Hispanic nations: it began in 1899, the year after Spain lost its remaining overseas colonies, and it ended in 1903, the year before Ramón Menéndez Pidal published his emblematic *Manual de gramática histórica española*. The skirmish between Cuervo and Valera neatly underscores the value that linguistics acquired as a source of legitimacy in cultural and political debates – in particular, in the debate over the nature of Hispanic identity during the early years of the twentieth century.

The polemic

In 1899 the Argentinean poet Francisco Soto y Calvo published his *Nastasio*, a narrative poem that related the awful misfortunes of a gaucho. The text was preceded by a letter, a prologue written by Colombian philologist Rufino José Cuervo. In the prologue, after summarizing and praising Soto y Calvo's work, Cuervo alluded to the glossary included at the end of the book, which contained a number of typically Argentinean terms that might be unknown to speakers of other varieties of Spanish. These "regionalismos" – whose use in literature, by the way, had become fashionable at the time – were, for Cuervo, the seeds of future independent languages, and foreshadowed the unfortunate fragmentation of Spanish – which would thus emulate the tragic destiny of Latin. Cuervo attributed the distant but inevitable fragmentation of the language to three factors: the natural differentiation brought about by distinct environments, lifestyles and matters of race; the collapse of Spain as a unifying center and source of intellectual inspiration for all Hispanic nations; and the lack of contact among Latin American countries. All of this Cuervo expressed with great sadness, insisting that these processes of division "may be very long in the life of nations," and that "we should not forget that we are brothers" (Cuervo 1899: x).

In those years, Juan Valera, Spanish writer and diplomat, assiduously contributed to *La Nación* of Buenos Aires as a literary columnist and cultural commentator. In August or September of 1900 Valera must have received a copy of *Nastasio*. So vehemently did he oppose Cuervo's beliefs, that without delay (on 24 September) he published a response, titled "Sobre la duración del habla castellana" (Valera 1900), in *Los Lunes de El Imparcial* of Madrid (Valera's review of *Nastasio* finally appeared in *La Nación* on 2 December of the same year). Valera's openly sarcastic article rejected the possibility of the fragmentation of the Spanish language. Provincialisms, he affirmed, were also common in Spain and in the life of any normal language, and did not by themselves constitute a threat to its unity. Moreover, he argued, the very same book that served as the anecdotal origin of the polemic, the *Nastasio*, offered a notable example of the uncorrupted persistence of Spanish in America: "Its language is very pure Castilian" (Valera 1900: 1037). Valera added that, if the language persists, it is because the causes of differentiation adduced by Cuervo do not exist. For Valera, the political independence of the Latin American nations had not caused an erosion of the unity of the Hispanic race, which was, in essence, identical on both sides of the Atlantic.[2]

Valera's article fell nowhere near the texts produced within the disciplinary boundaries of linguistics (nor did he intend it to do so). It was clearly a journalistic and polemical piece in which the author framed the few linguistic facts he adduced in cultural, historical and philosophical ideas. Underlying Valera's article was the ideological pillar of his thought. In response to the economic and political crisis that Spain was experiencing in the nineteenth century, intellectuals should affirm their patriotic pride; such patriotism was fully justified, Valera claimed, by Spain's imperial past and by the present health of the Spanish language and culture. Consequently, Valera responded to Cuervo that the Spanish language must continue to be spoken without corruption; that the mere existence of seventy million speakers should silence those who maliciously dwell on the decadence and fragmentation of the race; and, finally, that "los españoles" – both from Spain and Latin America – should have confidence in their men of letters, who should, in turn, demonstrate that they merit such confidence (Valera 1900: 1038).[3]

Cuervo's reaction was prompt (cf. Guitarte 1981). In 1901, volume three of the *Bulletin Hispanique* included an article by the Colombian entitled "El castellano en América" (I cite this article by Cuervo 1950: 273–332). First, Cuervo tried to put aside the discussion of the cultural models – Iberian or non-Iberian – that Latin Americans should follow; and he did it with a sharp comment that clearly echoed the skepticism with which Sarmiento and the members of his generation saw the state of Spain's intellectual life (cf. chapter 2):

> Yo lamento también, como el que más, y sin poderlo remediar, que si en América quiere uno estar al tanto del progreso científico y literario, desde la gramática hasta la medicina, la astronomía o la teología, no se le ocurra acudir a los libros españoles, y que si tiene los recursos necesarios para trasladarse a las universidades europeas, no escoja las de Madrid o Salamanca.[4]
>
> (Cuervo 1950: 275)

Having said this – in order to elude the political tone of the polemic and to legitimize his own discourse against Valera's – Cuervo declared his scientific independence and his intent to respond to the Spaniard with scientific arguments (Cuervo 1950: 281). From this point onwards, the article offered an impressive display of linguistic erudition. Throughout the central body of the text, Cuervo insisted on the validity of the comparison between the fragmentation of Latin and the future of Spanish; he used abundant philological evidence that showed the slow, yet natural and inevitable, process of linguistic change, and provided dialectal data that confirmed the presence of the seeds of separation. Cuervo concluded that when, in addition to the internal dynamics of the linguistic organism, we add historical and geographical circumstances which favor the relative isolation among regions, divergence is inevitable: "It is clear that everything conspires to dismantle unity" (ibid.: 306).

Linguistics and philology effectively served Cuervo to establish certain facts with a solid empirical base. Nonetheless, he would have been unable to sustain his fragmentation thesis without wrapping the linguistic facts in cultural, political, and social arguments all pointing to the relative isolation among Hispanic nations. We must not lose sight either of the fact that a great part of the article was destined to demonstrate that certain linguistic forms considered by Spaniards to be "American degenerations" were, in reality, consistent with the natural evolution of Spanish, often having their origin in dialects of Spain; and that words marked as "americanismos" in the dictionary of the RAE could actually be found in the classics of Spanish literature. Cuervo's intention in presenting these data and linguistic-philological arguments was therefore to unveil the discrepancies between Spain and Latin America in questions of linguistic and, by extension, cultural legitimacy: "Los españoles, al juzgar el habla de los americanos, han de despojarse de cierto invencible desdén que les ha quedado por las cosas de los criollos" (1950: 288).[5] But this contempt, according to Cuervo, was not exclusive to Spaniards. Naturally, the old colonies, upon gaining independence from Spain, had developed a certain "irresistible disdain for everything that came from it, including grammatical correctness" (ibid.: 307). The Colombian insisted again that this mutual distrust, the formation of national cultures in America, the development of their own codes of conduct, literary nationalism – that caused the appearance of popular speech in domains traditionally reserved for the educated – and the massive immigration of foreigners, may very well be social and cultural phenomena that would favor the eventual fragmentation of the Spanish language (Cuervo 1950: 308).

After a reference in passing to this topic, in the prologue to the book *Reminiscencias Tudescas* by the Colombian Santiago Pérez Triana (Valera 1902: 1110–12), Valera returned to the polemic with full force. The Spaniard's new critique of Cuervo was published in Mexico's *La Tribuna* on 31 August and 2 September 1902 (I cite them as Valera 1902a and 1902b, respectively).[6] I will not detain myself in summarizing the contents of these articles, except to say that they contained a restatement of the ideas expressed two years earlier. It is worth mentioning, nevertheless, that Valera did not yield before the erudition demonstrated by Cuervo and that, as the good polemicist that he was, he ignored, and even ridiculed, the professional stance of the Colombian philologist: "Yo creo que el Sr. Cuervo, en su eruditísimo artículo, a fuerza de dar razones y de emplear argumentos para demostrar la instabilidad de los idiomas, no prueba nada, porque prueba demasiado" (Valera 1902a: 2).[7]

In 1903 – again in the *Bulletin Hispanique* – Cuervo, irritated by Valera's inability to discuss the matter in scientific terms and offended by the Spaniard's manipulation of his words, put an end to the polemic with a most revealing statement:

[Valera] pretende que las naciones hispanoamericanas sean colonias literarias de España, aunque para abastecerlas sea menester tomar productos de países extranjeros, y, figurándose tener aún el imprescindible derecho a la represión violenta de las insurgentes, no puede sufrir que un americano ponga en duda el que las circunstancias actuales consientan tales ilusiones: esto le hace perder los estribos y la serenidad clásica. Hasta aquí llega el fraternal afecto.[8] (1950: 332)

Thus, throughout the polemic, Valera defended the unity and uniformity of Spanish culture on both sides of the Atlantic over political division and used, as the principal weapon for its defense, the purity and indivisibility of the language. Cuervo, for his part, questioned the possibility of maintaining the unity of culture, and consequently insisted upon his interpretation of the dialectal differences as embryos of a fragmented linguistic future.

The contradictory linguistic-historical theses that these two intellectuals defended were products of the different conceptions of language that they adopted, but most importantly, of the incompatible notions of "Hispanidad" that they held. The acrimonious character of the polemic – from Valera's initial sarcasm to Cuervo's final abruptness – is an indication of the difficulties experienced by the post-colonial reconstruction of the idea of Hispanic culture.

The linguistic-cultural context: Valera

Considering the incredibly intense literary, journalistic and political activity of Juan Valera, it is quite admirable that he had such familiarity with the state of language science in the second half of the nineteenth century.[9] His linguistic thought was based on a romantic conception of language derived from Humboldt and possibly mediated, given the frequency with which he cited them, by Steinthal and Renan:

> No se crea que hago por acaso, sino adrede y muy de propósito, esta especie de identificación y de unificación del espíritu nacional y del habla nacional, porque el habla es una misma con el espíritu; es su emanación, es su *verbo*.[10]
>
> (Valera 1862: 1055)

In his essays, he frequently insisted on the close relation between language and spirit of the nation; for him, the evolution of language was a reflection of the historical development of the national spirit. He also admired the work of comparativists, provided that they did not question the equation between language, thought and nation. Specifically, he praised Grimm and Bopp, who had demonstrated "the extraordinary virtues that the Indo-European languages have to impose themselves on others" (1869: 1108). In a similar vein, Valera affirmed that "the history of the language in Spain demonstrates this vitality and persistence" (1108), having preserved its Indo-European essence, having rejected loans from Semitic, Basque and Arab sources, and having demonstrated its capacity for expansion (1869: 1109; cf. 1905: 1176)

In addition to assuming a Humboldtian conception of language and accepting the explanatory potential of comparative linguistics, he praised – although with some reservations – the descriptive accomplishments of historical linguistics. This he did in a brief article published in 1905 (1176–81), in which he reviewed, in generally laudatory terms, the historical grammars of José Alemany (1903), Ramón Menéndez Pidal (1904), and Salvador Padilla (1916), published in the early years of the century. He accepted, as I said, the descriptive character of historical grammars, specifically, of the so-called phonetic laws; but he denied that they possessed any explanatory power. Valera was very suspicious of any possible naturalistic, deterministic philosophy that could lie behind the notion of phonetic law, and flatly negated the mechanical character and inevitability of linguistic change (Valera 1905: 1176; cf. 1869: 1105).

> A primera vista, para los profanos en gramática histórica, en cuyo número modestamente me incluyo, no hay ley fonética que valga; para la transformación de los vocablos no hay más que el uso persistente, fundado en el capricho instintivo.[11] (1905: 1179)

Linguistic evolution was thus, for Valera, a product of the "capricious instinct," of the ingenuity and inspiration of the speakers (1869: 1106). Nonetheless, not all changes produced in this way triumph without the contribution of some other factor. According to Valera, innovations should be sanctioned or rejected by the genius of the nation, or by those who embody it; by those who can discern changes that enrich the language from mere vices and corruptions.

The capacity and will of a nation to control the destiny of its language, and consequently its spirit, are central to the linguistic thought of Valera. For the Spanish writer, the language, aside from being a reflection of the genius of a race or culture, is a symbol of unity and seal of fraternity among its members: "the great writers are those who create this seal" (Valera 1862: 1055), and the "académicos" are its "custodians and defenders" (1055).

Valera's linguistic ideas, as well as his attitude towards language science, are closely connected with his vision of the cultural and political reality of Spain and the Hispanic world. Joining "that part of Spain not resigned to decadence" (Tuñon de Lara 1980: 97), he proposed that in order to confront the economic and political decay in which Spain found itself, it was the responsibility of all Spaniards to affirm the greatness of Spanish civilization and defend its unity.

Valera identified the defense of the *unity* of the Hispanic world with the defense of linguistic and cultural *uniformity*. To a certain extent, his ideology was a result of what Joan Ramon Resina has called "one of the greatest equivocations of Spanish history: the superordination of the Castilian identity as the identity of the Spanish state" (Resina 1996: 101). Valera promoted the trans-oceanic projection of the superordination of Spanish identity, and for this reason, conceived of Latin America as a simple extention of Spain. Throughout his life, as a founding member of the *hispanismo* movement, he defended the unity and uniformity of Hispanic culture and eagerly promoted the strengthening of bonds and forms of communication between both continents: "La unidad de civilización y de lengua, y en gran parte de raza también, persiste en España y en esas Repúblicas de América, a pesar de su emancipación e independencia de la metrópoli"[12] (Valera 1958 : 313).[13] The unity and uniformity between "españoles de España" and "españoles de América" carried with it a latent hierarchical order, and necessarily implied a condemnation to silence, an erasure – to use Irvine and Gal's term (cf. 2000) – of the Indian and Black as elements constitutive of Hispanic identity:

> Lo que yo sostengo es que ni el salvajismo de las tribus indígenas en general, ni la semicultura o semibarbarie de peruanos, aztecas y chibchas, añadió nada a esa civilización que ahí llevamos y que ustedes mantienen y quizá mejoran y magnifican.[14]
>
> (Valera 1958: 365)

In his defense of the greatness and unity – which, I insist, implied uniformity – of the race, Valera vigorously condemned the Francophilia (Valera 1958: 264, 424, 523) and the excessive anti-Spanish sentiment in Latin America (ibid.: 362–3, 372–3). Yet, for the Spaniard, the dangers that stalked and menaced the purity and unity of the race did not only come from America. In his discussions of the cultural and political life of Spain, he flatly rejected federalism (ibid.: 388), and warned against the excesses of Catalan and Galician regionalism (ibid.: 276, 412, 442, 815, 819), not only political but also philological (Valera 1961: 907–10). He rebelled for the same reasons against all forms of naturalism and, whenever the occasion arose, against any expression of end-of-the-century pessimism (Valera 1958: 413).

Reading Valera's essays reveals to us, in summary, a man with a mission of Quixotic shades – that of restoring the pride to a nation suffering from economic backwardness, military demoralization, political unrest and cultural decay. The solution, once again, required pride in the defense of unity and – anticipating Pidal's vision of cultural and linguistic development – the *will* of Spaniards to be respected (cf. chapter 5):

> Todo lo que acabo de decir, refiriéndome a un individuo, puede aplicarse también a las naciones, por donde el concepto que ellas forman de sí y el que de ellas forman los extraños importan a su valer real, a su acrecentamiento o a su caída.[15]
>
> (Valera 1868: 741)

We can now better understand the importance that the romantic conception of language had for Valera. The fragmentation of the language would inevitably be an unquestionable symptom of the collapse of Spanish culture. Hence his praises of the language, and his defence of its purity and indivisibility. His blind faith in the will of the human being and of the power of self-esteem always led him to negate, with the harshness and vehemence that may have been necessary – e.g. the polemic with Rufino José Cuervo – the possibility of the division of Spanish into multiple languages.

The linguistic-cultural context: Cuervo

Cuervo's linguistic thought is characterized primarily by his assimilation of the dominant linguistic ideas in the second half of the nineteenth century (Martinez 1954: 106–11). After the formulation of the principle of the genealogical relation among languages, nineteenth-century linguistics was dominated by the comparative method (based on the comparison of the formal elements of languages) and historical linguistics (based on the analysis of the evolutionary system of each). Even at its earliest stages, historical linguistics demonstrated a clear preference for the study of the evolution of the formal dimension of language. But this type of study did not yet constitute an end in itself. Responding to romantic impulses, linguistic change was interpreted as an indicator of the intellectual history of a nation. However, little by little, the growing accumulation of data and the calls for methodological rigor produced a greater understanding of the formal structure of language, as much as of its physiological and mental base. Moreover, originally clarifying metaphors – that compared, for example, language with a natural organism, or linguistic processes with laws – came to structure the perception of the object of study and the study itself (cf. Joseph 1989). It would be in the last third of the nineteenth century when, by the hand of the neogrammarians, language would come to be studied as an end in itself (Jankowski 1972: 196) gaining independence, not from human beings, but from human will, and certainly from the will of nations. Language was conceived, then, as a changing entity whose evolution was determined by natural laws: fixed, constant and inexorable.

Although, as indicated above, Cuervo was well acquainted with and followed the dominant academic trends, we cannot ignore, if we want properly to characterize his attitude toward language, the impact that another tradition had on his linguistic thought: that is the tradition represented by Bello, which put language science at the service of the cultural ideal of linguistic unity. The convergence of these two traditions in Cuervo's intellectual and professional development planted the seed of a contradiction that would mark the evolution of the great philologist's linguistic thought. On one side, the objective study of language demonstrated its changing nature; but on the other, the historical circumstances in which he lived, as well as his cultural convictions, resulted in his assuming an intellectual responsibility to defend the unity of the language. The first phase in his intellectual evolution, which can be situated between 1867 and 1872 (the dates of the publication of the first edition of *Apuntaciones*), is characterized by the will to resolve the above-mentioned contradiction. Conscious of the danger implicit in the distance between the scientific description of language and the prescription of its use – especially in its most conservative, latinized versions – Cuervo tried to reconcile them (Martínez 1954: 122–6). The preservation of the unity of a language before the presence of "vices," "deviations," or plain variation, made it necessary to distinguish correct from incorrect forms. The traditional solution consisted of resorting to prescriptive grammar; in contrast, Cuervo proposed the elaboration of a norm based on historical-linguistic investigation. He defended a *dynamic norm*, since "every epoch has to be necessarily innovative with respect to earlier ones" (Cuervo 1907: x) and based on "respectable, general and *actual use* as it is manifest in the most famous writers, and in the speech of people of very *high education*" (Cuervo 1907: xi, emphasis added). This use that has to serve as a normative model should have historical justification "and no rule or theory should be proposed if it does not represent facts" (Cuervo 1907: xii). In view of the changing character of language and the vast territory in which Spanish is spoken, Cuervo demands linguistic consensus:

> Tal evolución se realiza por fuerza en todas partes, en España como en América, y si con sinceridad se desea mantener la unidad del habla literaria, única posible, tanto españoles como americanos han de poner algo de su parte para lograrlo.[16]
>
> (Cuervo 1907: xiii)

The second phase in Cuervo's linguistic thought, which we can situate during the period when the polemic with Valera occurred, is dominated by the idea of the inevitable fragmentation of the Spanish language. The change in Cuervo's views regarding the future unity of Spanish has been explained in different ways. For Fernando Antonio Martínez, when Cuervo defended "this thesis of the fragmentation of Spanish in America, he did nothing but be consistent with the principles and postulates of the science he practiced" (1954: 136). For Menéndez Pidal the final pessimism of Cuervo had to be a result of the alleged emotional weakness that overcame the Colombian during the last decade of the nineteenth century ("la naturaleza del sabio colombiano se vio prematuramente minada por los achaques de la senectud" [Menéndez Pidal 1944: 5]). According to Pidal, this emotional weakness associated with age made Cuervo prone to fall under the influence of the "fragmentationist" ideas, expressed during those times by the French linguist Louis Duvau, and by Luciano Abeille (who was also French, though he emigrated to Argentina), author of *El idioma nacional de los argentinos* (1900) (cf. chapters 2 and 5).

As indicated above, and as stated by Fernando Antonio Martínez (1954: 136), the ideas expressed by Cuervo during the polemic with Valera were consistent with the conception of language that he espoused from very early in his career as a philologist. This leads us to remove to a second plane, if not to abandon, Pidal's explanation, which attributed the change in Cuervo's views to his mental decline or premature senility, and to the influence of a couple of second-rate linguists (cf. chapter 5 on Pidal's "analysis" of Cuervo). The fear of fragmentation was ever-present in Cuervo's work with the same latency with which it was present in Bello's grammar. But what explains Cuervo's evolution throughout the years was his loss of confidence in the future maintenance of a linguistic norm common to the whole Hispanic world. Fernando Antonio Martínez's explanation, although correct, is insufficient. We should not lose sight of the time when Cuervo changed his position with respect to fragmentation. In the decades of the 1860s, 1870s, and until the 1880s, Cuervo believed in the possibility of a consensus over an educated norm that would channel the natural evolution of the Spanish language in the vast territories where it is spoken; towards the end of the century he lost faith in such possibility. Without the common norm, the evolution that historical linguistics predicts, in combination with the differentiation demonstrated by dialectology, forced Cuervo to conclude that the fragmentation of Spanish into different languages was, although not imminent, certainly inevitable. The key to the change in Cuervo's thought was therefore the loss of faith in the capacity of educated classes in Spain and Latin America to produce a common norm; and this loss of faith was, in my view, associated not with senility, or with Abeille's book, or with any shift in theoretical orientation, but with two other phenomena: the recognition of Spain's lesser role after 1898, and the inability of Hispanic intellectuals at the turn of the century to generate an attitude of tolerance and dialogue that would facilitate the development of an integrated and pluralistic concept of Hispanic culture; and, more concretely, the paternalistic and hegemonic attitudes that Spain projected toward America.

In order to fully understand the implications of the Valera–Cuervo polemic, it is necessary to take into account the nature of the cultural relations between Spain and Latin America from independence until the first decade of the twentieth century (cf. Fogelquist 1968; Pérez de Mendiola 1996; Pike 1971; C. M. Rama 1982). As Donald F. Fogelquist has indicated, "after the wars, everything tended toward separation" (1968: 11). The young Latin American nations looked for inspiration in European philosophical doctrine and political models, while Spain found itself confronted by the challenges of its development as a modern nation-state in the middle of economic hardship and a crisis of conscience.

The interruption of material and spiritual commerce between the metropolis and its old colonies accentuated the ignorance and disinterest that, in Spain, existed toward all things American:

> En la segunda mitad del siglo XIX lo que menos interesaba al español eran los países hispánicos de allende el mar. Los periódicos traían noticias de Francia, Inglaterra, Alemania, Italia y otros países europeos, pero casi nada de América o sobre América.[17]
>
> (Fogelquist 1968: 19)

There certainly were reconciliatory efforts that came from the Iberian Peninsula: publications such as *La Revista Española de Ambos Mundos* (published from 1853), *La América* (created in 1859), or *Unión Ibero-Americana* (founded in 1885 by the group of the same name). It was precisely this institution that organized the Ibero-American congresses of 1892 and 1900 with the goal of strengthening the ties between Spain and Latin America.

In general, these efforts entailed a "hispanoamericanismo" similar to Juan Valera's, that is, a defense of the unity of Spanish civilization that implied a vision of Latin America as an extension of Spain. Along with the assimilating embrace of "hispanoamericanismo" and the ignorance and lack of interest of the majority, there were also, in Spain, openly hostile attitudes toward Latin American culture, and, specifically, toward its literary manifestation. Julio Cejador y Frauca, in *Cabos Sueltos*, expressed his opinion on Latin American literature in the following terms:

> Es tan floja, por término general, la literatura americana, tan ligera y tan híbrida en el fondo y en la forma, en el pensamiento y en el lenguaje, ... que no hay paladar español capaz de arrostrar diez estrofas o tres capítulos de tan desaborido manjar.[18]
>
> (quoted in Fogelquist 1968: 60)

As this quote illustrates, one of the sources of tension between Spanish and Latin American intellectuals – a tension that would eventually be transferred to Spanish literary circles – was the penetration of modernism in the Spanish cultural venue, and the renovation of language that it implied. Obviously, literary modernism had its detractors in all parts, but in Spain, anti-modernism acquired a special character: anti-Americanism. The modernist movement was seen as confirming the conception of Latin Americans as linguistic saboteurs (Fogelquist 1968: 50 and 337).

The polemics of language in nineteenth-century Latin America – particularly intense in the Southern Cone, as we saw in chapter 2 – probably fed the puristic fears of some Spanish intellectuals. These polemics developed in the context of a cultural movement eager to affirm the Latin American identity and proclaim literary autonomy (Caballero Wanguemert 1989: 180). But within Latin America, and beyond the dominant spirit of Americanism, there were significant differences with respect to the thorny issue of linguistic emancipation. On one hand, figures such as Gutiérrez, Alberdi, Echeverría, or Sarmiento saw fragmentation as naturally linked to the development of American national identities, and they conceived of linguistic evolution as a necessary result of the intellectual progress of those nations (cf. chapter 2): "Ya que lengua y pensamiento constituyen un binomio inseparable, se aceptarán todas aquellas innovaciones lingüísticas que supongan un crecimiento intelectual"[19] (Caballero Wanguemert 1989: 181). On the other hand, personalities such as Florencio Varela or Andrés Bello defended the idiomatic order and warned against linguistic populism and the corruption implied in the fragmentation of the language (cf. chapter 3). With this latter tradition that defended linguistic unity we could associate the early Cuervo, the Cuervo who, at the end of the 1860s, published the *Apuntaciones*. In fact, the Colombian would never abandon the desire to maintain the unity of the language and Hispanic community. We should recall his attitude in the prologue to the *Nastasio*: Cuervo made his fateful prophecy with deep sorrow, stating that it would not occur but in a very distant future, and reaffirming the brotherhood among all Hispanic nations. What did disappear from Cuervo's thought, as already mentioned, was his faith in the capacity and the will of the Spanish and Latin American leading intellectual classes to develop a consensus and agree on a single norm. This change must have been determined by the cultural tensions mentioned above, and by the differences in tone of the declarations defending linguistic unity made on both sides of the Atlantic.

In sum, the present analysis of the polemic between Cuervo and Valera offers several keys for the understanding of the cultural relations between Spain and Latin America, and for the contextualization of the recent history of Hispanic linguistics. First, it shows the profound implication of language science in the elaboration of unquestionably ideological cultural discourses. Second, it illustrates how, at the beginning of the twentieth century, Spanish philology had to reconcile scientific linguistics with a romantic conception of language that retained a connection with human will (we must not forget that, at the time of the controversy, Menéndez Pidal was launching his philological career and acquiring the intellectual legitimacy and the institutional support necessary for the development of the Madrid School of Philology; cf. next chapter). Lastly, the polemic illustrates the difficult relationship between the old metropolis and its former colonies in the process of configuring a common identity, adjusted to the new post-colonial reality: Valera insisted in the survival of a pan-Hispanic spirit associated with the forces of civilization, and called on all Spaniards and Latin Americans to defend it; Cuervo voiced his skepticism regarding the glorious future of a united Hispanic community and his disappointment in face of the persistent attempts by Spanish intellectuals to retain their hegemonic position in the concert of Hispanic nations.

Notes

1 "Every science or subject has had its madmen, but one of the most dangerous for those that possess weak brains and poor judgment is this science of linguistics."

2 It is not surprising that Valera is considered one of the founders of the *hispanismo* movement to which we referred in chapter 1.
3 This is one of the several points in which Valera's thought anticipates Menéndez Pidal's. In this particular case, the similarity between Valera's position and Pidal's views on the role of the intellectual elite is striking (cf. first and second sections in chapter 5).
4 "I too regret, like anyone else, and without being able to help it, that, if in America one wants to be abreast of scientific and literary progress – from grammar to medicine, and astronomy to theology – one does not go to Spanish books; and that, if one has the resources to attend a European university, one does not choose Madrid or Salamanca."
5 "Spaniards, upon judging the speech of Americans, have to strip themselves of certain irresistible disdain that they still feel for things having to do with Criollos."
6 I want to express my gratitude to Dr. Juan M. Lope Blanch and to Dra. Marcela Uribe for assisting me in acquiring the articles that Juan Valera published in Mexico's *La Tribuna*.
7 "I believe that Mr. Cuervo, in his most erudite article, in his great attempt to give reasons for and employ arguments to demonstrate the instability of idioms, proves nothing, because he proves too much."
8 "Valera wants Latin American nations to be literary colonies of Spain, although in order to supply them he must resort to foreign products; and, thinking that he still has the unalienable right to violent repression of the insurgent colonies, he is unable to tolerate that an American questions such possibility in the present circumstances: that makes him lose his temper and his traditional serenity. Here ends the fraternal love."
9 In 1856, he published two lengthy articles on Pedro Felipe Monlau's *Diccionario etimológico de la lengua castellana*; in 1869, he gave a lecture entitled "Sobre la ciencia del lenguaje" at the RAE's reception of Francisco de Paula Canalejas – whose entrance speech was "Las leyes que presiden la lenta y constante sucesión de los idiomas en la historia indo-europea;" in 1905, he wrote a review of Pidal's famous *Manual de gramática histórica española*.
10 "Do not think that I do this by chance, but rather with reason and purpose, this identification and unification of the national spirit and the national language, because speech is one and the same with the spirit; it is its freedom, its verbal expression."
11 "At first glance, for those who are not experts in historical grammar, in whose number I modestly include myself, there are no phonetic laws; the transformation of the language is the result of persistent use, founded in capricious instinct."
12 "The unity of civilization and language – and to a great extent, of race – remains in Spain and in those American Republics, in spite of their emancipation and independence from the metropolis."
13 For the quotations taken from letters in Valera's "Cartas americanas" and "Nuevas cartas americanas" I refer to the year and page of the *Obras Completas*.
14 "What I claim is that neither the savagery of the indigenous tribes, nor the semi-culture or semi-barbarism of the Peruvians, Aztecs and Chibchas, added anything to this civilization in which we find ourselves, and that you maintain and perhaps improve, magnify and enhance."
15 "All that I have just said about individuals also applies to nations; since the concept they form of themselves and the concept that others have of them matter to their real value, to their growth or decay."
16 "Such evolution necessarily occurs everywhere, both in Spain and in Latin America; and if we sincerely want to maintain the unity of the literary language, both Spaniards and Spanish Americans must contribute to the task."

17 "In the second half of the nineteenth century, Spaniards could not care less about the Hispanic nations across the ocean. Newspapers had news about France, England, Germany, Italy and other European countries, but practically nothing from or about Spanish America."
18 "Spanish American literature is usually so weak, so light, so hybrid in both content and form, thought and language, . . . that no Spanish palate can endure ten stanzas or three chapters from such an insipid dish."
19 "Since language and thought constitute an inseparable pair, all linguistic innovations that entail intellectual growth will be accepted."

5 Menéndez Pidal, national regeneration and the linguistic utopia

José del Valle

> La función histórica de la utopía no consiste precisamente en traducir a la realidad aquí y ahora . . . sus contenidos; sino en ensanchar las posibilidades históricas de un pueblo a través de un enriquecimiento de su conciencia colectiva.[1]
>
> (Jover Zamora 1991: 189)

Pidal and the turn-of-the-century crisis

When at the end of the nineteenth century Menéndez Pidal emerged as a distinguished intellectual figure in the Spanish academic and cultural scene, his beloved nation was in the midst of a most disconcerting crisis of identity. As the Spanish Empire finally crumbled, Spain's image in the international arena reached an all-time low. Most of its American colonies had become politically independent a few decades earlier, and their leaders had begun to build their own cultural and political destinies with models from nations other than the former metropolis. Pidal earned his professorship at the University of Madrid in 1899, a few months after the last remnants of the empire were lost in 1898's heart-wrenching defeat against the United States, the new economic and military power that now spread its dominance over the American continent. Within Spain, regionalist and nationalist movements – with both cultural and political fronts – were emerging in parts of the north, in regions such as the Basque Country, Catalonia and Galicia, threatening Spain's cultural and political unity and its viability as a nation, and hurting the pride and aspirations of liberal Spanish nationalism.[2] In addition to the colonial disaster and the nationalist outbreak, Pidal also experienced how the social order and lifestyle conceived by liberalism – not to mention conservatism – were placed in jeopardy, as the anarchist and socialist movements gained political influence and as the voices of the lower classes found their way to the privileged discursive spaces of politics and literature.[3]

Knowing that their country was perceived, both inside and outside its borders, as intellectually and politically decadent, Spanish intellectuals (*regeneracionistas*, *noventayochistas*, etc.) of the turn-of-the-century generations set out to diagnose the illness and concoct remedies that would allow the nation to overcome the trauma (cf. chapters 4, 6 and 7 on Valera, Unamuno and Ortega).

In this chapter, I will argue that Pidal's linguistic oeuvre can be read as a response to this complex crisis, and as an attempt to help the Spanish intellectual elite – and ultimately the whole nation – overcome its trauma. Pidal's role was rather unique and outstanding among his contemporaries: in contrast to authors who searched for the causes of the crisis, he was interested not so much in making a diagnosis as he was in minimizing the symptoms of the illness in order to boost the morale of the Spanish people. In an interview with his disciple Federico de Onís, he expressed an optimistic faith in the spirit of the Spanish people and in the ability of the selected minorities to liberate the nation from its temporary setback:

> A esta idea de la incapacidad originaria y fatal de la raza (madre de un pesimismo mortal e injustificado), sustituyen otros la de que la raza ha degenerado (pesimismo relativo, pues deja la puerta abierta a la posibilidad de regeneración). Yo, más optimista aún, no veo segura esa supuesta degeneración. . . . La virtud, el vigor [de la nación], han quedado atenuados, sí, más bien dormidos, latentes; pero a poco que se acerque uno al pueblo encuentra vivas las fuentes de la energía que esperan ser suscitadas, vigorizadas, encauzadas por elementos directores capaces de representar el espíritu de todo un pueblo. . . . nunca han faltado ni faltan ahora grandes españoles capaces de tomar las riendas y dirigir los esfuerzos espontáneos por los caminos seguros de la reconstitución nacional.[4]
>
> (quoted in Pérez Pascual 1998: 147)

Thus Pidal, in his role as linguist, historian and philologist, assumed his share of the responsibility to produce the spirit of leadership that Spain so badly needed. As I will try to argue in the following pages, the ultimate objectives of his linguistic work were to counter anti-Spanish sentiment and secure the loyalty of the Spanish and Latin American intellectual elite to the project of constructing a *modern* Hispanic community in which Spain's leadership would be recognized. More precisely, through his philological investigations he attempted to neutralize the impact of the discourses that disrupted the dominant linguistic order, both in Spain and in the Hispanic community as a whole. He produced an impressive body of scientific work and, with it, a magnificent conceptualization of the Spanish language as a monument that perfectly balances a tribute to tradition and a symbolic representation of modernity.

Pidal and the language battle

Previous chapters have illustrated that language was one of the fronts in which Hispanic intellectuals were waging the prestige war. Debates over which individuals or institutions should control the linguistic norm and over the desirability or inevitability of fragmentation – that is, the language battle – had come to symbolize the argument over Spain's modernity and its potential role in the maintenance and development of a united Hispanic culture. As we discussed in chapter 1, throughout the nineteenth century, the convergence of romanticism, nationalism and linguistics had consolidated the equation language = culture = nation. In this context, it was only natural that language would become one of the privileged platforms from which to launch the project of cultural revitalization that the state of crisis demanded.

We have also seen in previous chapters – and will continue to see in the rest of this book – how acutely aware of the changing nature of language were the participants in the language battle that we are analyzing. However, they held sharply contrasting views regarding the degree to which language change could or should be controlled and about how it could or should be channeled. Some language commentators, as we saw in chapters 2 and 4, identified change with fragmentation. As Velleman indicated, for Sarmiento the fragmentation of Spanish and the development of new languages in Latin America were a desirable goal that would free the American nations' spirit from the constraints of a worthless and antiquated Spanish culture. For Cuervo, as I explained in the previous chapter, the split would be the unfortunate outcome of Spain having lost its power to unify Hispanic nations and of intellectuals on both sides of the Atlantic to reach a consensus that would preserve the existing unity. In any event, the idea of the possible fragmentation of the Spanish language, whether it was desired or not, was being interpreted as a practical consequence and as a distressing sign of Spain's cultural decadence and political weakness.

However, acceptance of fragmentation was only one of the many possible responses to the challenge posed by the evidence of a constant evolution in language. In fact, numerous Spanish and Latin American intellectuals desired and believed in the preservation of linguistic unity. Yet, even among them, two key questions still demanded answers. First, who should control change, that is, the selection, codification and elaboration of the Spanish language? Second, who should dominate the public discourse on language and manage the complex web of associations between language and cultural referents? The intensely felt need to preserve linguistic and cultural unity could only be met with an agreement or *consensus* between Spanish and Latin American intellectuals regarding how the Spanish language was to be conceptualized and standardized. However, the tensions surrounding that linguistic consensus (most visible in the Valera–Cuervo controversy or in the Palma episodes; cf. chapters 1 and 4) were often the product of diverging views by Spanish and Latin American intellectuals regarding the hierarchical configuration of Hispanic culture.

In sum, champions of the Spanish cause, such as Pidal, had to fight the language battle on two fronts. On one hand, they had to neutralize the assault of *fragmentationists* and safeguard the Hispanic community's unified image. On the other, they had to hold the high ground for Spain against the charges of peripheral nationalisms and of those Latin Americans who either proclaimed their linguistic independence or demanded their legitimate share of linguistic power.[5] In either case, the language battle was being fought over Spain's hegemony – its viability as a nation and its international prestige in the cultural-linguistic map of the Hispanic community.

Regaining hegemony

Pidal's power and prestige, and consequently, his ability to share with his contemporaries his vision of the Spanish language, certainly derived from the resources that he controlled as a result of his association with and leadership role in various cultural institutions of the State. He earned his professorship at the University of Madrid in 1899; became a member of the Board for the Expansion of Studies and Scientific Research ("Junta para la Ampliación de Estudios e Investigaciones Científicas") in 1907; directed the Center for Historical Studies ("Centro de Estudios Históricos") between 1910 and 1936; was accepted into the Spanish Royal Academy in 1902 and directed this institution after 1926; and became a member of the Spanish Academy of History in 1916.[6]

However, Pidal's most efficient source of power – the reason behind his appointment to the above-mentioned positions – was his brilliant and prolific scientific production, that is, the intellectual capital he had so painstakingly earned. As a nationally and internationally recognized scientist of language and history, he earned a level of public admiration that invested him with what Pierre Bourdieu has called *symbolic power*, "that invisible power which can be exercised only with the complicity of those who do not want to know that they are subject to it or even that they themselves exercise it" (1991: 164).[7] Thus, Pidal entered the language battle well entrenched in the institutions of cultural power, and armed with the finest weapon of language science.

The high quality of his work and his well-deserved stature as a linguist and philologist inevitably predispose us to interpret his linguistic discourse as objective and ideologically neutral. However, it is my contention – as I anticipated in the previous section – that the impulse behind his scientific endeavors was intensely patriotic, as José Luis Abellán has suggested:

> Su exaltación de Castilla y su preocupación por todo lo referente al espíritu castellano le sitúan en un lugar privilegiado dentro del 98, que

no sólo no le impidió, sino que de algún modo inspiró su obra científica de historiador y filólogo.[8]

(quoted in Pérez Pascual 1998: 86)

Pidal firmly believed in the ultimately cultural and political consequences of his scientific work: "[C]onfío mucho en la eficacia del trabajo científico, que lentamente labra la conciencia de un pueblo elevando su cultura"[9] (quoted in Pérez Pascual 1998: 244). From the conceptual and methodological frameworks of historical linguistics and philology, and from the privileged position of intellectual and political power that he held, Pidal contributed to the creation of a monumental image of the Spanish language that would symbolize the greatness of Spanish civilization. He used the rhetorical power of science to produce and spread a vision of Spanish as the perfectly harmonious creation of a forward-moving culture and as an instrument of civilization that could only be disdained or rejected while disdaining or rejecting culture and civilization themselves. We will see how, in Pidal's linguistic work, the trauma narrative that reflected Spain's misfortunes was gently put aside and the insults to Spain's honor elegantly yet unforgivingly dismissed. The fear of linguistic fragmentation was dispelled as the contours of the Spanish language were drawn against the backdrop of a well-structured sociocultural system. The integrity and dignity of this system – Hispanic civilization – were and would always be guaranteed as long as an illuminated and loyal cultural elite assumed the responsibility of safeguarding the traditions that define it (language among them).

Holding the *skeptron*

> The discourse of authority . . . exercises its specific effect only when it is *recognized* as such: . . . it must be uttered by the person legitimately licensed to do so, the holder of the *skeptron*, known and recognized as being able and enabled to produce this particular class of discourse.
>
> (Bourdieu 1991: 113)

Throughout the nineteenth century, just before Pidal's time, linguistics had been rapidly developing in Europe as an independent academic discipline. As linguistics grew in academic prestige and as language matters became more and more prominent in cultural and scientific debates (Robins 1990: 187–8), Spanish intellectuals experienced with much preoccupation their nation's delay in incorporating this new and successful science to their universities (Mourelle Lema 1968: 155–209). Their concern was not unjustified, since, as late as the beginning of the twentieth century, no historical grammar of Spanish had been produced, and no worthy study of the history of Spanish following the dominant paradigm had yet been published. It would be precisely Pidal who, in 1904, would fill this vacuum by publishing his *Manual de gramática histórica española*, a most successful text that would be updated in several editions until the last one in 1941.[10]

The theoretical development of comparative and historical linguistics in Europe throughout the first half of the nineteenth century had culminated in the 1860s with the formulation of the neogrammarian program by a group of German scholars: Hermann Osthoff, Karl Brugmann and their collaborators (Jankowsky 1972). In the 1904 *Manual*, Pidal demonstrated, as he described the history of the Spanish language, that he was conversant with the most current advances in historical linguistics by following rather faithfully and successfully the neogrammarian model and principles. After a brief introduction of the languages that contributed to the development of the Spanish lexicon, the *Manual* presented the phonetic laws that had shaped the Spanish language, that is the changes that describe the evolution from Latin to Standard Spanish. This section was followed by one dedicated to exceptional changes, explained mainly as the result of analogical processes. A final section was devoted to morphological change, and again analogy played a central role. Pidal's adsorption to the neogrammarian model in the *Manual* is quite explicit, as the following quote – so reminiscent of the regularity principle – illustrates:[11]

> Esta historia nos ha dado a conocer leyes o direcciones que obraron sobre todos o sobre la mayoría de los casos en que cada sonido se daba en igualdad de condiciones dentro de palabras . . . El descubrimiento de esas leyes fonéticas ha sentado el estudio del origen de las palabras sobre una base firme capaz de servir al trabajo científico.[12] (1941: 175)

In sum, the general organization of the book, the methodology it proposed, and the conception of language change that it espoused were highly consistent with the neogrammarian doctrine, that is to say, with language science. The rigidly academic configuration of this text and its compliance with the neogrammarian program underscored its ideological power: the *Manual* demonstrated – in this case, to its Spanish readers – that the Spanish language could, and consequently should, be studied scientifically. By doing it (and by doing it so well) Pidal assumed control of the writing of its history, and took an important step toward the construction of its modern scientifically based public image. But the publication of the *Manual* further demonstrated – in this case to both its Spanish and international readers – the ability of Spanish academics to produce high quality scientific work.[13]

Pidal's elaboration of a documented history of the Spanish language and his growing international recognition did not stop with the *Manual*. In 1926, the Spanish philologist published the first edition of what would quickly come to be recognized as his linguistic masterpiece: *Orígenes del español: estado lingüístico de la península ibérica hasta el siglo XI*. The book contained four sections: it began with a critical edition of texts through which the preliterary phase of the Spanish language could be studied; it continued with a linguistic analysis – a grammar – of those texts and was followed by a chapter that discussed the relevance of the previously-presented linguistic evidence for the social and political history of Spain. Finally, the concluding section presented the implications of these findings for language-change theory in general.

The scholarly accomplishments of Pidal in *Orígenes* were many. For example, he intervened in the theoretical discussions in which the polemics between neogrammarians and dialectologists were grounded. As I mentioned above, due in part to the prominence of the neogrammarian school, the concept of phonetic law had become central in linguistic theory. The radical nature of Osthoff and Brugmann's regularity principle was the product of a desire by nineteenth-century linguists to associate themselves with the scientific method and to define their object of study – i.e. language – as highly systematic. However, some contemporary scholars, mainly dialectologists, had voiced their opposition to a method based on such a rigid conception of the phonetic law, on a principle so flagrantly false. In contrast with neogrammarians, many linguists decided to focus on heterogeneity – e.g. Rousselot or Gauchat – or on the protagonism of the word – e.g. Curtius or Schuchardt – (cf. Iordan and Orr 1970: 24–75 for a lengthy discussion of this matter). In *Orígenes*, Pidal responded to the objection of dialectologists; while he accepted their evidence and arguments, he accused them of shortsightedness:

> El espejismo . . . no se producirá si afirmamos la existencia de la ley fonética; se produciría si la negásemos, por no considerar el conjunto de una evolución secular sobre un territorio lingüístico de cierta unidad, y por limitarnos a la intensa contemplación de un solo instante del dialecto de una aldea.[14] (1950: 531)

The defective nature of the regularity principle was accepted; however, Pidal's solution was not to discard it but to redefine it. The concept of phonetic law was valid as long as it was not taken at face value or interpreted as "natural." For Pidal, a sound law is a phonetic phenomenon that operates historically under the impulse of social and cultural forces; it is a *symbol* of linguistic trends that can only be understood by taking into account the *socio-cultural* history of the community under consideration.[15]

As I have argued somewhere else (del Valle 1999a), Pidal's redefinition of the phonetic law and the historical-dialectological method that he developed – in which the evidence of the evolution of forms in time was crossed with their distribution in space – placed him among the scholars who anticipated some of the conceptions of language change that became prominent in linguistics only after the advent of sociolinguistics and lexical diffusion.[16] *Orígenes* was therefore a linguistic masterpiece, recognized as such by his contemporaries – both in Spain and abroad – that further strengthened Pidal's already-established authority in linguistic matters. His integrative reworking of the phonetic law and its application in *Orígenes* to the writing of a history of Spanish allowed him to hold on to the *skeptron* of language science while producing an ideologically charged discourse with direct implications for the language battle, that is, for Spain's attempt to regain its hegemonic position.

Spreading the word

While the intellectual magnitude of the Spanish philologist should certainly be measured by his scientific accomplishments – which were many – his acute awareness of the political implications of his linguistic-philological enterprise must not be taken lightly. He clearly understood the need to create a body of knowledge and a school of thought that would elevate the prestige of Spanish scholarship and legitimize a specific view of the Spanish language, the Spanish nation and the Hispanic community. But his vision of the role he had to play did not end there. As we saw in the first section of this chapter – in his own words – he also realized the political significance of his work and saw the need to personally intervene in the social propagation of that language ideology.

Consequently, Pidal's linguistic work was not exhausted by academic writings such as the *Manual* and *Orígenes*. He also produced a number of texts for a wider audience of educated readers not necessarily versed in linguistic and philological matters. They were popularizations of Pidal's linguistic ideas, of the conclusions he had reached in his less-widely-read linguistic and philological research. One such text is "La lengua española," published in 1918 in the first issue of the journal *Hispania* of the American Association of Teachers of Spanish. It was presented as a letter to Aurelio Espinosa and Lawrence Wilkins, distinguished founders of this association. Interestingly, several years later, Pidal would publish a very similar piece, *La unidad del idioma*, a speech given at a meeting of the Spanish Association of Book Publishers. It was printed and released in 1944 by that same group, and reproduced a year later in Pidal's *Castilla, la tradición, el idioma*, published in Espasa-Calpe's Austral series – a widely read and fairly inexpensive collection geared towards the general public.[17] The content of both articles is similar: it provides abundant arguments to dissipate any fears of fragmentation and describes Spanish as a uniform and stable language that symbolizes the historical accomplishments and the promising future of Spanish civilization. The deeply rhetorical character of these articles and the highly imaginative nature of the theses and arguments they present are quite evident (as I will try to show below), and *seem to be* in sharp contrast with the nature of his academic texts, which were consistent both in content and structure with the dominant trends in historical linguistics and dialectology. However, the academic and popular texts show a thematic continuity and coherence of argument that allows the latter to draw their legitimacy from the former. They are all in some way alleged descriptions of the Spanish language as unitary and uniform and of its history as an inevitable process of convergence. Linguistic unity and uniformity are presented as a natural result of the superior vision (civilizing model) offered by Castile first and Spain later to the whole Hispanic community. In sum, the popular texts are surrounded by a halo of respectability and legitimacy that is only possible as a result of the author's symbolic power and their association with the academic texts.

Unity and uniformity: the academic texts

Most of Pidal's linguistic oeuvre pivots around the concept of the past, present and future unity of the Spanish language. Just as the idea of fragmentation, enthusiastically promoted by Sarmiento and sadly predicted by Cuervo, reflected a negative or pessimistic view of Hispanic culture – especially Spanish culture – Pidal's insistence on the unity and uniformity of the language was part of his effort to neutralize the possible spread of the fragmentation theory and to forge a positive image of Spain and the civilization it had created throughout history.

The existence of dialectal differences within Spanish was the material basis for all claims that fragmentation would occur, in conjunction with the new aesthetic trend that was bringing non-standard forms and varieties to the realm of literature. The argument was that, if the educated classes adopted dialectal forms, new standard languages might emerge in each Hispanic nation (cf. Sarmiento's and Cuervo's positions in chapters 2 and 4 respectively). Pidal's stature as a linguist and philologist, his knowledge of the Spanish language in particular and of linguistic phenomena in general, was too sharp to plainly deny the existence of dialects and variation. Therefore, he faced the task of defending unity while acknowledging diversity. He responded to this challenge by opening two fronts: on the one hand, he had to argue that variation was minimal, that is, that there was not only *unity* but also a high degree of *uniformity* among Spanish dialects. On the other, he had to show that the existing variation was consistent with the life of a *normal* modern language and that in no way should it threaten its unity, diminish its value or tarnish its image (cf. Valera's response to Cuervo in chapter 4).

Pidal's stance on unity and uniformity was grounded in his historical-linguistic work. As I have indicated, in the elaboration of these texts, he complied with the most current methodologies and conceptual systems, and met the highest standards of historical linguistic research. But in addition, he took full advantage of the unifying potential of the philosophical principles underlying the historicist outlook.[18] As Julia Kristeva has indicated, historicism was, at least in part, a consequence of the eighteenth-century revolutions that made it necessary to reconcile with those radical transformations the rationalist concept of a natural order (1989: 193–5). This reconciliation produced the idea that order generates evolution: "Historicism gave its reason for the rupture in order to find continuity after division" (ibid.: 194).

But, within the conceptual framework of historicism, the notion that change can be interpreted as permanence is not considered to be universally valid: continuity is only guaranteed by "natural" changes. In other words, since an object contains within itself the seeds of its own transformation, continuity is secured if the impulses of change remain within the organic structure of the object.

In the *Manual*, Pidal's diachronic portrait of Spanish was clearly consistent with the principles of historicism. His description focused on two elements of the language: the continuity of its hereditary traits and its stability which was ultimately accomplished when, under the thrust of Castile, it reached maturity:

> Sólo será objeto de nuestra atención preferente el elemento más abundante, más viejo, el que nos puede ofrecer la evolución más rica: el del latín vulgar o hablado, que forma, por decirlo así, el *patrimonio hereditario* de nuestro idioma.
>
> (1941: 30, emphasis added)

> Este idioma hispano-romano, continuado en su natural evolución, es *el mismo* que aparece constituído ya como lengua literaria en el Poema del Cid, *el mismo* que perfeccionó Alfonso el Sabio y, sustancialmente, *el mismo* que escribió Cervantes.[19]
>
> (1941: 8, emphasis added)

For Pidal, the early stages of the development of modern Spanish begin with the collapse of the unifying force of the Roman Empire. At this point in the history of the language, the seeds planted by dialectal variation within Latin begin to grow. But after the disappearance of the Latin norm, not all Romance languages grew equally. In the Ibero-Romance territory, it was Castile's expansionist spirit and its ability to develop a literary variety that brought the language to maturity and gave it the stability that distinguishes all healthy languages:

> El castellano, por servir de instrumento a una literatura más importante que la de otras regiones de España, y sobre todo por haber absorbido en sí otros dos romances principales hablados en la Península (el leonés y el navarro-aragonés), recibe más propiamente el nombre de *lengua española*.[20]
>
> (1941: 2, emphasis in the original)

As we have seen, stability, according to the principles of historicism and historical linguistics, cannot be identified with immobility. Language inevitably evolves; but while it does, the preservation of its essence – i.e. its stability, mostly manifest in lexicon and grammar – can be guaranteed by what Pidal calls its "natural evolution," that is, the *internal* evolution experienced by healthy mature languages. For Pidal, Spanish clearly exhibits the power to reject external, unnatural influences:

> Lo que el español tomó de otros idiomas extranjeros fué ya en época más tardía, y por lo tanto es menos importante que lo que tomó de germanos y árabes, pues el *idioma había terminado su período de mayor evolución y era menos accesible a influencias externas.*
> (1941: 24, emphasis added)

> Llegarán acaso a olvidarse, como se han olvidado ya cientos de palabras que usaban los galicistas del siglo XVIII . . . *un idioma, como un cuerpo sano, tiene facultad de eliminar las sustancias extrañas* no asimiladas e inútiles.[21]
> (1941: 25, emphasis added)

As we know, Pidal further developed his historical image of the Spanish language in *Orígenes*. As he commented on the language of the documents from the period immediately preceding the birth of Spanish, he stated that that they displayed a "disconcerting variety of forms," a language that lacked a clear self-conscience, a personality, a soul, a life of its own (1950: 517–29). In the middle of this chaotic scenario, he claimed, Castile and its language emerged as a model of order, as a civilizing force to which all others could not but submit:

> Ciertos paises muestran una orientación más espontánea hacia la *estabilización* más decididamente que otros. Castilla se adelanta a todos los dialectos hermanos.
> (1950: 529, emphasis added)

> Castilla muestra *un gusto acústico más certero*, escogiendo desde muy temprano, y con *más decidida iniciativa,* las formas más eufónicas de estos sonidos vocálicos.
> (1950: 486, emphasis added)

> El dialecto castellano representa en todas esas características una nota diferencial frente a los demás dialectos de España, como una *fuerza rebelde y discordante* que surge en La Cantabria y regiones circunvecinas.[22]
> (1950: 487, emphasis added)

Thus, from his philological analysis he concluded that Castilian was born with certain inherently superior qualities – stability, a special aesthetic sense, and a spirit of entrepreneurship – offering a superior model to its neighbors. As these neighbor regions adopted the model, or as they were absorbed by it, contributing modestly to its orderly evolution, its sheer superiority functioned as a guarantor of unity.

Unity and uniformity: the popularizing texts

The idea of unity and uniformity also pervades, in an even more explicit manner, Pidal's popularizing texts; in fact these articles directly address the question of the unity and uniformity of the Spanish language (the title *La unidad del idioma* speaks for itself). In general, in these essays, Pidal insists on Spain's special loyalty to the true spirit of the language, stresses the existing linguistic uniformity both within Spain and across the Atlantic, and affirms the power of human institutions to control language:

> El tipo europeo prolonga más directa y firmemente la línea evolutiva antigua; la sociedad peninsular . . . continúa más fielmente su mismo estilo lingüístico; . . . El tipo americano pertenece a pueblos que se han formado previo el desgarrón de la vida peninsular . . . ; pueblos que . . . sienten con menos viveza la tradición idiomática. (1944: 29)

> El español peninsular es entre las lenguas romances la más unitaria; la lengua hablada en la Península, salvo en Asturias y en Alto Aragón, no muestra verdaderas variedades dialectales. (1944: 30)

> Ahora nos basta el hecho para comprender que las hablas populares hispano-americanas no representan una desviación extraordinaria respecto de la castellana. (1918: 2)

> La conversación de las personas educadas de la América española es, mirada en sus más salientes rasgos, el habla culta de Andalucía. (1918: 6)

> Con los progresos de la comunicación y con los de la cultura va alcanzando nuevos caracteres lo que se llama fijación del idioma . . . La acción del individuo y de la colectividad sobre el idioma se va haciendo cada vez menos inconsciente. (1944: 23)

> [L]os medios disponibles para propagar las normas lingüísticas son hoy increíblemente superiores a los de antes.[23] (1944: 23)

The effect of Pidal's intense insistence on the homogeneity of all varieties in his popularizing texts is that all descriptions and references to dialectal variation – both scientific and popular – are bound to be absorbed or overpowered by the master narrative of unity and uniformity. This is precisely one of the strategies with which he strives to neutralize the fragmentationist interpretation of dialectal variation as potentially divisive.

In addition to insisting on homogeneity, Pidal's main strategy for countering the fragmentation theory was integrating variation in his language image:

> La separación que media entre el español culto común, representante de la unidad, y el español popular de las varias regiones, representante de la diversidad, no puede simbolizarse en la creciente divergencia, cuya diferencia llegue a ser tanta que el español literario quede ininteligible para el pueblo, sino que debe figurarse por dos líneas ondulantes que caminan a la par en la misma dirección y cuyos altibajos tienden frecuentemente a la convergencia y se tocan muchas veces, sin llegar nunca a confundirse. El habla literaria es siempre la meta a que aspira el lenguaje popular, y, viceversa, la lengua popular es siempre fuente en que la lengua literaria gusta refrescarse.[24] (1944: 10–11)

In order to respond to the claims of fragmentationists, Pidal resorts to a conceptualization of language in general and the Spanish language in particular that views variation – at least a certain degree of variation – as consistent with the life of a healthy and stable language. The chosen metaphor is most revealing in this sense: the language is visualized as a two-tiered structure in which the standard is on top and popular varieties or dialects underneath. The life of the language is represented as two wavy lines (standing for the educated and popular varieties respectively) with the bottom one (the dialects) running parallel but always tending to move closer and closer to the top (the standard) without ever merging. Guided by this image, Pidal's readers are more likely to perceive variation not as a wild and disruptive phenomenon, or as an inevitable symptom of fragmentation, but as a process actually controlled by the laws that govern the life of language.

But perhaps the most surprising aspect of Pidal's language image is that he manages to create a positive notion of variation: not as a lesser evil, as one might expect, but as an essential component of the language. As we saw earlier, one of the legacies of linguistic historicism is that language can only be conceived as a dynamic entity, one that necessarily evolves over time. However, in the dominant linguistic culture of modern society (cf. chapter 1), variation and change are supposed to be, on the one hand, moderate and controlled and, on the other, organic (i.e. internal). External influences – coming from other languages, from other cultures – are usually seen with suspicion and considered to be most dangerous for the preservation of the language's identity. They must therefore be curbed. Similarly, internal variation, while recognized as inevitable, is only accepted with great reluctance. Pidal addresses the issue of internal variation in the dialects of the uneducated classes by distinguishing between *popular* and *vulgar* speech: "Lo popular supone la compenetración del elemento culto con el pueblo en general; lo vulgar supone la mayor iniciativa del pueblo inculto"[25] (1918: 5). Thus, external influences and vulgar forms – those which, in the language of the uneducated, significantly deviate from the established norm – constitute a serious threat to the integrity of the language and the culture it represents, especially if they are adopted by disloyal or unqualified members of the speech community who may somehow gain undue protagonism. Yet languages, even the healthiest ones, must change. What better source of innovation for the language than the language itself? Here resides the crucial value of dialects, of variation, of the *popular* speech represented in the lower tier: still part of the same tradition, of the same history, popular forms offer to the language "the fountain in which the standard is to refresh itself." In other words, change from within.

But there is still something missing for this linguistic picture to be perfect. As stated above, for Pidal, variation is not to be feared as long as it is subject to the laws that control the life of healthy languages; evolution – change from within – is normal as long as it is "natural." But what are those laws of linguistic gravity that keep the popular language always running parallel to the standard preventing it from making any sudden turns?

Laws of linguistic gravity

Pidal insisted that, contrary to the dominant views developed within linguistics in the nineteenth century, language is not a natural phenomenon controlled by inevitable laws totally independent from human will:[26] "La historia del lenguaje . . . pareció estar regida por leyes independientes de la voluntad humana" (1944: 17); "Debemos ahora insistir en desechar toda semejanza de los principios que rigen el lenguaje como función del espíritu, con las leyes naturales"[27] (ibid.: 16). Instead, he maintained that language is a social activity, one of the traditions that define a *community*'s identity. As such, it must be the result of a collective consensus:

> Si volvemos nuestra consideración a la canción popular y tradicional, una actividad social también muy extensa, . . . vemos que la participación del individuo es libérrima dentro de ciertos límites que la tradición le señala; . . . jamás un romance se repite exactamente de igual modo, sino con variaciones individuales, aunque, sin embargo, a pesar de tantas modificaciones, *el texto tradicional se conserva sin esencial alteración, ajustado al patrón heredado que a todos recitadores se impone como modelo ejemplar y superior.*[28]
>
> (1944: 17, emphasis added)

The development of folk songs and traditional ballads is therefore connected with human will. In their origins, we find the efforts of the human beings who created the tradition: the "patrón," the "modelo ejemplar y superior." Throughout their lives, we find the compliance of the individuals, who, in spite of their superlatively free ("libérrima") participation, maintain the tradition unaltered. Language, also a social phenomenon and a defining element of a community's identity, is subject to the same forces that explain the history of folk songs and traditional ballads:

> La lengua está en variedad continua y en permanencia esencial. Cada hablante moldea los materiales que en su memoria ha depositado la tradición . . . pero a pesar de eso, la lengua permanece en su identidad esencial.[29] (1944: 17)

We see then that the linguistic image produced by Pidal is characterized by an essential tension – almost by an internal contradiction. On one hand, language lives in the variable actions of superlatively free individuals; but on the other, it retains its essential identity. Such conception of language contains a built-in frailty: individual freedom, as much as it is natural, is also dangerous, since individuals may be exposed to and adopt undesirable linguistic forms such as external influences or vulgar speech. It is therefore essential for the guardians of the community's identity to keep them at bay, lest these undesirable forms generalize and enter the common patterns of linguistic behavior changing the essential identity of the language:

> El individuo por sí solo es impotente para alterar el curso de las modificaciones que el lenguaje tienda a sufrir; pero también es evidente que los cambios que se produzcan en el lenguaje, siendo éste un hecho humano, serán siempre debidos a la iniciativa de un hombre, de un individuo que, al desviarse de lo habitual, logra la adhesión o imitación de otros, y éstos logran la de otros.[30] (1944: 17–18)

For this very reason it is necessary to summon the loyal linguistic elite. These individuals are granted special status, since, as long as they are capable of earning the consent of the people, they can control the life of language – its formation, evolution and maintenance. Therefore, for Pidal, control over a language's identity cannot be taken for granted; it requires securing the loyalty of all members of the community both to the proposed linguistic norm and to the proponents of that norm. The power of the linguistic elite to generate collective loyalty to a given language and to the culture it represents – to create the social will to preserve a certain view of tradition – is the force that maintains the hegemonic vigor of the top tier – the standard – always pulling the lower tier – the popular dialects – towards it.

We have thus come to a crucial point in Pidal's dispute with the fragmentationists. The prestige and dignity of the Spanish language and the conditions of its future existence rest solely on the *will* of the members of the Spanish and Hispanic communities. After a long rhetorical trip through the land of historical linguistics, dialectology and the history of ballads and folk songs, Pidal is back where he started, standing next to Juan Valera (cf. previous chapter) telling his contemporaries – a very select group among them – that nothing bad will happen if *we* do not want it to happen:

> Mientras la sociedad *quiere* conservar su lengua, la vitalidad de ésta es perdurable, y si bien la sociedad recibe de la lengua una conformación

mental dada, antes la voluntad social conformó la lengua y sigue conformándola.[31]

(1944: 9, emphasis in the original)

The future of the Spanish language and Spanish culture depends therefore not so much on *what it is* as on *what we say it is, what we want it to be*. If the members of the intellectual elite construct a linguistic utopia, a united and harmonious image of the Spanish language and Hispanic culture, and if they demonstrate their loyalty to it, the people will follow suit and unity and harmony will be guaranteed.

"We"

But who is the implicit "we" in Pidal's linguistic image? Who embodies the tradition that defines the community? Who has the responsibility of establishing the norm and safeguarding it against any possible illnesses by serving as an active model of behavior? The criteria on which Pidal based his choice of the select group did not differ greatly from the ones Bello had used several decades earlier (cf. chapter 3). In the Spaniard's language ideology, social, educational and geographic factors also combined to produce a fairly precise sketch of the ideal speakers:

> En Madrid la «ll» suele articularse entre *las clases más educadas*, y el yeísmo domina completamente en *las clases populares*.
> (1944: 26, emphasis added)

> Es forzoso que una reacción correctiva empiece por *las clases educadas*, pero de ellas se propaga a *las clases que tienen menos tiempo para su educación*.
> (1944: 20–1, emphasis added)

> La escuela chilena, siguiendo las enseñanzas de Bello, había conseguido que el "tú" predominase sobre el "vos" en *la clase culta* de la sociedad; veinte años después, el "voseo" había desaparecido por completo de *la clase media* y se estaba perdiendo aún entre *la clase obrera*: los trabajadores de Santiago, observaba un sabio lingüista alemán, se tratan de "usted" aunque a veces cuando se acaloran en disputa echan mano del "vos."[32]
> (1944: 21, emphasis added)

Education and intellectual sophistication are therefore crucial criteria for determining who is to be included in the linguistic elite, in the group that carries the highest responsibility to monitor their speech and to launch the "reacción correctiva" that would trickle down to reach the less-educated members of society. We must take additional notice of the fact that Pidal associates the use of standard forms not only with individuals who have had access to a high level of formal education; his reference to the German linguist's statement – pointing out the association of the "undesirable" *vos* with the rowdy behavior of the working class – also links the linguistic elite with what we might refer to as civilized behavior, with the controlled and rational conduct that is expected of the ideal citizen of the modern nation (cf. "Spanish: a *modern* language" below).[33]

As we have seen, for Pidal, while a certain degree of variation was deemed normal in popular speech, the educated variety had to exhibit the highest possible level of uniformity. In the case of the Spanish-speaking community, Pidal insisted that the differences in the speech of the educated classes in Latin America and Spain were few; however, he saw them as constituting two separate norms and threatening the unity of the language.[34] Therefore, as in Bello's, in Pidal's linguistic model the socio-educational criterion did not suffice to precisely define the ideal speaker, since, by itself, it did not guarantee the level of uniformity required of the standard. In order to resolve this inconvenience, Pidal resorted to historical and geographic reasons that favor one of the educated varieties: the educated speech of Castile:

> [E]l tipo etimológico [the Castilian norm], valido de sus razones históricas y prácticas, hará importantes *reconquistas* en el terreno que le ha hecho perder el tipo derivado [the Andalusian and Latin American norm].[35]
>
> (1944: 28, emphasis added)

The practical motives adduced by Pidal for the adoption of the Castilian variety as the Spanish norm – multiple homonyms caused by *seseo* and *yeísmo* – were, in reality, very few ("multitud de homonimias enfadosas que el seseo y el yeísmo ocasionan" (ibid.: 27)). Instead, he allowed the historical reasons to carry greater weight in the justification of his choice. For Pidal, Spaniards, inhabiting the soil where the language was born, naturally had closer ties with it, and displayed stronger loyalty to its essence – as the preservation of an etymologically correct variety proves. In contrast, the Latin American norm had emerged among "pueblos que . . . sienten con menos viveza la tradición idiomática" (ibid.: 29). The circumstances of the colonization were such that a relative disruption of the linguistic order in America could not but be expected:

> España llevó a América sus instituciones religiosas, sus colegios, universidades y academias, su imprenta, su literatura, su civilización entera; pero las dificultades de administrar un territorio inmenso . . . imponían inevitables deficiencias a la obra gigantesca. En la colonización abundaron las clases bajas.[36] (1918: 5)

In order to properly describe the function of the linguistic elite in Pidal's language image, we must insist on the *necessarily active* role that he assigned to them. We have just seen how he selected a fairly specific group whose speech should serve as a model for grammarians or language planners in the process of elaborating the standard; but he also insisted that the members of this group should play an active role in the spread and maintenance of the selected variety. Spaniards (educated Spaniards) must be active agents in the process, and it is incumbent on them to do what it takes to deserve the privileged position they occupy. The loyalty of the educated elite to the language and to the model of civilization that it represents is the first step in the direction of securing its prestige and continuity:

> Castilla habría de emprender la corrección de su habla corriente, que no es modelo y guía más que cuando tiene razones para serlo. (1944: 30)

> Todo esto [Castile-based standardization] implica un esfuerzo grande,... para que no salga verdad la frase de un cineasta allá en California: "España ha perdido el *control* del idioma castellano". No pretendamos vivir en pereza fatalista, dejando el trabajo de corrección sólo a los otros.[37]
>
> (1944: 28, emphasis in the original)

Let us recapitulate. Pidal's linguistic ideology is based on the following assumptions. Since languages are inevitably bound to change, the linguistic elite must channel the evolution of the Spanish language: they must maintain control of the selection, codification and elaboration of the standard. As a general rule, changes are to be curbed: foreign influences must be avoided and changes from within encouraged only when they contribute to furthering uniformity. The general *acceptance* of the standard in the Hispanic community as a whole is the responsibility of the linguistic elite, who must secure linguistic control by earning the consent of the people. The construction of social consent depends on the linguistic elite's ability to create an appealing image of the language and to present themselves as the true interpreters of the community's collective will and linguistic identity: Grammarians, linguists and philologists – as holders of the *skeptron* of language science – are in a privileged position to claim that title. In sum, for Pidal, the unity and dignity of the Spanish language ultimately rested on the ability of the linguistic, cultural and political elite to control change by creating a linguistic utopia, and by selling it to the community, like "any political idea:"

> Cabe la propaganda en favor de tal o cual uso lingüístico, lo mismo que cabe en favor de tal o cual idea política, económica, jurídica o literaria cuyo triunfo se desea; así que un individuo puede influir poderosamente en el lenguaje de la comunidad hablante lo mismo que puede influir en una propaganda electoral: captándose adhesiones.[38] (1944: 18)

Erasing dissent

A crucial element in Pidal's construction of his language vision, and a key strategy for guaranteeing the dominance of his language ideology, is the minimization of the value and cultural weight of the perpetrators of linguistic subversion. Sarmiento and Cuervo (cf. chapters 2 and 4) are the main two such figures that Pidal discredits.

The Argentine's position on fragmentation is mentioned in passing by Pidal, and is easily dismissed as simple resentment in the aftermath of the bitter process of independence: "En vano Sarmiento, en quien los rencores que la emancipación dejó tras sí eran muy vivos . . ."[39] (Menéndez Pidal 1944: 19).

However, Cuervo's fragmentationist ideas were more difficult to discard since the Colombian had presented his views at the beginning of the twentieth century, long after the wars of independence (cf. chapter 4 on the Valera–Cuervo controversy). Pidal's handling of Cuervo takes place primarily in his 1944 article. His concern with the Colombian's views had to do less with the ideas themselves than with the fact that a linguist, someone *holding the skeptron* had produced them:

> No hay duda de que en esta polémica entre el sabio colombiano y el insigne don Juan Valera el mayor interés brotó bajo la pluma del gran lingüista y no bajo la del gran literato; . . . los extremados conocimientos que Cuervo poseía sobre la historia lingüística de América, dan a su razonamiento una densidad que todavía pesa sobre nuestros ánimos como amenazadora nube y reclama nuestra atención después de cuarenta años.[40] (1944: 4)

As we can see, Pidal was concerned with Cuervo's legitimacy, which was a direct result of his reputation as a linguist and philologist. The strategy that Pidal used to discredit such a well-regarded linguist – one that he himself much admired – was to create two Cuervos and deal with them separately. First, he praised the younger Cuervo, the great linguist who had gloriously worked for the unity of the Spanish language, and who had acknowledged Castile's dominance by opening his *Apuntaciones* with Puigblanch's famous words:

> [E]l avance de éste [criollismo] es considerado por Cuervo con noble melancolía, sin olvidar nunca, como lema de todos sus trabajos, el dicho de Puigblanch: "Los españoles americanos, si dan todo el valor que dar se debe a la uniformidad de nuestro lenguaje en ambos hemisferios, han de hacer el sacrificio de atenerse, como a centro de unidad, al de Castilla, que le dió el ser y el nombre."[41] (1944: 7)

He then went on to criticize the older Cuervo, linking his pessimistic attitude with his senility – "La naturaleza del sabio colombiano se vio minada prematuramente por los achaques de la senectud"[42] (5) – and with the possible influence of *El idioma nacional de los argentinos* written by Lucien Abeille, a French immigrant who settled in Argentina (cf. chapter 2). In this book, Abeille had presented a description of Argentinean Spanish that emphasized the differential features of this dialect. Abeille had also pointed out, even with his suggestive title, that such considerable differences justified speaking of the possible development of an Argentinean language. Pidal said of this book that it was stillborn, "un libro muerto al nacer"; and of the author: "en todo se mostraba falto de los conocimientos científicos y prácticos pertinentes, y sobre todo, falto de buen gusto"[43] (1944: 7).[44]

But the crucial criticism with which Pidal tackled Cuervo's position was the latter's conception of language, that is, the linguistic theory underlying his work. According to Pidal, "Cuervo, en la senectud, erró su camino científico sumándose a una teoría de 'fatal evolución' que ya entonces comenzaba a caer en descrédito"[45] (Menéndez Pidal 1944: 10). Let us return briefly to Cuervo's pessimistic prognosis for the Spanish language (cf. previous chapter for more details). Although Cuervo, in keeping with dominant trends of nineteenth-century linguistics, did maintain the inevitability of change in language, he never claimed that constant evolution *necessarily* entailed fragmentation. His pessimistic outlook was the outcome of his having lost faith in the ability of Spanish and Latin American intellectuals to build the necessary consensus to preserve a common standard. For the Colombian, the force that would keep the popular dialects running parallel to the educated norm was simply exhausted. His moderately stated position on fragmentation was grounded in his view that the conceptions of Hispanic culture and attitudes toward its construction held by Spaniards on the one hand and Latin Americans on the other were outright irreconcilable. Consequently, Cuervo and Pidal – contrary to the latter's statements – did in fact share the same conception of language and disagreed only about their beliefs concerning the preservation of the common social will. When Pidal claimed that he would respond to Cuervo's linguistic arguments from a linguistic perspective, he was manipulating both Cuervo's and his own discourses. On the one hand, he distorted the Colombian's position by claiming that it was based on an obsolete theory of language; and on the other – as I argued earlier – he used exactly the same arguments Valera had used against the Colombian, although, granted, camouflaged with the rhetoric of language science.

Thus, Sarmiento and Cuervo's dissent was explained away by attributing it to unique, individual circumstances: Sarmiento was angry in the postcolonial fever, and Cuervo was under the effects of a premature senility. What is the place then, in Pidal's linguistic oeuvre, for the claims made by some Latin American intellectuals, such as Sarmiento or Gutiérrez in the nineteenth century (cf. chapter 2) and Arguedas or González Prada in the twentieth (cf. chapter 8), that Spain did not offer an appropriate cultural and linguistic model for the young nations? And what about the complaints by authors such as Ricardo Palma and Cuervo who, willing at first to construct a pan-Hispanic future, became skeptical as a result of the paternalistic and dominating attitude of Spaniards? In order to sustain the linguistic utopia, these claims must be dismissed and never openly addressed.

Spanish: a *modern* language

The centrality of the notion of progress in the discourse of modernity has given this mode of social organization an unquestionable future-oriented character. At the end of the nineteenth century, this modern condition must have posed a serious problem for a nation such as Spain whose greatest glory seemed to be a question of the past. Yet Pidal – displaying a lucid intuitive understanding of the requirements of modernity – did not respond to the present crisis by simply basking in the nation's glorious history, by constructing a "monument" to its past; instead, he constantly projected national history onto the future, defining the Spanish language not only as the symbol of a great old civilization, but as an instrument that could build the bridge of progress for the Hispanic community. For example, as he rejected Cuervo's comparison between the collapse of Latin and the possible fragmentation of Spanish, he subtly portrayed the latter as the instrument that would open the gate for the Hispanic community's participation in the activities of modern times:

> [C]uando la intercomunicación de las Repúblicas americanas llegue a hacerse tan difícil que para los negocios importantes se practique con intervalos de un año, cuando en ellas la producción literaria enmudezca por espacio de un siglo o más, entonces podremos entristecernos sobre una suerte de la lengua, semejante a la del latín . . . Cabe en lo posible que la Humanidad caiga otra vez en la barbarie, que pierda la *universalidad* de su *ciencia* y de su *comercio*, que el *aeroplano* se olvide y la *locomoción* se reduzca al asno. Pero estamos tan lejos de esto que no es sensato pensar en ello más que en el enfriamiento del sol y el apocamiento de la vitalidad en la especie humana.[46]
>
> (1944: 14–15, emphasis added)

Similarly, as he justified the hierarchical distinction between educated and popular speech – which brilliantly foreshadowed contemporary discourses on the need to face the challenges of globalization – he reminded his readers, once again, that they must embrace the norm if they are to have access to the universal thought of modernity: "La lengua culta y literaria es tan connatural al hombre cuando quiere universalizar sus pensamientos, como la lengua local lo es cuando piensa las cosas más cotidianas y caseras"[47] (1944: 20).

In Pidal's history of Spanish, the language's association with the forces of civilization and with their universalizing tendencies was not a recent development. The language's history demonstrated the presence of Spain's – more precisely, Castile's – courageous spirit from quite early. As indicated above, in his historical-linguistic works, Pidal insisted that Spanish had its roots in the speech of Castile, which had emerged at a time when this kingdom, rebellious and energetic, offered its neighbors a *future*, an ambitious political project and the spirit to bring it to completion. In Pidal's linguistic oeuvre, the birth of Spanish in medieval Spain was presented as the emergence of the paradoxical combination of socio-cultural stability and rebelliousness that would provide the Hispanic community with a sense of identity, with an *hecho diferencial*. The birth of Spanish symbolized the establishment of a solid identity that would give impulse to an inexorable march towards modernity:

> La falta de una norma romance sentida con gran eficacia por los hablantes es falta de un *alma* o principio personal en la lengua nueva, falta de un *vivir* propio, apartado del de la lengua latina. Ese espíritu propio va formándose lentamente en la lucha de las varias tendencias o fuerzas. Ciertos paises muestran una orientación espontánea hacia la *estabilización* más decididamente que otros. Castilla se adelanta a todos los dialectos hermanos . . . también fue la que primero desarrolló una literatura propia.
> (1950: 529, emphasis added)

> El dialecto castellano representa en todas esas características una nota diferencial frente a los demás dialectos de España, como una *fuerza rebelde y discordante* que surge en La Cantabria y regiones circunvecinas.[48]
> (1950: 487, emphasis added)

In Pidal's language ideology, the inherently superior qualities of the dialect of Castile explained its projection not only in time but also in space, as it spread outside its original territorial boundaries. Spanish, therefore, while rooted in a specific place and time, established its truly modern nature by overcoming temporal and spatial limitations, by proving to be endowed with the superlatively modern quality of universality:

> La lengua culta . . . se difunde donde quiera que llega la actividad de los hombres de acción o el brillo de las inteligencias más eficaces que se sirven del mismo idioma. *Aventureros, comerciantes, magistrados, capitanes, tribunos, pensadores* . . . cualquiera que necesita hacer vivir una idea, útil y bella, . . . se esfuerza en crear y conservar ese lenguaje de más poderosa virtud . . . logrando el mayor alcance en el espacio y en el tiempo.[49]
> (1918: 2, emphasis added)

Entrepreneurship ("aventureros"), commerce ("comerciantes"), order ("magistrados, capitanes, tribunos"), knowledge ("pensadores") ... catchwords of modernity, universally admired activities and aspirations that the Spanish language has made possible and that it has come to symbolize.

Throughout history, it has been customary for great political and military powers to symbolically show off their strength by building architectural masterpieces and engineering wonders. Such displays of national discipline, technological prowess and, often, aesthetic sensibility became particularly conspicuous in modern times when technology reached an unprecedented peak and communications expanded the potential ideological impact of those awesome structures. Could Pidal's construction of an image of the Spanish language have performed a function analogous to that of those architectural and engineering feats? As a Spanish intellectual of the turn-of-the-century generations, he did not merely engage in the objective description of the language, but in the construction of a spectacular icon: glorious symbol for the nation's past and sophisticated vehicle for its race towards a brilliant future.

> La tarea que históricamente nos toca es, primero, la de no menoscabar, por desidia, la vigencia de esa forma [the Peninsular Spanish norm]; después, el llevarla constantemente a nueva perfección literaria, con el oído siempre atento a los pueblos hermanos ... tendiendo a un futuro en que aparezca más espléndida la magnífica unidad lingüística creada a un lado y otro de los mares, una de las más grandiosas construcciones humanas que ha visto la historia.[50]
>
> (Menéndez Pidal 1944: 33)

Notes

I want to express my gratitude to my friend and colleague Alberto Medina Domínguez for his careful reading and insightful comments on an earlier version of this chapter.

1 "The historical function of utopias is not the immediate realization – here and now – of their content, but the broadening of the historical possibilities of a people through the enrichment of their collective conscience."
2 By Spanish nationalism I refer to the nineteenth-century liberal project of construction of a modern nation – as described for example by Hobsbawm (1990); cf. chapter 1. The political ideas and practices associated with liberal nationalism – of which Pidal, in my view, was an important ideologue – must be clearly distinguished from the fascism-inspired Spanish nationalist movement. Unfortunately, the cultural dimensions of both projects, while not identical, bear some uncomfortable resemblances (which, I must insist, do not justify their identification).
3 "Desde mediados del siglo XIX se da franca entrada en la literatura al habla dialectal ... Y ya en 1882 Juan Ignacio de Armas ... hacía notar el hecho de que la literatura costumbrista adquiría una extensión mayor cada día" (Menéndez Pidal 1944: 2; "From the middle of the nineteenth century, dialectal speech is

brought into literature ... As early as 1882, Juan Ignacio de Armas ... pointed out the fact that *costumbrista* literature spread more every day.")

4 "While some hold the idea of the race's original and fatal unfitness (source of an unjustified and deadly pessimism) others suggest that it has degenerated with time (a relative pessimism that leaves the door open for regeneration). I am even more optimistic; I do not see any degeneration ... The virtue and vigor [of the nation] have weakened, or rather, have become asleep and latent; but as soon as one approaches the people, one finds the live sources of energy waiting to be aroused, strengthened and channeled by leaders capable of representing the spirit of a whole people. ... we have never lacked – and we do not lack now – great Spaniards able to take control and direct spontaneous efforts along the sure paths of national reconstruction."

5 The emergence in the late nineteenth century of regionalist and later nationalist movements in the Basque Country, Catalonia and Galicia constituted serious challenges to Spain's status. How could the prestige of the nation be maintained when its value as a modern national entity was being questioned both from the outside (by the former colonies) and from the inside (by Basque, Catalan and Galician separatists)? Pidal's position with respect to the Catalan question was fairly clear: in the 1920s, he signed, with other Spanish intellectuals, a manifesto in defense of the Catalan language in response to General Primo de Rivera's restrictive measures. He also publicly expressed his sympathy towards the Catalan cultural revival and even his support of a reconfiguration of the state that would grant some regions a certain degree of autonomy (Pérez Pascual 1998: 233–49). However, he vehemently opposed any regional demands that in any way denied or undermined the unity and relative uniformity of the Spanish nation, "el hecho magno y secular de la pacífica y perdurable penetración del castellano, desde la Edad Media, tanto en Galicia como en Cataluña y Vasconia" (Menéndez Pidal quoted in Pérez Pascual 1998: 248; "The magnificent and historical fact of the peaceful and durable penetration of Castilian, from the Middle Ages, in Galicia, Catalonia and the Basque Country.")

6 For Pidal's biography cf. Hess (1982), Malkiel (1970), the already-mentioned Pérez Pascual (1998), and Pérez Villanueva (1991).

7 A clear example of the symbolic power with which Pidal, as a linguist, was endowed was Miguel de Unamuno's expression of satisfaction when Pidal – a linguist, one truly equipped to deal with language – was elected to the RAE.

8 "His intense praise of Castile and his concern for everything that had to do with the Castilian spirit give him a prominent position among the members of the generation of 98; this did not hamper – in fact it somehow inspired – his scientific work as a historian and philologist."

9 "I greatly trust the value of scientific work, which slowly cultivates the conscience of a people elevating their culture."

10 "Pocas obras de este tipo pueden vanagloriarse de haber resistido tan bien el paso del tiempo, hasta el punto de que aún hoy en día es un texto de obligada consulta para especialistas y estudiosos de la evolución del castellano" (Pérez Pascual 1998: 81; "Few works of this kind can boast of having resisted so well the passage of time; even nowadays it is an essential text for scholars and specialists in the history of Castilian.")

11 The most crucial element of Osthoff and Brugmann's theory of language change is the so-called regularity principle: "[E]very sound change, inasmuch as it occurs mechanically, takes place according to laws that admit no exception" (Osthoff and Brugmann [1878] 1967: 204).

12 "This history has allowed us to see laws or directions that were effective in all or the majority of cases in which a sound occurred in the same context within a

word ... The discovery of those phonetic laws has established the study of the origin of words on a firm basis capable of serving scientific work."

13 Pidal was greatly concerned about the quality of Spanish academic life: "La Universidad ha mejorado algo, quizá bastante; pero en rigor no ha habido en ella una mejora esencial, que la haga levantarse de la decadencia en que hace siglos ha caído (como otras tantas manifestaciones de la vida nacional)" (Pidal quoted in Pérez Pascual 1998: 132; "The University has improved a little, maybe a lot; but in reality there has not been an essential improvement that will help raise the institution from its long decadence (like many other aspects of national life).")

14 "The illusion ... would not be to state the existence of a phonetic law; the illusion would be to deny it, and not consider the complete historical evolution in a relatively united linguistic territory; the illusion would also occur if we limited ourselves to the intense contemplation of one single instant in the dialect of a village."

15 "Propendí a considerar inseparables la historia lingüística con la historia literaria (crónicas métricas, poesía épica) y con la historia política y social (personajes, instituciones, sucesos)" (Pidal quoted in Pérez Pascual 1998: 36; "I tended to treat as inseparable linguistic and literary history (chronicles and epic poems) and political and social history (characters, institutions, historical events).")

16 Cf. Lloyd (1970) for the connections between Pidal's doctrine and sociolinguistics and del Valle (1999a) on his foreshadowing of lexical diffusion.

17 Pidal's renewed intervention in the fragmentation debate may have been stimulated in the 1930s and 1940s by the publication of *El problema de la lengua en América* by Amado Alonso (1935) and *La peculiaridad lingüística rioplatense y su sentido histórico* by Américo Castro (1941). In these books Alonso and Castro, two of the most distinguished disciples of Menéndez Pidal, discussed what they considered to be the linguistic chaos of Argentina (cf. del Valle 1999b). Argentinean writer, Jorge Luis Borges, responded to Castro's book with an article that has become a classic: "Las alarmas del doctor Américo Castro." For the ideological dimension of these dialectological discussions cf. del Valle (1998).

18 The political use of the unifying potential of linguistic history was a widespread phenomenon, to which Tony Crowley – studying the development of the history of the English language in England – has referred in the following terms: "'the history of the language' belonged to the discourse of cultural nationalism which stressed continuity, that which is known, a sense of history, and gradual evolution. ... 'the history of the language' and discourses like it were centripetal" (Crowley 1996: 152).

19 "We will only pay special attention to the more common and old elements, the ones that may offer us the richest evolution: spoken or vulgar Latin, which is the *hereditary patrimony* of our language, so to speak" (emphasis added). "This Hispano-Roman language, continued in its natural evolution, is *the same* found as a literary language in the 'Poem of the Cid,' *the same* brought to perfection by Alfonse the Sage and, essentially, *the same* in which Cervantes wrote" (emphasis added).

20 "Castilian, having been the instrument for a literature more important than that of other regions of Spain, and having absorbed the two main Romance languages spoken in the Iberian Peninsula (Leonese and Aragonese), receives the more appropriate name *Spanish*."

21 "What Spanish borrowed from foreign languages came at a later date, and it is therefore less important than what it took from Germans and Arabs; *the language had completed its period of more intense evolution and was less accessible to external influences*" (emphasis added). "They may even be forgotten, just like the hundreds of words

used by gallicists in the eighteenth century . . . *a language, like a healthy body, has the ability to eliminate foreign substances that are not assimilated and useless*" (emphasis added).

22 "Certain countries display a more spontaneous inclination towards *stabilization* more decisively than others. Castile was faster than its brother dialects" (emphasis added). "Castile shows a *more proper acoustic taste*, selecting rather early and *with greater initiative*, the more euphonic variants of these vocalic sounds" (emphasis added). "The Castilian dialect displays in all its characteristics a unique character in comparison to the other dialects of Spain, as a *rebellious and dissenting force* that emerges in Cantabria and adjacent regions" (emphasis added).

23 "The European type is more directly and firmly consistent with the old line of evolution; Peninsular society . . . maintains more faithfully its linguistic style; . . . The American type belongs to peoples that developed after breaking away from peninsular life . . . peoples who feel less intensely the linguistic tradition." "Peninsular Spanish is the most unitary of all Romance languages; the language spoken in the Peninsula, with the exception of Asturias and High Aragon, does not have any true dialectal varieties." "This fact suffices to understand that Spanish American popular speech does not significantly deviate from Castilian." "The speech of the educated in Spanish America is, if we look at its most prominent features, the educated speech of Andalusia." "With the progress of communication and culture the stabilization of language acquires a new character . . . Individual and collective influence on language becomes less and less unconscious." "The means to spread the linguistic norm are today incredibly superior to what they used to be."

24 "The distance between general educated Spanish, which represents unity, and the popular Spanish of various regions, which represents diversity, cannot be interpreted as a process of growing divergence, whose differentiation will be such that literary Spanish will be unintelligible to the people. Instead, it should be conceived of as two wavy lines that run side by side in the same direction and whose peaks and valleys frequently tend towards convergence, often touching but without ever merging completely. The literary language is always the goal towards which popular language aspires, and, vice versa, the popular language is always the fountain in which the literary language likes to refresh itself."

25 "The *popular* always entails the mutual understanding between the educated and the people in general; the *vulgar* a greater initiative on the part of the uneducated people."

26 Cf. Joseph 1995: 221.

27 "The history of language . . . seemed to be governed by laws independent from human will." "We must now discard any similarity between the principles that govern language as a function of the spirit and natural laws."

28 "If we turn our attention to traditional and folk songs, another very common social activity, . . . we see that the individuals' participation is free within certain limits established by tradition; . . . a romance is never repeated exactly in the same manner; instead it is reproduced with individual variations, although, however, in spite of so many modifications, the traditional text remains without essential alterations, respecting the inherited standard imposed on all singers as a superior and exemplary model" (emphasis added).

29 "The language lives in a state of constant variation and essential permanence. Each speaker moulds the materials deposited in his mind by tradition . . . but in spite of that, the language remains with its essential identity."

30 "The individual by himself is unable to alter the course of the modifications that language will tend to suffer; but it is also evident that the changes that affect language – being as it is a human phenomenon – will always be the product of an

individual's initiative, of an individual who, deviating from what is usual, manages to earn the support of others; they imitate him, and subsequently others will imitate them."

31 "While society *wants* to preserve its language, its vitality is guaranteed; and while society receives from language a given mental conformation, befor, social will conformed language and continues to conform it" (emphasis in original).

32 "In Madrid, 'll' is usually pronounced [as a lateral sound] among *the most educated classes*, and *yeísmo* [the non-lateral pronunciation] is widespread among *the popular classes*" (emphasis added). "It is necessary that a corrective reaction begin with *the educated classes*, and from them spread to *the classes that have less time for their own education*" (emphasis added). "Chilean schools, following Bello's teachings, had imposed the pronoun 'tú' over 'vos' among *the educated class* of society; twenty years later, the 'voseo' had completely disappeared from the *middle class* and was being lost even among the *working class*: workers in Santiago, said a German linguist, use "usted" to address each other, although sometimes in the heat of a dispute they resort to 'vos'" (emphasis added).

33 I have discussed the role that grammar and language planning play in the configuration and domestication of the ideal subject of the modern nation-state in del Valle (1999b) (cf. also González Stephan 1995).

34 Any consideration of Pidal's use of the geographic criterion must be placed in the context of *hispanismo* (cf. chapter 1) since his firm belief in the indisputable cultural unity between Spain and Spanish America is central to his linguistic ideology: "Simper la onda vital de España y de Hispano-América vibrará con misteriosos unísonos, y responderá al común atavismo. Toda la civilización hispanoamericana descansa principalmente en su base española" (Menéndez Pidal 1918: 9). As was the case with *hispanismo* in general, in Pidal's view of the Hispanic community Spain, and more specifically Castile, is the *alma mater* of the Hispanic world which also justifies the special position it occupies and the major responsibility it has: "Lengua española, creada por cima de todas sus variedades dialectales, aunque con la colaboración más o menos sensible de ellas. Claro es que *la variedad castellana fué principalísima en esa labor*" (Menéndez Pidal 1918: 3, emphasis added).

35 "The etymological type [the Castilian norm], legitimized by practical and historical reasons, will *reconquer* the terrain lost to the derived type [the Latin American norm]" (emphasis added).

36 "Spain brought to America its religious institutions, its schools, universities and academies, its printing presses, its literature, its entire civilization; but the difficulties of governing such a vast territory . . . produced inevitable deficiencies in the gigantic enterprise. In the colonization, the lower classes were abundant."

37 "Castile should begin to correct its speech, since it will only be a model and a guide when it deserves it." "All of this [Castile-based standardization] requires great effort, . . . so that that statement made by a famous movie personality over there in California doesn't turn out to be true: 'Spain has lost *control* of the Castilian language.' Let's not live in fatalistic laziness, leaving the corrective work only for others."

38 "It is possible to campaign for a type of linguistic usage; just as it is possible to campaign for a political, economic, legal or literary idea whose success we want; therefore an individual may powerfully influence the language of a speech community just as he can have influence during an electoral campaign: by gaining the support of others."

39 "In vain Sarmiento, for whom the resentment left by the emancipation was great . . ."

40 "Undoubtedly, in this polemic between the Colombian scholar and the distinguished Juan Valera, the most interesting views were produced by the great

linguist and not by the great writer; . . . Cuervo's breadth of knowledge of the linguistic history of America gives his ideas great weight; a weight that we still feel over our spirit as a threatening cloud, and which demands our attention after forty years."
41 "The advance of this *criollismo* is considered by Cuervo with a noble melancholy, without forgetting, as the epigraph to his works, Puigblanch's words: 'Spanish Americans, if they value as they should linguistic uniformity in both hemispheres, must sacrifice and respect Castile as the center of unity, since it gave the language its being and name.'"
42 "The nature of the Colombian scholar was prematurely mined by the ailments of senility."
43 "He lacked the necessary practical and scientific knowledge, and especially, he lacked good taste."
44 Again, we must take notice of the fact that Pidal is concerned not so much with refuting Abeille's ideas as with discrediting him, with pointing out that he could not speak legitimately: he did not hold the *skeptron*.
45 "Cuervo, in his old age, went the wrong scientific way by subscribing to a theory of fatal evolution that was beginning to be discredited."
46 "When communication among the American Republics becomes so difficult that important businesses take a year to complete, when literary production disappears for over a century, then we may be sad about the destiny of our language, similar to that of Latin . . . It is perhaps possible that Humanity will fall again into barbarism, that it will lose the *universality* of its *science* and of its *commerce*, that the airplane is forgotten and *transportation* is limited to donkeys. But we are so far from this that it is not more sensible to think about it than it is to think about the freezing of the sun or the fainting of the vitality of the human species" (emphasis added).
47 "The educated and literary language is as natural to man when he wants to universalize his thoughts, as the local language is when he thinks about the more mundane and domestic."
48 "The absence of a Romance norm intensely felt by speakers is the absence of a *soul* or personal principle in the new language; absence of a life of its own, separate from Latin. That unique spirit slowly develops in the struggle among different tendencies or forces. Certain countries show a more spontaneous inclination than others towards *stabilization*. Castile is faster than its brother dialects . . . it was also the first one to develop a literature of its own" (emphasis added). "The Castilian dialect displays in all its characteristics a unique character in comparison to the other dialects of Spain, as a *rebellious and dissenting force* that emerges in Cantabria and adjacent regions" (emphasis added).
49 "The educated variety of the language . . . spreads as far as the activities of men of action or the spark of the most efficient intelligences which use the language go. *Adventurers, traders, magistrates, captains, tribunes, thinkers* . . . anyone who wants to give life to an idea, useful and beautiful, . . . strives to create and preserve that more virtuously powerful language . . . reaching as far as possible in space and time" (emphasis added).
50 "The task that has been handed down to us by history is not to destroy, out of neglect, the validity of this form [the Peninsular Spanish norm]; then, we must constantly bring it to a new literary perfection, with our ear always open to our brother nations . . . moving towards a future in which, more splendid, will appear the magnificent linguistic unity created on both sides of the ocean, one of the grandest human constructions that history has ever seen."

6 "For their own good"
The Spanish identity and its Great Inquisitor, Miguel de Unamuno

Joan Ramon Resina

> Sean cuales fueren las deficiencias que para la vida de la cultura moderna tenga el pueblo castellano, es preciso confesar que a su generosidad, a su sentido impositivo, a su empeño por imponer a otros sus creencias, debió su predominancia. . . . Gran generosidad implica el ir a salvar almas, aunque sea a tizonazos.
>
> (Unamuno 1905b: 1293)

> En bien espiritual de Cataluña, en bien de su mayor cultura, hay que mantener la oficialidad irrestringida e incompartida de la lengua española, de la única lengua nacional de España.
>
> (Unamuno 1908d: 377)

> El inquisidor es más caritativo que el anacoreta.[1]
>
> (Unamuno 1908d: 375)

Centennials, it seems, are a function of history: a turning back, an awareness of elapsed time, a recollection of elements that time has dispersed and pious evocation brings back to life for as long as the rite lasts. History, though, is a double-edged word. It stands both for action in the past and for the retrospective consciousness of that action in the minds of those who have suffered its consequences, who *are* the consequences of action as well as the agents of memory. Yet consciousness is not just the residue of past events or impressions; it is itself constitutive of history. It is by knowingly producing the conditions of human action that history arises, by acting in knowledge of the effects of one's action. This means that historical discourse is never purely retrospective, that it never records or traces the past for its own sake, but produces itself in order to establish the conditions in which the present is experienced. Organized to honor or remember the past, centennials can also serve to expand the range of its agency, building a bridge to the future by anchoring it in present rhetoric. Or they can stabilize an order inaugurated by the historical agent being commemorated or remembered. In such cases a centennial can legitimize a conservative option that has stalled ideologically, even as the time gap is acknowledged and differences of context are stressed. It seems to me that the large-scale centenary of the Generation of 98, activated, financed, and to some extent organized by the Spanish government, partakes of this goal.

During 1997 and 1998 Spain has been the stage for an ideological return of the past, not just by way of centennial celebrations, but above all through vindications of the political culture of the previous turn of the century. These vindications began during the 1996 electoral campaign, when the Popular Party's leader, Jose María Aznar, in the course of an interview declared that Castile is the avant-garde of Spain. This strange notion, burdened with aesthetico-political overtones, can only be understood as an ideological inheritance from the Generation of 98 via Falange Española and the National Movement. When the 98ers tried to imagine the Spanish nation, they conceived it metonymically in the image of Castile. For them Castile was indeed the essence of Spain, but did that also make it its vanguard? The 98ers were confronted with the problem of historical decadence; hence, in their view, Castile's backwardness, its status as a hinterland, privileged its image and lent a vanishing aura to values that had proven refractory to modernity. Aznar, however, seemed to call on those values as if, by virtue of their confrontation with modernity, they were themselves modern, nay ultramodern, by analogy with the artistic avant-garde's challenge to modernity. After the elections that returned the conservatives to power, Aznar, seeking a historical referent for his government (and debarred from identifying with the Francoist regime from whose shreds his party had grown), extolled the period of corrupt democracy known as the Restoration. This long period of conservative rule is certainly, in some ways, reminiscent of the current Restoration. At the start of the last quarter of the nineteenth century, and again in 1975, situations of force (a *coup d'état* and a long dictatorship, respectively) were legitimized by a constitutional monarchy and a formal democracy tightly controlled by the political class and buoyed by economic growth. The political culture of that Restoration – as of the current one – was based on bipartisan hegemony moderately influenced (some might say disturbed) by the nagging interference of a Catalan political front. Admittedly, these parallelisms are crude, but the unequivocal will to reconnect with the past at a time when the political and economic centers of gravity are being dispersed must have some significance; especially when the references are so broad and unfocused that they encompass elements as varied as a parliamentary system convicted of rigging the elections, Catalan reformism, and the Castilian mystique of the 98ers. In view of such ambiguity and its inherent contradictions, we may wonder what is gained by staking one's ideological capital on the production of such a disheveled view of the past.

Commenting on Marx's concept of *Eskamotage*, Derrida notes that this form of legerdemain consists of making something disappear by producing "apparitions" or visions (Derrida 1993: 204). Although more subdued than the postmodern hype of the 1980s, the recent vindications of turn-of-the-century politics are continuous with the debauchery of the spectacular in the socialist era. Both regimes knew how to produce visions that took the place of events, precisely because the events themselves – among which the dismantling of a national economy and the long road towards the liberalization of the labor market are not the least prominent – had to pass unfocused and preferably unnoticed. The socialists produced images of change to mask how much of the inherited relations of power was preserved in their conception of the state. The conservatives, by whose timetable the single European currency will be implemented along with other transferences of state power, disguise the political and economic shifts by creating a mirage of stability and deploying an identity politics: decree on the national anthem, a unified Humanities curriculum centered around a mandated version of "national history," an intensified language marketing policy designed to challenge the hegemony of English as the medium for international communication (cf. chapter 9), and, last but not least, a renewed opposition to the reestablishment of the Catalan language as the ordinary vehicle of communication in its native areas. This opposition refers not only to the conservative party's negative vote on an extremely cautious law seeking legal parity for the use of Catalan in Catalonia, or to its role in fostering Valencia's linguistic secession from the Catalan-speaking lands, but also to a spate of allegations, disinformation, and alarming declarations given vent by the Spanish media. Fears about the potential reestablishment of Catalonia's pre-1939 linguistic situation are hard to understand in a Spain that is no longer politically circumscribed and culturally sealed. Since Spain is now not merely adjacent to but interrelated with different linguistic communities in a converging European political and economic space, even the semblance of a reason is lacking for not tolerating a transitional linguistic group situated between Spain's Castilian core and the multilingual reality beyond the state's vanishing borders.

The entire issue is based on *Eskamotage*, on making the actual object of politics disappear behind apparitions. These apparitions or specters, about which Derrida gives a gripping account in *Specters of Marx*, are shadows in search of a body, of a social body. Being inherently social, the specter is involved in competition and war from its first appearance (Derrida 1993: 241). Although the specter is always a plurality, as the title of Derrida's book avers, let me say outright that the shadow I am concerned with here and now is the Spanish identity forged by the Generation of 98. This shadow haunts the entire century, not as a continuous vision but, in revenant fashion, at concatenated intervals, as a spooky rumble of chains coinciding with various crises. The staccato character of this revelation agrees with the phantasm's mode of self-production. I mean first of all the phantasm of ideology, but also the past as revenant. Is there a privileged form of return for the collective past? I suppose the answer depends on a number of factors, not least on time and place, as well as on the version of the past that turns around and walks back up from Hades. But for us, witnesses of Spanish society at this other turn of the century, there is an unequivocal answer: the dead become a spectacle for the living in the profane rituals of institutions.

In rituals such as the centennial we face a deliberate practice of identity politics as anachronism. By anachronism I do not mean the obvious fact that a politics of identity is inherently dependent on a time which is not *this* time, that it depends on memory, personal and collective. I mean, rather, the importation into the present of a past that was itself out-of-joint, displaced, disembodied so to speak, an apparition from somewhere or *somewhen* else. Uchronism is the extreme form of anachronism, and timelessness in its variegated forms (eternal values, intrahistory, suspension, geographic determination, universality) has been called upon to found the Spanish identity. There is something cosmic in this ever-expanding timelessness which feeds on time. Is not this mode of self-production equivalent to the phenomenon known to physicists as a black hole? Yet a key difference between both phenomena is that, while the black hole is the negation of appearance, ideological timelessness depends on the ineluctable return of something like an appearance, the epiphany of a spectral past that continues to feed on the present. If this reappearance resembles cosmic phenomena, then the relevant comparison would be to those long extinguished stars which from millions of years away continue to shine on unwitting terrestrial beings, their cold light blinding them to the perception of other stars that may be just flaring up into existence.

A Spanish identity constructed from the disembodied and dehistoricized memories of a Castilian past was already misdated in its original formulation. Glaringly anachronistic was the claim that a unitary identity preexisted its construction, that it went back to a time when national formations had not arisen as a key concept of social organization and power. But then such historiographic claims were part of the business of dissipating histories and making realities disappear. The very generalization of the name "Spanish" for the Castilian language, a generalization which is itself part and parcel of the ideological legerdemain, though going back several centuries in the Castilian imaginary, is, institutionally speaking, largely a twentieth-century development. Evidence that this generalization did not translate linguistic reality is abundantly present in the numerous linguistic laws against the use of Catalan decreed by all Spanish governments since 1715, and in the compelling fact that its ample social use in the 1930s had to be suppressed *manu militari*. Not unplanned or incidental, as Dionisio Ridruejo suggests in his account of the propaganda operation set up for the impending conquest of Barcelona, the attack on Catalan is explicit in fascist doctrine and was launched at the beginning of the Civil War. For this reason it affected first of all those right-wing Catalans who fled to Franco's territory and even those who participated in the fascist Crusade. Much less did Republican Catalans entertain any illusions about the tolerance of their adversaries. The historian Miquel Tarradell spent part of the war reading Catalan books in Barcelona's Ateneu, obsessed with the thought that the Spanish nationalists would burn everything they could lay their hands on (Roig 1978: 169). And subsequent events justified his fears.

Spanish nationalists were acting on principles laid down by the Generation of 98, those principles which a century later still impede recognition of Spain's multinational composition and the implicit plurality of national rights. Eigtheenth- and nineteenth-century legal encroachments on the use of Catalan lacked a systematic ideology. This ideological base first appears around the turn of the century and is given its starkest expression by Miguel de Unamuno. From this moment it spreads into Spanish intellectual and political life irrespective of political affiliation. It becomes a dogma for the nationalistic liberals of Madrid's *Centro de Estudios Históricos* as well as for the Falangists, linking up with the annihilation policies of the Franco era and the *ABC* campaigns and COPE broadcastings of the 1990s.[2] In this decade anti-Catalan sentiment has been deliberately whipped up and used as a vote-catching net, first by the conservatives in a sustained assault culminating in the 1996 electoral campaign, and more recently, by the so-called left-wing Spanish opposition, tempted by this strategy's success to test it with diminishing degrees of self-restraint.

Unamuno's attitude towards the non-Castilian languages of Spain was a function of his early disillusion with the cultural possibilities of the Basque language, which in his view was unfit to express a modern culture. It is of course possible that Unamuno restated as inherent linguistic limitations what were in fact objective social hindrances, and that Euskera appeared to him intellectually confining because its institutional exclusion and stunted currency among the middle and upper classes hindered his opportunities for social advancement. Such transferences are commonplace. As a young man, Unamuno vied unsuccessfully for a chair in Basque linguistics at a public high school in Bilbao. Also competing for that chair was Sabino Arana, the founder of the Basque national movement.

While resentment cannot be ruled out as a source for Unamuno's later aversion to Euskera, his condition of state employee (as rector of Salamanca's university) goes a long way to explain his alienation from the language of his native region. As Rafael Ninyoles explains, civil servants tend to embrace the generalizing point of view of the state bureaucracy, perceiving historical and cultural heterogeneity as an obstacle to the deployment of state power and, consequently, to their own (social and geographic) mobility on the strength of that power (1997: 91). But it may not be superfluous to recall, in view of Unamuno's later positions, that in the 1880s he supported some form of autonomy for the Basques, even if this support was already plagued by his characteristic individualism. In a speech delivered in Bilbao on 3 January 1887, he defends, in typically ambiguous fashion, personal rather than collective self-determination: "El que combatió contra el derecho divino, justo es combata contra lo que llaman soberanía nacional; ni el despotismo de un hombre, ni el despotismo de la masa"[3] (Unamuno 1887: 174). On this very occasion he warned Basques that Catalonia's fate at the hands of the Castilian troops in 1715 entailed not just the destruction of Catalan institutions but also of Spanish freedom in general. Political unity was achieved but it was a despotic unity (Unamuno 1887: 172). Admittedly, this is a far cry from the Unamuno who will eventually adopt a shrill Spanish nationalism driven by antimodernism, authoritarianism, and profound antipathy towards the other Iberian cultures. Let us trace this development.

In 1896, when the Cuban War was still raging, Unamuno claimed that the unhindered expression of Spain's multilingual reality would enhance communication and provide a sure basis for civilian freedom and political integration. In an article on the use of the Catalan language, published in Barcelona's *Diario Moderno*, Unamuno asserts:

> Todo castellano, y llamo aquí castellano al que piensa en lengua de Castilla, todo castellano de espíritu abierto e inteligencia sesuda y franca debe desear que los catalanes escriban en catalán, porque produciéndose más como ellos son, nos darán más, y obligándonos a esfuerzos para entenderlos, nos arrancarán a las solicitaciones de la pereza mental y del exclusivismo. Sacan más uno de otro los pueblos autónomos en absoluto libre cambio que sometidos a una unidad centralizadora, vejatoria para uno y otro, aun en el caso en que sea uno de ellos aparentemente el unificador y el otro el unificado.[4]
>
> (Unamuno 1896b: 503)

Let us repeat it: every open-minded Castilian must not only suffer but also desire the expansion of literary Catalan, and not as a marginal and at best indifferent phenomenon but for precisely this reason: that Castilians will gain both intelligence and tolerance from the acknowledgment *and* knowledge of this other culture. Unamuno demands absolute freedom of exchange, and this can only mean that reciprocal knowledge cannot be based on the unilaterally imposed duty of speaking the victor's language. But this is not all. Unamuno speaks of written Catalan. If he says nothing of oral practices, this is because in 1896 Catalan was still the language of everyday communication in Catalonia. A Civil War and a cultural genocide would be necessary before the opposite could be assumed to be true. Yet, as we will see, Unamuno *did* challenge the right of Catalans to use their language as official language, that is to say, as a national language and, therefore, as a language of politics. And this happened not far down the road.

The title of an article published in 1908 is in itself a declaration of principles: "Su majestad la lengua española." If Unamuno had earlier advocated complete ethnic autonomy and linguistic freedom, now he declared Castilian the cornerstone of an authoritarian linguistic politics which, at this time, took its cue from the monarchical principle. An anecdote gave him the pretext to proclaim his new position. Barcelona's mayor had used Catalan in welcoming the King to the city, claiming that only the vernacular could convey the citizens' sentiments and aspirations unaffectedly. This had also been Unamuno's claim in 1896, when he asserted that translation deforms the original thought. Now, however, he denounces this idea as "one of many Catalan pedantries."[5] Catalans, he says, can express themselves flawlessly in Spanish, especially when they want to ask for something (Unamuno 1908d: 374). Catalans, it would seem, betray their excellent knowledge of Spanish in the very act that reveals their dependence.

By 1908 free exchange has gone by the board, together with free communication. Unamuno's Castilianization has made him a zealot. Besides chastising the mayor's audacity, he deprecates the King's reassurance that all the national languages are pleasing to his ear, and that he prefers on each occasion the language that best conveys the spontaneous feelings of his subjects. A national language, Catalan?, thunders an irate Unamuno. Absolutely not! In Spain there is only one national language, and that is the Spanish or Castilian language (Unamuno 1908d: 375). If his majesty the King has been ill advised, her majesty the Spanish language knows her privileges:

> En esta cuestión de la lengua nacional hay que ser inflexibles. Cobren toda la autonomía municipal y provincial que quieran, puertos francos, libertades y privilegios y fueros de toda clase; pero todo lo oficial, en español, en español las leyes, en español los contratos que obliguen, en español cuanto tenga fuerza legal civil, en español, sobre todo y ante todo, la enseñanza pública en sus grados todos.[6]
>
> (Unamuno 1908d: 377)

The mayor's speech is for Unamuno a crime of *lèse majesté* against the fatherland as he understands it, and against culture, which he deems inseparable from the state apparatus:

> No puede haber más que una lengua para dirijirse [sic] pública y oficialmente al jefe del estado, que es órgano de cultura, y esta lengua es la lengua de cultura, la única lengua de cultura moderna que hay en España, su única lengua nacional, la lengua española.[7] (378)

The significance of these opinions does not lie in their power to take stock of the situation – for example, the claim that Spanish is the only vehicle for a modern culture is plainly reactionary after the Catalan modernist movement has been saluted abroad as the avant-garde of Spanish modernization. Their effect lies in their substitution of hardened political clichés (which speak directly to the hardened conception of the centralist state) for sober evidence or rigorous thought. Verification is left to a younger generation of activists who will take to heart the teacher's intransigence. In the 1930s, young Castilian intellectuals will make good on Unamuno's claim that the inquisitor is more charitable than the hermit (Unamuno 1908d: 375).

Unamuno does not approach language as a philologist; he is engaged in a *Kulturkampf*. By aggressively insisting on cultural hegemony, he pioneers cultural jingoism in Spain, acclimatizing a new form of intolerance that has been gathering strength in the last quarter of the nineteenth century:

> Porque es en nombre de la cultura, no sólo del patriotismo, es en nombre de la cultura como debemos pelear por que no haya en España más lengua oficial, más lengua de cultura nacional, que la lengua española que hablan más de veinte naciones. Y esto, sean cuales fueren las hermosuras, los méritos y las glorias de otros lenguajes españoles, a los que se debe dejar a su vida doméstica.[8]
>
> (Unamuno 1907e: 522)

Unamuno is the clearest Spanish instance of a new kind of European intellectual, one who reacts to a perceived destruction of the old world by fanatically opposing change. He is in many ways a product of the nineteenth century's uprooting of traditional certainties: a Christian who can't believe but yearns to do so, a fervent nationalist who can't assume nationhood for his community of origin. Despair tinges his fanaticism. When he rails against the non-Castilian languages one senses his dejection, caused by disbelief in the rebirth of Basque. At first Unamuno's longing for community directed him towards his Basque roots. But the Basque language, still in the first stages of reclamation, could not offer the rewards required by his ambition. Concluding that Basque was in its death throes, Unamuno recommended euthanasia. The rational and *moral* attitude, he said, was to wish it a speedy demise. In his view even bilingualism is deleterious. Since language is subject to Darwinian laws, once Basque has been displaced by Spanish in everyday communication it can never be brought around as a live language (Unamuno 1902b: 1060–1). But anxious that he might be proven wrong, he opposes efforts to revive it at the same time that he rationalizes its necessary extinction:

> Es absolutamente imposible hablar hoy en vascuence vivo y verdadero de proyectos ningunos de Hacienda. Y mañana, más imposible aún, merced a los enterradores de esa lengua milenaria y ahistórica que son los que se empeñan en galvanizarla con trabajos de gabinete para impedir su muerte inevitable.[9]
>
> (Unamuno 1917b: 546)

Having renounced this source of identity, Unamuno looks to the Spanish language for cultural survival, embracing the mediated sense of selfhood with the convert's fanaticism: "Por mi parte declaro que siento cada vez mayor fanatismo por la lengua en que hablo, escribo, pienso y siento" (Unamuno 1911d: 598).[10] As a result of this conversion he transferred his longing for community to an abstract, spectral, but for that reason expandable Hispanic race. Disembodiment confers on the specter an inflationary existence in the course of which it haunts other bodies. Being neither flesh nor blood, the Hispanic body is not circumscribed by "natural" borders. Unamuno is very clear on this issue. In order for him, a Basque, to be able to commune with this sacramental presence, the nation must not be physically confined to Castile; nor can it be the sum of the various nationalities of the Spanish state. He wants a Hispania high above the petty determinations of origin, a mystical union in a spectral body irrigated by spiritual blood (Unamuno's words): the Castilian language. Transmuted into metaphors for the soul, language and landscape, both of them Castilian, reach out for absolute existence in a pleonastic Hispanic Spain. But for identity to be, there must be a return, a parousia or disclosure of sameness in time. Yet time undoes the body and destroys sameness. Hence Unamuno conceives identity as the return of a disembodied political entity: *Hispanidad*, the ghost of the Spanish empire.

As Derrida remarks, "For there to be a ghost, a return to the body is required, but to a body more abstract than ever before" (Derrida 1993: 202). In order to be, the phantom of empire vampirizes the emerging patriotisms of the new nations, which Unamuno wants to hitch to a struggle for world dominance of and through the Spanish language (Unamuno 1911d: 599). An idol, in the etymological sense of an apparition, haunts the new political bodies of America, spiriting away their aboriginal flesh. Since birth is a condition of bodies, the ghost preys upon whatever is native: ethnicity, indigenous languages, ancient identities, orality, not in order to incorporate them but to occupy their disincarnated hull. Cannibalism, which entails the incorporation of the other's body under the law of affinity and the consumption of real difference as potential identity, is the native sin upon which the empire legitimizes itself. Built upon the dogma of the transubstantiation of the flesh, the empire communes in a mystical body whose real presence is the word. Ruling this idol, ventriloquizing through it, are the souls of the dead, the intrahistorical community about which Unamuno still waxed lyrical toward the end of his life. One recalls the tolling of the bell in the submerged village in *San Manuel Bueno, mártir*, a charnel house of history rattling in Manuel's haunted soul (Unamuno 1995: 140). This phantasmal village comes alive in the reflection of the living village on the specular surface of enclosed water. This image, in which presence and absence overlap, illusory like a *trompe l'œil* and thus not properly an image, captures the ghost's tangible intangibility. Ghosts can be recognized by their lack of reflection in the mirror. Autonomous likenesses and tapering wraiths of time, they do not re-present, do not summon the co-presence of an object. Unlike the village of the living, whose reflection on the lake's surface makes it an object of representation, the village of the dead is invisible. Present only to the ear when the wind (*spiritus*) blows, it exists, like

Atlantis, in myth and poetry. That it is continuous with the living village is an article of faith, San Manuel's faith.

Such a faith in a phosphorescent life radiating from the bones of history exchanges social and political realities for a dreamy mixture of power and poetry. One of the adherents of this dream, Américo Castro, called this faith Unamuno's Hispanic Gospel (1948: 640).[11] This is a felicitous expression, for Unamuno's legacy raised Spanish nationalism to the status of a religion, a metaphysics of identity whose internal mechanism his last novel lays bare. Inextricable from the sense of historical crisis, Unamuno's national theology implicitly contains the ideas of heresy, holy cause, and the coming of a redeemer:

> Se habla mucho de la religión del patriotismo; pero esa religión está, en España por lo menos, por hacer. El patriotismo español no tiene aún carácter religioso, y no lo tiene, entre otras razones, por una, la más poderosa de todas ellas, y es que le falta base de sinceridad religiosa. . . . Es la raíz de las raíces de la triste crisis porque está pasando España, nuestra patria.[12]
>
> (Unamuno 1905b: 1296)

True to a type of European intellectual who emerged in the 1880s and included Charles Maurras, Maurice Barrès, Knut Hamsun and Julius Langbehn, Unamuno mistrusted reason's capacity to further the community he longed for.[13] But where reason fails, authority steps in. To be sure, Unamuno insists on spiritual authority, "el imperio espiritual sobre las almas," which Lazaro admires in San Manuel. But such empire is merely the obverse of imposition raised to a spiritual principle. Although Unamuno refrains from discussing the means needed to implement his patriotic religion, his vehemence suggests coercion at every turn.

Calls for inflexible imposition and constraints alternate with sneers and ridicule fired with an anxious intensity. We have already seen his opposition to the philological evolution of Basque, a language he deemed ahistorical because he wished it that way. Galician he disallowed on the grounds that it could not reconquer the urban middle class. Although its literary use could not be gainsaid, it was restricted to the low style, a trademark of the uneducated:

> Y *La Veu de Catalunya*, por su parte, cuando trata del movimiento lingüístico en otras regiones españolas, pierde los estribos y da aire a los mayores absurdos. Hace poco traía una carta de Galicia llena de ridículas consideraciones sobre el uso de la lengua gallega. Si lo hubieran leído en la tierra de la Pardo Bazán y de Valle-Inclán, ¡no se habrían reído poco de ello! Porque en Galicia tampoco hay, digan lo que quieran cuatro exaltados, cuestión del gallego. El gallego mismo que cultivan,

sobre todo en el género festivo, algunos escritores gallegos no pasa de ser algo artificial. Es como esos trajes regionales que cuando van desapareciendo o cuando han desaparecido, los visten los señoritos en Carnavales. En Galicia no volverá a ser el gallego la lengua corriente de las clases medias e instruídas de las ciudades.[14]

(Unamuno 1917b: 548–9)

Leaving aside the class prejudice and the limiting conception of culture exhibited in this judgment, it is impossible not to notice the double standard. While Unamuno disparages here a language that is still alive in rural Galicia, elsewhere he preaches the need to revitalize Spanish by giving wider currency to expressions garnered from the Castilian peasantry. Why the double standard? Why the impatience with peripheral languages that refuse to give up (and give themselves up to) the ghost? He gives us a clue by insisting on his Basque identity, but asserting time and again that this identity can only be articulated in Spanish. Unamuno is afraid that history might prove him wrong. Therefore he fights with tooth and claw any suggestion that Euskera and Galician may gain a foothold in print, and thus in culture as the nineteenth century understood it. He must deny the possibility in order to disown that which he fears most: in his own religious terms, the sin against the spirit, against the Basque spirit. And since denial requires universal connivance, Catalans are reproved ostensibly for exaggerating the significance of these languages, in truth, however, for encouraging them through their own exemplary literary renaissance. The stirring of languages that he deems and wishes historically condemned must be neutralized at any cost. To that purpose he denies and ridicules, blasts and cajoles by turns. Appeals to realism and acceptance of the inevitable alternate with emotional rantings and an unwavering tactic of delegitimization. He encourages dialectal forms with the aim of fragmenting and atomizing, denounces derivations and neologisms as so many falsifications, and attacks the formation of standard codes as a vestigial archaism driven by political reaction (Unamuno 1902b: 1060; 1905b: 1296).

Eskamotage plays a decisive role in Unamuno's view of cultural evolution. First of all *Eskamotage* of the political function of the state, which he construes as essentially cultural. *Eskamotage* also of the fact that, at a certain stage of development, languages do not die a natural death but are killed through legal and ideological means. And *Eskamotage*, finally, of the evidence that oppressed languages can endure long-standing imperial pressures if they preserve or regain a political space. The fall of two empires, the Third Reich and the Soviet Union, has been necessary to expose the ideologeme hidden in Unamuno's liquidation of the Basque linguistic question by analogy with another oppressed language:

Que se vaya hoy a los habitantes de la antigua Lituania y se les pregunte si quieren volver a hablar lituánico [*sic*], dejando el alemán, y se verá lo que contestan. Así sucederá con los vascos de mañana, cuando hayan abandonado por completo el vascuence. Por mi parte me compensa de los torpes insultos que algunos de mis paisanos me hayan dirigido el pensar que sus nietos me darán la razón algún día.[15]

(Unamuno 1902b: 1061)

Unamuno finds solace in the thought that some day there will be no Basque-speakers left. Veiled and withdrawn is not only the issue of a language's political relevance but also the status of the linguistic factors juggled with. In 1908, in his article on Her Majesty the Spanish language, Unamuno had imputed to Catalan the same faults that he presses against Basque and Galician in 1917: artificiality, lack of fit between the vernacular and a high culture which, in a blatant begging of the question, he defines as consubstantial with the state's administrative culture. The Basque language lacks a proper term for "Internal Revenue Service" ("Hacienda"), Galician is the language of the peasantry, and Catalan is strange to the monarchical dignity of Spanish. Yet *Eskamotage* fails when the objects to be concealed are juggled against each other. The silk handkerchief cannot facilitate the sleight of hand and at the same time *prestissimo* disappear behind itself. That trick will not work; something else must catch the eye while the object is removed from view. Catalan, which after all does have a print culture, and a modern one to boot, whose public use is extensive, and *is* the language of an urban middle class, cannot be both conjured away and played against the other languages. So, how does Unamuno get out of this pass? The stock ruse is to magnify the paradox by scapegoating the Catalan language. Regionalized and isolated, it is made to bear the sins of artificiality and subculturalism imputed to the other peripheral languages. Denounced as socially fractured, it will be loathed for *naturally* producing an *unnatural* cleavage in the Spanish identity. A bad example, whose exceptionality is conceded in order to keep other potentially renascent languages on their vanishing course:

> No, en eso de la lengua regional – o si quieren nacional; por una u otra palabra no hemos de reñir – los catalanes están solos. Ni los valencianos están con ellos, porque en Valencia, en la ciudad, todas las personas cultas se expresan y piensan en castellano. Los versos valencianos de Vicente Wenceslao Querol, tan exquisito poeta en castellano, suenan a falso y a artificio de erudito.[16]

(Unamuno 1917b: 549)

The sleight of hand includes the regionalization of Catalan by severing its territories. "Regional," however, is a conflictive term. Of what linguistic circumscription would Catalan be a regional variant? What map could include it as a dialectal variant of a dominant language? It is neither a variant of Spanish, nor circumscribed by a single administrative division in political maps. In the past this language benefited from the political sovereignty of its speakers; today it is spoken in several circumscriptions within and beyond the Spanish state. A national language, then, Unamuno concedes – a word here or there changes nothing. Yet, a few years earlier Unamuno had been emphatic: words are everything. Only Her Majesty the Spanish language deserved to be called a national language; there was no national salvation, no culture, no education, no law outside this language. Unamuno takes back with one hand what he feigns to give with the other. He, a philologist who certainly knows better, produces a supposedly self-contained Valencian language, only to declare it unfit for social and cultural life. Yet this same language is very much alive in Catalonia; renaming it Valencian does not change either its code or its scope. Nevertheless, the recognition that Catalan and Valencian are regional variants of the same national language is implicit in Unamuno's triumphant assertion that *not even* Valencians ("not even" ratifies a contrary assumption) follow Catalans in their effort to preserve their language. Unamuno's quandary is that, like every juggler, he must show that which he would occlude and name that whose existence he would deny.

Faithful to the tactic of conceding in order to refuse, and inverting the relation between action and reaction, he denounces Catalans as exporters of linguistic revolt. They might have a usable vernacular but others do not. If they respond in solidarity with the awakening of other national languages, they are acting in bad faith, since there is nothing to respond to where Spanish reigns supreme. Casting Catalan as the linguistic problem of Catalans, Unamuno dissembles the fact that the problems experienced by Catalans with their language stem from the intransigence of Castilian Spain. In other words, the language problem of Catalans dissembles Unamuno's (and the state's) problem with languages other than their own:

> No sé si es un bien o un mal para los catalanes el que en eso de la lengua regional se encuentren solos, pero es así. Su problema lingüístico es único en España, y querer transferirlo a otras regiones es algo así como si quisieran predicar en Chile los derechos del araucano, en el Perú los del quechua o en Paraguay los del guaraní.[17]
>
> (Unamuno 1917b: 549)

Unamuno would turn in his grave if he could know that at the end of the century at least Quechua and Guarani are slowly but steadily asserting their rights and reconquering social space.

Unamuno's jingoism was due at least in part to Spain's colonial "Disaster."[18] Before the end of the war he had declared himself a free trader, a confused one to be sure, capable of invoking socialism and free trade, humanism and dialectical materialism in the same breath (Unamuno 1896a: 980–1). As so often with Unamuno, it is best to bypass the confused reasoning and focus on the emotional clamor. It is 1896 and the pathos is still libertarian: "Libertad, libertad ante todo, verdadera libertad. Que cada cual se desarrolle como él es y todos nos entenderemos. La unión fecunda es la unión espontánea, la del libre agrupamiento de los pueblos" (Unamuno 1896a: 982).[19] Things will change quickly. Still, Unamuno's initial response to the military defeat in Cuba was not a nationalistic reaction but a condemnation of history and a flight out of time. At this moment skepticism towards the national idea anesthetized the wound inflicted by history. In his article "La vida es sueño," published in *La España Moderna* in November 1898, he asserts that the people "lo que tiene no es nación, es patria, tierra difusa y tangible" (Unamuno 1898: 941).[20] As long as people have a material culture of their own the problem of identity does not arise. Why not? Because the tangible fatherland defines a natural community, which in keeping with Ferdinand Tönnies' distinction between *Gemeinschaft* and *Gesellschaft*,[21] guarantees a sense of organic belonging, as opposed to the abstract relations that obtain in a national society, in which the uprooted and anonymous individual first discovers the problem of identity. At this time to sacrifice individuals to the idea of the nation seemed to Unamuno a pagan idolatry, more congenial with the Germanic than with the Hispanic mind (Unamuno 1898: 942). He could still soberly assess the political instrumentalization of culture as a ghostly affair, and reckon the obsession with cultural expansion a function of the metaphysical egotism which the later Unamuno would fully share:

> Y por debajo de tales ideas palpita su alma oculta, el deseo de que nuestra nacionalidad cobre relieve y se extiendan nuestra lengua y nuestra literatura, se lean más nuestros libros, los de cada cual de los que así sentimos, y duren más nuestros nombres en los anales y los calendarios. . . . [H]ay que inmortalizar nuestro fantasma aquí abajo, tenemos que pasar a la Historia. ¡Hay que alcanzar los favores de la sin par Dulcinea, la Gloria![22]
>
> (Unamuno 1898: 945)

In the same article he notes that the Spanish people seem unaffected by the collapse of the empire, and interprets this indifference as a source of strength. But is this the true meaning of apathy? Does strength really underpin this blasé attitude? Could the masses that had vibrated with chauvinism just a few months before have been truly insensitive to the humbling experiences of Cavite and Santiago? Feigning to reject national pride (but concealing, in effect, the wounded national pride), Unamuno proclaims that the ethnic spirit must now go on sleeping and dreaming the slow, dark dream of its healthy, healing routine (Unamuno 1898: 943). Such a reaction is not untypical of traumatic experiences. A state of suspension and insensitivity to suffering is typical of trauma. Due to a surplus of pain, the traumatic event impacts the psyche below the threshold of consciousness. Pain, however, does not remain indefinitely quiescent but replays itself in a constantly displaced, phantasmagoric likeness of the originating event. Geoffrey Hartman speaks of "a kind of memory of the event, in the form of a perpetual troping of it by the bypassed or severely split (dissociated) psyche" (Hartman 1995: 537). Unamuno, like the Spanish masses he describes, appears unaffected by the traumatic image, but the latter veils, without effacing it, the experience of loss that is already burrowing its way into his rhetoric. The day after the defeat, the collective ghost ("nuestro fantasma") of Spanish nationalism begins to haunt a country bereft of its empire. Repressed from consciousness, the historical meaning of the empire and its demise returns as a ghost to lead a dissociated existence as a lyrical ideologeme. Taking on a literary identity, that of Don Quixote (a revenant from the feudal past), the meaning of an empire at odds with reality spookily reenters history by religious fiat.[23] By inverting the hierarchy between the phenomenal and the ontological, Unamuno substitutes poetics for history and dresses politics as religion. Eeriest of all is the anticipated return of the repressed in the shadows of the departed. The nightmarish vision of the living dead returning from an extinct empire, the "cadáveres vivientes" (Unamuno's words) who reach the Spanish ports after a miserable voyage over the waters of oblivion calls on fantasy to heal the agony of the eyes (Unamuno 1898: 941). Fantasy soothes by troping the affliction, that is, by causing the traumatic impact to reappear (*phantasia* means literally "apparition") as symptom and no longer as event. The real revenants, wounded, maimed, and sick with malaria, vanish behind a parade of shadows from the historical beyond. It is the time of specters, and Unamuno, like others, seeks in a phantasmagoria of Segismundos and Quixotes consolation for the wound inflicted by history.[24]

> A medida que se pierde la fe cristiana en la realidad eterna [one is tempted to translate: to the extent that the empire's collapse becomes manifest], búscase un remedo de inmortalidad en la Historia, en esos Campos Elíseos en que vagan las sombras de los que fueron. Perdida la visión cordial y atormentados por la lógica, buscamos en la fantasía menguado consuelo. Esclavos del tiempo, nos esforzamos por dar realidad de presente al porvenir y al pasado.[25]
>
> (Unamuno 1898: 946)

History as a pretext for poetry. The gods, he says recalling the *Odyssey* in the wake of Cavite and Santiago, devise the destruction of men so that there may be song (Unamuno 1898: 946). History's injury is not avowed as historical but rendered a metaphysical failure – a loss of faith in eternity – or a mythical *fatum* – the whim of the inscrutable gods. Then the injury takes an ominous turn as the imperial consciousness spins a gauze of timelessness over the sores of time. In the depths of military humiliation and with Spain's utter want of political, economic, or scientific sway staring Unamuno in the face, language appears to him as the only means of patriotic affirmation. Thus history returns under a new guise. Just one year after Spain's defeat in Santiago de Cuba, Unamuno, writing for the Buenos Aires newspaper *El Sol*, links the end of political empire to the founding of a language empire and the achievement of linguistic supremacy over historical and geographic contingencies.

> Recluídos de nuevo a nuestra Península, después del gloriosísimo ensueño de nuestra expansión colonial, volvemos a vernos como Segismundo, vuelto a su cueva, según decía Ganivet. Y ahora es cuando nos acordamos de nuestra raza. Mas esta nuestra raza no puede pretender consanguinidad; no la hay en España misma. Nuestra unidad es, o más bien será, la lengua, el viejo romance castellano convertido en la gran lengua española, sangre que puede más que el agua, verbo que domina el Océano.[26]
>
> (Unamuno 1899b: 571)

Race, blood, and the old dream of an overseas domain are given new course by salvaging from the ruins of history that form of hegemony which Pierre Bourdieu has called symbolic domination. In a fatal mixture of the conquistador and the nationalist theologian,[27] Unamuno demands *Lebensraum* for the Spanish spirit: "Una tierra no agota la potencialidad de una casta" (Unamuno 1899b: 572).[28] Spain's historic destiny, which he had challenged only one year earlier – "A todas horas oímos hablar de la realización de nuestro destino (¿cuál?)" (Unamuno 1898: 945)[29] – will now be fulfilled when every language submits to Castile's accent in homage to the empire that Spain cannot let go.

> En tan vastos y variados dominios se cumplirá una diferenciación mayor de nuestra raza histórica, y la lengua integrará las diferencias así logradas. Italianos, alemanes, franceses, cuantos concurren a formar las repúblicas hispanoamericanas, serán absorbidos por nuestra sangre espiritual, por nuestro idioma, y dirán *mi tierra*, así, en robusta entonación castellana, al continente que oyó *¡tierra!* como saludo de otro mundo.[30]
>
> (Unamuno 1899b: 572)

While other forms of nationalism are also inextricable from the cult of the national language, none – with the possible exception of French nationalism – has been so obsessed with its imperial expansion. The Falangist slogan "por la lengua hacia el Imperio" merely gave programmatic form to a Darwinian conception of language that, in the case of Spanish, originated in the clash between a rising and a fading empire. A defeated empire can hope to retrieve some of its losses through symbolic self-assertion, and Unamuno became prophet and crusader of requital through language. On 14 October 1914, in the Buenos Aires paper *La Nación*, he extols "nuestro español, que tiene en sí, por inermes que seamos los que le hablamos, tantas y tan excelentes cualidades, no ya para resistir, sino hasta para imponerse"

(Unamuno 1914b: 535).[31] Are these military expressions merely metaphorical? Hardly. Language is for Unamuno the continuation of war by other means.

> En el fondo los pueblos que pelean unos con otros no pelean, aunque ellos no lo sepan ni lo crean, sino por el predominio de una lengua. Que A conquiste a B o B conquiste a A sólo significa que los de A hablen la lengua B o los de B hablen la lengua A.[32]
>
> (Unamuno 1914a: 528)

And once war becomes not of words but for words, once the religious and the political are displaced by the cultural, the road is open to the new experience of the twentieth century: programmed cultural genocide. The idea of language as a weapon and as the target of aggression became a key element in the fascist armory during the Spanish Civil War.[33] This idea still feeds the language race in which many Spanish philologists and politicians engage, both on the global and on the Iberian level. In 1898 conclusive defeat and irretrievable loss did not break the spell of the past on that part of Spain that was wont to identify with the country's history of mastery. From the eddies of the ships sunk in Santiago Bay rose the ghost of cultural supremacy, the ghost of a ghostlike empire. From that time Spanish became for Unamuno "la lengua que compartirá un día con la inglesa el predominio mundial. Y quién sabe... Quién sabe..., digo" (Unamuno 1911d: 598–9).[34]

In the absence of the necessary work of mourning, melancholy took hold of the Spanish soul, giving it up to visions of power haunted by the consciousness of defeat. Back in the cave, Segismundo dreams of new conquests: but he now knows that the epic of gold and blood has passed into legend and can return only as poetry. Promising a second release from the cave, poetry transfigures the bid for power of dreamy Segismundos, and our lord Don Quixote guides their historical despair in search of glorious Dulcineas. During the Spanish Civil War, the servants of the new Francoist state were required to swear their allegiance on this Hispanic bible. But what does it mean to swear by Don Quixote? What holy principle was invoked? What inner commitment did the pledge call upon? Unamuno had made it abundantly clear: performative faith, faith in one's own fictions, irrational faith in faith. Or rather, since faith is inherently tautological, as Unamuno incessantly claimed, the Quixotic principle stood for faith in the irrational, for self-affirmation unperturbed by the violence it may exert on the empirical world. Hallucinated trust in the return of a bygone age justified in advance the warrior-poets who would soon rise in arms in the historically insolvent towns of rural Castile. If Falange Española conceived itself, in the words of its founder, as a "poetic movement," this was not by virtue of an avant-garde rejection of the past, but because the movement's imagination was possessed by the ghosts of yore. The Spanish fascists wrote sonnets in the manner of Garcilaso and titled their chief literary journal *Escorial*. A reference, certainly, to the emblem of Spain's imperial architecture, but above all to the burial place of the Spanish kings, who, as Unamuno remarked, are never really buried, never put to rest (Unamuno 1923: 638). As Werner Krauss perceptively observed:

> the root of such confusion between poetics and politics was already planted in the possibilities of the Generation of 98. The rejection of political rhetoric led to the double affirmation of the lyrical word and pure action, the unmediated act, to a now aesthetic now emotional transfiguration of a dynamic will to action.
> (Krauss 1997b: 50–1)

The path of cultural despair has a traumatic origin in the clash between two different experiences of time. As in the sixteenth century but in reverse, anachronism assigns their respective historical roles to Spain and America. In 1898 ideological modernity and technological superiority were clearly on the American side, while Spain was a mere vestige of the past. A possible way to relieve the traumatic friction between radically different cultural cycles is to flee from time and to take refuge in timelessness. In 1898 Unamuno signed his earliest attacks on progress and modernity. But flight is only the first defense against history. In a second moment, culture, disguised as nature in the quasi-biological process of intrahistory, is called upon to heal the historical wound and to reassert some form of hegemony. Why the cultural path? And why through despair? The answer lies in Catalonia, Unamuno's greatest political obsession. Admired and scorned, and the latter because of the former, Catalonia had emerged from 1898 not into timelessness but into modernity. In the two decades after the colonial disaster, it forged a distinct national culture, which Unamuno, like other Castile-oriented intellectuals, both admired and resented. In 1901 ambivalence turned into apprehension when political Catalanism defeated the liberal-conservative alliance of the Spanish parties at the municipal polls in Barcelona. And it grew into anxiety when in April 1907 a broad Catalan front, Solidaritat Catalana, swept those parties from Catalonia. The reaction was predictable: Spain, Castilian Spain, must not be humiliated a second time. Catalonia must not be a second Cuba.[35] Yet how could it be? Catalonia was not coveted by any rising empire and, unlike Cuba, it did not confront the rest of Spain with an insurrectional army but a civilian culture demanding political empowerment. But this, alas, the wounded imperial consciousness could not suffer. It was one thing to be overpowered by an emerging economic and technological empire, and a very different one to be challenged by a region twice defeated in the previous two and a half centuries and forced to beg for basic rights. A region whose culture rises or falls with its language, kept at bay through ordinances like the one which in 1896 forbade its use in telephone conversations.

Unamuno came up with two solutions for what many were already calling "the Catalan problem." The first one was to turn Spain into a larger Catalonia purged of the Catalan element, so that the problem might disappear together with the cultural difference. In a letter to his friend Joan Maragall, Unamuno speaks of his fear (and thus of his despondent hope) that the Catalan Solidarity (the newly united Catalan political front) will not claim leadership in Spain (Unamuno 1907d: 514). Repeatedly Unamuno urged Catalans to Catalanize Spain, yet posited as a necessary condition the renunciation of the key to their identity: the Catalan language. The second, more practicable solution, was to call for a reactive culture: "A los esfuerzos de Cataluña por crearse una cultura propia no ha sabido responder el resto de España con una cultura española" (Unamuno 1916: 437).[36] Both solutions, inspired by mistrust towards the cross-fertilizing powers of independent cultures, merged seamlessly with the dream of settling the score with the Anglo-American imperial rival. The Castilo-Hispanic response to Catalan and Basque efforts to define their respective national cultures came in the early 1930s with Ernesto Giménez Caballero's call for national salvation through the reassertion of the Spanish genius, with Onésimo Redondo's Juntas Castellanas de Actuación Hispánica (Castilian Juntas of Hispanic Action) and with other microgroups agitating for a reactive Spanish nationalism which vowed to destroy the peripheral nationalities along with liberalism, the bourgeois economy, and the political weight of the industrial cities. On 29 October 1933 Falange Española gathered the strands of various reactive formations, merging Unamuno's vision of the cultural empire with his unitarian view of Iberian cultures.[37]

Unamuno's relentless offsetting of the peripheral nationalisms with an exalted Spanish nationalism reappears (via Ortega y Gasset) in José Antonio's definition of Spain as a unity of universal destiny.[38] Like Unamuno then and many a contemporary Spanish intellectual today, the Falange's founder filled his doctrine with nationalist content while rejecting the concept of nationalism, which seemed compromised by the claims of the detested Basque and Catalan nationalities. Thus appeared a form of supernationalism whose political expression was the corporatist state. José Antonio Primo de Rivera proclaimed nationalism "a complete stupidity" and declared: "We are not nationalist, because nationalism is only the individualism of peoples. We are Spaniards – one of the few serious things that one can be in the world!" (quoted in Krauss 1997a: 433). And soon the only thing one was allowed to be in the new Spain. For the Falangists, as for Unamuno, the peripheral nationalities were defined by anthropological factors such as archaic customs and residual languages. Hence, while amiable as a natural foundation for the spiritual fatherland, the historical nationalities were contemptible as the expression of an autonomous political will. At play in this ultranationalist anti-nationalism is Unamuno's distinction between intuition and concept, feeling and mind, an antithesis whose political translation opposes the "sensible fatherland," defined by one's physical horizon, to "the mental or historic fatherland," a product of national education, and the higher of the two in the spiritual order (Unamuno 1905b: 1288–9). Applying these criteria, José Antonio criticized the love of the immediate and contingent in the name of a national idea purified of the dross of history: "Those who love their fatherland because it pleases them love it with a will to touch, love it physically, sensually. . . . We love the eternal and immovable metaphysic of Spain" (quoted in Payne 1961: 80). The Falange's neo-imperialism, strung between the hope for absolute Castilian hegemony and dreams of Spanish expansionism, found inspiration in Unamuno's own bizarre imperialism, indeterminate between the assertion of the intrinsic generosity of conquest and a diffuse and limitless self-affirmation through the Spanish language.[39] This mixture of boundless ambition and disregard for the concrete and limited forms of social life explains the threadbare articulation of history in Falangist doctrine, its substitution of a sinister compendium of historical clichés for the complexities of past and contemporary existence on the Iberian peninsula. In this context imperialism means a blurring of the confines between concrete political spaces and the ideal projection of dreams of grandeur. Looking from a mountain range on the Castilian expanse below, Unamuno claims that the scene dematerializes before his eyes and turns into the predestined stage for "los más excelsos personajes de la tragedia de la Historia" (Unamuno 1915: 432). In a similar vein, the Falangists fought a transcendent battle above and beyond the misery of circumstantial reality. For them, as Werner Krauss observed, "[t]he stage of Spanish history has no boundaries. It is the Universe" (Krauss 1997a: 434).

The Universe as tragico-historical stage implies a cast of characters and a script.[40] Alarmed by the spectacle of revenant cultures, Unamuno fell prey to the specters of tradition and to delusions of revealed destiny. His descriptions of the Castilian landscape are haunted by the glories of the past and insinuations of a nationalist mission. High up on the hallowed Castilian range, like Moses on Mount Sinai, he receives the revelation from his national God: "Viendo ceñir los relámpagos a los picachos de Gredos se me reveló el Dios de mi Patria, el Dios de España, como Jehová se les reveló a los israelitas tronando y relampagueando en las cimas del Sinaí" (Unamuno 1909: 285).[41] This is a transcendent deity. The allegedly perennial Spain of the chosen Castilian tradition speaks to Unamuno from the historical beyond with a voice unheard by those who are distracted by present events.[42] Not only the living trees, "espejo de nuestra vida y de nuestro pensar," teach him an ideal lesson (Unamuno 1915: 433),[43] but even dead wood, the paradigm of matter in Western metaphysics (*hylē*, the root concept of the Aristotelian hylemorphic doctrine, means 'wood' in Greek), communicates to him metaphysical messages.

> Las dos veces que he visitado Yuste . . . sentí adentrárseme el corazón patrio al contemplar aquella caja de madera que guardó una docena de

años el cuerpo del que fue emperador antes que le trasladaran a ese horrendo panteón del Escorial. Mejor allí, entre seis tablas de madera de la sierra, de árboles que arraigaron entre rocas españolas. ¡Ah, ser enterrado entre seis tablas de una de estas robustas encinas castellanas, de hoja perenne inmoble al viento de la tormenta, de flor que se esconde entre las hojas y de rojo corazón con que hacen melodiosas chirimías los zagales! Pero a los reyes propiamente no se les entierra; ni muertos se les deja tener contacto íntimo con la madre tierra.[44]

(Unamuno 1923: 638)

Like a seance table, the planks or "tablas" of this empty coffin, which is therefore not a coffin but a resonance box for the spirits, speak to the patriot-medium. And the message with which this box informs him – like spirit informs wood in the hylemorphic doctrine – is the death drive as completion and accomplishment. Death as mystical fusion with the Castilian landscape *and* the Castilian tradition. A fusion both aided and impeded by the casket, whose planks remind him of the empire: the wood girdles the body – just as the body constrains the soul in Unamuno's neo-Orphism – while metonymy-cally linking it to the woods and the mountains, where the roaming spirits of kings communicate the empire's universality to the landscape. For mystical purposes, however, metonymy is an imperfect trope. Matter cannot totally seal the spirit. Through their woodenness, the planks assimilate the body (Unamuno's imagined corpse) to the earth. It is only through their form, through their symbolic function as a (vacant) casket, that they interrupt the flow between body and earth. This interruption creates a difference within matter, a meaningful threshold whose historical mark (Yuste) can only be crossed patriotically, with an "innering" or (in geopolitical terms) "self-centralizing" heart. A heart that Unamuno feels "adentrárse[l]e," seeking the deeper recesses of the body, where matter becomes synonymous with *mater*, the mother earth of Spanish rocks and Castilian oaks whose perennial leaves are forever still and whose trunks, turned into corpselike but corpseless planks, resonate with spirit. Spirited away, the body is neither here nor there, least of all in the pantheon that will later inspire so much fascist rhetoric. Kings cannot be properly buried, they cannot merge with the ground or rest in a locality. Only as ghosts haunting the landscape can they fulfill the patriotic work to which they were divinely appointed. As Unamuno insisted and his fascist disciples repeated, Spain was beyond the sensual, material, temporally bound contingencies of particular traditions. Spain was a universal entity, a metaphysical essence unfolding in the realm of spirit. One decade later, Ernesto Giménez Caballero received this "Hispanic Gospel" as he stood on his chosen Tabor mountain, Madrid's *El Pardo*, watching the world's transfiguration through the rebirth of the Spanish genius (Giménez Caballero 1971: 213). In the flaming Castilian dusk, another fascist commonplace, he heard the command of the dead: "¡Sed católicos e imperiales! ¡César y Dios!", and understood that geniuses, like clouds in the sky, like ghosts too, are vaporous self-identical forms. They do not really pass away, but unfailingly return in battle and storm-ready arrays (Giménez Caballero 1971: 212).

What Unamuno did try to bury, to assimilate to a plot of earth and to quarantine, were the non-statal Iberian languages and cultures. He combated efforts to rekindle the social use of Basque from the position of a self-appointed undertaker: "Más daño le hacen los curanderos que le asisten en su lecho de agonía que los que nos disponemos a cantarle los funerales y a embalsamarlo" (Unamuno 1902b: 1061).[45] His diagnosis of terminal illness was, however, less confident than he cared to admit. While feigning pious concern for the impracticality of the non-Castilian languages as vehicles for modern culture and for culture *tout court*, Unamuno showed considerable alarm at the potential revival of these prostrate languages and at the limiting effect they might have on Spanish, in spite of the latter's post-imperial scope:

> Creo entender, siquiera por mi cargo, en cosas de enseñanza un poquito menos mal que en otras cosas, y le digo a usted, mi querido don Telesforo, que si se descentralizase en España la enseñanza, dejando a los Municipios, o siquiera a las regiones, o provincias, el proveer a ella, sufriría gravísima herida la causa de la cultura – de la cultura, no del patriotismo solamente –, y la sufriría hasta en las regiones que se creen más capacitadas para la autonomía pedagógica y probablemente más en éstas que en las otras. Pueblo habría en que no se enseñara más que lo de "eso no me lo preguntéis a mí que soy ignorante . . ." y lo que sigue. Y nuestro órgano de cultura, la lengua, no ya nacional, sino internacional de España, sufriría rudo golpe. Porque nuestra lengua es internacional, como lo son el inglés y el alemán y el francés.[46]
> (Unamuno 1907e: 523)

Unamuno's logic is more instinctive than sound. How could a language boasting the demographic and political rostrum that Spanish commands be threatened by languages that were and still are legally, demographically, and ideologically hemmed in? Why should the state's "organ of culture" be diminished by internal and enormously disadvantaged competition, unless it is not secure in the culture it transmits? And what is one to make of the anxious assertion that Spanish, like English, French and German, is an international language too? Unamuno argues from the weakness of a post-imperial nationalism in the heyday of European empires. Not the Castilian language but the post-imperial Spanish nation was a feeble, incomplete affair. Conceived in the nostalgic image of its forfeited empire *and* in the coveted image of the modern empires it could not emulate, Spain – the idea of Spain launched by the 98ers – militates against the modern concept of the plurinational and plurilinguistic state advanced by certain intellectuals and politicians with a prescient discernment of the European future. Gone, after

1898, was Unamuno's free market approach of yore, having turned into a rigid statalism: "Lo que más falta hace es robustecer el poder central, que si de algo peca es de débil; robustecerlo y a la vez flexibilizarlo y enriquecerle con los jugos de la vida toda difusa de la nación" (Unamuno 1907e: 523).[47]

Unamuno's post-98 political philosophy is best characterized as bad Hegelianism, with the state, or more precisely, the centralist state, driving the wheels of the civilizing process: "El Estado ha venido a ser el supremo órgano de la cultura" (Unamuno 1907e: 525).[48] Unamuno conceived this process as an extension of the Castilian historical experience. With this statement he did more than document a political fact. He sanctioned a notion of culture as centralized regulation and of civilization as expansive domination. In this way he kept open the old route of the conquistadors for the dawning age of communications, in full awareness that the post-imperial struggles of the twentieth century would be for the creation of a cultural world-system and for the definition of post-historical totalities:

> Necesitamos hablar castellano, ante todo y sobre todo, para imponer nuestro sentido a los demás pueblos de lengua castellana primero, y a través de ellos, a la vida toda histórica de la Humanidad.[49]
> (Unamuno 1905b: 1292)

Notes

This essay was presented at the conference "De nuevo el 98" held at UCLA on 29–31 October 1998. It has been previously published in the proceedings of that conference, edited by Jesús Torrecilla (Amsterdam: Rodopi, 2000).

1 "Whatever shortcomings the Castilian people may have to confront modern culture, we must admit that it owed its predominance to its generosity, sense of authority, and determination to impose its beliefs on others. . . . Saving souls, even with the help of the firebrand, implies great generosity." "For Catalonia's own spiritual good, for their own greater cultural good, it is necessary to maintain the exclusive and unrestricted official character of the Spanish language, the only national language of Spain." "The inquisitor is more charitable than the anchorite."

2 [Editors' note: *ABC* is a national newspaper of conservative leaning; COPE is a radio broadcasting company owned by owned by the Spanish Catholic Church.]

3 "It is fair that, he who fought against the divine right, should also fight against the so-called national sovereignty; neither the despotism of a man, nor the despotism of the mass."

4 "All Castilians – and by Castilians I mean those who think in the language of Castile – all Castilians with an open spirit and a sincere and judicious intelligence should want Catalans to write in Catalan; because if they express themselves in their own way, they will give us more, and by forcing us to strive to understand them, they will save us from the temptations of mental laziness and close-mindedness. Autonomous peoples get more from each other when they exchange freely than when they are subject to a centralizing unity which offends all; even in cases in which one is the apparent unifier and the other the unified."

5 Unamuno actually says "Catalanist pedantries," but it is clear from the context that Catalan is meant, since speaking preferentially one's mother tongue is not tantamount to embracing a political credo. Unamuno's extension of Catalanism to the mere claim of linguistic rights automatically politicizes the condition of being Catalan.
6 "On the issue of the national language we must be inflexible. Let them get as much local or provincial autonomy as they wish, free ports, freedoms, privileges and regional laws of all sorts; but everything official must be in Spanish: laws, binding contracts, anything that has civil legal force, and above all, public education at all levels."
7 "There can only be one language to address publicly and officially the head of the state, who is an organ of culture; and this language is the language of culture, the only language of modern culture in Spain, its only national language, the Spanish language."
8 "Because it is in the name of culture, not only of patriotism, that we must fight so that Spain has no official language, no language of national culture, other than the Spanish language, which is spoken by more than twenty nations. And this regardless of the beauties, the value and glories of other Spanish languages, which must remain in their domestic life."
9 "Today it is absolutely impossible to speak in real Basque about any finance projects. And tomorrow, it will be even more impossible thanks to the gravediggers of that millennial and ahistorical language, who are determined to galvanize it with studies and reports in order to prevent its inevitable death."
10 "Each day I feel more fanaticism about the language in which I speak, write, think and feel."
11 Toward the end of his life, Castro explicitly acknowledged Unamuno's imperialist attitude towards language: "a Unamuno le interesaba la extensión y 'soberanía' de la lengua, horizontal y verticalmente" (1973: 384). Castro, however, did not go as far as recognizing that the imperialist attitude is never a matter of language alone, since symbolic domination does not take place in the Platonic ether.
12 "There is a lot of talk about the religion of patriotism; but that religion, at least in Spain, is still uncreated. Spanish patriotism lacks religious character; and it lacks it, among other reasons, for the most powerful of all, namely that it lacks a bedrock of religious sincerity . . . It is the source of all sources of the sad crisis that Spain, our fatherland, is undergoing."
13 Stern (1965) rightly includes Unamuno in this type of intellectual. His characterization of pre-Nazi German intellectuals like Lagarde, Langbehn and Moeller applies verbatim to Unamuno, with the obvious substitution of Spain for Germany: "They exemplified and encouraged what they sought to combat and annihilate, the cultural disintegration and the collapse of order in modern Germany. They were the accusers, but also the unwitting proof of their charges. As a consequence, they were forever wrestling with themselves even as they were fighting others" (Stern 1965: 328).
14 "And *La Veu de Catalunya*, when it deals with the linguistic movement in other Spanish regions, runs amok and airs the greatest absurdities. Not long ago, it published a letter from Galicia full of ridiculous considerations about the Galician language. Had they read it in the land of Pardo Bazán and Valle-Inclán, they would have had quite a laugh! Because in Galicia, regardless of what a couple of radicals may say, there is no Galician language question. The Galician used, mostly for droll purposes, by some Galician writers is artificial. It is like those regional costumes which, as they become obsolete and disappear, young aristocrats don during the Carnival. In Galicia, Galician will never again be the normal language of the educated urban middle class."

15 "Go ask today the people of the old Lithuania if they want to speak Lithuanian again instead of German, and see what they answer. The same thing will happen with Basques tomorrow, after they completely forsake Basque. As far as I am concerned, it is enough compensation for the clumsy insults that many fellow Basques have addressed to me, knowing that their grandchildren will some day prove me right."
16 "No, in the issue of the regional language – or national, if that is what they want to call it; we won't fight over a word – Catalans are alone. Not even Valencians are with them, because in Valencia, in the city, all educated people speak and think in Castilian. The Valencian poems of Vicente Wenceslao Querol – an exquisite poet when he writes in Castilian – sound false and like a scholar's contrivance."
17 "I do not know whether it is good or bad for Catalans to be alone in the issue of the regional language, but they are. Their linguistic problem is unique in Spain, and transferring it to other regions would be like defending in Chile the rights of Araucanian, the rights of Quechua in Peru, or those of Guarani in Paraguay."
18 Years later, speaking of his religious crisis in March 1897, he says that since that time he became convinced that he was "un instrumento en la mano de Dios y un instrumento para la renovación de España" ("an instrument in God's hand and an instrument for Spain's renewal": letter to Mújica of 2 December 1908; Fernández Larrain 1972: 291). I am grateful to Javier Herrero for this reference.
19 "Freedom, freedom above all, true freedom. Let each one develop their own way and we will manage to understand each other. A fertile union is a spontaneous union, the free union of peoples."
20 "What they have is not nation, but fatherland, tangible and diffused land."
21 Tönnies' theory of modernization as a loss of communal structures of experience and the formation of societal structures appeared in 1887. See Ferdinand Tönnies, *Community and Society*, trans. Charles P. Loomis (East Lansing, Michigan: Michigan State University Press, 1957).
22 "Under such ideas throbs their hidden soul, the desire that our nation become prominent and that our language and literature spread in such a way that our books are more widely read, the ones by those of us who feel this way, and that our names last longer in histories and yearbooks. . . . We must immortalize our ghost down here, we have to make History. We must earn the favors of the matchless Dulcinea, Glory!"
23 Unamuno's elevation of Don Quixote to national sainthood is programmatic. The idealist would-be knight becomes the redeemer in the patriotic religion of which Unamuno, in 1905, considered himself prophet and harbinger (Unamuno 1905b: 1296).
24 [Editors' note: Segismundo is the main character in Calderón de la Barca's famous play, *Life is a dream*.]
25 "As the Christian faith in eternal reality dwindles, we look for a substitute for immortality in History, in those Elysian Fields in which the shadows of those who were now roam. Having lost the cordial vision and tormented by logic, we seek paltry consolation in fantasy. Slaves of time, we strive to endow the future and the past with the reality of the present."
26 "Confined once again to our Peninsula, after the glorious dream of our colonial expansion, we see ourselves again like Segismundo back in his cave, as Ganivet used to say. It is now that we remember our race. But this race of ours cannot claim a common blood; it is no consanguinity even in Spain itself. Our unity is, or rather will be, the language, the old Castilian Romance turned into the Spanish language, a blood more powerful than water, word that rules the Ocean."
27 Unamuno's probable model would be Paul de Lagarde, the father of the German nationalist religion and theorizer of the Germanic expansion beyond Germany's

borders. Lagarde had asserted that "Germanism is not a matter of the blood, but of the spirit" (Stern 1965: 91).
28 "The potential of a race is not exhausted within the limits of its land."
29 "We constantly hear people talk about the realization of our destiny (which destiny?)."
30 "In such large and diverse territories will take place the greatest differentiation of our historical race, and the language will integrate the differences. Italians, Germans, French, all those who arrive there to form the Spanish-American republics, will be absorbed by our spiritual blood, by our language, and they will say *my land*, just like that, with a robust Castilian intonation, in reference to the continent that heard *land!* as the greeting from another world."
31 "Our Spanish language, which, regardless of how powerless those who use it are, has within itself so many excellent qualities not only to resist but even to impose itself."
32 "In the last analysis, even if they do not know it or believe it, the peoples who fight each other only fight for the supremacy of their language. That A conquered B or B conquered A only means that those from A must speak B or those from B must speak A."
33 On 16 April 1937, the *Diario Vasco* warns that Castilian "es un arma contra el enemigo. No emplearla en estos momentos es señal de tibieza patriótica" (Solé i Sabaté 1994: 35: "[Castilian] is a weapon against the enemy. Not using it these days is a sign of patriotic weakness.")
34 "The language that will share one day with English world dominance. And who knows . . . who knows . . ."
35 The ghost of Cuba began to haunt the Spanish imaginary after 1901, and did so increasingly after the creation of the Catalan Solidarity in 1905. The Madrid newspaper *El Imparcial* compared this development with the Cuban independence movement: "Exactamente así se hizo en Cuba la propaganda separatista." Cited in *La Correspondencia Militar*, 10 December 1907 (Solé i Sabaté 1990: 98; "This is exactly how separatist propaganda was presented in Cuba.")
36 "Spain has not been able to respond with a Spanish culture to Catalonia's efforts to create its own culture."
37 Unamuno's opinion that Portugal is an artificial nation wrongly excised from Spain reverberates in José Antonio Primo de Rivera's confidence in Spain's eventual reabsorption of Portugal (Payne 1961: 44). "Me pongo a pensar en la agorera suerte de esta nación [Portugal] tan poco naturalmente formada, y a la vez agólpanseme a las mientes dolorosos pensamientos sobre lo que en nuestra España está hoy ocurriendo. ¡Portugal y Cataluña! ¡Qué mundo de reflexiones no provoca en un español el juntar estos dos nombres!" (Unamuno 1908c: 211; "As soon as I think about the ominous fortune of this nation, of this unnaturally created nation [Portugal], my mind is flooded with painful thoughts about what is happening in Spain today. Portugal and Catalonia! What a world of thoughts come to the mind of a Spaniard upon putting these two names together.")
38 [Editors' note: José Antonio Primo de Rivera (1903–36) was the founder of the Spanish fascist movement and organized its political action through *Falange Española*.]
39 "Oponen en Inglaterra al pobre sentido de la *little England* el vasto imperialismo del pueblo que habla inglés, *the English speaking Folk*; tengamos también los vascos nuestro imperialismo, un imperialismo sin emperador, difusivo y pacífico, no agresivo y guerrero. Rebasemos de la patria chica, chica siempre, para agrandar la grande y empujarla a la máxima, a la única, a la gran Patria humana" (Unamuno 1901c: 240; "In England, they oppose the vast imperialism of the people who speak English, *the English speaking Folk*, to the menial *little England*; let

us Basques have our own imperialism, an imperialism without an emperor, expansive and peaceful, not aggressive and warring. Let us go beyond the small hometown, always small, in order to push it towards the biggest, the only, the great human Fatherland.")

40 Unamuno explains the transition from his *intuitive* Basque nationalism to his *conceptual* Spanish nationalism as a result of his consideration of Spain's history (Unamuno 1905b: 1288–9). He is obviously unaware that the triumph of what he calls *conceptual* nationalism presupposes the nationalist conception of Spanish history. The opposition between "intuitive patriotism" and "conceptual patriotism," along with the in-built connotations of nature versus culture, primary versus complex, etc., is not only a mainstay of nationalist doctrine but a consequence of hegemonic nationalism.

41 "While contemplating the lightning over the peaks of Gredos, I had a vision of the God of my Fatherland, the God of Spain, just as the Israelites had a vision of Jehova in the thundering and lightning peak of the Sinai."

42 "¡La sugestión de estos viejos claustros en que se cree uno liberado del peso de los siglos! Al llegar a Torrelavega nos encontramos con un periodista madrileño, que empezó a darnos noticias de los sucesos de Barcelona y de Melilla [the reference is to Barcelona's Tragic Week, one of the salient events in twentieth-century Spanish history]. ¡El sempiterno suceso! ¡La devoradora actualidad! Todo anecdótico, todo fragmentario, sin que haya modo de sacar sustancia ni contenido a nada. ¡Cuánto más no me decían del alma de la Patria el sombrío silencio del valle de Pas y la quietud soleada del viejo claustro de la colegiata de Santillana! (Unamuno 1909: 284; "How suggestive are these old cloisters where one feels liberated from the weight of centuries! When we arrived in Torrelavega we met a journalist from Madrid, who gave us news about the events in Barcelona and Melilla [the reference is to Barcelona's Tragic Week, one of the salient events in Spain's twentieth-century history] The eternal incident! The devouring present! Everything is anecdotal, everything is fragmentary, and there is no way to see any substance or content in anything. The somber silence of the Pas valley and the sunny peace of the old cloister in Santillana's *Colegiata*, told me so much more about the soul of the Fatherland!")

43 The trees, "mirror of our life and thought."

44 "The two times that I visited Yuste . . . I felt the patriotic heart come over me as I contemplated that wooden box that held for a dozen years the body of the emperor before it was moved to that horrible pantheon in El Escorial. It would have been better there, enfolded by six boards of wood from the mountains, from trees that grew among Spanish rocks. How great to be buried in a casket made of wood from one of those robust evergreen Castilian oaktrees, their leaves undaunted by the stormy wind, their flowers hiding in the leaves, their red-hearted wood ready to turn into melodious flutes in the hands of shepherd lads! But kings are not really buried; not even in death are they allowed to be in intimate contact with mother earth."

45 "The medicine men that attend it in its deathbed hurt it more than those of us who are ready to sing at its funeral and embalm it."

46 "Because of my position, I think that in matters of education I am a little less ignorant than about other things; and I tell you, my dear don Telesforo, that if Spanish education becomes decentralized, entrusting it to municipalities, regions or provinces, the cause of culture – and not just of patriotism – would suffer a serious injury. And it would suffer this injury even in those regions that consider themselves more capable of implementing an autonomous pedagogical system; in fact, the injury would probably be greater in those regions than in others. There would be towns where nothing would be taught but the saying 'don't ask me, I'm

ignorant . . .' and all the rest. And our organ of culture, the language, not only national but international, of Spain would suffer a serious blow. Because our language is international, like English, German and French."
47 "What we need most is to strengthen the central power – which is now weak if anything – strengthen it and at the same time make it flexible, with the the sap of the difuse life of the nation."
48 "The State has become the supreme organ of culture."
49 "We must speak Castilian, first and above all, in order to impose our sense of things to the rest of Castilian-speaking peoples first, and through them, to the whole historic life of Humanity."

7 A nobleman grabs the broom

Ortega y Gasset's verbal hygiene

Luis Gabriel-Stheeman

La gente habla muy mal, y cuando habla bien no se le entiende nada.[1]
(José Luis Coll quoted in *El País*, 28 September 2000)

Ortega as a language maven

In 1910, a 27-year-old José Ortega y Gasset dedicated a short essay to the literary style of Spanish novelist Pío Baroja. Focusing specifically on the novel *El árbol de la ciencia*, Ortega began his analysis by pointing out that, no matter where one opened Baroja's book, it would not be long before at least two or three taunts sprang from the page:

> llegándonos a la [página] 68 tenemos que "aquel petulante idiota ... era un macaco cruel este tipo" y "Aracil no podía soportar la bestialidad de aquel idiota".
> Pasemos a la 69: "'¡Canalla! ¡Idiota!' – exclamó Aracil, acercándose al médico con el puño levantado: 'Sí, me voy, por no patear las tripas a ese idiota miserable'".
> En la página 87: "Julio le presentó a un sainetero, un hombre estúpido, fúnebre" ... En la 89: "El amante de Pura, además de un acreditado imbécil, fabricante de chistes estúpidos ... En fin, en la página 100: "Pero usted es un imbécil, una mala bestia".[2]
> (Ortega 1910: 104)

According to Ortega, "words that express the greatest irritation are characteristic of Baroja's literature" (105). In order to understand an author's style, and see where they go in search of inspiration, stated Ortega, it is important to determine their preferred vocabulary. In Baroja's case, it was clear to Ortega that he descended "to the dregs of the dictionary."

Why? – Ortega asked himself – how could a writer show preference for words such as "wretch," "stupid," "imbecile" or "repugnant" – words with little or no specific meaning, yet at the same time so hard, so blunt, so excessive? Searching for an answer, Ortega proceeded to sketch a "theory of the insult" which could clarify the role such words play in language. He concluded that all words can be placed, according to their meaning, somewhere between two extremes: the technical term and the interjection. While the first expresses "a maximum of idea and a minimum of emotion" (106), the second conveys "a minimum of idea and a maximum of emotion" (107). These two poles provided him with the framework for a biological metaphor of language: "Entre ambos extremos flota la vida del idioma; la interjección es su germen, el término técnico es su momia" (107).[3] With their interjectional nature, insults belong to the early, primitive stages of language, although Ortega was careful to point out that their emotional overload does not originate in the words themselves, but rather in the use we make of them:

> los improperios son palabras que significan realidades objetivas determinadas, pero que empleamos, no en cuanto expresan éstas, sino para manifestar nuestros sentimientos personales. Cuando Baroja dice o escribe "imbécil", no quiere decir que se trate de alguien débil, *sine baculo*, que es su valencia original ... Lo que quiere expresar es su desprecio apasionado hacia esa persona. Los improperios son vocablos complejos usados como interjecciones; es decir, son palabras al revés.[4] (107)

I will not reproduce here Ortega's conclusions about Baroja; as the reader might have guessed, they were not very positive. More important to me is the fact that, in Ortega's eyes, *Spaniards* in general tend to use insults much too frequently: "[E]s sabido que no existe pueblo en Europa que posea caudal tan rico de vocablos injuriosos, de juramentos e interjecciones, como el nuestro" (108).[5] Since the abundance of insults in any given language is a symptom of that language's regression into its infancy (107) – a reminder of the aforementioned biological metaphor – it seems safe to infer that Ortega perceived Spain as an enormous and quite unruly verbal kindergarten: "Como para Baroja, suele ser para nosotros los demás iberos cada palabra un jaulón, donde aprisionamos una fiera, quiero decir un apasionamiento nuestro" (111).[6]

The views and concerns expressed by Ortega in the 1910 article are consistent with a significant number of statements he made on language and language use throughout his life. Usually restricted to lexical issues, these remarks were often limited in their scope, offering assessments or reports on the fate of a certain word or expression, or even on the grammatical or lexical incorrectness of another:

> La palabra 'amoralismo', usada por algunos escritores en los últimos años, no es sólo un vocablo bárbaramente compuesto, sino que carece de sentido.[7] (1908a: 93)

> La palabra 'encanto', tan trivializada, es, no obstante, la que mejor expresa la clase de actuación que sobre el que ama ejerce lo amado.

> Conviene, pues, restaurar su uso resucitando el sentido mágico que en su origen tuvo.[8] (1925: 472)

> Es irritante la degeneración sufrida en el vocabulario usual por una palabra tan inspiradora como 'nobleza'.[9] (1930: 182)

> La palabra 'típico', 'típica' se ha desviado en nuestro idioma e importa mucho corregir su uso que es un abuso.[10] (1939a: 425)

> Todas las demás especies viven adscritas a un restringido 'habitat', para emplear esta palabra que han dado en usar todos los biólogos, que me parece una palabra ridícula tomada del alemán, el cual no hace sino emplear torpemente un vocablo latino.[11] (1948: 183)

> Y digo españolía porque no logro acomodarme al erudito término que funciona estos últimos años y que suena 'hispanidad', el cual me parece un error desde el punto de vista de la lengua castellana.[12] (1948: 226)

Frequently, however, Ortega's comments on individual words would lead into broader statements on the general communicative effectiveness of our vocabulary:

> No es indiferente que en el repertorio de los nombres con que aludimos a las cosas llegue a ser demasiado grande el número de ellos que no designan con precisión y fuerza denominativa sus objetos. . . . [N]uestra habla reclama una reforma a fondo.[13] (1939b: 358–60)

> [N]o es posible . . . seguir usando el habla a la buena de Dios. Urge ya una higiene y una técnica del hablar.[14] (1939a: 434)

> [C]onversar sobre cualquier tema importante es hoy sobremanera difícil, porque las palabras mismas han perdido su sentido eficaz. Como acontece siempre al fin de un ciclo cultural, los vocablos de las lenguas están todos envilecidos y se han vuelto equívocos.[15] (1949: 249)

> [L]as palabras, como los navíos, necesitan de cuando en cuando limpiar fondos.[16] (1950b: 510)

> [E]l vocablo 'individuo' se ha convertido en una palabra opaca, sin vivacidad expresiva. Si esto aconteciese sólo con ella, el mal no sería digno de atención, pero me he servido de este caso como ejemplo de lo que acontece hoy con casi todas las palabras más importantes de la lengua. Todo el que hoy se ocupa en pensar y se arriesga a escribir, se siente deprimido al advertir que la parte más decisiva del vocabulario se ha hecho inservible porque sus vocablos están demasiado cargados de

sentidos anticuados, cadavéricos y no corresponden ni a nuestras ideas ni a nuestra sensibilidad.[17] (1953b: 676–7)

All of these remarks share three essential characteristics: (a) they are, very obviously, evaluative comments; (b) they bring forth a picture of language decay, an image which implies the existence of better times in the past; and (c) they call for immediate corrective action in order to prevent some sort of imminent cultural collapse. Together, these common traits should suffice to inscribe the Spanish philosopher in what James and Leslie Milroy have called "the complaint tradition," that is, a line of thought for which language is "always on a downhill path," and for whose defenders it is "up to experts (such as dictionary-makers) to arrest and reverse the decline" (Milroy and Milroy 1999: 4). Aside from prescriptive lexicographers, it is quite common to find among these "experts" a number of "writers . . . who set themselves up as public guardians of usage" (1999: 10), and who have received such names as *language mavens* (a title given to himself by the *New York Times* columnist William Safire – cf. Pinker 1995: 373; Cameron 1995: vii) or *language shamans* (Bolinger 1980: 1). Due perhaps to the impressively varied range of his intellectual undertakings, Ortega y Gasset was not nearly as dedicated to this task as the aforementioned Safire or as today's most renowned Spanish language guardian, Fernando Lázaro Carreter (cf. chapter 9). Nonetheless, statements like the ones quoted above, together with the following self-description, should grant Ortega, at the very least, the title of part-time maven:

> [L]os señores del tópico quieren reducir la política a problemas *particulares o parciales*; por lo tanto, abstractos; pero les llaman 'problemas concretos', maltratando el idioma como podía hacerlo un carabinero – sea dicho sin enojo para este Cuerpo, ya que su misión se limita a evitar el contrabando de cosas, como la mía es a ratos evitar el contrabando de palabras.[18]
>
> (Ortega 1931: 149)

On understanding Ortega's verbal hygiene

There are a number of models a critic can follow when deciding how to read Ortega as a language maven. One may try for instance Steven Pinker's way, utterly dismissive from its starting point – "Maven, shmaven!" he decries, making good use of the Yiddish word (1995: 373). This approach, excessive and irreverent as it may seem,[19] might be quite understandable if one shares the opinion of most contemporary linguists and endorses descriptivism ("grammars and dictionaries should describe how people talk") over prescriptivism ("grammars and dictionaries prescribe how people should talk"). After all, it can be said that linguists for whom berating the "misuse" of *hopefully* makes as little sense as censuring chickadees for constructing their nests incorrectly (Pinker 1995: 370), have themselves frequently become the targets of the mavens' wrath (cf. Bolinger 1980: 164; Milroy and Milroy 1999: 7; Cameron 1995: xi), or at the very least of their derision: "Los lingüistas . . . son, después de los aviadores, los hombres menos dispuestos a asustarse de cosa alguna" (Ortega 1937a: 129).[20] In any case, it cannot be ignored that today's linguistic science would be very skeptical of Ortega's urgent summons to restore language. The tendency has been, to the contrary, "to posit speaking subjects acted on by language and largely unable to act upon it themselves" (Cameron 1995: 18).

The careful reader, on the other hand, may also consider the view held by different scholars who are fonder or at least less disdainful of Ortega's remarks on language. These critics – who, by the way, would favor terms such as "language reformist" over "maven " or "shaman" (cf. Rosenblat 1958: 32) – prefer to interpret Ortega's concern for language in the light of the philosopher's sociohistorical context. Born in 1883, Ortega belonged to a generation of intellectuals – the "novecentistas" – who imposed on themselves and demanded of their society a "doble imperativo de rigor y precisión" (Senabre 1964: 29), in order to overcome the pervasive crisis of the turn of the century. In their eyes, to achieve this goal Spain required drastic improvements in all areas, from science and technology to the very language spoken by the people. Seen from this perspective, then, Ortega's efforts to modernize Spanish can be interpreted not merely as a hygienic mission but also as a patriotic one:

> [Ortega] revitaliza el valor originario de algunas palabras y expresiones desgastadas atendiendo a su etimología, ya que "la vida del lenguaje, por uno de sus lados, es continua degeneración de las palabras," [Ortega 1943: 355] y hay que evitar la desaparición de lo que en ellas haya de castizo y positivo.[21]
>
> (Senabre 1964: 36; cf. also Huerta 1956 and Rosenblat 1958: 33–4)

The Pinkerian critic would probably set about the long and painful task of dismantling Ortega's warnings and complaints, all the while maintaining a strictly linguistic perspective and ultimately rejecting the maven's claims. His more benign readers, however, have not been so keen on double-checking the legitimacy of the maestro's specific assertions. On the contrary, they tend to be rather acritical in their approach, keeping their thorough and detailed studies bound to a descriptive account of Ortega's ideas on language. Their primary purpose is to explain these linguistic views within the general philosophy of the author and to place them in the context of his cultural milieu. Testing the soundness of any of Ortega's complaints, however, has been considered secondary or even irrelevant to the understanding of what they see as the thinker's master mission: "hacer apto el castellano para la faena filosófica" (Maldonado 1957: 125; cf. also Senabre 1964: 35 and Pascual 1985: 74).[22]

Finally, there is a third possible line of analysis, one in tune with the ideas laid out by Deborah Cameron in her 1995 book, *Verbal Hygiene* – note the fortunate coincidence between the title and Ortega's words as quoted above (1939a: 434). This "third way" situates itself somewhere between the two preceding views. In contrast with Pinker and the descriptivist tradition, for example, Cameron is reluctant to censure all evaluative considerations of language. Instead, she aligns herself with other linguists and philosophers such as Baker and Hacker (1984), Harris (1980, 1981) or Taylor (1990), and exposes the "instability of the descriptive / prescriptive opposition" (Cameron 1995: 8) – a binarism which "sets the parameters of linguistics" as a science concerned with "objective facts and not subjective value judgements" (5). In the first place, as Cameron proves, "value-laden attitudes" are common to both sides of the contention, neither of them being "neutral with respect to what is 'good' linguistically speaking": *perfection* as a value that needs to be pursued or protected (prescriptivists) or *naturalism* – that is, unguided *variability* – as a concept that is incompatible with tampering or preservation (descriptivists) (4). In the second place, Cameron and the authors mentioned above seriously doubt that the objective facts investigated by linguists can be reduced to "descriptive rules." As Talbot Taylor pointed out, there is a critical mistake

> in assimilating the assertion of the truth of normative statements such as "'Soporific' means *tending to produce sleep*" to the assertion of the truth of a descriptive statement like "Grizzly bears hibernate in the winter". Asserting the truth of a normative statement is asserting that that statement is normatively enforced (within some context, by some individual or group) . . . Such statements are not descriptions of facts, but rather citations of norms.
>
> (Taylor 1990: 24)

What follows from this argument is that if Pinker's tenets are not as solid as they appear, his disregard of language mavens may need other reasons to prevail. For Deborah Cameron, on the other hand, the blurring of the borders between descriptivism and prescriptivism justifies a careful analysis of verbal hygiene: "practices like these, born of an urge to improve or 'clean up' language, . . . [are] as basic to the use of language as vowels are to its phonetic structure, and as deserving of serious study" (Cameron 1995: 1). Actually, even if one supported *naturalism* – the descriptivists overriding value – it would turn out to be just another good reason to consider prescriptivism seriously: "If 'natural' here means something like 'observed to occur in all speech communities to a greater or lesser extent', then the kind of norm-making and tinkering linguists label 'prescriptive' is 'natural' too" (5).

The view synthesized above would thus reject any swift dismissal of Ortega's evaluative comments on language, calling instead for a careful consideration of his writings on the matter. In contrast with those critics closer to Ortega, however, it would also reject any acritical kind of attention. If it is true that, as Cameron warns, we cannot escape normativity (1995: 10), then we can neither avoid the questions of authority nor the ideologies behind it. Who decides and enforces or tries to enforce these norms? What justifies these norms? Why should these norms be accepted and followed? (cf. Taylor 1990: 24–5). The fact that there are different answers for each of these questions only proves that "all attitudes to language and linguistic change are fundamentally ideological" (Cameron 1995: 4) and that, in consequence, there is no reason to accept uncritically any given set of norms (11). This is precisely why it is so important to subject verbal hygiene practices to a scrupulous analysis, carrying out an active and critical search for what Cameron calls their "unspoken assumptions" (11) or even their "hidden ideological presuppositions" (232). Any statement on what is "wrong" about language (or about *a* language), as well as any suggestion on how to "fix" it, are ultimately based on a particular vision of what society is or should be. The authors of such statements assume there is a portion of that society more prone to do what is "wrong" and another portion that is either more apt or better prepared to do what it takes to "fix" it (cf. also Kroskrity 2000: 8). Inevitably, then, these linguistic statements will shape a discourse that favors a certain social hierarchy.

The kind of critical inquiry proposed by this "third way" is basically the same as the one formulated by students of language ideologies. For Bauman and Briggs the goal is "to identify ways that key texts seek to delegitimate particular practices of discourse production and reception while promoting others" (2000: 139–40). And that is exactly the purpose of this chapter. In the pages that follow I will pursue a critical approach to Ortega's linguistic reasoning as it relates to his calls for verbal hygiene. Many of these statements are rather impersonal in the phrasing of their demands: "conviene, pues, restaurar..." (1925: 472), "importa mucho corregir..." (1939a: 425). By exploring the ideological framework that supports them, I intend to find the faces Ortega imagined on the agents of his proposed changes, as well as those he painted on the "culprits" of verbal decay. This probe will also require assessing the soundness of the philosopher's arguments. For if it is true that "there is scope, albeit not unlimited scope, for effective intervention in language" (Cameron 1995: 18), an appraisal of Ortega's complaints and of the feasibility of his proposed solutions should be quite illuminating about the present situation in his own country; one must not forget that Ortega is a model for our contemporary language mavens and authorities (cf. chapter 9).

Ortega's linguistic reasoning

Desde hace tiempo – y aunque de lingüística sé poco más que nada – procuro, al desgaire de mis temas, ir subrayando aciertos y fallos del lenguaje, porque, aun no siendo lingüista, tengo, acaso, algunas cosas que decir no del todo triviales.²³

(Ortega 1943: 357)

One shortcoming that linguists perceive in language mavens refers to the limited knowledge the latter usually have of the subject, being as they are for the most part *amateurs* or professionals whose expertise is not directly related to linguistics – "professional language users" is how Cameron describes them (1995: 14; cf. also ix, xi and Bolinger 1980: 5–6; Milroy and Milroy 1999: 10; Pinker 1995: 372, 398–9). This reproach, however, does not seem to apply to José Ortega y Gasset. As a postdoctoral student in Germany, and already prepared with a prolonged and very solid philological education in both Latin and Greek (cf. Díez del Corral 1968), he decided to dedicate himself professionally to linguistics (Ortega 1991: 599–601). Granted, this resolution did not survive the test of time – he gave up on the idea only a few months later (Díez del Corral 1968: 275) – but it did signal the beginning of a close and extended contact with the discipline. The lengthy list of linguists that appear throughout the pages of his complete works should be evidence enough of this life-long interest in the discipline: Bréal, Bühler, Brugmann, Hronzn, Humboldt, Lapesa, Lerch, Meillet, Menéndez Pidal, Paul, Saussure, Sievers, Trubetzkoy, Vendryès . . . (cf. Araya 1971: 83; Pascual 1985: 79; and Martín 1999: 303). This close contact, however, should not be mistaken for a sustained respect towards the profession. Even before being admitted into a seminar led by Brugmann in Leipzig, the young Ortega had chosen linguistics only as a "scientific springboard towards subsequent intellectual endeavors" (Díez del Corral 1968: 276), and he did not intend to spend his life absorbed by its inner details: "[E]l filósofo tiene que buscar su materia en una ciencia especial . . . Ahora que hace falta mantener siempre el espíritu a temperatura filosófica y no ser un erudito o un mero botánico o geólogo" (Ortega 1991: 600).²⁴ The study of phonetic laws and other neogrammarian principles, therefore, must not have particularly impressed him. From this moment on, Ortega's ceaseless interest in the question of language coexisted with a growing skepticism toward the science of linguistics, a progressive falling-out that lasted until the end of his life. Ten years after making the statement just quoted, the still young university professor questioned during an academic lecture the boundaries between the linguistic discipline and his own, thereby suggesting that a linguist's scope fell short of addressing the *whole* question of language, and reclaiming his stake in the matter: "¿Hasta dónde llega en el fenómeno 'lenguaje' la jurisdicción del lingüista y dónde empieza la del filósofo?" (Ortega 1915: 445).²⁵ Twelve years after posing that question, in a book review of Menéndez Pidal's *Orígenes del español*, the critic warned once more against the futility of mere erudition, urged for a reform in linguistics and expressed a glimmer of hope that mostly underlined the wide discrepancy between his views and those of this discipline:

> Al complicar con la evolución de cada sonido en el tiempo su traslación en el espacio, la vieja lingüística renace convertida en *cinemática* o ciencia de movimientos. Ya está, pues, más cerca de lo que debe ser una ciencia de realidades. Sólo le falta un paso para transformarse en la física del lenguaje. Ese paso consistirá en añadir a la determinación de los movimientos o cambios tempoespaciales del lenguaje la investigación de <u>las fuerzas que los engendran</u>. La lingüística cinemática de este libro demanda, como su coronación, una lingüística dinámica. (Algún que otro germen de ella asoma en las postreras páginas.)[26]
>
> (Ortega 1927: 517; underline added)

Clearly, Ortega was not very interested in a descriptive account of a language's history. "La laboriosidad de un erudito empieza a ser ciencia cuando moviliza los hechos y los saberes hacia una teoría," he stated in the same article (516).[27] Linguists, therefore, would not be real scientists until they focused on theorizing, that is, on going *beyond* phonetic and lexical evolution and inquiring into the *forces* that generate language change. In this light, Pidal represented for Ortega a promising yet still uncertain case. On the one hand, the philosopher recognized in the linguist "un gran talento combinatorio, compuesto en dosis compensatorias de rigor y de audacia" (516),[28] and he celebrated this boldness whenever it manifested itself (519). On the other hand, not only was this audacity still a little weak – "Desearíamos, sin embargo, que Menéndez Pidal se explayase un poco más" (519)[29] – but it was also hampered by a most unscientific trait: insufficient curiosity. Having stressed the notion that a theory must open to doubt any received or unquestioned knowledge (516–17), Ortega made sure to point out that Pidal was less surprised than him by what he himself saw as a striking fact: the relative linguistic uniformity of the Iberian Peninsula during the ninth century (518). I will return to this criticism later, but for now the following quote should suffice to illustrate Ortega's reservations concerning the linguist:

> Un hombre tan cuidadoso, tan rigoroso, tan *científico* en el tratamiento del detalle, parte siempre de dos enormes supuestos que contrajo en la vaga atmósfera intelectual de su juventud, y que usa sin previo examen, sin precisión.[30]
>
> (Ortega 1927: 519)

Sadly for Ortega, the few seeds of hope he observed in Pidal's work did not seem to grow and bear fruit. Ten years after his book review, Ortega wrote the joke quoted earlier on linguists' incapacity for surprise (1937a: 129). The reason for his likening of linguists' "lack of fear" to that of aviators was that none of the former seemed to turn pale in the face of Latin's blatant lack of diversity throughout the territories of the Late Roman Empire. This homogeneity was, according to Ortega, Vulgar Latin's most terrifying characteristic (we will see the others later), and a telling sign of that language's sudden incapacity for innovation. Again, the fact that linguists did not care to explain *what* had arrested those innovative *forces* made them deserving of Ortega's intellectual contempt.

The nature of linguistic change, thus, the *reasons* behind it, lie at the core of Ortega's interest in language, and ultimately explain most of his specific reproaches to the members of the linguistic discipline. Through the years, as a reaction to their indifference toward the matter, Ortega went from merely calling for a new linguistics to actually setting up the principles on which this reformed science could be founded. Bolstered by a rediscovery of Humboldt's ideas on language (a source of inspiration that many critics have revealed – cf. Martín 1999: 302–9), the Spanish philosopher intensified his reflections on the subject from 1937 onward, producing an increasing amount of material which culminated in his 1949–50 course on *Man and People*. The last two lessons or chapters of what would later become his posthumous sociological treatise, contain a number of linguistic propositions that are usually formulated after related attacks on linguists. As anybody should expect after having read thus far, the first of these charges constitutes a return to and an elaboration of what Ortega saw as the language professionals' inability to properly understand their subject in its whole, dynamic nature:

> La lingüística ... ha estudiado bajo el nombre de lenguaje una abstracción que llama la "lengua" ... [Pero] eso que llama lengua no existe en rigor, es una figura utópica y artificial creada por la lingüística misma. En efecto, la lengua no es nunca "hecho" por la sencilla razón de que no está nunca "hecha", sino que está siempre haciéndose, o, dicho en otros términos, es una creación permanente y una incesante destrucción.... [La] llamada "historia de la lengua" no es, en verdad, sino una serie de gramáticas y léxicos del aspecto que, en cada estado pretérito, la lengua hecha ya en aquella fecha mostraba. La historia de la lengua nos muestra una serie de lenguas sucesivas, pero no su hacerse.[31]
> (Ortega 1950a: 247–8)

The postulation of language as a process and not as a product – a notion completely in tune with Humboldt's *enérgeia* as opposed to *érgon* – lead Ortega to suggest that linguistics should study its object at a deeper level, that is, "antes de estar hecha la palabra, en sus raíces, en sus causas genéticas" (248).[32] These roots, naturally, reach back to the origins of language, a subject whose consideration had been long dismissed by linguists. However, as Ortega readily pointed out, the reasons for this dismissal were based on the erroneous assumption that language was a *datum* – without enough primitive data, linguists had decided it would be impossible to trace its origin. If one considered language as a process, instead, it would only be logical to assume the same *forces* that originated it should also be at work at the present time (251). Ortega's understanding of these "potencias genitrices" drove him to dissociate the idea of language into two different concepts: *to speak* ["hablar"] and *to say* ["decir"].

To *speak*, for Ortega, is "to use a language as constituted and as our social environment imposes it on us" (Ortega 1957: 243; 1950a: 248). When we *speak*, we benefit from a "vast system of verbal usages established in a collectivity" (1957: 251; 1950a: 253). We absorb that system in our childhood by listening to the others, by learning it unconsciously. Consequently, we also use it in a very mechanical way, more or less "like a series of phonograph records" at our disposal (1957: 258; 1950a: 259). To *say*, on the other hand, is "to invent new modes of the language . . . because those that exist and that it already possesses do not satisfy, do not suffice to say what needs to be said" (1957: 243; 1950a: 248). When we *say*, we try to externalize something we have inside and we look for any possible way to express it – for Ortega, all the fine arts are ways of *saying* (1957: 258; 1950a: 259). To *say* represents thus the creative, innovative force behind language: "[It] is a deeper stratum than speaking, and it is to this deeper stratum that linguistics should now apply itself" (1957: 243; 1950a: 248). In fact, as Ortega argued, this energy constantly exposes the inherent inadequacy of grammars, since, in order to *say* something new, we need to find expressive ways that are not already registered by those texts. In other words, we cannot say anything new without "offending against grammar and outraging the dictionary" (1957: 240; 1950a: 246). Although Ortega did not mention it explicitly in this work, it is clear that by "outraging the dictionary" the author could not have meant the careless utterance of a solecism but rather a more elegant and wilfully creative act. To illustrate this act, he gave his audience the example of *manda-más* ("commands more," "top boss"), an expression whose origin he dated back to the recent Spanish civil war, when somebody had decided to refer ironically to the abundance and diversity of people "in command" (1950a: 260; 1957: 259–60). For Ortega, though, there are many ways of *saying* in language, and a mere compound like the one just quoted did not belong to his favorite kind. More than twenty-five years before *Man and People*, he had already defined *metaphor* as an "improper use" of a pre-existing word, a deliberate inaccuracy chosen to convey a new concept that was difficult not only to express but also to conceive without the trope (1924: 390). Ortega considered metaphor as an invaluable tool in science and philosophy, but it is certain that he also deemed it a language's strongest engine. Otherwise he would not have called it "la comparación menuda y latente que dio origen a casi todas las palabras" (1909: 454);[33] nor would he have referred to "esas venerables metáforas que se han convertido ya en palabras del idioma" (1929: 418–9);[34] nor would he have stated that "toda la lengua es metáfora, . . . toda lengua está en continuo proceso de metaforización" (1947: 284).[35]

Ortega's conceptual dissociation between to *speak* and to *say* provided him with a powerful argument against another tenet held by linguists: the equality between all languages. The author answered specifically to Meillet's statement of 1922 – "Every language expresses whatever is necessary for the society of which it is the organ. . . . With any phonetics, with any grammar, anything can be expressed" (Meillet quoted in Ortega 1957: 246; 1950a: 250). According to Ortega, the error in this assertion lies in assuming that language is "the expression of what we want to communicate and manifest, whereas the fact is that a great part of what we want to manifest and communicate remains unexpressed" (1957: 244; 1950a: 248–9). Otherwise put, linguists mistake the words people *speak* for what they truly want to *say*, thereby missing the real question: "whether all languages can [formulate every thought] with the same ease and immediacy" (1957: 246; 1950a: 250). For Ortega, the answer to this question is flatly negative. Language does not allow us to say everything we want and, since it is impossible to say it all, "each people leaves some things unsaid *in order to* be able to say others." This "equation between manifestations and silences" gives each different language its own, peculiar shape, and constitutes an excellent source of information about the collectivity who uses it (1957: 246; 1950a: 250). Ortega's line of thought thus points to the identification between language and culture, another idea that he shared with Humboldt and which he held from the beginning of his career: "Como no se abren todas las puertas con la misma llave, no todos los pensamientos se pueden pensar en una lengua . . . Un espíritu de gran potencialidad se creará un idioma multiforme y sugestivo; un espíritu pobre, un idioma enteco, reptante, sin moralidad ni energía" (1911: 548; cf. Pascual 1985: 74–5).[36]

To *say* and to *speak* are, in the eyes of the philosopher, two facets of language tied together in a seemingly endless cycle. What somebody succeeds in *saying* only enters language once it is accepted by the *speaking* collectivity, that is, once it becomes a mechanized usage (1950a: 254; 1957: 252). The dynamic system thus revealed works as the engine that keeps language alive and "it is the normal form in which a language exists" (1957: 252; 1950a: 254). This "normal form," nevertheless, is not exactly balanced:

> El individuo, prisionero de su sociedad, aspira con alguna frecuencia a evadirse de ella intentando vivir con formas de vida propias suyas. Esto se produce a veces con buen éxito, y la sociedad modifica tales o cuales de sus usos adoptando formas nuevas, pero lo más frecuente es el fracaso del intento individual. Así tenemos en el lenguaje un paradigma de lo que es el hecho social.[37] (1950a: 254)

For Ortega, the disproportionate tension between the forces of *saying* and those of *speaking* implied that an eventual halt in language evolution was not inconceivable. In fact, according to him, this had already happened in History. As I already pointed out, what he saw as the pervasive uniformity of Latin throughout the Late Roman Empire was proof that its speakers had become unable to reinvigorate it. According to him, this could only be explained by one reason: "los hombres se han vuelto estúpidos" (1937a: 128).[38] In other words, people had run out of new things to *say*, and had fallen from then on into mere repetitions and stereotypes, stuck in a persistent state of stupor that left no one out: "¿Cómo podían venir a coincidencia el celtíbero y el belga, el vecino de Hipona y el de Lutetia, el mauretano y el dacio, sino en virtud de un achatamiento general, reduciendo la existencia a su base, nulificando sus vidas?" (1937a: 129–30).[39]

We do not need to reach such extreme situations in order to be accused of stupidity by the Spanish philosopher, for the very act of *speaking* is, according to him, already stupid: "La vida del lenguaje, por uno de sus lados, es continua degeneración de las palabras. Esta degeneración, como casi todo en el lenguaje, se produce mecánicamente, es decir, estúpidamente" (1943: 355).[40] When we *speak*, we use words in a manner that is progressively unaware of the meaning those words had when they were *said*. This ever-increasing distance finally breaks the connection between the word and its origins, and reduces our use of it to an ignorant, mechanical repetition (1950a: 260). Our stupidity, therefore, resides not only in not innovating but also in not realizing to its full extent the wealth of knowledge left to us by those who over the ages have had something to *say*: "Como buenos herederos, solemos ser bastante estúpidos" (1937b: 445).[41]

Ortega's accusations of stupidity, not surprisingly, were also meant for those who dedicated themselves to the study of linguistics. They were, in the first place, critically aloof regarding one of the worst consequences of verbal degeneration as just described: "el fenómeno de la equivocidad, multiplicidad de significaciones de las palabras o polisemia" (1946: 763).[42] In our author's eyes, polysemy constituted a congenital sickness of language, while linguists in contrast considered its ubiquitous presence as the most natural thing in the world, not one ounce stranger than metasemia or change of meaning (763). To make matters worse, linguists could not even admit that words have a "true" meaning: "Es increíble que la lingüística actual ignore todavía que las cosas tienen, en efecto, un 'nombre auténtico'" (1943: 386; cf. also 1953a: 637).[43] For Ortega, the only meaning that deserved such a designation was the one received by the word when it was first *said*, when it signaled a creation that made sense "to its inventor and for its immediate recipients" (1957: 259; 1950a: 260). In his eyes, thus, the search and recovery of this authentic meaning or *etymology* represented a most valuable practice, not only for historical and philosophical inquiries,[44] but also, and more importantly in the context of this chapter, for *verbal hygiene*:

> Todo el que lea a Heidegger [another well-known friend of etymologies, cf. Adkins 1962: 236] tiene que haber sentido la delicia de encontrar ante sí la <u>palabra vulgar transfigurada</u> al hacer revivir en ella esa su significación más antigua. Delicia, porque nos parece como si sorprendiésemos al vocablo en su *statu nascendi*, todavía caliente de la situación vital que lo engendró. Y al mismo tiempo recibimos la impresión de que

en su sentido actual la palabra apenas tiene sentido, significa cosas triviales y está como vacía. . . . Más aún, nos parece que <u>su uso cotidiano traicionaba a la palabra, la envilecía</u>, y que ahora vuelve a su verdadero sentido.[45]

(Ortega 1953a: 636–7; underline added)

For our language maven, then, not everything *said* was irreversibly stained once it had been *spoken*. In spite of linguists, etymology could still provide the kind of deep, thorough cleansing needed to bring the shine back to words.

The social dimension

As the above mentioned diagnosis of polysemy illustrates, Ortega's evaluative statements on language often seemed to refer to it as an autonomous entity, with its own virtues and downfalls (cf. also, for example, 1943: 355). In these cases, consequently, all humans, and not just some of them, appeared equally responsible for the inherently degenerative nature of *speaking*. Hence Ortega's use of the first person plural when alluding to "us the inheritors" (cf. 1937b: 445), or when explaining that "*nuestro* ordinario lenguaje [usa las palabras] sumaria y mecánicamente, sin entenderlas apenas . . . *las manejamos* por de fuera, resbalando sobre ellas velozmente, sin *sumergirnos* en su interior abismo" (1935: 210; emphasis added).[46] In light of other comments made by Ortega, however, the actual scope of this "we" needs to be reconsidered. In fact, after reading the following assertions, taken from the beginning and the end of his career, it should become clear that, in the author's opinion, some of "us" tend to use language more stupidly than others:

> El hombre vulgar e ineducado acentúa preferentemente, al conversar, las partes semimuertas, casi inorgánicas de la oración, adverbios, negaciones, conjunciones, al paso que el discreto y culto subraya los sustantivos y el verbo.[47] (1908b: 99)

> [H]ay los que hablan sin reflexionar sobre su modo de hablar, en puro abandono y a como salga; es el grupo popular. Hay los que reflexionan sobre su propio hablar, pero reflexionan erróneamente, lo que da lugar a deformaciones cómicas del idioma . . . Hay, en fin, el grupo superior que reflexiona acertadamente. . . . Lerch nos hace ver cómo el "culto", que suele pertenecer a las clases superiores, habla desde una "norma" lingüística, desde un ideal de su lenguaje y del lenguaje en general. El plebeyo, en cambio, habla a la buena de Dios. . . . [L]os selectos, las aristocracias, al ser fieles a aquella norma fijan y conservan el idioma impidiendo que éste, entregado al mecanismo de las leyes fonéticas que rigen sin reservas el hablar popular, llegue a las últimas degeneraciones.[48] (1950a: 240)

In complete agreement with Lerch, Ortega tied "degenerative" change – in both its semantic *and* phonetic dimensions – to a habit he attributed mostly to the common, uneducated person: carelessness. Negligent phrasing of one's ideas *entailed* inattentive pronunciation, which in turn led to a "language of ambiguous monosyllables, many of them identical" (1957: 233; 1950a: 241).

The linguistic dismissal of common people was present too in Ortega's description of the decadence of Latin throughout the Late Roman Empire. In this case, the author also made them responsible for what he perceived as a rudimentary grammar, an aspect which completes the portrait of the commoner as a verbally inept individual:

> La sabrosa complejidad indo-europea, que conservaba el lenguaje de las clases superiores, quedó suplantada por un habla plebeya, de mecanismo muy fácil, pero a la vez, o por lo mismo, pesadamente mecánico, como material; gramática balbuciente y perifrástica, de ensayo y rodeo como la infantil. Es, en efecto, una lengua pueril o *gaga* que no permite la fina arista del razonamiento ni líricos tornasoles.[49]
>
> (1937a: 129, underline added)

This rendition of the lower, uneducated classes as linguistically immature and irresponsible complemented quite adequately Ortega's idea of *saying* as a precious, invaluable creation. Brilliant metaphors that transfigured older words, deliciously complicated structures that allowed for subtle and penetrating thought, were gems that should not be left in the careless hands of a child. Plebeians, like infants, were not yet far enough from the primitiveness of animals – hence their fondness of the "almost inorganic" parts of the sentence, or their penchant for monosyllables. Like children, also, they were to be watched and monitored by mature and well-prepared individuals, guardians who could lead them by example while ensuring the safety of their language. As the reader has surely noticed in the preceding quotes, Ortega attributed to the refined, cultivated and usually aristocratic minorities the ability to fight and contain the people's leveling of language by acting precisely as its custodians: through a thoughtful use of words and an exemplary commitment to the established norm. In all fairness, however, a caveat must be expressed regarding the role Ortega gave to the common person in the life of language. Like children, again, uneducated people can also be very creative. Although incapable of configuring a language fit for thought and poetry, as we saw above (1937a: 129), once in a while they can have inspired glimpses of reality that drive them to *say* something, thereby creating a new word or expression. Poets (1918: 16–17) and philosophers (1943: 384) are the sublime *sayers*, but it is the "anonymous mind" (1926b: 584), the entire "Humanity" who shapes in words the experience of life and builds the treasure of a language (1947: 292). A treasure that, naturally, needs a few, select keepers.

Ortega's evaluative thoughts on language, and particularly his attribution of positive and negative energies to socially defined speakers, are quite consistent with the social tenets he formulated in his landmark work, *The Revolt of the Masses* (1926–8). According to the author, any type of society, whether democratic or authoritarian, "is always a dynamic unity of two component factors: minorities and masses" (1932a: 13; 1998: 132). The minorities, identified here as "individuals or groups of individuals which are specially qualified," *stand out* in their communities for constantly aiming at self-improvement, that is for imposing on themselves higher standards and expectations. The masses, in contrast, are defined as a uniform collectivity – so uniform, in fact, that Ortega refers to them as *the mass*: "The mass is the average man . . . man as undifferentiated from other men, but repeating in himself a generic type" (1932a: 13–14; 1998: 132). To summarize this lack of personal distinction in an effective and decidedly pejorative manner, Ortega referred to the common people with a term laden with negative connotations: "lo *mostrenco* social" (1998: 132, emphasis added),[50] a scornful expression which is echoed in the following quote:

> Y es indudable que la división más radical que cabe hacer en la humanidad es esta en dos clases de criaturas: las que se exigen mucho y acumulan sobre sí mismas dificultades y deberes, y las que no se exigen nada especial, sino que para ellas vivir es ser en cada instante lo que ya son, sin esfuerzo de perfección sobre sí mismas, *boyas que van a la deriva*.[51]
> (1998: 133, emphasis added)

In principle, Ortega denied any correspondence between the division into masses and select minorities on the one hand, and the division into upper and lower social classes on the other. One can find, he argued, "unqualified pseudo-intellectuals" among the higher levels of society, while it is also possible to identify "nobly disciplined minds" among the working class (1932a: 16; 1998: 134). However, as the author readily admitted, the latter are far more likely to be found among "these 'upper' classes, when and as long as they really are so . . . whereas the 'lower' classes normally comprise individuals of minus quality" (1932a: 15–16; 1998: 133), a fact that necessarily excludes them from higher social responsibility. Indeed, under normal circumstances, the masses should understand that

> existen en la sociedad operaciones, actividades, funciones del más diverso orden, que son, por su misma naturaleza, especiales, y, consecuentemente, no pueden ser bien ejecutadas sin dotes también especiales. Por ejemplo: ciertos placeres de carácter artístico y lujoso, o bien las funciones de gobierno y de juicio político sobre los asuntos públicos.[52]
> (1998: 134)

Taking into consideration Ortega's linguistic reasoning as presented thus far, there should be no doubt that nurturing and safeguarding a society's language was for the philosopher one of those special functions that should be reserved for the qualified minorities. One can easily realize that, in Ortega's mind, those select individuals who demand more of themselves and have a higher purpose in life will experience much more often than the rest the need to *say* something, thus becoming the main lifeline of language: as Francisco José Martín put it, Ortega's select person is constantly "remontando la caída de la lengua en *hablar* para portarla al *decir*" (1999: 398).[53] Conversely, the mass of ordinary people who live quite happily, feeling themselves to be as "one with everybody else" (Ortega 1932a: 15; 1998: 133), will be less likely to experience that same need to *say*. Far from testing the limits of language, thus, these passive *speakers* constitute the homogeneous community that, if left alone, could bring language to a halt.

The Spanish dimension: society

In *The Revolt of the Masses*, Ortega's opposition between mass and minorities provided him with a theoretical framework for his interpretation of the modern world's crisis. To put it in a nutshell, the author perceived and indicated an alarming change of attitude in the masses. Traditionally, the latter had recognized and accepted their submissive role in society's more important functions, realizing that, if they wanted to participate in them, they would have to become qualified and therefore stop being "mass." Modern democracy and the economic progress that accompanied it during the nineteenth century, however, had altered that "healthy dynamic social system" (1932a: 16; 1998: 134). Given access to the security, comfort and pleasures that were once reserved for the select few, the masses had overlooked the responsibilities and moral obligations that those benefits historically entailed. As a result of that negligence, "the mass, without ceasing to be mass . . . [was] supplanting the minorities," imposing on them by sheer pressure, not only its sociopolitical desires and aspirations, but also its esthetic and intellectual likes and dislikes, as well as its shallowly conceived opinions in all orders of life (1932a: 17–18; 1998: 135–6). Moreover, the masses were imposing themselves on society *believing* they had the right to do so: "*The characteristic of the hour is that the commonplace mind, knowing itself to be commonplace, has the assurance to proclaim the rights of the commonplace and to impose them wherever it will*" (1932a: 18; 1998: 136, emphasis in the original). In this context, Ortega's book was to be understood as an urgent call to restore society's sanity in the wake of a more than likely disaster.[54]

Ortega's concepts of the "mass" and the minorities did not appear for the first time in *The Revolt of the Masses*, however. In 1921, the Spanish philosopher had already used them in *Invertebrate Spain* to offer his diagnosis for a previous, more immediate crisis: that of his own country. The image that resulted from this earlier analysis was substantially gloomier than the one that followed. Whereas the crisis delineated in *The Revolt of the Masses* was historically recent – a vintage of modern democracy – the one that afflicted Ortega's land was not only much older: it was endemic. The people of Spain had always been "aristophobic" (1921: 108), that is, they had felt "puro odio y torva suspicacia frente a todo el que se presente con la ambición de valer más que la masa y, en consecuencia, de dirigirla" (122).[55] This hatred, frequently mistaken for a democratic impulse (122), had had its origin in the effective absence or dire scarcity of the "country's best." Deprived of the opportunity to interact with a truly select minority, the people had become blind and could not distinguish the better individuals, who in consequence were often annihilated (121). The reason Ortega gave for the "absence of the best" can be called, at the very least, highly peculiar: The "embryonic stage" of the Spanish nation, in his opinion, had been defective (119).

According to Ortega, the genesis of the European nations was not a product of the fusion between different peoples but the result of the conquest of the various autochthonous populations by different Germanic tribes after the fall of the Roman Empire. These tribes had imposed their "social style" on the "subjugated mass," they had been the "mold" that had shaped the indigenous, "formless matter." The qualitative differences between the various conquerors, and not those between their respective native subjects, determined therefore the different nature of the European nations (1921: 112). In this distribution, the Iberian Peninsula could not have suffered a worse lot. Whereas the Franks who settled in the old Gaul possessed the highest degree of "historic vitality," the Visigoths who entered the former Hispania had already lived side by side with the Romans, sharing the latter's "most corrupt hour." As a result, they had been irreparably tainted: "Eran, pues, los visigodos germanos alcoholizados de romanismo, un pueblo decadente que venía dando tumbos por el espacio y por el tiempo cuando llega a España, último rincón de Europa donde encuentra algún reposo" (113).[56] For Ortega, there was a strong similarity between what the feudal minority represented for the germinal stages of the European nations and what the intellectually superior minority represented for his own time (117). While the Franks' energetic nature yielded a myriad of powerful feudal lords – foreshadowing, we have to assume, *la grandeur de la France* – the exhausted, degenerated Visigoths were not able to engender a strong, select minority. Swept away from the Peninsula by a mere "African breeze," they left behind a handful of Christian kingdoms that never developed the necessary "few good men" – a fact which, in Ortega's opinion, explains why the Reconquest took no less than eight centuries to complete (118). After that, the lapse between Spain's discomfiting gestation and its present times can be summarized in just one sentence: "[L]a historia de España entera, y salvas fugaces jornadas, ha sido la historia de una decadencia" (118).[57]

A clear corollary to this historical rendition is that, in Spain, "lo ha hecho todo el 'pueblo', y lo que el 'pueblo' no ha podido hacer se ha quedado sin hacer" (1921: 109).[58] Since, as the philosopher argued, "the people" are unable to realize sophisticated feats such as science, high art, advanced techniques or solid, cohesive political states, it is no wonder that none of these are to be found on Spanish soil (110). From a linguistic point of view, it should not take much time to realize the implications this line of thought has in regard to the birth and development of the Spanish language. As a Romance tongue it was mothered by Vulgar Latin which, as we saw, Ortega derided as childish, rudimentary and stereotypical; and as a medieval dialect it was fathered by the offspring of the tired, impotent Visigoths. The remains of a plebeian, intellectually vacant language, spoken by a people with no enterprising, distinguished and exemplary minds: that was the Spanish Visigothic vernacular of the ninth century, the very same vernacular Menéndez Pidal unquestioningly characterized as uniform. Not surprisingly thus, Ortega hailed Pidal's philological findings of 1926 as a confirmation of his own theory, while regretting at the same time the linguist's lack of curiosity – a trait that, in Ortega's eyes, not only would have made Pidal a real scientist, but would have put them both in agreement about the Spanish problem. Furthermore, Ortega's kind of curiosity would have helped the linguist to reconsider what the philosopher called one of his two groundless assumptions: "la sobreestima de lo 'popular'" (1927: 519).[59] Indeed, from Ortega's point of view, Pidal's rendering of the Spanish language as a monument and a symbol of Spain's modern *grandeur* (cf. chapter 5) would be nonsensical: if everything in Spain had been done by the people, and what the people could not do had not been done, that also meant that everything in Spanish had been *said* by the people and what the people could not *say* had not been *said*. Given Ortega's lack of confidence in what the people can *say*, his pessimism about what happens to what they *say* once they start to *speak*, and given the fact that, for the author, the entire history of Spain had been that of a constant decadence, his 1910 consideration of Spain as a verbal kindergarten – inferred at the beginning of this chapter – was only logical.

Somber as it was, Spain's outlook as painted by Ortega was not entirely hopeless. According to the philosopher, History is a process moved by a perpetual alternation of two periods: one in which the aristocracies are formed (and thus society is formed); and another one in which those same aristocracies degenerate, causing society to stagnate and dissolve. In this last period, the masses rebel against the old minority and, identifying that particular aristocracy with *any* type of aristocracy, try to live without exemplary leaders. Once this is proven "positively impossible," the masses, humbled by their failure, recognize again their need to follow the best, and a new exemplary minority appears (Ortega 1921: 97–8). In the last pages of *Invertebrate Spain*, Ortega claimed to have perceived a few – albeit weak and sporadic – signs of "spontaneous repentance" in the Spanish "mass." If this was true, the author ventured, then one could still hope for a "radical conversion" of the people and a glorious, rapid revival of Spain (1921: 125–6). Although Ortega did not offer any information that might help ascertain what those specific "signs" were, the warning at the end of his book was loud and consistent with his lifelong, patriotic thought: the recovery of the Spanish nation could only be accomplished through the creation of a select, solid and beloved minority, a group of excellent individuals who would then educate, by example, the rest of the population. From what has been presented thus far, it should be clear that one of the responsibilities Ortega's leading minority would have to assume was the improvement and safeguarding of the Spanish language. As a distinguished member of that minority, Ortega himself needed to be a role-model. He had to set an example with his own use of language,[60] *and* he had to keep a shepherd's eye over his speaking flock: thus his contributions as a language maven.

The Spanish dimension: geography

Ortega's analysis of the Spanish crisis, and the project he proposed as its solution, were not limited to the sociopolitical sphere. As Andrew Dobson has stated, the philosopher "was well aware that the disintegration of Spain was not only social but also geographical" (1989: 91). *Invertebrate Spain*, in fact, began with a historical reading of the peripheral separatism that was progressively jeopardizing the nation's unity. Inspired by the German historian Theodor Mommsen, Ortega posited two complementary principles: on one hand, the history of a nation can be understood as a vast process of incorporation; on the other – and this was the Spaniard's own addition – the history of a nation's decadence can be read as a process of disintegration (Ortega 1921: 51–4). A nation, therefore, does not need to be built on any kind of ethnic identity but rather depends on what Ortega called a people's "nationalizing talent" (55): a non-intellectual quality that the philosopher recognized in Rome and that he defined as the ability some peoples have to present their neighbours with a "*proyecto sugestivo de vida en común*" (56, emphasis in the original). Enticing as it may be, though, in Ortega's eyes this project did not preclude the use of force. Without the slightest mention of oppression, injustice, massive destruction and the like, the author offered the following explanation:

> Por profunda que sea la necesidad histórica de la unión entre dos pueblos, se oponen a ella intereses particulares, caprichos, vilezas, pasiones, y más que todo esto, prejuicios instalados en la superficie del alma popular que va a aparecer como sometida. Vano fuera el intento de vencer tales rémoras con la persuasión que emana de los razonamientos. Contra ellas sólo es eficaz el poder de la fuerza, la gran cirugía histórica.[61]

(Ortega 1921: 57)

The application of these ideas to the history of Ortega's own country had rather remarkable implications. Not only was Spain the exclusive work of Castile but, since *no other people on Spanish soil* had its "nationalizing talent," it followed that, in general, "sólo cabezas castellanas tienen órganos adecuados para percibir el gran problema de la España integral" (61).[62] Moreover, if Castile was solely responsible for the creation of Spain, it was equally accountable for its undoing (69). After its finest hour (the sixteenth century) Castile soon slipped into a "perdurable modorra de idiotez y egoísmo" (70)[63] and practically abandoned its "seductive project." If Catalonia and the Basque country had really been the "razas formidables" they now claimed to be, wrote Ortega, they would have grasped that opportunity to pull away from Castile and start their own national projects (70). The fact that they had not done so proved that peripheral nationalism was not truly *the* problem but only a specific symptom of the illness that afflicted the Spanish nation: "particularism." With this term, Ortega referred to a pervasive phenomenon in which "cada grupo deja de sentirse a sí mismo como parte, y, en consecuencia, deja de compartir los sentimientos de los demás" (68).[64] Note that the expression "cada grupo" encompasses all the different groups that can be perceived within a large community: territorial, ethnic, social, political and even professional. The challenge posed by regional nationalism was thus diminished, dissolved in Ortega's argumentation, and, in consequence, its self-justification was effectively dismissed. That in turn allowed the philosopher to present his own antidote for the Spanish problem – "nacionalización" – as a process above any kind of difference, be it social, political *or* territorial. Based on Renan's definition of a nation as a daily plebiscite (71), "nacionalización" would be the process by which all those different groups would become actively involved in the resumption of that forsaken "*proyecto sugestivo de vida en común.*" And this enterprise, as we have seen already, could not be undertaken until a strong, respected, exemplary minority was created.

Once again, Ortega's reasoning, as summarized above, allows for some important inferences regarding his language ideology. If, in general, only "Castilian heads" are apt to comprehend the problem of Spain as a whole, and if the formation of a motivated, truly involved national consciousness can only be achieved through the exemplary guidance of a minority, it is a necessary conclusion that, in general at the very least, the minority must be Castilian-minded. Likewise, the language in which the Spanish nationalizing project is articulated must necessarily be Castilian, and that language must be used by anyone who wishes to contribute significantly to the project.

The word "significantly" is especially relevant to Ortega's argumentation as it relates to Spain's linguistic diversity. In fact, after reducing the disquieting elements of peripheral nationalism to particularism, which he also perceived at every other level in his entire country, Ortega added the following observation:

Lo demás, la afirmación de la diferencia étnica, *el entusiasmo por sus idiomas*, la crítica de la política central, me parece que, o no tiene importancia, o si la tiene, podría aprovecharse en sentido favorable.[65]

(1921: 71; emphasis added)

From *La redención de las provincias* (1927-8), as well as from many articles dating all the way back to 1917 (Dobson 1989: 91), it is quite clear that the philosopher considered political decentralization as one of the fastest ways to engage individuals from all regions in the revival of the Spanish nation: involvement in local politics, even if not "having more than a minimal influence on national policy" (Dobson 1989: 93), would be effective in creating the sense of civil responsibility that the country lacked. In contrast, ethnic differences and – more importantly for this chapter – love for one's autochthonous language did not seem to be of any importance for the construction of a national project. A latter confirmation of this idea in Ortega's work can be found in his staunch opposition to the establishment of a bilingual university in Catalonia:

[E]l Estado no puede abandonar en ninguna región el idioma español; puede inclusive, si le parece oportuno, aunque se juzgue paradójico, permitir y hasta fomentar el uso de lenguas extranjeras o vernaculares, es decir caseras (eso es lo que significa la palabra), . . . pero lo que no puede es abandonar el español en ninguno de los órdenes, y menos que en ninguno en aquel que es el que tiene mayor eficacia pública, como el científico y profesional; es decir, en el orden universitario.[66] (1932c: 505)

For the author, there should be no question about the monopoly of Spanish as *the* language of the Spanish state: "el Estado español, que es el Poder prevaleciente, tiene una sola lengua, la española" (505).[67] Since the intellectual elite was the fundamental piece in the process of *nacionalización* that Spain must undergo in order to heal, and since the linguistic vehicle for that *nacionalización* was the Spanish language, it was imperative that the future elites from every corner of the Peninsula receive their instruction in Spanish. To invest a local language with more significance than it deserved (according to Ortega) would necessarily hamper the national project the Spanish philosopher so adamantly defended.

A careful look at Ortega's statements regarding the question of the Catalan language can open a new interpretive window on the author's linguistic argumentation. The adjective he used to allude to the Mediterranean tongue – *casera* – has almost the same meaning that the word *vernacular* had in its origin: *vernaculus* in Latin was a homeborn slave, whereas *casero/a* is anything that is home-made or relates to the household. However, as I have already pointed out elsewhere (Gabriel 2000a: 129), *casero/a* carries in Spanish strong connotations that cannot be detached from its meaning, and which can no longer be found in *vernacular*. While the latter means "indigenous" and simply refers to the language of one's native country, the former brings to mind images of home-made pies, household chores, slippers and pyjamas. Thus, to call Catalan a "lengua casera" – instead of "autóctona" or "nativa" – when discussing the possibility of its coexistence with Spanish in the university, effectively diminishes, nullifies even its stature *vis-à-vis* "la lengua del Estado español." In other words, Ortega's choice of words fulfilled a strongly rhetorical function. It equated Catalonian linguistic aspirations with the "intereses particulares, caprichos [and] vilezas" of those too shortsighted to comprehend the Spanish nation, and it sought to bring them down, if not with the power of force (1921: 57), at least with a forceful argument.

The rhetorical factor

The fragment quoted above (Ortega's reference to Catalan as "lengua casera") belongs to one of his parliamentary speeches, thus to the kind of discourse where persuasive stratagems such as the one just analyzed are common, even expected. Yet, they are not in the least an exclusive trait of our philosopher's political writings. On the contrary, rhetoric permeates his entire oeuvre to such an extent that the latter cannot be fully comprehended without taking into consideration the former. As Thomas Mermall has indicated (1994: 73–4), there is a constant tension between *epísteme* and *doxa* in Ortega's work, that is, an ambivalence between his aspiration to create a rigorously scientific discourse and the call he felt to promote cultural enterprises and to encourage the intellectual revival of his own country. The Spanish author himself provided a fundamental clue to understanding his printed legacy from this perspective:

> He aceptado la circunstancia de mi nación y de mi tiempo. España padecía y padece un déficit de orden intelectual. . . . Era preciso enseñarla a enfrentarse con la realidad y transmutar ésta en pensamiento, con la menor pérdida posible. . . . Ahora bien, este ensayo de aprendizaje intelectual había que hacerlo allí donde estaba el español: en la charla amistosa, en el periódico, en la conferencia. Era preciso atraerle hacia la exactitud de la idea con la gracia del giro. En España para persuadir es menester antes seducir.[68]

(Ortega 1932b: 367)

A rhetorical reading that limits its scope to Ortega's graceful expression, however, will merely scratch the surface of the matter, and will in the end only serve to confirm the patriotic mission alleged by the Spanish philosopher. To avoid this, the reader should refrain from making any conclusions until analyzing, not only the *elocution*, but also the *invention* and *disposition* of Ortega's arguments. In other words, to be minimally probing, one should try to identify how the author organized and/or manipulated ideas and opinions that, while not being ultimately supported by empirical evidence, were likely to be shared by the community to which the author belonged (cf. Mermall 1994: 75).

It is from this standpoint that rhetorical analysis can yield results very similar to those sought by students of language ideologies. In fact, much of Ortega's linguistic reasoning owes its apparent coherence to two semiotic processes mentioned in the introduction to this book and defined by Irvine and Gal as *erasure* and *iconization* (2000: 37–8). The workings of erasure are plainly visible in Ortega's description of the Late Roman Empire as a linguistically stagnant territory. Irvine and Gal point out that, by disregarding or transforming "facts that are inconsistent with the ideological scheme . . . a social group or a language may be imagined as homogeneous, its internal variation disregarded" (2000: 38). This is exactly what the Spanish philosopher did with Vulgar Latin. For Thomas Mermall, Ortega's tendentious or distorted interpretation clearly ignored that the quick transformation of that language into the different romance tongues was "testimonio de su naturaleza *heterogénea*" (Mermall 1996: 188; emphasis in the original). Likewise, in order to correlate linguistic uniformity with a supposedly pervasive social stupefaction (Ortega 1937a: 128), the Spanish philosopher needed to be oblivious to "las diferencias entre el idioma oral y el escrito, entre clases sociales, de formación intelectual, etc" (Mermall 1996: 188).

Ortega's totalizing vision of language required other notorious erasures. His conceptual dissociation between *to say* and *to speak*, for example, paid no attention to most of the ways in which *new* things can be *said*. In fact, in order to claim that we can only say something new by creating an entirely new expression (Ortega 1950a: 246), one must first ignore something as essential to language as its combinatory nature: the power of a limited number of elements to generate virtually endless permutations. But Ortega's hyperbolical distinction was a necessary step towards another rhetorical maneuver. Through *iconization*, "[l]inguistic features that index social groups or activities appear to be iconic representations of them, as if a linguistic feature somehow depicted or displayed a social group's inherent nature or essence" (Irvine and Gal 2000: 37). The identification of "positive" and "negative" forces in language change and, subsequently, their respective attribution to (intellectual) noblemen and plebeians, allowed Ortega to depict phonetic and semantic negligence (1950a: 240) – as well as grammatical primitiveness (1937a: 129) – as *icons* of the commoners. Likewise, it ultimately justified his representation of the careful, creative and selected few as the exemplary guardians of language.

I stated earlier in this chapter that, being a prominent member of Spain's enlightened minority, Ortega y Gasset regarded himself as a linguistic role-model, that is, he felt the responsibility to improve and safeguard the Spanish language by setting an example with his own work. In this sense, aside from his impressive mastery of the language (cf. Senabre 1964), it was the philosopher's abundant etymological inquiries and arguments that earned him his prestige as a linguistic renovator. As the reader will recall, etymology was for Ortega the true, authentic meaning of all words (1943: 386), a meaning that their present usage falsified and even vilified (1953a: 636–7). It is not surprising then that he thought of etymology as the way to restore clarity and authenticity to the Spanish language; or, in other words, as the ultimate tool for verbal hygiene. A closer look into Ortega's etymological labor, however, reveals a more mundane aspiration next to his quest for rigor and clarity: the commitment to persuade his interlocutors. This bent, in fact, is so powerful that it often annuls his explicit purpose, contradicting even his own theoretical premises.

Rhetorically, etymology acts as a *legitimizer*. Its presence strenghtens the apparent validity of an argument by offering as proof a conceptual "birth certificate:"

> [D]oxa significa la opinión pública.... ¿No parece más verosímil que el intelectual existe para llevar la contraria a la opinión pública, a la *doxa*, descubriendo, sosteniendo frente al lugar común la opinión verdadera, la paradoxa?[69]
>
> (Ortega 1937b: 441)

At the same time, though, by revealing the disparity between the word's root and its current meaning, etymology highlights the "degradation" suffered by the word, its loss of authenticity in the hands of *usage*. Moved by these joint forces, readers will feel strongly inclined to adhere intellectually to what the text is asserting, much in the same way Ortega described himself when reading Heidegger (as quoted earlier in this chapter – cf. Ortega 1953a: 636–7).

More than occasionally, however, the Spanish philosopher also used the legitimizing technique just described to reinforce arguments that were *not so legitimate*. It so happened, for example, that common usage – the biggest villain in Ortega's linguistic ideology – could serve him explicitly as a scapegoat and implicitly as a very convenient support. We already saw, for example, how Ortega's description of Catalan as a "lengua casera" was in fact a sly connotative manipulation of *vernacular*'s etymological meaning. The following quote should serve as an additional case in point:

> [L]as gentes protestan inmediatamente contra la verbosidad parlamentaria, obstáculo a todo mejoramiento nacional. Porque estaba reservado a la perspicacia española descubrir que es intolerable que el Parlamento parle. Por lo visto, la misión de los parlamentarios es más bien hacer gimnasia sueca o cualquier otro mudo menester.[70] (1922: 15)

In order to counter effectively the accusation made by "the people" against parliamentary verbosity – that is, the habit of speaking excessively – Ortega resorted to the etymological connection between *parlar* and *parlamento*. But, in all strictness, the *parlar* that gave birth to *parlamento* meant simply "to speak," which is what it still means in its language of origin – French (Corominas 1983: 434). In contrast, the sense in which Ortega used *parlar* ("to speak a lot and without any substance," according to the dictionary of the RAE) was acquired by this word only much later, precisely through the people's *usage* of it once it became a Spanish word (Corominas 1983: 433). As it turns out, then, Ortega dismantled the people's arguments by offering as "authentic" a meaning that, from the standpoint of his own theory, was nothing but "degeneration," *usage*. If, according to what the word *parlament* "says," its members meet to speak (*parler*) and not to chatter (*parlar*), one must conclude that the philosopher did not properly reject the people's accusation.

There is enough evidence that Ortega's open disparagement of usage ran parallel to his covert exploitation of it (Gabriel 2000b: 199–203). Moreover, his adamant vindication of the original meaning of words lies in sharp contrast with the large quantity of pseudo-etymologies that appear throughout his works (Gabriel 2000b: 203–8). Ortega's fondness for words with clearly recognizable roots often drove him to follow too blindly his own intuition, and to fall prey to popular etymology:

> Pero si todo es importante, no lo es en la misma medida. Vayamos alegremente, pero con seriedad. No hay contradicción. Seriedad no es lo que suele decirse. Seriedad, como el vocablo indica, es sencillamente la virtud de poner las cosas en serie, en orden, dando a cada problema su rango y dignidad.[71]
>
> (Ortega 1926a: 94)

This statement offers a perfectly reasonable and coherent point of view: seriousness does not imply lack of cheer, inasmuch as an organized soul is not necessarily devoid of joviality. But this perspective – which, if taken as an opinion, would question the austere connotations of the word – is not posited as reasonable but *imposed as necessary* and *legitimized* by its own "origin." There is, however, no etymological relationship between "serio" (<SERIUS) and "serie" (<SERIES) (Corominas 1983: 532). Ironically, therefore, the ultimate fallacy of this origin disavows the philosopher's argument.

Ortega's passion for suasion did not only lead him to venture into daring etymological explanations; occasionally, it also led him to metathesize the process and change etymology into . . . *emythology*. An adequate example of this would be the account he offered for *carnaval*. This word comes, according to Corominas, from the old Italian form *carnelevare*, a compound of *carne* ("meat") and *levare* ("to remove," "to confiscate") that referred to the onset of fasting at Lent (Corominas 1983: 134). However, the explanation offered by Ortega – and for which I have not been able to find any sources or support – is radically different:

> El carnaval, hoy ya moribundo, ha sido la perpetuación en las sociedades cristianas occidentales de la gran fiesta pagana dedicada a Dionysos, el dios orgiástico que nos invita a despersonalizarnos y a borrar nuestro yo diferencial . . . [S]egún el mito helénico, Dionysos llega . . . de Oriente en un navío sin marinería ni piloto. En la fiesta, este navío, con la figura del dios, era transportado por calles y campos en un carro, en medio de la muchedumbre embriagada y delirante. Este *carrus navalis* es el origen de nuestro vocablo *car-naval*, fiesta en que nos ponemos máscaras para que nuestra persona, nuestro yo, desaparezca.[72]
> (Ortega 1950a: 195–6)

If one forgets, for one moment, *carnaval*'s correct etymology, the coherence of Ortega's tale will be undeniable; the idea of an orgiastic and pagan origin of dance cannot be discarded as inconsistent or unreasonable. That is, the story is verisimilar . . . but its etymological confirmation is false. With respect to the possibility of an honest, unintended mistake from Ortega, one question should suffice: if he was discussing a Hellenic myth, why did he offer a Latin etymology? An indirect source, perhaps? None is given and none is known.

The question of authority

By reading Ortega in Ortega's terms – that is, by looking at the exemplary practice of his own linguistic reasoning – the observations laid out in the previous section have fulfilled an important purpose of rhetorical analysis: to "detect the tensions between figural scheme and propositional content" (Mermall 1993: 164). These tensions, we have seen, do not arise from minor conflicts or ambiguities, but from major discursive contradictions – one should not forget, for instance, that the *emythology* of *carnaval* appeared in the same volume where Ortega denounced the crime of usage and invoked its redemption through etymology. It is indeed perplexing to surprise such a distinguished individual – and one who insisted so fiercely on the exemplarity of the selected few – in the act of benefiting from what he publicly despised, and even in the middle of forging his own example. This bewilderment, however, should give way to some conclusive inferences, not the least of which – but certainly the most obvious – are the questioning of Ortega's linguistic authority and the dismissal of his verbal hygiene. How much credibility can we now bestow upon his complaints about the trivialization, degeneration, abuses and misuses of words? How will we trust his promise to honor and protect our language? How can we lend our blind confidence to anyone of Ortega's kind?

"In order to challenge verbal hygiene practices we find objectionable," Deborah Cameron has written, we must "pose searching questions about who prescribes for whom, what they prescribe, how, and for what purposes" (1995: 11). Throughout the present chapter, it has become clear that Ortega y Gasset advocated for a linguistic hierarchy that faithfully replicated his own vision of a "healthy society." This image placed the common people at the bottom, looking toward the top, where a few individuals – with a striking resemblance to the philosopher's persona – indicated the way to be followed. Ortega's very interest in proclaiming his authority in a persuasive manner, however, led him to hyperbolize his own discourse, and to incur contradictions that ultimately annulled its alleged legitimacy. Curiously, Ortega's case – that of his illegitimate exemplarity – might still be exemplary. After finishing the last chapter of this book, the reader should be able to decide.

Notes

1 "People don't know how to speak properly and, when they do, nobody understands them."
2 "if we look at page 68, we find that 'that petulant idiot . . . that guy was a cruel buffoon' and that 'Aracil could not stand that idiot's stupidity.'

   Let's move on to page 69: 'You swine! Idiot!' – Aracil cried out while approaching the doctor with raised fist: 'Yes, I'm leaving so I don't have to kick that miserable idiot's guts.'"

   On page 87: 'Julio introduced him to a farceur, a stupid lugubrious man,' . . .

   On page 89: 'Pura's lover, on top of being a certified imbecile, a stupid teller of stupid jokes . . .' Finally, on page 100: 'But you are an imbecile, a great idiot.'"
3 "The life of a language fluctuates between both extremes; interjections are its seed and technical terms are its mummy."
4 "Taunts are words that refer to a specific, objective reality, but we use them to express our personal feelings rather than this objective reality. When Baroja says or writes 'imbecile,' he does not mean to say that somebody is weak, *sine baculo*, which is its original valency . . . What he wants to convey is his passionate contempt for that person. Taunts are complex terms used as interjections; that is, they are words backwards."
5 "It is a known fact that there is no other people in Europe with a wealth of offensive terms, swearwords and interjections as rich as ours."
6 "In the same way as for Baroja, for the rest of us Iberians, each word is a cage where we lock up a beast, I mean, a passion of ours."
7 "The word 'amoralism,' used by some writers in the last few years, is not only a barbarically created term, but it also makes no sense."
8 "The word 'charm,' so trivialized, is nevertheless the one that best expresses the type of action exerted on the lover by the loved one. It is therefore important to restore its usage, reviving the magical meaning it had in its origin."
9 "It is annoying to see the degeneration suffered in ordinary speech by a word so inspiring as 'nobility'" (Ortega 1932a: 64).
10 "The word 'typical,' has gone astray in our language and it is very important to correct its use, which is an abuse."

11 "All the other species live assigned to a restricted 'habitat,' to employ this term that all biologists have gotten into the habit of using – in my opinion, a ridiculous word borrowed from German, which in turn is clumsily using a Latin term."
12 "And I say 'españolía' [Spanishness] because I cannot get accustomed to 'hispanidad' that learned term which has been used in the last few years and which is, in my opinion, a mistake from the point of view of the Spanish language."
13 "It is not indifferent that, among the words with which we refer to things, the number of those not designating precisely and powerfully their objects has become too big . . . Our way of speaking demands a thorough reform."
14 "We cannot . . . keep on using language any old way. Verbal hygiene and a proper speaking technique are urgently needed."
15 "Nowadays it is extremely difficult to talk about any important topic, since words themselves have lost their effective meaning. As at the end of any other cultural cycle, words in all languages are degraded and have become ambiguous."
16 "Words, like ships, need to have their hulls cleaned from time to time."
17 "The term 'individual' has become an opaque word, one with no expressive vigor. Had this happened to this word alone, the fact would not be worth mentioning. But I have used it precisely as an example of what is happening today to the most important words in the language. Those who think and dare to write today become depressed when they realize that the most decisive part of the vocabulary has become unusable because its terms are overloaded with outdated, cadaverous meanings that do not correspond to our ideas nor to our sensibility."
18 "The lords of the commonplace want to reduce politics to *particular* or *partial* problems; therefore abstract problems; yet they call them 'concrete problems,' mistreating language like only a revenue guard would – this said without wanting to offend this Body, since, after all, its mission is limited to preventing people from smuggling goods, just as mine is, from time to time, to preventing people from smuggling words."
19 Pinker does make a point of keeping an informal, rather "unscholarly" tone throughout his book.
20 "Linguists . . . are, after aviators, the people least prone to being scared of anything."
21 "Ortega revitalizes the original value of some worn-out words and expressions attending to their etymology, since 'the life of a language is, in one aspect, the continuous degeneration of its words' and we must prevent the loss of their authentic and positive qualities."
22 "to make Spanish a language fit for philosophical endeavours."
23 "For some time now – and even though I know next to nothing about linguistics – I have tried in a most incidental way to point out accomplishments and errors of language, since, even though I am not a linguist, I have, perhaps, some things to say that are not utterly trivial."
24 "Philosophers need to find their subject matter in a specialized science. . . . Nevertheless, they also need to maintain their spirit at a philosophical temperature and be careful not to become a pedant or a mere botanist or geologist."
25 "How far does the linguist's jurisdiction extend in the phenomenon called 'language'? Where does the philosopher's jurisdiction begin?"
26 "By interrelating the evolution of each sound in time with its progress across space, the old discipline of linguistics is reborn as *kinematics* or science of motion. It is thus closer now to what a science of reality must be. It only needs one more step in order to develop into the physics of language. This step will consist of adding to the determination of a language's movements or changes in space and time an inquiry into the forces that generate those changes. The kinematic linguistics that this book offers, demands as its culmination a dynamic linguistics. (One

or two glimpses of that science can be seen in the last pages of the book.)" (Underline added.)
27 "An erudite's diligence begins to turn into science when it mobilizes facts and knowledge towards a theory."
28 "A great talent for combination, formed by complementary doses of rigor and boldness."
29 "We would wish, however that Menéndez Pidal used that talent a little more."
30 "A man like him, so careful, so rigorous, so *scientific* in his handling of details, starts always from two tremendous assumptions that he made back in the vaguely intellectual environment of his youth, two assumptions to which he recurs imprecisely and without previous examination."
31 "Linguistics... has studied an abstraction that it *calls* 'language'... [But] what it calls 'language' really has no existence, it is a utopian and artificial image constructed by linguistics itself. In effect, language is never a 'fact' for the simple reason that it is never an 'accomplished fact' but is always making and unmaking itself, or, to put it in other terms, it is a permanent creation and a ceaseless destruction.... [The] so-called 'history of language' is really nothing but a series of grammars and dictionaries of the aspect that the language as constituted at each of its previous stages exhibited at that date. The history of a language shows us a series of successive languages, but not their making" (Ortega 1957: 242–3).
32 "before the word is made, at the roots, in the genetic causes of language" (Ortega 1957: 243).
33 "the brief and latent comparison that gave birth to almost every word."
34 "those venerable metaphors which by now have become part of the language" (Ortega 1960: 222).
35 "the entire language is a metaphor, ... every language is in a constant state of metaphorization."
36 "In the same way as not every door is opened with the same key, not every idea can be thought in one language ... A spirit of great potentiality will create for itself a suggestive and manifold language; a poor spirit will generate a frail language, a crawling one, without any morality nor energy."
37 "The individual, prisoner of his society, frequently aspires to escape from it in order to live by forms of life that are his own. This is sometimes brought off successfully, and the society alters one or another of its usages and adopts the new forms; but what usually happens is that the individual attempt is defeated. Thus we have in language a paradigmatic example of the social" (Ortega 1957: 252).
38 "men [people] have become stupid"
39 "How else could a Celtiberian and a Belgian, a neighbor from Hipona and one from Lutetia, a Mauritanian and a Dacian coincide if not by virtue of a general loss of intellectual fiber that reduced their existence to its base and nullified their lives?"
40 "The existence of language is, in a way, a continual denigration of words. This denigration, like almost everything in language, is produced mechanically, that is, senselessly" (Ortega 1967: 21).
41 "Like all good heirs, we tend to be quite stupid."
42 "the phenomenon of ambiguity, multiplicity of meanings in words or polysemy."
43 "It seems incredible that current linguistics still ignores the fact that things do have 'authentic names'" (Ortega 1967: 63).
44 "Universal history [appears] as a gigantic etymology. 'Etymology' is the concrete name for what is usually and abstractly called 'historical reason'" (1957: 203; 1950a: 220).
45 "Anyone who has read Heidegger must have been delighted to witness how the vulgar word is transfigured as its most ancient meaning is revived in it. We are

delighted because we feel as if we had caught the word in its *statu nascendi*, still warm from the vital situation from which it originated. And at the same time we get the feeling that, in its current meaning, the word hardly has any sense, it means trivial things and it looks empty... Even more, we feel that the word was betrayed, degraded by its daily usage, and that only now it comes back to its true meaning."

46 "*our* ordinary language [uses words] summarily and mechanically, hardly understanding them ... *we* handle them from the outside, quickly sliding along them, without *immersing ourselves* in their inner depths" (emphasis added).

47 "In their conversations, vulgar and uneducated persons tend to accentuate more the semi-inert, almost inorganic parts of the sentence – adverbs, negations, conjunctions – while discreet and cultivated individuals underscore nouns and verbs."

48 "[T]here are those who speak without thinking of how they speak, in pure freedom and just as they happen to; this is the lower-class group. There are those who reflect on their own speech, but reflect erroneously, which gives rise to comic deformations ... Finally, there is the upper group, which reflects and reflects correctly.... Lerch shows us how the 'cultivated man,' who usually belongs to the upper classes, speaks *from* a linguistic 'norm,' from an ideal of his language and of language in general. The people, on the other hand, speak as the good God puts it in their hands to speak.... [T]he select, the aristocracies, by being faithful to the norm, fix and preserve the idiom, and thus prevent it from reaching the final degeneracy at which it would arrive under the phonetic laws that completely govern popular speech" (Ortega 1957: 231–2).

49 "The delicious Indo-European complexity, which was maintained by the language of the upper classes, was supplanted by a <u>plebeian dialect</u>, very simple in its mechanism but, at the same time or because of it, clumsily mechanical, material-like; a <u>babbling</u> and periphrastic grammar, one of trials and circumlocutions, very much like that of <u>children</u>. It is, in fact, a <u>puerile</u>, *gaga* tongue that does not allow for sharp reasoning nor for lyrical effects" (underline added).

50 When applied to an object, "mostrenco" means "crude, roughly made," although in an informal conversation it can also be used to refer to ignorant, dense or slow people; in addition, "mostrenco" alludes to homeless or rootless persons (cf. Smith 1992: 491).

51 "For there is no doubt that the most radical division that it is possible to make of humanity is that which splits it into two classes of creatures: those who make great demands on themselves, piling up difficulties and duties; and those who demand nothing special of themselves, but for whom to live is to be every moment what they already are, without imposing on themselves any effort towards perfection; mere *buoys that float on the waves*" (Ortega 1932a: 15, emphasis added).

52 "There exist, then, in society, operations, activities, and functions of the most diverse order, which are of their very nature special, and which consequently cannot be properly carried out without special gifts. For example: certain pleasures of an artistic and refined character, or again the functions of government and of political judgment in public affairs" (1932a: 16).

53 "rescuing language from its fall into *speaking* and bringing it back to *saying*."

54 The argumentation in *The Revolt of the Masses* is much richer and more elaborate than my rough synthesis suggests. Cf. Mermall's introduction in Ortega (1998).

55 "pure hatred and fierce mistrust against anyone wanting to become better than the mass and, consequently, to lead it." NB: this fragment did not appear in the English translation of *Invertebrate Spain*.

56 "The Roman influence was the alcohol of the German Visigoths, a decadent people who came stumbling down across space and time until they reached Spain, the farthest corner of Europe, where they found rest" (Ortega 1937c: 76).
57 "[E]xcept for a few fleeting moments, the whole of Spanish history had been the history of a long decay" (Ortega 1937c: 81).
58 "Everything in Spain has been done by the people, and what they did not do has been left undone" (Ortega 1937c: 85).
59 The other one, less important for Ortega, was "la creencia, perfectamente arbitraria, de que lo español en arte es el realismo" (1927: 519; "the perfectly arbitrary belief that, in art, only realism is Spanish.")
60 Ricardo Senabre's thorough inventory of Ortega's "language and style" (1964) offers an accurate picture of the author's overwhelming mastery in this respect.
61 "However deep may be the historic necessity for a union between two peoples, it will be opposed by special interests, whims, passions, infamies, and above all, by collective prejudices on the surface of the popular soul [of the conquered people. It would be useless to try to overcome such obstacles with persuasive reasoning].... The only effective weapon against them is that form of political surgery, the power of force" (Ortega 1937c: 26–7). NB: the text between brackets did not appear in the English translation of *Invertebrate Spain*.
62 "only Castilian heads contain organs capable of perceiving the great problem of Spain as a whole" (Ortega 1937c: 28).
63 "long coma of egotism and idiocy" (Ortega 1937c: 39).
64 "each group ceases to feel itself part of a whole, and therefore ceases to share the feelings of the rest" (Ortega 1937c: 36).
65 "As for the rest – the affirmation of ethnic differences, *the enthusiasm for their own languages*, the criticism of Madrid's politics – it seems to me that, either it is of no importance or, if it is, it could very well be used in a favorable way" (emphasis added). NB: this fragment did not appear in the English translation of *Invertebrate Spain*.
66 "The State cannot abandon in any region the Spanish language; it can still, if it deems it opportune – even if it looks like a paradox – allow for and even promote the use of other languages, foreign or vernacular, that is, domestic ["home-made"] (for that is what the word means), . . . but what it cannot do is to abandon Spanish in any of its fronts, much less in the one that is most effective in the public sphere, like the scientific and professional; that is, in the university front."
67 "The Spanish State, which is the prevalent Power, has only one language: Spanish."
68 "I have accepted the circumstance of my nation and my time. Spain was and is afflicted with an intellectual deficit.... It was necessary to teach the country how to confront reality and turn it into thought, with the slightest possible delay.... But this intellectual training needed to be attempted there where the Spaniards were: in informal conversations, in newspapers, in lectures. It was necessary to attract them to the realm of exact ideas by means of the clever turn of phrase. In Spain, in order to persuade, one needs first to seduce."
69 "*Doxa* means public opinion . . . Is it not more likely that the intellectual exists to go against the public opinion, against the *doxa*, while revealing, holding up in the face of the commonplace, the true opinion, the paradox?"
70 "People complain immediately against parliamentary verbosity, which is, they say, an obstacle against any national improvement. Only Spaniards could be so shrewd as to discover that it is intolerable that members of the Parliament meet to parley. It seems that the mission of these politicians is in reality to do Swedish gymnastics or any other mute activity."

71 "But even if everything is important, not everything is equally important. Let's proceed joyfully, but in a serious way. There is no contradiction in this. Seriousness is not what is commonly said. Seriousness, as the word itself indicates, is simply the virtue of putting things in a series, in sequence, giving each problem its true weight."

72 "The carnival, which is moribund today, has perpetuated in the Christian societies of the West the great pagan festival dedicated to Dionysus, the orgiastic God who summons us to depersonalize ourselves and blot out our differentiating I . . . [A]ccording to the Greek myth, Dionysus arrived from the East . . . in a boat without sailor or pilot. In the festival this ship, with the image of the God, was borne through streets and fields in a cart amid the intoxicated and delirious crowd. This *carrus navalis* is the origin of our Spanish word *car-naval* ['carnival'], a festival in which we put on masks so that our person, our I, will disappear" (Ortega 1957: 169).

8 José María Arguedas
Peruvian Spanish as subversive assimilation

John C. Landreau

> Estamos asistiendo aquí a la agonía del castellano como espíritu y como idioma puro e intocado. Lo observo y lo siento todos los días en mi clase de castellano del colegio Mateo Pumaccahua, de Canchis. Mis alumnos mestizos, en cuya alma lo indio es dominio, fuerzan el castellano, y en la morfología íntima de ese castellano que hablan y escriben, en su sintaxis destrozada, reconozco el genio del kechwa.[1]
>
> (Arguedas 1939a: 33)

Introduction

Intellectual and political debates about Spanish – both in Spain and in its former colonies – have played an interesting and important role in the creation, representation and dissemination of collective identities, both national and transnational. As the previous chapters have shown, during the nineteenth century, after the constitution of the new Spanish American nations, significant discussion ocurred on both sides of the Atlantic over the question of whether Spanish would (or could or should) remain unified, or whether it might undergo a process of change and fragmentation analogous to the development of the vernacular Romance languages after the fall of the Roman Empire. Much of this debate was underwritten by concepts and vocabulary that emerged from the newly-formed science of linguistics.[2] By the early to mid-twentieth century, however, the fear that Spanish would become fragmented in America had largely subsided.[3] This was due in no small measure to the development of an international web of regulatory linguistic institutions such as state educational systems, grammars, textbooks, and the activist role of the *Spanish Royal Academy*. In any event, it is the case that most twentieth-century intellectuals share the assumption that a more or less unified Spanish language is (and will be) the common tongue of the nations of *Spanish* America. While there are disagreements about the specific contours of what constitutes "standard" Spanish, nonetheless it is clear that regional or national variations no longer occasion a serious threat to its unity. In fact, since dialectal differences are constructed against a theoretical norm, they become curiosities, sources of humor, aberrations, markers of class, status or origin – but, of course, not legitimate for use in formal institutional contexts such as courts of law or government documents.

In this context, it is understandable that one of the central themes of intellectual debate in twentieth-century Spanish America was, as Pedro Henríquez Ureña articulated it, how to create an *original* linguistic and literary identity from within the inherited (i.e. *unoriginal*) Spanish language:

> No hemos renunciado a escribir en español, y nuestro problema de la expresión original y propia comienza ahí. Cada idioma es una cristalización de modos de pensar y de sentir, y cuanto en él se escribe se baña en el color de su cristal. Nuestra expresión necesitará doble vigor para imponer su tonalidad sobre el rojo y el gualda.[4] (1960: 246)

Of course, Henríquez Ureña's influencial formulation of the problem of American identity and originality presupposes the existence of a unified Spanish language shared by an international community.

The focus of this chapter is on the intervention of the Peruvian novelist and anthropologist José María Arguedas (1911–69) in the debate on Spanish in the Americas. Arguedas' reflections on language and literature are eccentric in that he rejects the theoretical norm of an official, universal Spanish in the attempt to validate and give legitimacy to a local (Peruvian, *mestizo*) linguistic and literary field.[5] In the context of the broader, international debate about Spanish that is the topic of this book, Arguedas' perspective takes on a special significance because he is one of a handful of twentieth-century intellectuals whose work poses a serious challenge to the institution of a universal, standard Spanish. His preoccupations are local, but it is precisely from this perspective that his work encourages us to think about those communities and social groups that are disadvantaged, displaced and excluded when a certain version of Spanish is imposed and institutionalized as standard.

Spanish and the unification of Peru: 1880–1930

> Every time the question of language surfaces, in one way or another, it means that a series of other problems is coming to the fore.
> (Gramsci 1985: 183)

Subsequent to the Peruvian defeat by Chile in the War of the Pacific (1879–83), the question of how to constitute a nation-state became the central preoccupation of intellectuals and politicians in Peru. In particular, the war revealed a country divided between a fragile ruling class and a Quechua-speaking majority population for whom the word *patria* meant nothing. Thus, the urgent question for post-war intellectuals was how to integrate, or as it was often phrased how to "Peruvianize" the Indian masses (cf. Bourricaud 1989; Cotler 1978; Quijano 1978). Ironically, however, the question of Quechua and other Amerindian languages never entered the post-war language debates between *hispanists* and *indigenists*.[6] Both groups shared the assumption that Spanish would be the national language.

A representative example of the hispanist position on language can be found in José de la Riva Agüero's 1905 book *Carácter de la literatura del Perú independiente*. In this early text, he argues that *because they share a common language* Peruvian and Spanish literature belong to the same literary tradition. He writes:

> Para que la literatura peruana dejara de ser castellana, sería preciso que el castellano se corrompiera totalmente y se descompusiera en nuevos idiomas, y por fortuna, en el Perú (a pesar de nuestros numerosos provincialismos y a pesar de la inexplicaple intransigencia, del tenaz empeño que la Academia pone en no admitirlos) aquella amenaza es muy remota.[7] (1905: 261–2)

For Riva Agüero, Peruvian literature is in fact "literatura castellana provincial" (261). Thus, in his conclusion, he exhorts Peruvian writers to "conserve" the Spanish language and literary tradition rather than succumb to extraneous influences in the false search for originality or authenticity:

> Conservemos la lengua, esta magnífica lengua, fuerte como una encina, sólida como el mármol, brillante como el fuego, sonora como el mar; conservémosla en la integridad de su genio, pero adaptándola prudentemente a las nuevas necesidades, defendiéndola a la vez de la insensata irrupción de los galiparlistas y de los seniles caprichos puristas. El idioma es un vigoroso fundamento de tradición; y, mientras no se altera, un gran vínculo subsiste.[8] (1905: 286)[9]

In contrast to Riva Agüero, the influential indigenista intellectual Manuel González Prada takes a more flexible approach to language change. His late nineteenth-century reflections are based largely on his understanding of the findings of the nascent science of linguistics:

> Los idiomas se vigorizan y retemplan en la fuente popular, más que en las reglas muertas de los gramáticos y en las exhumaciones prehistóricas de los eruditos . . . Las multitudes transforman las lenguas, como los infusorios modifican los continentes.[10]
>
> (González Prada 1889: 261)

Here, González Prada sees language change in a positive light, as a product of social and historical processes. In turn, he is critical of essentialist approaches like that of Riva Agüero: Nothing is more "hygienic," he writes, than contact with foreign languages and foreign literatures. "Salir de la patria, hablar otro idioma, es como dejar el ambiente de un subterráneo para ir a respirar el aire de una montaña" (1889: 266).[11]

However, despite these reflections on the salutory character of language contact, and of changes wrought in the "fuente popular," González Prada does not seem to imagine that in Peru Quechua might be one of the languages with which Spanish would come into contact. His writings are absolutely silent on this matter.

Why doesn't the Quechua language enter the stage of González Prada's linguistic meditations? There are probably two reasons. First, González Prada, as all Peruvian intellectuals of his generation, simply cannot imagine that Quechua is anything other than a primitive language condemned to disappear. Second, he visualizes language change in terms of an ever-expanding, inclusive world idiom. He believes that those who advocate the cause of regional languages such as Provençal and Catalan are "retrograde:"

> [A]l verbo de gran amplitud, usado por millones de hombres I comprendido por gran parte del mundo intelectual, prefieren el verbo restrinjido, empleado por miles de provincianos i artificialmente cultivado por unos pocos literatos.[12]
>
> (González Prada 1889: 262)[13]

That is to say, for González Prada the proper historical direction of language change must, following the model of national languages, lead towards further generalization and unification of disparate populations. Thus, when he speaks of the "healthy" contact between languages, he imagines that the major European languages will exert influence on one another to the effect that one day they become – as he puts it – five streams that flow together to create a universal tongue (González Prada 1889: 261). Regional separations, or claims to distinction, are invalid because they contradict the direction of modernity. In this sense, they are backward and restrictive.[14] From this perspective, González Prada's position coincides with Riva Agüero's in the sense that both of them see as illegitimate any distinctive, local (regional or national) forms of Spanish in Peru.

The most influencial early-twentieth century Peruvian intellectual was José Carlos Mariátegui (1894–1930). Mariátegui's polemical writings argued both against the racist positions of the oligarchy as well as against what he regarded as liberal "defenses" of the Indian, which tended to frame the "Indian problem" as a moral/educational issue, or as a juridical issue of protection against gross exploitation. Instead, he underscored the fact that Peru was four-fifths Indian, and therefore Peru could not be a nation until Indians achieved political and economic participation. At the same time, Mariátegui's position was also radical in its departure from the strictly political-economic analysis of classical Marxism. In particular, the notion of "myth" as the driving force of history enabled Mariátegui to conceive of revolution as a problem of history and culture as much as a problem of politics and economy. José Guillermo Nugent observes that Mariátegui considered the most radical transformations of his time to be the change of symbols and the appearance of new representations (1991). It is in this arena of changing symbols and new representations that he sees the value of intellectuals and the importance of questions of literature, language and culture.

In this context, it is ironic that Mariátegui argued forcefully in favor of Spanish as the national language of Peru. In his *Siete Ensayos*, he argues that a national literature in Peru does not yet exist because of the "unresolved" problem of national language.

> El dualismo quechua-español del Perú, no resuelto aún, hace de la literatura nacional un caso de excepción que no es posible estudiar con el método válido para las literaturas orgánicamente nacionales, nacidas y crecidas sin la intervención de una conquista. Nuestro caso es diverso del de aquellos pueblos de América, donde la misma dualidad no existe, o existe en términos inocuos. La individualidad de la literatura argentina, por ejemplo, está en estricto acuerdo con una definición vigorosa de la personalidad nacional.[15]
>
> (Mariátegui 1979: 154)

Like Riva Agüero and González Prada before him, Mariátegui assumes an "organic" link between language and culture. This compromises the literature of societies which are the product of a conquest because they are written in the language of the conquerors. Furthermore, in America one must distinguish between countries like Argentina, where Spanish is universal, and cases like Peru where an indigenous language is still widely spoken.

Thus, Mariátegui argues, Peru must "resolve" the Quechua–Spanish conflict *in favor of Spanish* in order to become a nation.[16] He writes: "La lengua castellana, más o menos americanizada, es el lenguaje literario y el instrumento intelectual de esta nacionalidad cuyo trabajo de definición aún no ha concluido" (1979: 153).[17] Thus while Spanish is to be the national language, like Henríquez Ureña, Mariátegui argues that national literary originality is to be measured, almost ethically, in terms of its "exceptionality" to Spanish literature. These arguments underlie Mariátegui's famous distinction between *literatura indigenista* and *literatura indígena*. On the one hand, he praises *literatura indigenista* for representing Peru's native people. On the other hand, he cannot conceive of national literary expression in Quechua, and therefore assumes that what he calls *literatura indígena* does not exist.

> El indigenismo, en nuestra literatura . . . tiene fundamentalmente el sentido de una reivindicación de lo autóctono. . . . Y la mayor injusticia en que podría incurrir un crítico, sería cualquier apresurada condena de la literatura indigenista por su falta de autoctonismo integral o la presencia, más o menos acusada en sus obras, de elementos de artificio

en la interpretación y en la expresión. La literatura indigenista no puede darnos una versión rigurosamente verista del indio. Tiene que idealizarlo y estilizarlo. Tampoco puede darnos su propia ánima. Es todavía una literatura de mestizos. Por eso se llama indigenista y no indígena. Una literatura indígena, si debe venir, vendrá a su tiempo. Cuando los propios indios estén en grado de producirla.[18]

(Mariátegui 1979: 220–1)

When an inclusive national society is constructed (Peruvian socialism) then Indians will be in a position to represent themselves. But first, according to Mariátegui, those native Peruvians would have to become literate in Spanish.

Arguedas and the assimilationist position

Since the late sixteenth century, two clear positions have developed with respect to use of native Andean languages . . . One position, which we might wish to refer to as "liberal" or "soft assimilationism" was promoted by the Jesuits . . . The other, which we might call "Hispanist" or "hard assimilationism" was proposed on the model of peninsular linguistic unification . . . With a few remarkable exceptions . . . the "Hispanist" position has dominated national language policy and education since Independence from Spain (1821) . . . Despite the dominance of the "Hispanist" position, the "soft assimilationist" position has been consistently promoted by educators and social scientists.

(Mannheim 1991: 77)

By the 1930s most Peruvian politicians and intellectuals agreed that universal literacy in Spanish was key for creating the longed-for national unity. Thus, for example, the great legislative debates of the 1930s were concerned with questions regarding the suffrage of illiterates, obligatory national education, and the *castellanización* of non-Spanish speakers. In her reflections on these debates, Eve Marie Fell writes: "Si les modalités envisagées different, la scolarisation de la population indienne apparait vraiment après 1930 comme le grand recours contre l'atomisation culturelle, comme l'élément fondateur d'une nationalité que ne serait plus de façade" (Fell 1981–2: 21–2).[19] Again, the underlying assumption of these debates was that the only conceivable linguistic basis for national society was the Spanish language.

It is in this intellectual context that Jose María Arguedas initiates his professional and literary career, and carves out his unique position *vis-à-vis* the assimilation of Quechua-speakers into a Spanish-speaking Peruvian nation. In the late 1930s and early 1940s he served as a bilingual schoolteacher at the Mateo Pumaccahua school in the Andean town of Sicuani. It is from his perspective as a young writer and educator that Arguedas published his first reflections on the problem of language in Peru. Echoing the intellectual discourse of his day, Arguedas assumes that the linguistic unity of the nation, if ever to be achieved, must be constituted in Spanish. Spanish, he argues, is the language of modern political and economic life in Peru. Therefore, he writes in 1940, Spanish acquisition is necessary if Andeans are to become full participants in national social and economic life:

> [T]odo indio que desea y pugna por ingresar a la vida activa del país, todo hombre de la sierra que pretende superarse y progresar, debe antes aprender el castellano, porque el gobierno, los negocios, la cultura, la enseñanza, todo se da y se hace en castellano. Desde 500 años el castellano lucha contra del kechwa con todas estas ventajas.[20] (1935: 35)

Quechua-speakers, if they are unable also to speak Spanish, are automatically excluded from the world of business, government, law, education.[21] Andeans understand this and therefore *want* to learn Spanish:

> [E]l pueblo, que conoce mejor que sus observadores sus propias necesidades, ha avanzado ya bastante. Hay en el pueblo mestizo actual una verdadera desesperación por dominar el castellano. Mis alumnos, que son todos mestizos o indios, acuden a mí, con una ansiedad incontenible, para que les enseñe castellano.[22] (36)[23]

For these reasons, then, Arguedas argues vehemently for a program of *castellanización* in the southern Andes so that Peru might achieve a single, national language:

> A pesar de las consideraciones que he hecho sobre que los pueblos sólo se expresan legítimamente en el idioma creado por ellos, y a pesar de que acaso sería posible la resurrección del kechwa como idoma único en algunas regiones del Perú, yo soy fervoroso partidario de la castellanización total del Perú, y estoy convencido de que el castellano como idioma general del Perú es conveniente y de absoluta necesidad.[24] (36)

But why does Arguedas favor Spanish over Quechua? His "vote" in favor of Spanish clearly comes as a result of the fact that he regards the vexing question of language in the Andes as a subset of the political, economic and social problems of creating a viable nation-state. He makes it clear that he is opposed to legitimizing Quechua because he believes that such a position would serve as a means for continuing to exclude Andeans from the broader social, political and economic universe in which only Spanish is valid.

The practical, political result of these reflections is a commitment to transforming primary and secondary education in Peru so that it responds to the needs of Quechua-speakers. The urgent task of the schools, in Arguedas' view, is to carry out a program of *castellanización* so that Andeans can participate in national life. In this context, the most pressing question is that of method: how to teach Spanish to Quechua-speakers in a non-destructive fashion. Manuel Prado's government, in response to the dire conclusions about the condition of the national educational system drawn from the 1940 census data, undertook a reorganization of the Ministry of Education. As part of this reorganization a Consejo Nacional de Educación was established whose purpose was to develop concrete measures to train teachers and develop related curricula. In 1941 Arguedas, then a bilingual schoolteacher in Sicuani, was invited to participate in the Consejo's Reforma de los Planes de Educación Secundaria. He worked on this project for a year between 1941 and 1942. Previously, in 1940, he had been invited to travel to Mexico to represent Peruvian teachers at the Congreso Indigenista Interamericano de Patzcuaro. He remained there two months observing a pilot program in bilingual education, sponsored by the Mexican government, which was directed by a North American linguist and ethnographer, Mauricio Swadesh. Arguedas' 1944 article entitled "El método para el caso lingüístico del indio" argues for Swadesh's "cultural method" of teaching literacy.[25] In it he writes:

> Concluido el proceso, el indio habrá logrado adquirir por sí mismo la convicción de que el castellano es un idioma mucho más perfecto que su lengua aborigen, comprenderá en lo substancial de su conciencia la superioridad del español como medio de expresión. Y su castellanización ya no será entonces obra sólo exterior, ni de maestros, ni de brigadas especiales, ni de misioneros protestantes; será obra incontenible del propio indio, del indio sediento de mejorar, de alcanzar el más alto nivel humano; porque entonces sentirá con mucha más violencia y de manera más directa e imperiosa la convicción de que sólo el castellano podrá llevarles la cultura y la técnica universal.[26]
>
> (Arguedas 1944: 43)

Curiously, in addition to the political rationale for *castellanización*, in his early essays Arguedas also makes a cultural/historical argument in favor of Spanish on the basis that it is a superior, more "universal" tongue than "lenguas ágrafas" like Quechua. Spanish, he asserts, is better suited than Quechua to be the language of a modern nation.

> Pues, si bien el kechwa es el idioma con que mejor se describe el paisaje del Ande, con que mejor se dice lo más profundo y propio del alma india, el kechwa es reducido y pequeño, el espíritu de quien sólo habla kechwa se agita en un círculo estrecho y oscuro, donde vienen con subyugante fuerza imágenes de la tierra y del cielo y donde cada palabra despierta dominadores sentimientos, y donde no existe el horizonte infinito de las imágenes del espíritu. ¿Cuántos siglos de evolución necesitaría aún el kechwa para lograr la amplitud de horizontes del castellano, del alemán, del francés, que tienen siglos de habla al servicio del espíritu

en su ansia de belleza y de investigación? Creo que el kechwa como idioma único y propio retardaría la evolución del pueblo mestizo e indio. Porque es necesario que el pueblo mestizo e indio tiendan a ponerse al nivel de los pueblos más cultos en lo que se refiere al dominio de la ciencia y al dominio de los medios superiores de expresión, entre los cuales el idioma, un idioma de iguales recursos que el de los pueblos más cultos, es indispensable.[27]

(Arguedas 1935: 36)

Quechua here is conceived of as a language whose scope is too limited for a modern society. Neither in the sciences, nor in the expression of the soul, is Quechua adequate. Its primitive beauty, like that of Sarmiento's gaucho characters, lies outside of modernity, and remains linked to a pristine, but no longer viable, form of social existence. Quechua may be the "legitimate" language of the Andes, but it is not capable of becoming the language of science and technology. In short, it is not the language of a modern nation. Spanish is associated with writing and literary tradition, with modernity, with technology, and with urban life while Quechua is associated with pre-modern orality, rural life, and a primitive world-view.[28]

This juxtaposition between modern and pre-modern languages coincides with the anthropological story of Peruvian historical evolution in Jorge Basadre's *La multitud, la ciudad y el campo*, first published in 1929. Arguedas was undoubtedly familiar with the book. Basadre's historical narrative is organized around a scheme which traces universal human evolution from primitive collectivities (rural, "instinctive" forms like the *ayllu*) to more civilized societies (the rational form of the city). Basadre, quoting Levy-Bruhl, sees the country as feminine, passive, never changing, and associates it with a "primitive," collective mentality. The primitive mind is conformist and attributes hidden mystical powers to all things (animism, magical rituals, etc.). The city, on the other hand, is associated with progress, rationality and advanced culture. Thus Basadre's history tells a contradictory story. On the one hand, it tells the brutal story of European invasion and conquest. On the other hand, it relies on Levy-Bruhl's anthropology to explain, and perhaps one might argue to justify, the inevitability of the domination of the Quechua-speaking country by the Spanish-speaking city.

Arguedas represents linguistic conflict in the Andes from a similarly contradictory perspective. He sees Quechua as the authentic, original language of the region while Spanish is the imposed language of the invader:

En el wayno, se ve muy claro esta lucha del kechwa y el castellano por convertirse en el idioma definitivo del hombre del Ande. Pero esta lucha es más bien de defensa por parte del kechwa y de conquista por parte del castellano.[29]

(Arguedas 1935: 35)

In contrast, he employs a conceptual framework which organizes languages, like Levy-Bruhl/Basadre organize cultures, along a continuum ranging from primitive to modern. Quechua, from this perspective, is both circumscribed, and at the same time valorized, for its primitivity.

Transculturation and Peruvian Spanish

As we have seen, Arguedas' "soft assimilationist" argument for *castellanización* is based on political and social considerations concerning the exclusion of Andeans, as well as on a notion of modern versus primitive cultures that emerges from his first readings in history and anthropology. In short, he believes that the institutionalization of Spanish will contribute significantly to national political unification and equality, and he also believes that Spanish is the only possible choice for a modern Peru.

However, despite his vote in favor of Spanish, Arguedas' experience as a bilingual teacher in the Andes, together with his growing intellectual interest and professional training in anthropology during the 1940s and 1950s, lead him to believe that this will not be a simple process.[30] As a mid-century anthropologist, he regards language as a sign of culture, the organic product of a people and a place. For this reason, as I indicated earlier, he believes that Quechua not Spanish is the legitimate language of the Southern Peruvian Andes.

> El kechwa es la expresión legítima del hombre de esta tierra, del hombre como criatura de este paisaje y de esta luz. Con el kechwa se habla en forma profunda, se describe y se dice el alma de esta luz y de este campo, como belleza y como residencia.[31]
>
> (Arguedas 1939a: 31)

For Andeans Spanish is still a tongue which belongs to a foreign landscape, and to a foreign experience; they have not yet dominated it and adapted it to their world. It is not "legitimate" in the sense that it does not have the native, deep-rootedness of Quechua. From the vantage point of "we Andeans" Arguedas writes: "Si hablamos en castellano puro, no decimos ni del paisaje ni de nuestro mundo interior; porque el mestizo no ha logrado todavía dominar el castellano como su idioma y el kechwa es aún su medio legítimo de expresión" (31).[32]

On the other hand, to argue in favor of Quechua as the national language would contradict the process of *mestizaje* in Peru which the 1940 census had detected so dramatically (cf. Valcárcel 1981: 350): "Iniciar la alfabetización del kechwa para su imposición como idioma definitivo del pueblo mestizo e indio sería pues una medida reaccionaria, artificial y contraria a la normal y justa evolución del mestizaje y del pueblo peruano del Ande" (Arguedas 1939a: 31).[33]

Here, Arguedas' perspective on language shows the direct influence of North American anthropology, especially functionalism. According to functionalism the variety of institutions and behaviors which characterize a culture form an integrated, functional whole in which every item fits together like the pieces of a complex, dynamic puzzle. While cultural change is ubiquitous (and each change produces alterations in the entire system) at the same time each culture has a "core" or "focus" which remains relatively unaffected. Culture is active, it is a creative response to changing conditions and situations, but at the same time it possesses a unique, identifiable character:

> A culture, like an individual, is a more or less consistent pattern of thought and action. Within each culture there come into being characteristic purposes not necessarily shared by other types of society. In obedience to these purposes, each people further and further consolidates its experience, and in proportion to the urgency of these drives the heterogeneous items of behavior take more and more congruous shape.
>
> (Benedict 1934: 42)

From this perspective, in which each culture is seen as an organic whole, external sources of change, produced in the contact between distinct cultures, do not fundamentally alter the receiving culture:

> One of the most important factors in connection with the diffusion of cultural elements is that they transfer from one society to another almost exclusively in terms of their form. In other words, the borrowing society copies particular patterns of behavior as it appends them, usually without understanding their original culture context. The new element is thus transferred at the objective level and comes into the receiving culture stripped of most of the meanings and associations which it carried in its original context.
>
> (Linton 1955: 459)

Ruth Benedict argues that cultures vary in terms of their degree of "integration," that is their "purpose" is more or less coherent and fortified. Since cultures range between the poles of relative strength and weakness with regard to their unity and purpose, they are "disoriented" in varying degrees by change.

Interestingly, from this perspective Arguedas sees the historical continuity or "survival" of Quechua culture not as resistance to influence or transformation, but rather as a sign of its capacity for change, and its ability to absorb foreign elements. Thus, Arguedas argues, the process of *mestizaje* in Peru (which began with the conquest), including the imposition of Spanish as the national language, does not threaten the fundamental cultural character of the Andes. "Lo indio es ya dominio en la psicología del mestizo peruano; ha ganado la contienda porque le ayudaron todo este mundo del Ande: la tierra, el aire, la luz . . ." (Arguedas 1939a: 31).[34]

Andean culture will continue to be dominant in Peru despite modernization and *castellanización*. In fact, he argues, Spanish will come to be "legitimate" in the Andes, when Andeans can effectively modify it until it is capable of translating their vision of the world:

> Esta ansia de dominar el castellano llevará al mestizo hasta la posesión entera del idioma. Y su reacción sobre el castellano ha de ser porque nunca cesará de adaptar el castellano a su profunda necesidad de expresarse en forma absoluta, es decir, de *traducir* hasta la última exigencia de su alma, en la que lo indio es mando y raíz.[35] (1939a: 32)

In that sense the duality of language in Peru will be resolved not when Spanish is imposed as the national language but rather when Andeans come to possess Spanish as their own. When they have transformed the foreign tongue into an Andean tongue, then they will be able to translate their sensibility into the new language:

> Estoy pues convencido de que el mestizo y el indio, es decir, el peruano del Ande, llegará a poseer el castellano con toda propiedad, después de un período más o menos largo de lucha y de reacción recíproca entre el idioma y el hombre.[36]
>
> (Arguedas 1935: 37)

This is a radical argument in that it absolutely rejects the dominant language ideology (standard Spanish) as appropriate or valid for Peruvians. In fact, Spanish, if it is to become the national language, must undergo profound transformations. An authentic and legitimate Peruvian Spanish, Arguedas argues, will be "intimately" influenced by Quechua:

> Estamos asistiendo aquí a la agonía del castellano como espíritu y como idioma puro e intocado. Lo observo y lo siento todos los días en mi clase de castellano del colegio Mateo Pumaccahua, de Canchis. Mis alumnos mestizos, en cuya alma lo indio es dominio, fuerzan el castellano, y en la morfología íntima de ese castellano que hablan y escriben, en su sintaxis destrozada, reconozco el genio del kechwa.[37]
>
> (Arguedas 1939a: 33)[38]

Thus, even though the Spanish/Quechua conflict in the Andes is "resolved" in favor of Spanish, its "conquest" by Quechua speakers means that its character will be transformed profoundly. It will be a hybridized

Spanish that is the result of its appropriation and transformation by Andean culture.

This is a utopian vision of the future of culture and language in Peru. It inspires an intellectual and political project whose goal is to create a *mestizo* national culture in which Andeans will be full citizens. The difficulty of Arguedas' project comes out of his dual fidelity in the first place to Quechua language and culture as the primary sources of national identity, and in the second place to the political idea of a nation from which Andeans are no longer excluded. His analysis clearly emerges from his understanding of the theories of cultural contact and change that he found in the work of Fernando Ortiz[39] as well as in North American cultural anthropologists. In Arguedas' contradictory, utopian vision, a truly Peruvian Spanish will be a hybrid tongue that provides a linguistic home for all Peruvians, including Quechua-speakers. Quechua in fact becomes the in-dwelling spirit of Peruvian Spanish. This hybrid Spanish, transformed by Quechua rhythms and meanings, becomes generalized in turn as the authentic national language.

Partha Chatterjee has stressed the ideological tension which the twin sources of nationalist thought produce in a "post-colonial" context:

> The problem of nationalist thought becomes the particular manifestation of a much more general problem, namely, the problem of the bourgeois-rationalist conception of knowledge, established in the post-enlightenment period of European intellectual history, as the moral and epistemic foundation for a supposedly universal framework of thought which perpetuates, in a real and not merely a metaphorical sense, a colonial domination. It is a framework of knowledge which proclaims its own universality; its validity, it pronounces, is independent of cultures. Nationalist thought, in agreeing to become "modern," accepts the claim to universality of the "modern" framework of knowledge. Yet it also asserts the autonomous identity of a national culture. It thus simultaneously rejects and accepts the dominance, both epistemic and moral, of an alien culture.
>
> (Chatterjee 1993: 11)

As we have seen thus far, Arguedas' efforts to think through the enormous problems of language, culture and social justice in Peru suffer tremendously from the tension described here by Chatterjee. Still, in spite of this conflict as reflected in his theoretical discussions, as we will see in the following section, his literary practice goes much further towards a questioning and subversion of the "rationalist conception of knowledge" – which, according to Chatterjee, underlies nationalism.

Spanish as translation: the utopia of language

We have seen that Arguedas promotes the imposition of Spanish as the national language of Peru because he believes that this will create social and economic opportunities for previously marginalized Quechua-speaking Andeans. At the same time, however, he soundly rejects the notion that the subordination of Quechua to Spanish poses a threat to Andean cultural integrity. On the contrary, he views the process of *castellanización* as one in which Andeans will appropriate Spanish for their own purposes. As a site of *translation*, Peruvian Spanish, he argues ebulliently, will become Quechuized. It is in his literary reflections that Arguedas most rigorously works through this possibility of realizing what Alberto Escobar has called "the utopia of language" (cf. Escobar 1984).

For Arguedas, the problems of literary expression and language conflict in the Andes are organically related:

> En nosotros, la gente del Ande, hace pocos años ha empezado el conflicto del idioma, como real y expreso en nuestra literatura; desde Vallejo hasta el último poeta del Ande. El mismo conflicto que sintiera, aunque en forma mas ruda, Huaman Poma de Ayala. Si hablamos en castellano puro, no decimos ni del paisaje ni de nuestro mundo interior; porque el mestizo no ha logrado todavía dominar el castellano como su idioma y el kechwa es aun su medio legítimo de expresión. Pero si escribimos en kechwa hacemos literatura estrecha y condenada al olvido.[40]
>
> (Arguedas 1939a: 31)

The unresolved conflict between Quechua, as the "legitimate" language of expression in the Andes, and Spanish, which is by necessity the language of literary expression, is what has caused the poverty of Andean literary expression historically. For Arguedas, Felipe Guaman Poma de Ayala, the early seventeenth-century Andean chronicler, in a fitful, uneven way, exemplifies this problem of linguistic conflict and writing:[41]

> No sabía expresarse en español; y en las mil páginas que escribió se siente la tremenda lucha de este indio con el idioma en que se ve obligado a expresarse. En muchas páginas no encuentra la palabra necesaria, y entonces se decide a hablar en kechwa; de ahí el gran desorden de su estilo y de sus informaciones.[42]
>
> (Arguedas 1939b: 40)

However, it is not until the appearance of César Vallejo[43] that a *mestizo* literature attempts to constitute itself out of the matrix of conflict between Spanish and Quechua. Vallejo exemplifies the linguistic homelessness of the Andean writer:

Vallejo marca el comienzo de la diferenciación de la poesía de la costa y de la sierra en el Perú. Porque en Vallejo empieza la etapa tremenda en que el hombre del Ande siente el conflicto entre su mundo interior y el castellano como su idioma.[44]

(Arguedas 1939a: 31)

Vallejo was raised in the late 1800s in the northern Peruvian Andes, which was not generally Quechua-speaking even at that time. Nonetheless, it is an area in which Andean oral traditions were still vital. It is in this context that Arguedas reads the strangeness and charged quality of Vallejo's poetry in Spanish. In Vallejo's literary Spanish he hears the unmistakable voices of Andean orality that must have been a fundamental aspect of his provincial Andean upbringing.[45]

Thus, for Andean writers, the problem of language is necessarily a problem of translation. The writings of Quispe Alancoa, one of Arguedas' Quechua-speaking students at the Mateo Pumaccahua school in Sicuani, exemplifies the linguistic dilemma of the mestizo writer. "Quispe se expresa bien y limpio en kechwa, es su idioma genuino y legítimo; y cuando se ve obligado a traducir sus inquietudes y todo su mundo interior en castellano, se confunde. De ahí lo oscuro de su idioma" (Arguedas 1940: 93).[46]

Arguedas describes his own efforts as a bilingual writer in similar terms. Quispe's "confusion" also plagues Arguedas and it is the same "confusion" which he attributes to Guaman Poma. The danger in this contact zone between languages is not silence but disorientation. And yet, at the same time, bilingualism harbors tremendous creative possibilities, as is also evident in Quispe Alancoa's writing:

> En el fondo de su estilo oscuro se siente una doble ansiedad: la del indio que se duele de la miseria de su vida y la del indio que sufre por traducir ese dolor en un idioma todavía extraño. Sin embargo, la exigencia de traducirse es tan profunda en Quispe, que en la última parte de su artículo, habla ya en nombre propio, porque en verdad es su vida la que cuenta, recurre al símbolo y su artículo logra una extraordinaria hermosura.[47] (1940: 93)

The urgency of what he is trying to say, coupled with the struggle for expression which he must necessarily pass through because he writes in Spanish, produces an extraordinary effect. It is this unique possibility, so painfully linked to the threat of babble, that lies at the heart of Arguedas' poetics of translation.

This utopian poetics of translation is most clearly elucidated in Arguedas' canonical literary statement entitled "La novela y la expresión literaria en el Perú," which was first published in 1950. This is a retrospective essay which takes stock of, and defends, the style of *Agua* (1935) and *Yawar fiesta*

(1941) as experiments in translation related to the bilingual social context of the writer (Arguedas) and the social world which is the referent of the texts.

"La novela" tells the story of Arguedas' literary beginnings which are linked to the circumstances of his childhood. "Una bien amada desventura," he explains, "hizo que mi niñez y parte de mi adololescencia transcurrieran entre los indios lucanas; ellos son la gente que más amo y comprendo" (1950: 67).[48] This experience, inscribed autobiographically in so many of Arguedas' texts, legitimizes the hybrid style of his writing. The narrator's feelings, and his linguistic dilemmas, are represented as being inextricable from those of the collectivity which is the referent of his discourse. Thus, through autobiography, Arguedas explains and defends the style of *Agua* and *Yawar fiesta* as reflective of Andean bilingualism.

Conventional, "literary" Spanish is incapable of adequately representing a universe in which Quechua is the legitimate language. "Muchas esencias, que sentía como las mejores y legítimas, no se diluían en los términos castellanos construidos en la forma ya conocida. Era necesario encontrar *los sutiles desordenamientos* que harían del castellano el molde justo, el instrumento adecuado" (Arguedas 1950: 70).[49] This kind of transformation is different from the case of the appropriation of regional Spanish like the kind Arguedas presumes to find in Güiraldes' *Don Segundo Sombra*. Although he is clearly inspired by Güiraldes' use of popular speech, his problem is to fashion a fictional language (the "subtle disordering" of Spanish) which will be capable of representing a Quechua language world to a monolingual Spanish reader. The incongruities which separate Quechua and Spanish (the unequal power relations between them in the Peruvian context, the profound differences between orality and literacy, and so on) make translation particularly problematic. In this context, the question of "universality" becomes secondary:

> [L]a angustia primaria ya no es por la universalidad sino por la simple realización. *Realizarse, traducirse, convertir en torrente diáfano y legítimo el idioma que parece ajeno; comunicar a la lengua casi extranjera la materia de nuestro espíritu. Esa es la dura, la difícil cuestión.* La universalidad de este raro equilibrio de contenido y forma, equilibrio alcanzado tras intensas noches de increíble trabajo, es cosa que vendrá en función de la perfección humana lograda en el transcurso de tan extraño esfuerzo. ¿Existe en el fondo de esa obra el rostro verdadero del ser humano y de su morada? Si está pintado ese rostro con desusados colores no solo no importa; puede tal suceso concederle mayor interés al cuadro. Que los colores no sean solo una maraña, la grotesca huella del agitarse del ser impotente; eso es lo esencial. Pero si el lenguaje así cargado de extrañas esencias deja ver el profundo corazón humano, si nos transmite la historia de su paso sobre la tierra, la universalidad podrá tardar quizá mucho; sin

embargo vendrá, pues bien sabemos que el hombre debe su preeminencia y su reinado al hecho de ser uno y único.[50]

(Arguedas 1950: 69–70)

In the case of the Andean writer to translate means to "charge" Spanish with strange (or foreign) Quechua materials; thus transformed, the language becomes capable of comprehending the violent and conflictive social and linguistic reality of the Andes. The translation is therefore both a fiction (not an equivalence but a "disordering") and, at the same time, an embodiment of the world.

Arguedas elaborates on this notion of translation when he speaks of the problem of literary form. He argues that form, in the case of Andean writers, is a problem of culture, not of superficial stylistics:

¿Fue y es ésta una búsqueda de la universalidad a través de la lucha por la forma, solo por la forma? Por la forma en cuanto ella significa conclusión, equilibrio alcanzado por la necesaria mezcla de elementos que tratan de constituirse en una nueva estructura. . . . No se trata pues de una búsqueda de la forma en su aceptación superficial y corriente, sino como problema del espíritu, de la cultura, en estos países en que corrientes extrañas se encuentran y durante siglos no concluyen por fusionar sus direcciones, sino que forman estrechas zonas de confluencia, mientras en lo hondo y lo extenso las venas principales fluyen sin ceder, increíblemente.[51]

(1950: 71–2)

Form, in this difficult context, becomes a question of the conflicting cultural currents that constitute the social and linguistic space of the nation. In this sense, the co-presence of languages in Arguedas' style is not a sign of harmony, nor of integration, but rather a measure of the continued incommensurability of the social and cultural worlds which exist side by side in Peru. This is why the problem of "universality" must be considered secondary: at this point the fundamental task of *mestizo* writers is to embody this linguistic and cultural conflict in the form and language of their texts. In this context, "universality" means the process of legitimization and validation that literary texts receive in relation to a dominant field or market. In this sense, for Arguedas the Peruvian novel, like Peruvian Spanish, must reject that international market in order to constitute itself. Its logic of composition responds to the conflictive cultural and linguistic matrix out of which it flows. Its literary value corresponds to its ability to house the voices of Peruvian people, not to its ability to compete in the international marketplace of literature in Spanish.

The language of translation embodies the violence of Peruvian history and culture, but at the same time it offers the prospect of healing as well, of future integration. Leónides Morales has astutely observed the way in which Arguedas' language, shaped by the tense relations between Spanish and Quechua, runs simultaneously in these two directions. In the first place, he argues, linguistic tension between Quechua and Spanish is an attempt to represent, on the level of content, the antagonisms of the social world which is depicted. But, at the same time, Arguedas' language is also an attempt to project itself beyond those antagonisms in order to model the possibility of a harmonious future:

> Pensaba que la estructura de su estilo, que fundaba una perfección estética, era el *modelo lingüístico* de una estructura social que, superando las contradicciones entre los dos pueblos y las dos culturas, fundaría a su vez una perfección humana: el hombre y el pueblo nuevos con que soñaba.[52]
>
> (Morales 1971: 141)[53]

The idea that language (and literature) might express the contradictions of the nation and at the same time serve as a utopian model of "human perfection," that is serve as a model of national cultural integration, is inspired to a significant degree by Arguedas' "oral" sense of language as motivated rather than arbitrary. Language, for Arguedas, has a mythological power. This sense of language is associated with Quechua.[54]

In his analysis of the *Ollantay*, for example, Arguedas comments that the language of the Quechua play is "untranslatable" because of its total integration with its referent and with human consciousness:

> No es posible traducir con equivalente intensidad la ternura doliente que su texto quechua transmite. La repetición de los verbos que llevan en su fonética una especie de reflejo material de los movimientos que en lo recóndito del organismo se producen con el penar, el sufrir, el llorar, el caer ante el golpe de la adversidad implacable, causan en el lector un efecto penetrante, porque los mismos términos están cargados de la esencia del tormentoso y tan ornado paisaje andino y de cómo este mundo externo vive, llamea, en lo interno del hombre quechua. Una sola unidad forman el ser, el universo y el lenguaje.[55]
>
> (Arguedas 1952: 139-40)

This is not necessarily a naive view of language, but rather an attempt to describe fundamental differences in function and character between orality and writing. Walter Ong describes these differences as follows:

> [T]he contact of an oral culture with truth, vague and evanescent though it may seem by some literate standards, retains a reality which literate cultures achieve only reflexively and by dint of great conscious effort. For oral-aural man utterance remains always of a piece with his life situation. It is never remote. Thus it provides a kind of raw, if

circumscribed, contact with actuality and with truth, which literacy and even literature alone can never give and to achieve which literate cultures must rather desperately shore up with other new resources their more spatialized verbal structures.

(Ong 1982: 33)

For Arguedas words in Quechua have an incantatory or mythological power: There is a bond not a separation between "words and things."

Peruvian Spanish, Arguedas claims, absorbs Quechua but at the same time is transformed by it; it serves as a meta-language for Quechua, and at the same time – and this is crucial – retains the Andean language's mythological power to name the world. By objectifying the composite, multilingual (and multidialectal) character of the nation, Arguedas' formal, literary innovations constitute, implicitly, an enactment in miniature of the ideal national community that he envisions. This idea rests on a sense of the magical, luminous power of language to transform what it touches. To name the nation by bringing its voices into contact, through the language of translation, is to transform it.

Conclusion

Arguedas believes that Spanish must be institutionalized as the national language in order for Peru to achieve social, political and cultural unification. At the same time, his writings and professional activities are dedicated wholly to the utopian project of buiding a national culture on the basis of Andean traditions, values and cosmovision. Moreover, his analysis of the character and direction of linguistic and cultural change in Peru – which emerges primarily from his study of (mostly North American) cultural anthropology, as well as his ethnographic fieldwork during the 1940s and 1950s – shows a process of *transculturation* in which Andean culture is not dominated and destroyed by Spanish culture, but rather is merged with it. Ultimately, then, what he promotes is a kind of subversive assimilation of Quechua-speakers into a Spanish-speaking Peruvian nation. It is subversive because, in his view, Spanish will become the national language only when Andeans fully appropriate it for their own purposes. In the process, the dominant language ideology will be transformed: Peruvian Spanish will be an Andean language in which one can still hear, as he wrote, *the intimate syntax of Quechua*.

Notes

1 "We are witnessing the death throes of Spanish as a spirit and as a pure and untouched language. I see it and feel it every day in my Spanish class at the Mateo Pumaccahua school in Canchis. My *mestizo* students, in whose spirit the Indian is dominant, strain Spanish, and in the intimate morphology of the

Spanish they speak and write, in their destroyed syntax, I recognize the genius of Quechua."

2 The significant debates in the nineteenth century were Bello/Lastarria, Valera/Cuervo, etc. For a discussion of the late nineteenth-century debate between Juan Valera and Rufino José Cuervo, cf. chapter 4.

3 In the 1930s and 1940s, some Spanish philologists still voiced their concern about the improper use of the Spanish language in Argentina (cf. Alonso 1935, Castro 1941). However, Argentinean writer Jorge Luis Borges was not so worried about the state of the language in the Río de la Plata region and responded to Américo Castro's concerns with an unforgettable article (1941).

4 "We have not forsworn to write in Spanish, and there begins the problem of how to achieve our own, original expression. Each language crystallizes modes of thought and feeling, and whatever is written in that language is bathed in the color of its crystal. Our expression will need to be doubly strong in order to impose its hue over the red and gold" (colors of the Spanish flag).

5 The notion of a linguistic field or marketplace comes from Pierre Bourdieu. He defines a linguistic field as a "system of specifically linguistic relations of power based on the unequal distribution of linguistic capital" (Bourdieu 1991: 57). For an overview of Bourdieu's notion of symbolic capital, and his application of economic concepts such as "market" and "capital" to spheres of culture, cf. Bourdieu (1977).

6 The distinction between "hispanists" and "indigenists" is a convention of early twentieth-century Peruvian intellectual history. For a summary review see Matos Mar (1974). For a more detailed analysis of intellectuals, ideas and politics in Peru see Salazar Bondy (1965).

7 "In order for Peruvian literature not to be Spanish, the Castilian language would have to be completely corrupted and split apart into new languages which, fortunately, in Peru (despite our numerous provincialisms and despite the indefensible resistance of the Spanish Royal Academy to recognizing them) is but a distant threat."

8 "Let us conserve our language, this magnificent language, strong as an oak, solid as marble, brilliant as fire, resonant as the sea; let us conserve the integrity of its genius, though adapting it prudently to new necessities, defending it at the same time from the idiotic outbursts of the Frenchifiers and from the senile whims of the purists. Language is a powerful foundation of tradition; and, as long as it is not changed, a strong connection remains."

9 In a very interesting (and enthusiastic) review of Riva Agüero's book, Miguel de Unamuno affirms Riva Agüero's contradictory view that Spanish culture and language are indivisible and, at the same time, need to be defended against malignant influences. He writes, "La lengua, he de repetirlo una vez más, es la sangre del espíritu; se piensa con palabras, y todo aquel que piense desde niño en español, pensará a la española, créalo o no, sépalo o no lo sepa, y aunque no corra ni una gota de sangre española en sus venas. La lengua es la sangre del espíritu social, y así como la sangre es como el ambiente interior del cuerpo, así la lengua es el ambiente interior del espíritu colectivo, el vehículo de su nutrición ideal" (Unamuno quoted in Riva Agüero 1905: 362; "Language, I must insist on this again, is the blood of the spirit; one thinks with words, and everyone who thinks in Spanish from childhood, will think *Spanish style*, believe it or not, know it or not, and even if not one drop of Spanish blood runs in his veins. Language is the blood of the social spirit, and just as blood is the internal environment of the body, language is the internal environment of the collective spirit, the vehicle of its ideal sustenance.")

10 "Languages are invigorated and re-tuned in popular usage, more than by the dead rules of the grammarians or the prehistoric exhumations of the scholars . . . The masses transform languages the way micro-organisms modify continents."
11 "To leave one's homeland, to speak another language, is like emerging from a cave to breath the mountain air."
12 "[T]o a great, open language, used by millions of people and understood by the great bulk of the intellectual world, they prefer a restricted tongue, used by only thousands of provincials and artificially cultivated by a few writers."
13 I reproduce here González Prada's orthography.
14 José Vasconcelos in Mexico takes a similar position in the 1920s. Cf. Vasconcelos (1927).
15 "The Spanish–Quechua duality in Peru, still unresolved, makes our national literature an exceptional case which cannot be studied with the method that is valid for organically national literatures, born and developed without the intervention of conquest. Our case is different than that of those American nations where the same duality does not exist, or it only exists in innocuous terms. The uniqueness of Argentine literature, for example, is in strict accord with a strong definition of its national character."
16 Hobsbawm, writing about European nationalism, comments that "Linguistic nationalism was the creation of people who wrote and read, not of people who spoke. And the 'national languages' in which they discovered the essential character of their nations were, more often than not, artefacts, since they had to be compiled, standardized, homogenized and modernized for contemporary and literary use, out of the jigsaw puzzle of local or regional dialects which constituted the non-literary languages as actually spoken" (Hobsbawm 1987: 147). The idea of a unified national language in Peru has always meant the suppression of Quechua and other native languages. But it has also served to suppress the distinctive regional dialects of Spanish (especially Andean Spanish) in favor of the Lima variety. Cf. Cerrón-Palomino (1987).
17 " A more or less Americanized Spanish is the literary language and intellectual instrument of this nation whose process of self-definition is still not finished."
18 "The meaning of indigenism, in our literature . . . is, fundamentally, that of vindicating the autochthonous . . . And the worst injustice a critic could commit would be a hasty condemnation of indigenist literature for its lack of true Indian character, or for the presence, more or less pronounced, of elements of artifice both in the interpretation and in the expression. Indigenist literature cannot give us a rigorously realistic picture of the Indian. It must idealize and stylize him. Neither can it give us his spirit. It is still a literature of mestizos. This is why it is called indigenist literature and not Indian literature. Indian literature, if it is ever to emerge, will come in its own time. When Indians themselves are capable of producing it."
19 " While the envisioned methods are different, the education of the Indian masses emerges after 1930 as the great solution to cultural dispersion, as the foundational element of a nationality that would no longer be just a façade."
20 "[A]ny Indian who desires and struggles to integrate himself into the life of the nation, anyone from the sierra who hopes to improve himself and to progress, first must learn Spanish, because government, business, culture, education, everything happens in Spanish. For 500 years, with all of these advantages, Spanish has opposed Quechua."
21 "[L]a urgencia de este proceso de incorporación del pueblo indio a la nacionalidad peruana es hoy angustioso y grave; la contemplación de la realidad humana presente nos parece que plantea un dilema casi mortal; o se actúa inmediatamente, con la energía y el fervor suficientes a fin de convertir a la gran población

kechwa y aymara en elementos activos del país; o ha de imponerse el ánimo de verlos convertirse, dentro de poco, en una masa definitivamente retrasada, detenida, y dejada sólo para la faena menor y ruda, para el menester sin esperanza, en cuyo curso acabará por momificarse y apagarse la luz de su espíritu" (Arguedas 1944: 44; "The urgency of this process of incorporation of Indian people into the Peruvian nation is today distressing and critical; the contemplation of our human reality presents us with an almost mortal dilemma; either we act immediately, with the necessary energy and the passion to convert the masses of Quechua and Aymara speakers into active participants in the life of the country; or, we allow victory to the desire to convert them into a backward, underdeveloped, repressed mass of people capable only the most menial and back-breaking labor, capable only of having needs but not hope, and in this process the light of their spirit will be mummified and extinguished.")

22 "[T]he people, who understand their needs better than their observers, have already advanced a lot. Today's *mestizos* are truly desperate to learn Spanish. My students, who are all *mestizo* and Indian, come to me, overwhelmed with impatience, to ask me to teach them Spanish."

23 Alberto Escobar cites a survey done during the 1960s in Quinua which confirms Arguedas' less "quantified" observations. To summarize: the survey revealed that the majority of monolingual Quechua-speakers in the community under age 50 clearly aspired to learn Spanish because they saw this as key to social mobility (cf. Escobar 1972: 24).

24 "In spite of what I've said about people only being able to express themselves legitimately in a language that they have created, and in spite of the fact that it might be possible to resurrect Quechua as the sole language of some regions of Peru, I am a passionate believer in teaching Spanish to everyone in Peru, and I am convinced that it is appropriate and an absolute necessity that Spanish become the general language of Peru."

25 The cultural method of *castellanización* is seen by Arguedas as a means for carrying the oral, Quechua side of the cultural equation into the national language by incorporating it rather than destroying it. In this context the mission of the teacher is to promote a process of cultural change which will result in national integration. The nationalizing mission of the teacher is linked, in Arguedas' early writings on education, to an exalted populism in which Quechua-speakers are integrated into the Spanish-speaking nation without "losing their souls." Arguedas' ardent nationalism is thus coupled with a passionate optimism in the perdurability of indigenous culture.

26 "Once the process is concluded, Indians will have acquired the conviction that Spanish is a much more perfect language than their aboriginal languages, and they will have a solid, conscious understanding that Spanish is a superior means of communication. And then their Spanish will not be a surface achievement, an achievement of teachers, and literacy brigades, and protestant ministers; it will be the achievement of Indians themselves, of those that are thirsty to better themselves, to achieve the highest levels; because at that point they will feel more violently and more directly and authoritatively that only Spanish will provide them with universal culture and technology."

27 "Though it is true that Quechua is the language with which one can best describe the Andean landscape, and with which one can best express the deepest and most authentic aspects of the Indian soul, nonetheless Quechua is diminished and small. The spirit of someone who only speaks Quechua moves in a narrow and dark circle where images of the earth and the sky come with oppressive force, and where each word awakens overwhelming feelings, and where one cannot find the limitless horizon of images of the spirit. How many centuries of evolution

would Quechua need in order to achieve the breadth of Spanish, German, or French, which have centuries of usage in the service of the spirit and in their quest for beauty and knowledge? I think as an exclusive language Quechua would retard the evolution of *mestizo* and Indian people. *Mestizos* and Indians must rise to the level of more educated peoples in terms of their understanding of science and their control of superior means of communication, among which language, a language whose resources are equal to that of the languages of the most advanced countries, is indispensable."

28 This perspective contradicts the erroneous – but nonetheless common – interpretation of Arguedas' world-view as a "manichean" opposition between good and evil where all things Quechua lie on the side of good and all things Spanish on the side of evil. Arguedas' position is far more complex and, in this instance, ambiguous. For examples of this erroneous interpretation cf. Castro-Klarén (1977: 8); and Vargas Llosa (1981).

29 "In the *huayno* [a kind of music (songs and dances) typical of the Andes], one can see clearly the struggle between Quechua and Spanish to become the definitive Andean language. But, for Quechua, this struggle is really one of survival, while for Spanish it is one of conquest."

30 Arguedas worked in the Folklore Section of the Ministry of Education from 1946 to 1952, and then assumed the post of Director of the Institute of Ethnological Studies at the newly created Museum of Culture, which he occupied until 1963. Also, 1946 he enrolled in graduate studies at San Marcos at the newly-created Institute of Ethnology. After completing the program in 1950, he went on to write a doctoral dissertation in 1958 based on rural field research in Spain. During the late 1940s and 1950s Arguedas published a number of significant ethnographic studies based on field research in the Southern Andes.

31 "Quechua is the legitimate expression of the people of this land, of the people born of this earth and this light. With Quechua one speaks deeply, one names the soul of this light and this earth, both as beauty and as a place of residence."

32 "If we speak pure Spanish, we can describe neither the landscape nor our inner world; because the *mestizo* has not dominated Spanish as a language and Quechua is still his legitimate means of expression."

33 "To begin a literacy campaign in Quechua, in order to impose it as the definitive language of the *mestizo* and Indian peoples, would be a reactionary measure. It would be artificial and contrary to the normal and proper evolution of *mestizaje* within the Andean people of Peru."

34 "The Indian is dominant in the psychology of the Peruvian *mestizo*; he has won the battle because everything in the Andean world helps him: the earth, the air, the light . . ."

35 "This desire to learn Spanish will enable the *mestizo* to dominate it entirely. And he will necessarily have an effect on Spanish because he will never cease to adapt it to his deep need to express himself totally, that is, to *translate* each last call of his heart, in which the Indian is leader and root."

36 "Thus I am convinced that *mestizos* and Indians, that is to say, Peruvians of the Andes, will come to possess Spanish entirely, after a more or less long period of struggle and mutual response between the language and the people."

37 "We are witnessing the death throes of Spanish as a spirit and as a pure and untouched language. I see it and feel it every day in my Spanish class at the Mateo Pumaccahua school in Canchis. My *mestizo* students, in whose spirit the Indian is dominant, strain Spanish, and in the intimate morphology of the Spanish they speak and write, in their destroyed syntax, I recognize the genius of Quechua."

38 Similarly, Arguedas wrote (1940: 94): "De esta pugna del mestizo por adaptar el castellano a la versión de su alma, en que lo indio es lo fundamental, el castellano saldrá intimamente influenciado por el kechwa." ("In this immense effort by *mestizos* to adapt Spanish to their innermost character, in which the Indian is predominant, Spanish will be intimately influenced by Quechua.")

39 Fernando Ortiz is considered to be the most influential Cuban anthropologist of the twentieth century. The bulk of his intellectual work focused on Afro-Cuban folklore. He created the term "transculturation" because he felt the then widely used "acculturation" did not account for the processes of mutual interaction and influence that occur between cultures under certain circumstances. From his point of view, Cuban culture was the product of the transculturation of African and European cultures.

40 "Over the past several years, there has emerged within us, the people of the Andes, a conflict of language, as something real and expressed in our literature; from Vallejo to the most recent Andean poet. This is the same conflict that Guaman Poma must have felt, although in a more crude form. If we speak pure Spanish, we cannot speak of the landscape nor of our inner world; because the *mestizo* has not dominated Spanish as his language, and Quechua is still his legitimate means of communication. However, if we write in Quechua we make literature that is narrow and condemned to be forgotten."

41 Guaman Poma was a local *cacique*, or leader, from the area around Ayacucho, Peru. In the early seventeenth century he wrote a "letter" of over 1000 pages to King Philip III of Spain in which he decried the Spanish abuses of Indian people, and called for a restoration of native lands and native rule in the Andes. His first language was Quechua, but he was literate in Spanish and familiar with the major Spanish historical and religious publications about the New World. In his text he intermingles Spanish and Quechua throughout. For a good introduction to Guaman Poma's writings, see Adorno (1986).

42 "He did not know how to express himself in Spanish; in the thousand pages that he wrote one feels the tremendous struggle of this Indian with the language in which he was obliged to express himself. On many pages he doesn't find the right word, and thus he decides to write in Quechua; this explains the great disorganization of his style and of his information."

43 César Vallejo (1892–1938) is widely considered the greatest Peruvian poet of the twentieth century. He was born in the Andean provincial town of Santiago de Chuco in northern Peru. His poetry is notable for its linguistic experimentation and its raw emotions. Also, his work is marked by a deep empathy for human suffering and a commitment to social justice. For a splendid English translation of his complex poetry, cf. Vallejo (1978).

44 "Vallejo marks the beginning of the differentiation of the poetry of the coast from the poetry of the sierra in Peru. Because with Vallejo there begins a tremendous period in which Andean people feel the conflict between their inner world and Spanish as their language."

45 George Steiner uses the notion of the "extraterritorial" writer to describe bilingual writers such as Nabokov or Becket. The extraterritorial writer is linguistically "unhoused," that is, "not thoroughly at home in the language of his production, but displaced or hesitant at the frontier" (Steiner 1971). Deleuze and Guattari expand on Steiner's notion of extraterritoriality in their notion of a "minor literature" which would include monolingual writers like Vallejo who nonetheless come to the socially dominant tongue from a marginal place. They write, "A minor literature doesn't come from a minor language; it is rather that which a minority constructs within a major language. But the first characteristic

of minor literature in any case is that in it *language is affected with a high coefficient of deterritorialization*" (Deleuze and Guattari 1986: 16).
46 "Quispe expresses himself cleanly and fluently in Quechua, it is his genuine and legitimate language; and when he finds himself obliged to translate his cares and feelings into Spanish, he becomes confused. That is the reason for the impenetrability of his language."
47 "At the bottom of his obscure style one feels a double anxiety: that of an Indian who suffers from the misery of his life and that of an Indian who suffers in the attempt to translate that pain into a language that is still foreign to him. Nonetheless, for Quispe, the need to translate himself is so profound that in the last section of his article he speaks in his own voice, because in truth it is his life story that he is telling, and he resorts to symbols and his writing takes on an extraordinary beauty."
48 "A wonderful misfortune caused me to spend part of my childhood among the *lucanas* Indians; they are the people I love most and understand best."
49 "Many essences, that I felt were the best and legitimate ones, could not be dissolved into Spanish words at least in their given forms. It was necessary to find *subtle disorderings* that would make Spanish a good mold, an adequate instrument."
50 "The most important concern is no longer universality but instead simply realizing the task. *To realize yourself, to translate yourself, to convert the seemingly distant language into a transparent and legitimate stream; to communicate to an almost foreign language the essence of our soul. That is the hard, the difficult question.* Universality is that rare equilibrium of content and form, an equilibrium achieved after intense nights of incredible labor, and it is something that will come as a result of the human perfection that is achieved through such a strange effort. Does one find at the bottom of that work the true shape of the human face? Does one find his dwelling-place? If that face is painted with outmoded colors not only does it not matter; rather, this fact might lend greater interest to the canvas. That the colors not be just a morass, the grotesque sign of an impotent being; that is the essential thing. But, if the language thus charged with strange essences makes visible the depth of the human heart, if it transmits to us the history of his existence on earth, universality might arrive late, perhaps very late, but it will arrive because we know that man owes his preeminence and his sovereignty to the fact that he is both universal and unique."
51 "Was and is this a search for universality by way of a struggle for form, for form only? Yes, for form in so much as form means closure, equilibrium achieved through the necessary mixture of elements attempting to constitute themselves as a new structure... However, this is not a search for form in its common and superficial sense. It is instead a problem of the spirit in countries like ours in which strange currents meet but for centuries never merge into one stream, but rather form close zones of confluence, while at the deepest and most extensive level their principle arteries flow without yielding, incredibly."
52 "He believed that the structure of his style, which established an aesthetic perfection, constituted a *linguistic model* for a social structure that, overcoming the contradictions of both peoples and both cultures, would establish in turn a kind of human perfection: the new human and the new collective that he dreamed of."
53 Angel Rama makes a similar point about the politics of Arguedas' poetics: "[L]a literatura operó ... como el modelo reducido de la transculturación, donde se podía mostrar y probar la eventualidad de su realización de tal modo que si era posible en la literatura también podía ser posible en el resto de la cultura" (Rama 1982: 202; "Literature functioned ... as a model of transculturation, wherein one might convincingly demonstrate and prove its eventual realization,

in so far as, if it were possible within literature, it also might come to pass within the culture at large.")

54 Arguedas often celebrates Quechua precisely in terms of what Lotman and Uspensky call the mythological: the correspondence of words and things, and the unalienated character of human speech. See Lotman and Uspensky (1977).

55 "It is impossible to translate with the same intensity the painful tenderness that is transmitted in the Quechua text. The repetition of verbs, that carry within their sound system a kind of material reflection of the movement that is produced in the most hidden recesses of an organism by pain, suffering, tears, and bending in the face of unending adversity, creates a penetrating effect within the reader because the words themselves are charged with the tortuous and ornate landscape of the Andes, and with the way this earth lives and burns in the heart of Quechua people. Being, universe and language form an undivided whole."

9 "Codo con codo"

Hispanic community and the language spectacle

José del Valle and Luis Gabriel-Stheeman

So . . .?

> No puede haber mayor concordia que el diálogo, el entendimiento, la comprensión para el respeto y la paz, y el instrumento fundamental, esencial, es la lengua, y las entidades que representan la lengua desde una perspectiva digamos oficial son las academias.[1]
> (Ignacio Chávez quoted in *El País*, 7 September 2000)

The careful reader may discern, in the background from which this image of language emerges, the shadowy silhouette of the *Other*. The image of harmony rendered by the existence of a Spanish-speaking community throughout the "mundo hispánico" forces to the margins the reality of the peripheral Peninsular tongues, the Latin American indigenous languages, and all contact varieties across the continent; it alienates them, it makes them unable to contribute to that harmonious dialogue.

In the past two centuries, Latin American nations and Spain have been involved in various processes of community construction: The creation of national cultures in a post-independence context; the development of the political and social institutions of the modern nation; the articulation of intellectual projects of cultural regeneration; and the post-colonial construction of a supranational Hispanic community. As we saw in the preceding chapters, these cultural, political and social contexts associated with community-building processes are closely intertwined with the language ideologies of Hispanic intellectuals.

One conclusion that can be drawn from the previous analyses is that these authors' visions of language shared certain fundamental principles, since they were all the product of the same monoglossic culture. They all assumed that peaceful coexistence within communities is possible inasmuch as they possess a stable and minimally variable linguistic system, and that this system must be known and accepted by those who belong or wish to belong. Consequently, they found that the specific projects of community-building in which they were engaged required the development and control of a well-defined and homogeneous language. They believed that this language would then serve as an instrument for the modernization of their community, as a symbol of that community's accomplishments, and as the unquestionable proof of its very existence. As we stated in chapter 1, different, even opposing, language ideologies, more often than not, are grounded in the same linguistic culture. We saw for example how Sarmiento's welcoming vision of linguistic fragmentation, while deeply monoglossic, was clearly different from Bello's ideal of a linguistically united Latin America; or how Arguedas' monoglossic language ideology – based on the *quechuaization* of Spanish in Peru – was in open contrast with Bello's, not to mention Valera's, Unamuno's, Pidal's and Ortega's.

Any credible analysis of language ideologies in the Hispanic world cannot obviate the hegemonic status of the vision of the Spanish language condensed in Ignacio Chávez's words: the common Spanish language, as defined by its self-appointed custodians, represents the historical and future unity of all Hispanic nations, and serves as the essential instrument for the preservation of that community as well as for the pan-Hispanic march across modernity: "Es realmente emocionante cómo la lengua está sirviendo de lugar de encuentro y no sólo como canal de comunicación. La lengua nos hace patria común en una concordia superior" (García de la Concha quoted in *El País*, 7 September 2000).[2] As the reader will surely recognize, this conception of the Spanish language shares *hispanismo*'s philosophy, in particular the idea that the Spanish language is the ultimate embodiment of the Hispanic community and the safest guarantor of its preservation. But the vision of Spanish as a communicative paradise also replicates what some intellectuals within Spain consider to be the condition *sine qua non* for the country's future as a cohesive community, a future that is constantly placed under threat by the aspirations and gains of peripheral nationalisms:

> La aceptación sin crítica de los propósitos nacionalistas, junto al oportunismo político de quienes se empeñan en que el plurilingüismo estatutario es bello, han hecho de la circunstancia española un caso único en el mundo: cómo se disuelve jubilosamente una *comunidad lingüística, que no es otra cosa que una comunidad humana y, sobre todo, es una comunidad económica*.[3]
>
> (Lodares quoted in *El País*, 19 May 2000, emphasis added)

Thus, the nationalists' demands for the promotion of their regional languages (themselves intensely monoglossic) are perceived by cultural critics such as Lodares as destructive, and as a menace to Spain's status within the concert of modern, developed nations.

As we attempted to show in previous chapters, this language ideology, predominant at the beginning of the twenty-first century, can be traced back to the writings of authors such as Valera, Unamuno, Pidal and Ortega. The unity and uniformity of the Spanish language, the responsibility of Spanish intellectuals to assume a leading role in its standardization, the importance of safeguarding its unity and purity, are recurrent themes in the linguistic discourse of these authors. Throughout the book we have seen how for the textual construction and legitimization of this ideology, Hispanic intellectuals often resorted in various degrees to the legitimizing power of science and rhetoric.[4] Their contemporary disciples continue to brace their discourse with the still legitimizing field of linguistics and philology; it is no coincidence that, in recent years, most of the public discussions of language matters have been authored by renowned Spanish professors of these disciplines: Manuel Alvar, Víctor García de la Concha, Rafael Lapesa, Fernando Lázaro Carreter, Juan M. Lope Blanch, Angel López García, Gregorio Salvador, etc. However, the power of these contemporary voices does not solely rest on the prestige of science any more; our contemporaries can now also invoke their intellectual predecessors (often their mentors) to legitimize their vision of language (and of themselves):

> Hace un siglo, cuando los hombres del 98 estaban preocupados por el problema de España, ¿qué hicieron? Preocuparse por el lenguaje. ¿Qué hizo Ortega en el programa de renovación? Convocar a lo que él llamaba la aristocracia en la plazuela.[5]
> (García de la Concha quoted in *El País*, 6 July 1999)

Here lies the reason behind the critical analysis that we have produced in the previous chapters. Only by reaching a clear understanding of the ideological foundations underlying the linguistic reasoning of authors such as Unamuno, Pidal and Ortega can we understand contemporary language ideologies and language conflicts in Latin America and Spain. The unquestioning rendition of these figures produces the "founding-father effect": not only a sanctification of the individuals but also a demonization of anyone who dares to question or challenge the absolute truth of their intellectual legacy.

Language *grandeur*: Spanish on three battlefronts

Although different language ideologies – different belief systems regarding the linguistic configuration of specific Hispanic communities and of the Hispanic community as a whole – have emerged throughout the nineteenth and twentieth centuries, the one produced by the *founding fathers* has successfully countered and overpowered all challenges to its hegemony. In fact, as we will attempt to show below, this persistent, and still prevailing, image is the very model against which contemporary intellectuals have delineated their own representation of Spanish.

In tracing the contours of this newer version of the older image we first encounter a determined insistence on the *grandeur* and *universality* of the Spanish language. Contemporary language authorities present Spanish as a symbol of the past accomplishments and bright outlook of Hispanic culture and as an instrument that will provide the means to attain that future (cf. chapter 5). At the outset of the twenty-first century, nothing represents the future – progress and modernity – better than computer technology. Consequently, any event that associates the Spanish language with the digital world is presented as a new landmark, as a new victory in the field of new information technologies. Recent feats such as the agreement between the RAE and Microsoft's mogul, Bill Gates, are displayed by the Spanish press as glorious victories for the Spanish language in the international arena.[6] Gates' 1999 visit to the Academy was hailed in Madrid's daily *El País* with the following headline: "BILL GATES Y LA ACADEMIA FIRMAN UN ACUERDO PARA *MEJORAR EL ESPAÑOL QUE USA MICROSOFT*: EL EMPRESARIO ESTADOUNIDENSE VISITA A LA REAL ACADEMIA ESPAÑOLA Y *ALABA SU NIVEL TECNOLÓGICO*" (*El País*, 16 October 1999, emphases added).[7] Gates' visit was a victory in a double sense: on one hand, he acknowledged the Academy's authority as an indisputable reference in any of Microsoft's undertakings involving Spanish; on the other, the Great Prophet of Silicon Valley augured the Academy's exemplary presence in the digital "road ahead":

> Microsoft está muy preocupada por mejorar siempre su calidad. Los usuarios de lengua española nos han dicho hace tiempo que quieren tener *el mejor español posible* en sus ordenadores. Así que estamos encantados de incorporar a nuestros programas el mejor español. Y entusiasmados de establecer una sociedad, que será muy fructífera en el futuro, con *esta institución, cuyo nivel tecnológico es formidable*.[8]
>
> (Bill Gates quoted in *El País*, 16 October 1999, emphasis added)

The RAE is not the only institution that has recognized the importance of associating the Spanish language with new technologies. Fernando Rodríguez Lafuente, Director of the *Instituto Cervantes* since 1999, stated that the spread of Spanish and the consolidation of its international prestige are fundamental objectives for his institution.[9] He made clear, in unforgiving military terms, his determination to "'ganar la batalla de la lengua'. 'Una batalla, por cierto, en la que unos suben y otros bajan: acabo de leer que se cierran 11 institutos Goethe'" (Rodríguez Lafuente quoted in *El País*, 4 October 1999).[10] A strategic high ground in this battle is precisely computer technology's most visible field of application: "[Lafuente] quiere que 'el español se convierta en el referente de la cultura castellana en el mundo, y como soporte para su expansión utilizaremos Internet'" (*El País*, 4 October 1999).[11] One of the most concrete steps taken in the direction of conquering cyberspace has been the recent agreement between *Telefónica* and the *Instituto Cervantes*.[12] As part of this agreement, the *Cervantes* will create a special office to promote technological research and e-trade, and to survey the presence of Spanish on the Internet.

In addition to the presence of Spanish in the field of new technologies, the public discourse on language consistently celebrates and highlights the international dissemination that Lafuente yearns for. Recently, summarizing the conclusions of the essays included in the *Instituto Cervantes' Anuario 2000* (Instituto Cervantes 2000), *El País* opened one of its editorials with a most optimistic prognosis:

> El castellano goza de muy buena salud en el mundo. En Estados Unidos se consolida como segunda lengua; sus perspectivas en Brasil son halagüeñas, sobre todo si se convierte en lengua obligatoria en la segunda enseñanza, y en muchos países de Europa y de Asia su aprendizaje es demandado por un número creciente de estudiantes. Cerca de cuatrocientas [*sic*] millones de personas hablan hoy castellano en el mundo.[13]
>
> (*El País*, 9 July 2000)

The presence and importance of Spanish in the United States are favorite topics among Spanish journalists and language authorities (the fact that one of the battles in the contemporary language war is being fought precisely against English is, of course, not unrelated). The presence of a large and seemingly growing Spanish-speaking population in the North American nation is interpreted and joyfully presented as a linguistic challenge to the almighty *lingua franca*. On 11 May 1999, *El País* introduced an article with the following headline: "LOS EXPERTOS CREEN QUE ESTADOS UNIDOS TIENE MIEDO A LA EXPANSIÓN DEL ESPAÑOL."[14] The undeniable tabloid-like tone in which the article is presented betrays the competitive impulses behind these reports. With such triumphal presentation of the alleged conflict between Spanish and English, the press contributes to the *agrandissement* of the former, to the creation of an image of international prestige and power. Another example of this rhetoric of rivalry comes from Spain's post-Almodóvar Oscar buzz. Stung by Billy Cristal's witty remark on the Spanish film director's unique rendering of the English language ("makes Benigni sound like an English teacher"), Juan Cruz counterattacked in the following terms:

> ¿Y Billy Cristal? ¿Habla español? Según se desprende de lo que se oyó estos días en Madrid es posible que lo necesite muy pronto para pedir una pizza en Nueva York o en Los Ángeles, para pedir el ticket del metro en Chicago, para circular por la vida e, incluso, por los platós de Hollywood. Porque ellos [Americans] creyeron que el inglés sería la lengua avasalladora y ya les está saliendo el tiro por la culata. ¿De veras? Hay datos, dicen, que llevan al optimismo sobre la lejana pero posible equiparación de las lenguas.[15]
>
> (Cruz quoted in *El País*, 6 May 2000)

Cruz's rhetorical manipulation of the presence of Spanish – the very complex life of this language – in the United States is not unique. In fact, this overstated linguistic prowess reaches at times the most unexpected levels of absurdity: "Seguramente Ricky Martin, en estos momentos, es una de las personalidades que más está influyendo en el imparable avance del castellano en el mundo, más en concreto en los mercados anglófonos" (*El País*, 27 April 2000).[16] We are very confident that millions of people all over the world are now familiar with the Spanish phrase "la vida loca" (in fact, what they are probably singing is "*living* la vida loca"). The author of this article seems to have overlooked the important fact that Ricky Martin is counted in the ranks of the cross-over artists, as an example of latinos who are able to succeed among the mainstream US public. We cannot help but wonder whether cross-over artists such as Mr. Martin are not in fact spearheading the prompt assimilation of Hispanics into the dominant anglo culture, thus doing very little for the promotion of Spanish in the United States.

The World Wide Web and the United States are, thus, two major fronts in which the language battle is being waged. Yet, in the public discourse that we are describing, a third front has been opened and given equal if not greater weight than the other two: "La trinidad que velará para que se consolide como segundo idioma universal tras el inglés, está formado [*sic*] por Brasil, Estados Unidos e Internet, según maneja el Instituto Cervantes" (*El País*, 27 July 2000).[17] In the last few years, the Spanish media have faithfully reported any news coming from Brazil on the presence of and growing interest in Spanish in that country. In the year 2000, reports have revolved around a specific issue: the possible passing of a law that would make the study of Spanish mandatory in Brazilian schools. Assuming a favorable outcome, openly triumphant headlines such as "EL ESPAÑOL *CONQUISTA* BRASIL" (*El País*, 5 August 2000, emphasis added) have reminded readers of long-gone colonial days when the Spanish Crown reigned over "almost" the entire American continent; for the author of this headline, at the beginning of the twenty-first century, the inexorable growth of the Spanish language seems to be completing the imperial mission that History had once stalled. But all empires must prove their strength by defeating worthy opponents and effectively manoeuvering against courtly intrigues. As an 18 June 2000 article reports, the fighting and scheming have already begun:

> Conscientes de la importancia de lo que está en juego, el Reino Unido e Italia, pero especialmente Francia, han movilizado su maquinaria diplomática para impedir que Brasil se decante, quizá de forma irreversible, hacia el mundo hispano. El resultado de esta feroz batalla se presenta incierto.[18]

(*El País*, 18 June 2000)

The "Brazil campaign" has indeed been intense, as Spanish institutions eagerly pursued the sympathy and trust of Brazilian legislators. President

Fernando Henrique Cardoso, for example, was awarded the *Príncipe de Asturias* prize for Cooperation, as a result of his efforts to promote Spanish in Brazil (*El País*, 14 July 2000); and the Spanish Monarchs visited the South American nation to stimulate "la cooperación económica y el auge del castellano" (*El País*, 14 July 2000).[19] The Spanish foreign-policy machinery seems to have effectively counterattacked, deploying its elite diplomatic team: the Crown.

The contemporary public discourse on language is thus projecting an image of Spanish that, as anticipated above, focuses on its *grandeur*. Like the modern nation conceived by nineteenth-century liberal capitalism, as defined by Hobsbawm (1990), contemporary Spain must prove its viability by associating itself with the forces of modernity and by demonstrating its capacity for expansion. The Internet, the Hispanic population of the United States, and Brazilian school children have become the new frontiers to be conquered, and the Spanish language has been presented as the avant-garde of the conquering armies: "Brasil tiene 165 millones de habitantes, de los que 50 millones son estudiantes, y hará falta preparar a cerca de 200.000 profesores de español. Detrás irán la industria del libro, del cine y de la música" (Rodríguez Lafuente quoted in *El País*, 4 October 1999).[20]

The fragility of language: the need for a linguistic elite

These skirmishes in which the Spanish language has engaged reveal that its importance goes well beyond that of a merely cultural phenomenon. The international prestige of Spain and the Hispanic community, as well as their economic prospects, are made to rely, to a great extent, on the language's qualities and accomplishments. The stakes are too high. Spanish is too valuable to be left at the mercy of its speakers: "El castellano no está empobrecido. Es riquísimo. Puede estarlo el uso que los hablantes hacen de él" (García de la Concha quoted in *El País*, 4 June 2000).[21] The implications of this last statement are clear: for Víctor García de la Concha, present Director of the RAE, people and their language live in fragile coexistence. It is therefore imperative that the populace be constantly surveilled by watchful sentinels, and that the language treasure be protected by heavily armed guards (cf. chapters 5 and 7).

Alex Grijelmo, author of *Defensa apasionada del idioma español* (1998) and Chief Editor of the Madrid daily *El País*, blames his own colleagues, journalists, for the deterioration of the Spanish language: "Jamás tan pocos tuvieron tanta capacidad para deteriorar el lenguaje" (quoted in *El País*, 24 January 1999).[22] For the former Director of the RAE, Fernando Lázaro Carreter, language decline "no sólo se da entre los periodistas, sino entre los curas, los notarios, los médicos . . . Los periodistas no son más que un espejo de lo que está ocurriendo en la sociedad" (quoted in *El País*, 24 January 1999).[23] Lázaro Carreter's successor, Víctor García de la Concha, identifies yet another culprit: "en el origen del problema está . . . el hecho de que los jóvenes se expresen cada vez peor y se hayan refugiado en el taco como única argumentación" (quoted in *El País*, 19 March 1999).[24] In July of 1999, during the opening ceremonies for Universidad Complutense's summer courses (in El Escorial, of all places!), García de la Concha voiced, once again, his concerns over the health of the Spanish language. The headline with which *El País* reported on don Víctor's speech read as follows: "GARCÍA DE LA CONCHA ALERTA SOBRE . . . EL EMPOBRECIMIENTO DEL LENGUAJE" (*El País*, 6 July 1999).[25]

But there seems to be hope. In the same speech, the Spanish professor offered as an inspirational example an old Chinese story: "Tzu-lu preguntó a Confucio: 'Maestro, si el duque de Wei te llamara para gobernar su reino, ¿cuál sería la medida que tomarías?'. Y Confucio le respondió: 'Cambiar el lenguaje del pueblo'" (*El País*, 6 July 1999).[26] For de la Concha, the role of the linguistic elite is crucial in the process of changing the language of the people: He deems essential the reconnection between the people and the illuminated intellectual elite – "cuando los hombres del 98 estaban preocupados por el problema de España, ¿qué hicieron? preocuparse por el lenguaje. ¿Qué hizo Ortega en el programa de renovación? Convocar a lo que él llamaba la aristocracia en la plazuela" (quoted in *El País*, 6 July 1999).[27] He also urges for the effective improvement of education: "[García de la Concha] añora los años en que se creó la Institución Libre de Enseñanza y cómo se potenciaba la calidad de la expresión en el ámbito educativo, algo de lo que hoy se carece" (*El País*, 1 November 1999).[28]

The first step towards behavioral change is self-awareness. The impressive commercial success of Lázaro Carreter's *El dardo en la palabra* (1997) – a compilation of articles addressing common doubts and censoring frequent "errors" of language use – was interpreted by the media as a clear indication that the worst is over, and that people are beginning to recognize their linguistic limitations and the need for an authority that leads the way. "LOS ESPAÑOLES RECUPERAN SU AMOR POR EL LENGUAJE"[29] claims the headline that celebrates the sale of 250,000 copies of *El dardo*. "¿A qué se debe este afán por el buen uso del idioma?" wonders the author of the article; and he allows Lázaro to answer: "Parece que ahora hay una conciencia colectiva, un mecanismo de alarma ante el deterioro de la lengua" (Lázaro Carreter quoted in *El País*, 24 January 1999).[30] A few months later, commenting on the enormous commercial success of three reference publications – *Diccionario del español actual*, *Ortografía de la lengua española* and *Gramática descriptiva de la lengua española* – Manuel Seco, member of the RAE, expressed the same view: "Hay un sentimiento generalizado de no dominar el idioma" (quoted in *El País*, 1 November 1999).[31]

The language pyramid, ignorance and disloyalty

As we discussed in chapter 1, all language standardization processes go through the stages of selection, codification, elaboration and acceptance; in fact, as Moré argued in chapter 3, the distinction between these phases is not always clear-cut as they often overlap and coincide. We also highlighted the strategic but often understated importance of the last phase, since without the successful implementation of acceptance strategies, selection, codification and elaboration become fruitless pursuits.

It is characteristic of monoglossic communities that the people and institutions involved in standardization produce an image of the language that evokes a pyramid-like structure. At the top of the pyramid we find the norm, that is, a minimally variable grammar that functions not only as the preferred system of communication but also as a symbol of the community and its culture. The linguistic behavior of the ideal community member is supposed to approach this model. The bottom of the linguistic pyramid represents folk varieties, the uneducated speech associated with the socio-economically unfit and the marginal. The natural divisiveness of the bottom varieties must be constantly countered by the unifying force of the superior norm holding the linguistic community together. Maintenance of the linguistic order of monoglossic societies thus requires the proper balance between these forces. In such communities, certain types of linguistic behaviors become highly stigmatized: traces of bottom varieties in contexts in which the norm would be expected tend to be considered signs of intellectual incompetence. Similarly, the appearance of linguistic forms alien to the language – coming from outside the linguistic pyramid – is perceived as a sign of disloyalty: "Por arriba, ese aluvión de anglicismos innecesarios, y, por abajo, el empobrecimiento del habla del pueblo, de las clases juveniles y de tantas capas de la sociedad" (García de la Concha quoted in *El País*, 6 July 1999).[32]

Spanish language authorities, as we saw above, must secure acceptance of the norm and the ideology that supports it, that is, they must perpetuate the hierarchy implicit in the pyramid metaphor. Just as Bello had justified the need for his grammar on the basis of improper use and the danger of fragmentation, contemporary speakers are constantly reminded – through the press and affordable publications – of their linguistic ignorance, of their position in the lower half of the pyramid: "En todas las épocas se ha acusado a las nuevas generaciones de maltratar el idioma, pero la situación ahora es más grave que nunca" (García de la Concha quoted in *El País*, 19 March 1999).[33] That is precisely the reason why a group of illustrious philologists, grammarians and men of letters are presented as the legitimate and zealous custodians of the linguistic order. Reporting in 1997 on the *Primer Congreso Internacional de la Lengua Española*, *El País* stated that:

> La armonía reina entre los académicos, lingüistas y periodistas reunidos desde el lunes en la ciudad mexicana de Zacatecas. La búsqueda de soluciones al deterioro del español en los medios de comunicación, objetivo del congreso, se realiza en un clima de comprensión mutua. Ayer mismo brotaron las primeras propuestas prácticas.[34]
>
> (*El País*, 10 April 1997)

In addition to displays of linguistic ignorance that alter the internal hierarchy of the linguistic pyramid, language custodians vehemently condemn anyone who dares to tamper with the integrity of the linguistic norm. In this sense, proposals of orthographic reform have been dismissed as extravagant, unrealistic and disruptive. The most highly publicized recent orthographic episode occurred in 1997, when Nobel laureate Gabriel García Márquez called for a radical reform of the Spanish writing system:

> Jubilemos la ortografía, terror del ser humano desde la cuna: enterremos las haches rupestres, firmemos un tratado de límites entre la ge y jota, y pongamos más uso de razón en los acentos escritos, que al fin y al cabo nadie ha de leer lagrima donde caiga lágrima ni confundirá revólver con revolver.[35]
>
> (García Márquez quoted in *El País*, 9 April 1997)

Three years after the fact, a simple inquiry in a popular Web search engine yielded dozens of links to sites that still discuss García Márquez's proposal. Given the stature of the Colombian writer and his status as one of the greatest representatives of contemporary literature in Spanish, his speech was obviously shocking to the linguistic establishment. How could one of the most distinguished users of the Spanish language perpetrate such a flagrant act of cultural irresponsibility?

> Es un tema que no se debía tomar a la ligera. García Márquez es un extraordinario novelista, pero no tiene por qué ser igualmente extraordinario cuando habla de política o de narcotráfico, o de lingüística. Lo que propone García Márquez supondría una fractura en la cultura del español.[36]
>
> (Francisco Albizúrez in http://www.el-castellano.com/zien.html)

Another orthographic polemic broke out in April 2000, when the Academies of the Basque, Catalan and Galician languages angrily contested a number of toponyms included by the RAE in the latest edition of its *Ortografía de la lengua española* (1999). In particular, they expressed their disagreement with Spanish translations of local toponyms that had no tradition – not even among the Spanish-speaking members of those communities – and with "inappropriate" orthographic representations of those geographic names.[37] The RAE's response was twofold. On one hand, they disavowed the regional academies by questioning their authority to intervene in a matter of *Spanish* orthography: "[L]o que tenga que decir la academia gallega, catalana y vasca, que se ocupan de esas tres lenguas, acerca de lo que decida la academia de otra lengua, es como tratar de gobernarle la casa al vecino" (Gregorio Salvador quoted in *El País*, 23 April 2000).[38] On the other hand, they took the opportunity to emphasize the universal status of the Spanish language, in contrast with the regional scope of Basque, Catalan and Galician:

[L]a oficialidad allí es una oficialidad regional, mientras que la ortografía española es una ortografía de 20 naciones. En España podría estimarse la posibilidad de oficializar un tipo de ortografía u otro, pero no les vamos a hacer escribir Baracaldo con 'k' a los argentinos o a los mexicanos.[39]

(Gregorio Salvador quoted in *El País*, 23 April 2000)

From this perspective, the intromission of the academies was tantamount to imposing on the rights of Latin American speakers of Spanish.

Another disruption of the linguistic order has come from intellectuals who have defended the legitimacy (rhetorical and communicative value) of hybrid linguistic behaviors. The most well-known variety of these is the so-called *Spanglish*, typically associated with Hispanic communities in the United States. The representatives of the dominant language ideology feel uncomfortable accepting the worthiness of Spanglish. In a recent event, Beatriz Pastor – a Spanish professor of Latin American literature at Dartmouth College (New Hampshire) – defended the practical and symbolic value of Spanglish: "[E]l spanglish no es una aberración ni una catástrofe, sino algo que fuerza la transformación del monolingüismo del poder" (Pastor quoted in *El País*, 23 November 2000).[40] Pastor's statements were received with uneasiness by Antonio Garrido, current director of the *Instituto Cervantes* in New York: "Antonio Garrido . . . se revolvía incómodo en su silla. . . . 'Dígase lo que se diga, el spanglish no es lengua canónica ni intelectual, y ningún documento serio de investigación será escrito jamás en spanglish,' comentó luego. 'O se escribe en español o se escribe en inglés'" (*El País*, 23 November 2000).[41]

The disjunction posited by Antonio Garrido reflects the distrustful and combative attitude with which Hispanic intellectuals, as we saw before, have tended to perceive the relation between the Spanish and the English languages. Much in the same way that nineteenth-century Spanish intellectuals, suspicious of French cultural influence, warned against the destructive effect of Gallicisms, their twentieth-century disciples decry the flood of Anglicisms threatening the Hispanic essence of their treasured lexicon. English loanwords are perceived both as aggressions to the dignity of Spanish and as threats to its unity: "La asunción creciente de extranjerismos y sobre todo de calcos del inglés está deteriorando nuestra lengua y está rompiendo la unidad del español," cautioned Alex Grijelmo (*El País*, 18 February 1998).[42] "El anglicismo es una injuria al español," sentenced García de la Concha in El Escorial (*El País*, 6 July 1999), with an outrage that still echoed a year later: "es vituperable . . . tomar préstamos innecesarios . . . Hay que salir al paso de esa actitud de esnobismo, que sobre todo practican los llamados ejecutivos, de decir en inglés lo que tiene 17.000 términos equivalentes en español" (García de la Concha quoted in *El País*, 19 March 2000).[43]

Of all the problems supposedly faced by the Spanish language, English loanwords have served like no other to promote the idea of unity. Grijelmo's concern, as stated in the previous paragraph, is shared by the Spanish and Latin American Language Academies. At a meeting held in Madrid in March 1999, the heads of these institutions reaffirmed their joint commitment in the battle against English: "Las academias de la lengua de los países de habla hispana están decididas a formar un frente común contra la avalancha de anglicismos innecesarios, y es en ese campo donde el futuro *Diccionario normativo de dudas* actuará 'como una fuerza de choque' y será 'muy beligerante'" (*El País*, 19 March 2000).[44]

Cultural unity and the language spectacle

In previous chapters, we saw that the unity of the Spanish language has been a central theme in the linguistic writings of Hispanic intellectuals. While some Latin Americans proposed specific national projects of linguistic regeneration, others subscribed to the maintenance of pan-Hispanic linguistic unity. However, in some cases, the defense of unity did not preclude a certain skepticism about the willingness of Spanish intellectuals to share their linguistic power with them. As recently as 1968, Argentinean philologist Angel Rosenblat still demanded equal participation for Latin Americans in the task of preserving the unity of Spanish:

> La unidad de la lengua española sólo puede ser obra de la cultura común ... La República del castellano está gobernada, no por los más, sino por los mejores escritores y pensadores de la lengua. ... Pueden participar y competir en ella, sin restricciones ni favoritismos, todos los países de lengua española.[45]
>
> (Rosenblat 1970: 69)

The voices of authors such as Cuervo, Palma and Rosenblat have certainly been heard. The rhetoric surrounding the standardization of Spanish has been intensely conciliatory in the most recent past. The moments most representative of the newly accomplished harmony were the publication and official presentation in October 1999 of the RAE's new edition of the *Ortografía*. The cultural significance of the book is noticeable even in the details of its external physical appearance. The front cover displays the title at the top and the name of the author, *Real Academia Española*, at the bottom. Between the two, in smaller but visible print, we find a most revealing statement: "Edición revisada por *las Academias* de la Lengua Española" (emphasis added).[46] The back cover is equally suggestive; the title sits at the top, followed by a list of all the Academies in the order of their foundation. Inside the book, the first two paragraphs of the prologue put into words the message conveyed visually by the front and back covers. The anonymous author of the prologue insists that this new edition has been prepared en estrecha colaboración con las corporaciones hermanas de América y de Filipinas . . . Los detallados informes de las distintas academias han permitido lograr una *Ortografía* verdaderamente panhispánica. *Apenas hay en ella novedad de doctrina*, pero se recoge, ordena y clarifica toda la que tenía dispersa la academia en los últimos tiempos, y se refuerza la atención a las variantes de uso americanas.[47]

(Real Academia Española 1999: xiii, emphasis added)

The pan-hispanist enthusiasm displayed by the *Ortografía* itself was shared by the press, which insisted in the landmark character of the publication. *El País* reiterated that the participation of all the academies in the revision of the text was final proof of the consolidation of the unity of the language: "Todos coinciden ahora en que el acercamiento de posturas entre unos y otros, junto a una mayor tolerancia en las reglas sobre acentos . . . despejan definitivamente cualquier temor sobre una fragmentación del español" (*El País*, 9 October 1999).[48] The most surprising aspect of the *Ortografía* spectacle – what actually turns the book presentation into a *mere* spectacle – is the fact that the "new" orthography changes practically nothing from the old orthography. Only a few accentuation rules affecting a small handful of words were modified. Yet, this publication was presented as the ultimate act of linguistic integration:

Rodeados por una espesa niebla matutina, los 22 responsables de las academias del español aprobaron ayer en el monasterio riojano de San Millán de la Cogolla, lugar al que se peregrina como cuna del castellano, la nueva Ortografía de la lengua española. Una edición revisada y consensuada por todas las academias, que, con algunos pequeños cambios en materia de acentos, acerca las normas de todos los países que comparten el idioma español.[49]

(*El País*, 9 October 1999)

In spite of the efforts of the *académicos* to project an image of Pan-Hispanic harmony and linguistic cooperation, the event betrayed itself. How to interpret the symbolic character of San Millán de la Cogolla and the nature of the "cradle" metaphor if not as a reproduction of the old linguistic hierarchies that placed Spain and its variety of Spanish in the privileged top of the linguistic pyramid? During the ceremony, the then minister of Education and Culture, Mariano Rajoy, sharing the enthusiasm of the *académicos* – and giving away the true ideological meaning of the event – insisted on the "'colosal' fuerza que significa el español y la 'potencia cultural que es España'" (*El País*, 9 October 1999).[50] At another point, with a different tone, García de la Concha celebrated the historical dimension of the event by reminiscing the transatlantic trip of La Pinta, La Niña and La Santa María: "Hoy retornan las naves" (*El País*, 9 October 1999).[51]

His master's voice

The ships are back. Given recent reports on the investments of Spanish multinational corporations in Latin America, one cannot help but wonder what the cargo of those ships might be. It is no secret that the economic interests of Spanish companies across this continent have grown exponentially. The presence of *Telefónica*, Spanish publishing companies, banks, etc. is conspicuous in most large Latin American cities. This presence has certainly been noticed by the Anglo-Saxon press and its potentially negative impact intensely felt by some Latin Americans. In an article entitled "Spanish firms revive Latin America conquest," *The Washington Post* (14 February 2000) reports on "what has been dubbed the reconquista – or reconquest – of Latin America". In this article, the president of the workers' union at Banco Santiago in Chile is reported to have said "every time I turn on the lights, make a phone call, cash a check or drink a glass of water, I'm putting money into pockets in Madrid... It's as if we're a colony again, paying taxes to the Spanish crown." Precisely because of the danger that attitudes like this one pose to Spanish investments, the leaders of Spain's economic foreign policy have understood the advantages of spreading and strengthening the idea of an essential cultural unity between Spain and Latin America:

> "Spain *understands* Latin America in a way that no other country outside Latin America possibly could," said Carlos Gasco, cabinet chief of Spain's Economy Ministry in Madrid. "We have used that to our advantage to build what we see as a long-term economic connection that is only going to keep binding us closer to Latin America."
> (*The Washington Post*, 14 February 2000, emphasis added)

Although the words we quoted earlier from Rodríguez Lafuente ("Detrás irán la industria del libro, del cine y de la música"; quoted in *El País*, 4 October 1999), referred to the specific case of Brazil, there is no doubt that they could be extended to the rest of the continent. In 1995, Jesús de Polanco, president of PRISA (a Spanish media and communications multinational corporate group), emphasizing the importance of the Spanish language as communicative capital for the Hispanic community, stated that Latin America is "un objetivo político, económico y empresarial *legítimo* para los españoles" (emphasis added).[52] He emphasized in particular the importance that Spain should have in the development of the publishing industry: "Nuestro grupo está en algo que es fundamental, la industria editorial, que en América Latina es fundamentalmente española y lo más importante que ha hecho España" (Jesús de Polanco quoted in *El País*, 24 July 1995).[53] The campaigns of Spanish publishing companies to control the Latin American market, and consequently the literary and intellectual production, seem to have been fairly successful (granted, according to the reports of the Spanish press): "El interés por la cultura española es enorme en Guadalajara y el sueño de todos los escritores mexicanos es publicar en una editorial española. Anagrama, Alfaguara, Tusquets, Seix Barral son las más deseadas" (*El País*, 29 November 2000).[54]

Nothing exemplifies the marriage between business interests and cultural institutions better than the already mentioned agreement signed between Fernando Rodríguez Lafuente, Director of the *Instituto Cervantes*, and Manuel García-Durán, President of Spain's *Telefónica Media*. On 26 July 2000, *El País* reported that the Spanish multinational had agreed to give 500 million pesetas to the *Cervantes* for the promotion of the Spanish language on the Internet. This generous donation, we suspect, is not unrelated to the fact that *Telefónica* "now operates one of every four phone lines across Latin America" (*The Washington Post*, 14 February 2000). In lay words, everybody wins: thanks to *Telefónica*'s contribution, the *Cervantes* can further promote the growth and protagonism of Spanish on the Internet and consolidate its international prestige; thanks to the *Cervantes*' promotion of Spanish as the constitutive element of the Hispanic community, *Telefónica* can present its intervention as legitimate (the "legitimacy" claimed by Polanco, and derived from the pan-Hispanic "understanding" assumed by Carlos Gasco).

The individuals and institutions that have produced the contemporary vision of the Spanish language – namely the RAE, and the *Cervantes* – are solidly grounded in the structures of political and economic power of contemporary Spain. The *Cervantes*' affiliation with the Spanish Ministry of Foreign Affairs, or this institution's reliance on generous donations by multinational corporations such as *Telefónica*, clearly tell us who the master is. With such powerful patrons, these cultural and linguistic institutions are able to project, loudly and clearly, their image of the Spanish language and the Hispanic community. The Spanish press, as our use of *El País* (owned by PRISA) has demonstrated, has been instrumental in spreading this language ideology and its hegemonic status.

Disruption and discipline

As we suggested at the beginning of the chapter, the powers that privilege this utopian image of communicative harmony muffle alternative visions, dismiss them, alienate them. Among the counterhegemonic cultural movements in the recent history of the Hispanic World we find struggles for the rights of the indigenous peoples of Latin America. Although these initiatives often demand due protagonism for the pre-Columbian languages, they have encountered little sympathy among some of the most prominent guardians of the dominant language ideology in the Spanish-speaking world. Manuel Alvar, former director of the RAE, expressed in the following terms his views on the "liberation" of the indigenous peoples of Latin America:

> México sabía mejor que nadie el valor de tener una lengua que unifique y que libere de la miseria y del atraso a las comunidades indígenas. . . .

> Salvar al indio, redimir al indio, incorporación del indio, como entonces gritaban, no es otra cosa que desindianizar al indio. Incorporarlo a la idea de un estado moderno, para su utilización en unas empresas de solidaridad nacional y para que reciba los beneficios de esa misma sociedad. ... El camino hacia la libertad transita por la hispanización.[55]
> (Alvar 1991: 17–18)

As has been common in Hispanic tradition, Alvar associates the Spanish language and culture with modernity, solidarity and freedom, that is with a model of society that guarantees progress and advancement. By the same token, he denies Indian cultures any possibility of participating in such enterprises in their own terms – in their own language and from within their own culture.

In addition to these external threats to the dominant linguistic order, recently, some internal challenges have arisen. As we have already seen, Gabriel García Márquez called in 1997 for a reform of the Spanish orthographic system. The prologue to the new *Ortografía* includes some observations that inevitably remind us of that episode:

> [S]on muchos los arbitristas de la Ortografía que acuden a esta Institución o salen a la palestra, con mejor intención que acierto, pidiendo u ofreciendo radicales soluciones a los problemas ortográficos o cebándose con fáciles diatribas en el sistema establecido.[56]
> (Real Academia Española 1999: xv)

The author of the prologue reminds those "well-intentioned individuals" who demand orthographic reform that people's customs are hard to break. More to the point, the prologuist recounts an 1843 orthographic crisis, when a group of Madrid schoolteachers ("Academia Literaria y Científica de Profesores de Instrucción Primaria") demanded and started to implement in their classrooms an orthographic system that suppressed the letters *h*, *v* and *q*.

> El asunto era demasiado serio y de ahí la inmediata oficialización de la ortografía académica, que nunca antes se había estimado necesaria. Sin esa irrupción de espontáneos reformadores con responsabilidad pedagógica, es muy posible que la Corporación española hubiera dado un par de pasos más, que tenía anunciados y que la hubieran emparejado con la corriente americana, es decir, con las directrices de Bello.[57]
> (Real Academia Española 1999: xvi)

This reference to the Academy's necessarily urgent intervention in 1843 constitutes, in our view, not a simple recollection of things past, but a reprimand and a warning to contemporary reformists such as García Márquez.

It manages to present their demands for reform as actual impediments for orthographic advancement, an objective that the RAE sees as consistent with its self-ascribed "espíritu progresivamente reformista" (Real Academia Española 1999: xviii). Is not the reference to the schoolteachers' proposal as "descabellada" (preposterous) a reprimand and a warning to past, present and future orthographic adventurers?

Another – barely publicized – challenge to the dominant linguistic order came from Arcadio Díaz Quiñones (native Puerto Rican and Professor of Spanish at Princeton University), in a series of articles written after the concession in Spain to the people of Puerto Rico of a prestigious and highly symbolic prize. The award, a recognition of the linguistic loyalty demonstrated when the island's governor declared Spanish the only official language, was denounced by Díaz Quiñones as an opportunity taken by the organizers to claim yet again Spain's spiritual power:

> Todo ello ha dado lugar, con nostalgia mal reprimida, a una rebosante oratoria que parece anunciar la recuperación de una hispanidad tendenciosa y tan abusivamente simple como la que se puso en práctica, hace ya un siglo, en el Cuarto Centenario.[58]
>
> (Díaz Quiñones 1996: 137)

This recovery of the Hispanic community is, for Díaz Quiñones, part of a *politics of forgetfulness* ("política del olvido"), a *politics of concealment* ("política de ocultamiento") (1996: 137–66). It is the result of the production of an overly simplified vision of the Spanish language and Hispanic culture that erases or displaces other memories not so peaceful, not so orderly, not so harmonic:

> A los españoles y a los puertorriqueños nos persigue demasiada historia, y demasiada historia de persecuciones y de crueldades. Nos une – y nos separa – la complicidad en el prolongado sistema esclavista que dominó hasta bien entrado el siglo 19, una historia casi totalmente ignorada en España.[59]
>
> (Díaz Quiñones 1996: 138)

Without rejecting the Spanish language as one of the elements constitutive of Caribbean identities, Díaz Quiñones asserts the existence of "una lengua española *diferente*, un *idioma blando y chorreoso*" (139).[60] This *other* Spanish, its value, its power as a communicative and symbolic instrument, is minimized when not forgotten by the dominant ideology: "Esto me lleva a lo que considero el olvido más inquietante en estas celebraciones del idioma oficial *único*, que es el posible olvido de la mezcla e hibridez de nuestra lengua, y de nuestros muchos grados de bilingüismo" (Díaz Quiñones 1996: 144).[61]

As the García Márquez episode and Díaz Quiñones' ideas illustrate, reprimands and warnings, and the power of the institutions that utter them, do not always deter perfectly able yet unorthodox thinkers who decide to voice their disagreement with the dominant linguistic culture. We indicated before how, in the orthography incident, the Colombian's intervention was countered with criticisms and diatribes intended to publicly ridicule and discredit his suggestions. The prestige of the Nobel laureate, the media attention he would inevitably attract, demanded such emphatic responses. However, in cases such as the Princeton professor's criticisms, the dissenting individuals may not be surrounded with the glamour and popular admiration of García Márquez; these disruptive voices are thus doomed to remain in the margins of the public discourse and are consequently barely heard.

The language monarchy

It is by no means insignificant that the prize awarded to the people of Puerto Rico was the *Príncipe de Asturias*. A survey of the recent recipients of this prize seems to indicate that it has become a valuable instrument for rewarding acts of loyalty to the Spanish language. In the year 2000, nine years after granting the honor to the Puerto Rican people, the *Fundación Príncipe de Asturias* again justified its choice of honorees on the basis of their role in the defense and promotion of the Spanish language. Brazilian President Fernando Henrique Cardoso was awarded the *Príncipe de Asturias de Co-operación* "por su 'empeño' en fomentar la enseñanza del español" (*El País*, 14 July 2000),[62] and the RAE and the *Asociación de Academias de la Lengua Española* were jointly given the *Príncipe de Asturias de la Concordia*.

Not surprisingly, the Honorary President of the *Príncipe de Asturias* Foundation is the Prince of Asturias himself, the Heir to the Spanish throne. Every year, the prizes are awarded by the Prince in person during a highly publicized ceremony held in Oviedo, Asturias. Images and reports of this event, of the Prince handing the prizes to the selected few, reach practically every Spanish home, and as citizens witness this ritual, the honorees become infused, in the public eye, with the symbolic power of the Crown. The Prince hands them their reward and their legitimacy grows, their intervention in the implementation of their ("the") language ideology becomes authorized by the highest institution of symbolic power. The celebrations themselves, their echoes heard and read throughout the Spanish media, become grand opportunities for the subtle – or not so subtle – transmission of the ideological foundations of cultural hegemony.[63]

The presence of the Crown in matters of linguistic relevance is not reserved to the Prince of Asturias.[64] In fact, his father, the King, has become a key element in an intense diplomatic campaign for the international advancement and defense of the Spanish language. In July 2000, for example, the Spanish Monarchs paid an official visit to Brazil to promote "cooperation" between the two countries: "El viaje de estado de los Reyes a Brasil ha servido para favorecer el auge del castellano en ese país ... y estimular la presencia empresarial de nuestro país, convertido en el primer inversor extranjero" (*El País*, 14 July 2000).[65] The importance of King Juan Carlos in the international spread of the Spanish language and culture is also attested by the fact that he is a distinguished member of the *Instituto Cervantes* Board of Trustees. His words during the year 2000 meeting of the Board could not be more eloquent: "Ahora os convoco a internacionalizar la cultura, a que las artes, las letras, el cine, la música, la ciencia y el pensamiento sean conocidos y apreciados por todos en todas partes" (quoted in *El País*, 12 October 2000).[66] We should not lose sight of the fact that the *Instituto*'s main contribution to the internationalization of Hispanic culture is, obviously, the promotion of the Spanish language.[67] But the King's words remind us of the ultimate objective behind the linguistic campaign: the association of the Spanish language with culture and science and the improvement of its international reputation.[68]

The *Royal* Academy of the Language seems to have understood the symbolic and legitimizing power of the King: they are now as royal as ever. Víctor García de la Concha has not failed to invoke His Majesty to justify the mission of the institution and to support the image of Spain's commitment to pan-Hispanic harmony: "Desde diciembre de 1998, la RAE no hace nada sin consultar con las restantes academias, tal y como me encargó el rey Juan Carlos cuando fui elegido director" (*El País*, 7 September 2000).[69] Don Víctor's relationship with the King seems to be moving along the most productive paths. Recently, in an interview with *El País*, the RAE's director made a humorous but most suggestive gesture: "Hasta comienzos de siglo todos los directores de la Academia fueron Toisón de Oro. Le he dicho al Rey que a ver si restaura la tradición" (*El País*, 4 June 2000).[70] The *Toisón*, an old chivalric order headed by the King of Spain, evokes in a beautifully revealing manner the structures of linguistic power, the distribution of linguistic legitimacy as they have been imagined by cultural institutions. The unity of the Kingdom, safeguarded by the figure of the King, mirrors the oneness of Hispanic culture that the Spanish language guarantees. Just as the Monarchs, using their prerogatives, fulfilling their responsibility, raise to knighthood the most honorable, courageous and dexterous among their subjects, the Spanish Crown knights its linguistic nobility, who are thus declared the true champions of the cause; they literally become the "aristocracia en la plazuela" that Ortega figuratively called for and that García de la Concha so fervorously invokes. Like the knights in King Arthur's court, the knighted language nobility sit at a round table; the *Real Academia Española* and the Latin American Academias, invested with the royal recognition of the *Príncipe de Asturias*, also sit in a circle, "codo con codo,"[71] posing for a perfect picture of equality and harmonious dialogue.

Notes

1 "There can be no greater source of harmony than dialogue, understanding, tolerance for respect and peace; and the fundamental, essential instrument is language; and the institutions that represent the language from an official perspective – so to speak – are the academies."
2 "It is truly moving to see how the language is functioning as a meeting point and not only as a means of communication. The language provides a common fatherland in superlative harmony."
3 "The uncritical acceptance of nationalist objectives, together with the political opportunism of those who insist that multilingualism is beautiful, have turned Spain into a unique case in the world: the jubilant dissolution of a *linguistic community, which is nothing but a human community, and above all, an economic community*" (emphasis added).
4 This is consistent with Hobsbawm's interpretation of nationalism as a modern phenomenon. While institutions such as the *RAE* or mythological linguistic figures such as Nebrija and Covarrubias already existed, and while Spain's status as one of the old European states was unquestionable, these turn-of-the-century intellectuals had to face the challenge of constructing the notion of Spain as a modern nation.
5 "A century ago, when the men of the Generation of 98 were concerned about the problem of Spain, what did they do? They concerned themsleves with language. What did Ortega do in the renovation program? He summoned what he called the aristocracy to the street."
6 The agreement signed between the *RAE* and Bill Gates consists of four points: (1) Microsoft will use the *RAE*'s 2001 Dictionary in its products; (2) Microsoft will have access to the *RAE*'s lexical database; (3) Microsoft will incorporate other *RAE* materials to its software; and (4) the *RAE* will participate in the analysis of Microsoft's grammar checking tool, "beta tester" (*El País*, 16 October 1999).
7 "GATES AND ACADEMY SIGN AGREEMENT TO *IMPROVE SPANISH USED BY MICROSOFT*: THE AMERICAN BUSINESSMAN VISITS SPANISH ROYAL ACADEMY AND *PRAISES ITS TECHNOLOGICAL LEVEL*."
8 "Microsoft is always concerned with improving the quality of its products. Spanish-speaking users have been telling us for a long time that they want *the best Spanish possible* in their computers. Therefore, we are delighted to incorporate to our programs the best Spanish; and we are excited to establish a collaboration, that will surely be very fruitful in the future, with *this institution, whose technological level is fantastic*."
9 The *Instituto Cervantes* was created by the PSOE Spanish government in 1991. Modelled – at least to an extent – after the Goethe Institute and the Alliance Française, the Instituto's most immediate mission is to promote the Spanish language as well as Spanish and Spanish American cultures in the world. While this book was in production, the Spanish press announced that Lafuente will be replaced by Jon Juaristi, Basque writer and journalist best known for his book *El bucle melancólico*, in which he dismantled the myths that sustain Basque nationalist ideology. The Madrid daily *ABC* (20 March 2001) opened the article that reported Juaristi's appointment with the following headline: "UN VASCO QUE DEFENDERA EL ESPAÑOL EN EL MUNDO."
10 "'to win the language battle.' 'A battle which, by the way, some are winning and some are losing: I just read that they are closing 11 Goethe Institutes.'"
11 "Lafuente wants 'Spanish to become the referent of Castilian culture in the world, and we will support its expansion with the Internet.'"
12 Telefónica is Spain's main phone company. As we will see below, in the past decade it has acquired interests throughout Latin America.

13 "Castilian enjoys very good health throughout the world. In the US, it consolidates its position as the second language; its prospects in Brazil are most optimistic, especially if it becomes a mandatory language in secondary education; and in many countries in Europe and Asia, it is requested by a growing number of students. Almost four hundred million people speak Castilian in the world today."

14 "EXPERTS BELIEVE THE USA FEARS THE SPREAD OF SPANISH."

15 "And what about Billy Cristal? Does he speak Spanish? From what some people said in the past few days it seems like he may need it very soon to order a pizza in New York or Los Angeles, to buy a subway ticket in Chicago, to walk around life and even in Hollywood's studios. Because they [Americans] thought that English would be the domineering language and it is beginning to backfire. Really? There is data, they say, that let us be optimistic about the distant but possible equality between both languages."

16 "I am sure that right now Ricky Martin is one of the people doing more for the unstoppable spread of Castilian in the world, and more specifically, in the anglophone markets."

17 "The trinity that will watch over its consolidation as the second universal language after English is made up by Brazil, the United States, and the Internet, according to the Instituto Cervantes."

18 "Conscious of what is at stake, the United Kingdom and Italy, but especially France, have set their diplomatic machineries in motion in order to prevent Brazil from leaning – maybe irreversibly – towards the Hispanic world. The outcome of this crude battle is still uncertain."

19 "economic cooperation and the growth of Castilian."

20 "Brazil has a population of 165 million people, 50 million of which are students; it will be necessary to train approximately 200,000 teachers of Spanish. They will be followed by the music, film and publishing industries."

21 "Castilian is not impoverished. It is actually very rich. Maybe what is impoverished is the way people use it."

22 "Never have so few had so much power to deteriorate language."

23 "can be found not only among journalists, but also among priests, lawyers, doctors . . . Journalists are just a reflection of what is happening in society."

24 "The source of the problem is . . . the fact that young people speak worse every day and have resorted to cursing as the only argument."

25 "GARCÍA DE LA CONCHA WARNS ABOUT . . . THE IMPOVERISHMENT OF LANGUAGE."

26 "Tzu-lu asked Confucius: 'Master, if the Duke of Wei called on you to govern his kingdom, what would your first decision be?' And Confucius said: 'I would change the language of the people.'"

27 "When the men of the Generation of 98 were concerned about the problem of Spain, what did they do? They concerned themsleves with language. What did Ortega do in the renovation program? He summoned what he called the aristocracy to the street."

28 "García de la Concha mourns the years when the Institución Libre de Enseñanza was created, and how they promoted the quality of verbal expression in education, something which is missing today."

29 "SPANIARDS RECOVER THEIR LOVE FOR LANGUAGE."

30 "Where does this urge for the proper use of language come from?" "It seems like now there is a collective awareness, an alarm system against language decay."

31 "There is a widespread feeling of not having a good command of the language."

32 "At the top, the flood of unnecessary anglicisms; and at the bottom, the impoverishment of the language of the people, the younger classes and so many other strata of society."

33 "In all eras, the younger generations have been accused of abusing language; but the present situation is more serious than ever."
34 "Harmony prevails among the académicos, linguists and journalists gatherered since Monday in the Mexican city of Zacatecas. The search for solutions to the decay of Spanish in the media – which is the objective of the conference – proceeds in a climate of mutual understanding. Yesterday the first practical proposals already emerged."
35 "Let us retire the orthography, that monster that terrorizes human beings from birth: let us bury the primitive hatchets; let us sign a border treaty between *g* and *j*; and let us be more reasonable about the use of accent marks; after all, nobody will read l*a*grima instead of *lágrima* or revolver instead of *revólver*."
36 "It is a topic that should not be taken lightly. García Márquez is an outstanding novelist, but he does not have to be so outstanding when he talks about politics, drug traffic, or linguistics. García Márquez's proposal would mean a fragmentation in the culture of Spanish."
37 "Euskaltzaindia menciona ejemplos de cada uno de los casos. Sant Boi de Llobregat ha sido traducido como San Baudilio de Llobregat, 'a pesar de que esa denominación no es utilizada ni tan siquiera por los vecinos castellanohablantes de esa localidad' de Cataluña. Y el pueblo guipuzcoano de Azkoitia y la ciudad vizcaína de Barakaldo figuran también como Azcoitia y Baracaldo, pese a que las que se escriben con k son las 'únicas denominaciones oficiales reconocidas'" (*El País*, 21 April 2000).
38 "Whatever the Basque, Catalan and Galician academies – which deal with their respective languages – have to say about the decisions made by the academy of another language, it is like trying to run your neighbor's house."
39 "Their officiality is regional, while Spanish orthography is an orthography in twenty nations. In Spain, we might consider officializing one type of orthography or the other; but we cannot make Argentineans or Mexicans write Baracaldo with *k*."
40 "Spanglish is neither an aberration nor a catastrophy, but something that forces the transformation of the monolingualism of power."
41 "Antonio Garrido . . . moved uncomfortably in his chair. . . . 'No matter what they say, Spanglish is not an intellectual or canonical language; no serious research document will ever be written in Spanglish,' he said later. 'You either write in Spanish or write in English.'"
42 "The growing adoption of foreign words, especially from English, is deteriorating our language and is breaking the unity of Spanish."
43 "Anglicisms are an insult to Spanish." "It is reprehensible . . . to adopt unnecessary loanwords . . . we must stop the snobbish attitude – especially common among the so-called business executives – of saying in English something for which there are 17,000 Spanish words."
44 "The language academies of all Spanish-speaking countries are determined to join forces to confront the flood of unnecessary anglicisms, and this is the field in which the forthcoming *Diccionario normativo de dudas* will function 'as an aggressive force' and will be 'very belligerent.'"
45 "The unity of the Spanish language can only be the work of a common culture . . . The Republic of Castilian will be governed, not by the majority, but by the best writers and thinkers in the language. . . . All Spanish-speaking countries may participate and compete in it, without restrictions or favoritisms."
46 "Edition revised by *the Academies* of the Spanish Language."
47 "'in close collaboration with the sister institutions in America and the Philipines . . . The detailed reports of the various academies have allowed us to accomplish a truly pan-Hispanic *Ortografía*. It contains practically no novelty, but it brings

together, organizes and clarifies everything that the academy had produced in the past years; it also pays more attention to the varieties used in America."
48 "They all agree that bringing their respective opinions closer, together with a greater tolerance toward accent rules . . . dissipate once and for all any fear about the possible fragmentation of Spanish."
49 "Surrounded by a thick early-morning fog, the twenty-two heads of the Spanish language academies approved yesterday in the Rioja monastery of San Millán de la Cogolla – pilgrimage site as the cradle of Spanish – the new orthography for the Spanish language. This edition, – revised by all the academies and the product of a consensus among all – with a few changes in the accentuation system, brings closer the norms of all the countries that share the Spanish language."
50 "'the colossal force' that Spanish is and 'the cultural power that Spain is.'"
51 "The ships return today."
52 "[Latin America is] a *legitimate* business, economic and political objective for Spaniards."
53 "Our group is involved in a fundamental area, the publishing industry, which in Latin America is essentially Spanish and the most important thing Spain has done."
54 "There is great interest in Spanish culture in Guadalajara and the dream of all Mexican writers is to be published by a Spanish publisher. Anagrama, Alfaguara, Tusquets, Seix Barral are the most desired."
55 "Mexico knew better than anybody else the value of having a language that unifies, that liberates the indigenous communities from their backwardness and misery . . . Saving the Indian, the redemption of the Indian, the incorporation of the Indian, as they used to say, is nothing but de-Indianizing the Indian; incorporating him into the idea of the modern state, in order to use him in projects of national solidarity and so that he receives the benefits from that same society. . . . The road to freedom runs through hispanization."
56 "There are many orthographic idealists who come to this institution or to some public forum – with better intentions than ideas – demanding or offering radical solutions to orthographic problems or producing simplistic diatribes against the existing system."
57 "The matter was too serious, and that was the reason for the immediate officialization of the academy's orthography, which had never before been necessary. Had it not been for the eruption of those spontaneous reformers with pedagogical responsibilities, it is very likely that the Spanish academy would have taken a couple of steps that had already been announced, and that would have brought it closer to the American trend, that is to say, with Bello's guidelines."
58 "All of this has generated – with a barely hidden nostalgia – a boasting oratory that seems to announce the recovery of a tendentious hispanidad and that is as abusively simple as the one practiced one century ago during the Fourth Centennial."
59 "Spaniards and Puerto Ricans carry too much history on our shoulders, too much history of persecutions and cruelties. We share a common complicity in the system of slavery that lasted well into the nineteenth century, a history almost completely ignored in Spain."
60 "a *different* Spanish language, a *liquid and juicy* language."
61 "This leads me to what I consider to be the most disquieting omission in this celebration of Spanish as the *only* official language; the possible omission of the mixed and hybrid character of our language and of our various degrees of bilingualism."
62 "for his determination in promoting the teaching of Spanish."
63 The citizen is presented, under the guise of a news piece, with what in essence is no more than an "infommercial". In other words, the news creates itself. One of the

principal goals of standardization processes is earning the consent of the people. As indicated in chapter 5, Ramón Menéndez Pidal – one of the founding fathers of the contemporary language ideology – clearly saw the importance of acceptance: "Cabe la propaganda en favor de tal o cual forma lingüística igual que cabe la propaganda en favor de tal o cual idea política."

64 Prince Felipe is also Honorary President of the Fundación San Millán de la Cogolla, another institution created in 1998 for the promotion of the Spanish language.

65 "The Monarchs' official trip to Brazil has served to promote Castilian in that country . . . and to stimulate the presence of companies from our country, which is now the main foreign investor there."

66 "Now I call upon you to internationalize our culture; to make our arts, letters, cinema, music, science and thought known and appreciated by everyone everywhere."

67 The emphasis on the international character of the Spanish language entails the erasure of the power relations which explain its history and its present status as a dominant language. While this book was in production, the contradictions implied in the discourse of universality came to the surface when King Juan Carlos, participating in the 2001 *Cervantes* prize spectacle, stated: "Nunca fue la nuestra lengua de imposición sino de encuentro; a nadie se le obligó nunca a hablar en castellano: fueron los pueblos más diversos quienes hicieron suyo, por voluntad libérrima, el idioma de Cervantes" (*El País*, 25 April 2001; "Ours was never an imposed language but one which represented the chance to meet on common ground. No one was ever obliged to speak Castilian, it was the free will of the different peoples and nations to make the language of Cervantes their own.") It is beautifully ironic that in response to the outraged reaction of Catalan and Basque nationalists, the Spanish Royal House hurried to clarify that the King's words referred not to the relationship between Spanish and other Iberian languages but to the expansion of Spanish in the Americas.

68 In the same vein, the King had also given his royal endorsement to the "Primer Congreso de la Lengua Española," held in April of 1997 in Zacatecas, Mexico, a gathering of Spanish and Latin American writers, linguists and journalists intended to strengthen the international image of the Spanish language and to discuss the issues associated with its presence and use in the media.

69 "Since December 1998, the *RAE* does not make any decisions without consulting with the other academies; just as King Juan Carlos asked me to do when I was elected director."

70 "Until the beginning of the century, all the directors of the Academy were members of the Toisón. I have asked the King to reinstate the tradition."

71 On 7 September 2000, *El País* reported on García de la Concha praising the Spanish and Latin American members of the language academies and describing them as working side by side ("codo con codo").

References

Abeille, L. (1900) *El idioma nacional de los argentinos*, Paris: Émile Bouillon.
Adkins, A. W. H. (1962) "Heidegger and Language," *Philosophy* 37: 229–37.
Adorno, R. (1986) *Guaman Poma, Writing and Resistance in Colonial Peru*, Austin: University of Texas Press.
Alemany, J. (1903) *Estudio elemental de gramática histórica de la lengua castellana*, Madrid: Revista de Archivos, Bibliotecas y Museos.
Alonso, A. (1935) *El problema de la lengua en América*, Madrid: Espasa-Calpe.
—— (1951) "Introducción a los estudios gramaticales de Andrés Bello," in A. Bello, *Obras completas*, Caracas, La Casa de Bello, 1981, vol. 4, ix–lxxxvi.
Altamirano, C. and Sarlo, B. (1994) "The Autodidact and the Learning Machine," in T. Halperín Donghi *et al.* (eds), *Sarmiento: Author of a Nation*, Berkeley: University of California Press, 156–68.
Alvar, M. (1991) *El español de las dos orillas*, Madrid: Mapfre.
Anderson, B. (1983) *Imagined Communities: Reflections on the Origin and Spread of Nationalism*, London and New York: Verso.
Araya, G. (1971) *Claves filológicas para la comprensión de Ortega*, Madrid: Gredos.
Arguedas, J. M. (1935) "El wayno y el problema del idioma en el mestizo," in *Nosotros los maestros*, Lima: Editorial Horizonte, 1986.
—— (1939a) "Entre el kechwa y el castellano la angustia del mestizo," in *Nosotros los maestros*, Lima: Editorial Horizonte, 1986.
—— (1939b) "Los doce meses. Un capítulo de Guaman Poma de Ayala, versión de las frases kechwas e interpretación del estilo," in *Indios, mestizos y señores*, Lima: Editorial Horizonte, 1985.
—— (1940) "Pumaccahua," in *Nosotros los maestros*, Lima: Editorial Horizonte, 1986.
—— (1944) "El método para el caso lingüístico del indio peruano," in *Nosotros los maestros*, Lima: Editorial Horizonte, 1986.
—— (1950) "La novela y el problema de la expresión literaria en el Perú," *Mar del Sur*, 3.9: 66–72.
—— (1952) "El Ollantay. Lo autóctono y lo occidental en el estilo de los dramas coloniales quechuas," *Letras Peruanas* 8: 139–40.
Arnoux, E. and Lois, E. (1996) "Retórica del discurso polémico y construcciones de identidad nacional (a propósito de derivaciones polémicas de la reforma ortográfica propuesta por Sarmiento en Chile)," Ms. of 12 pp. of a paper presented at "Polémiques et manifestes en Amérique latine, XIXe. et XXe. Siècles." Colloque international du CRICCAL, Paris, Sorbonne: 29, 30 and 31 March 1996.
Baker, G. and Hacker, P. (1984) *Language, Sense and Nonsense*, Oxford: Blackwell.
Barrenechea, A. M. *et al.* (1997) *Epistolario inédito Sarmiento-Frías*, Buenos Aires: Universidad de Buenos Aires, Facultad de Filosofía y Letras, Instituto de Filología y Literaturas Hispánicas "Dr. Amado Alonso."

Basadre, J. (1980) *La multitud, la ciudad y el campo en la historia del Perú*, Lima: Mosca Azul.
Bauman, R. and Briggs, C. L. (2000) "Language Philosophy as Language Ideology: John Locke and Johann Gottfried Herder," in P. V. Kroskrity (ed.), *Regimes of Language: Ideologies, Polities, and Identities*, Santa Fe, NM: School of American Research Press.
Bello, A. (1823) "Indicaciones sobre la conveniencia de reformar y uniformar la ortografía en América," in *Obras completas*, Caracas: La Casa de Bello, 1981, vol. 5, 69–87.
—— (1827) "Ortografía castellana," in *Obras completas*, Caracas: La Casa de Bello, 1981, vol. 5, 89–96.
—— (1830) "La oración inaugural del curso de oratoria del Liceo de Chile de José Joaquín de Mora. III," in *Obras completas*, Caracas: La Casa de Bello, 1981, vol. 9, 299–335
—— (1832) "Gramática castellana," in *Obras completas*, Caracas: La Casa de Bello, 1981, vol. 5, 173–84.
—— (1833–4) "Advertencias sobre el uso de la lengua castellana dirigidas a los padres de familia, profesores de los colegios y maestros de escuela," in *Obras completas*, Caracas: La Casa de Bello, 1981, vol. 5, 145–71.
—— (1835) *Principios de la ortología y métrica de la lengua castellana*, in *Obras completas*, Caracas: La Casa de Bello vol. 6, 3–546.
—— (1841) "Análisis ideológica de los tiempos en español," in *Obras completas*, Caracas: Ministerio de Educación, vol. 6, 3–67.
—— (1842a) "Ejercicios populares de lengua castellana," in J. Durán Cerda (ed.), *El movimiento literario de 1842*, Santiago de Chile: Editorial Universitaria, 1957, vol. 1, 241–3.
—— (1842b) "Ejercicios populares de lengua castellana," in *Obras completas*, Caracas: Casa de Bello, vol. 9, 435–40.
—— (1847) *Gramática de la lengua castellana destinada al uso de los americanos*, in *Obras completas*, Caracas: La Casa de Bello, 1981, vol. 4, 1–382.
—— (1849) "Reformas ortográficas," in *Obras completas*, Caracas: La Casa de Bello, 1981, vol. 5, 133–43.
—— (1981) *Gramática de la lengua castellana destinada al uso de los americanos*, edición crítica de Ramón Trujillo, Tenerife: Instituto Universitario de Lingüística Andrés Bello, Cabildo Insular de Tenerife.
—— (1997) *Selected Writings of Andrés Bello*, trans. F. M. López-Morillas, New York: Oxford University Press.
Benedict, R. (1934) *Patterns of Culture*, New York: Penguin Books.
Betancur, C. (1964) "Lenguaje y verdad en Unamuno," in P. G. Valderrama (ed.), *Unamuno en Colombia*, Bogotá: Instituto Colombiano de Cultura Hispánica, 69–89.
Blanco Aguinaga, C. (1954) *Unamuno, teórico del lenguaje*, El Colegio de México.
Blommaert, J. and Verschueren, J. (1991) "The pragmatics of minority politics in Belgium," *Language in Society* 20: 503–31.
—— (1998) "The Role of Language in European Nationalist Ideologies," in B. B. Schieffelin, K. A. Woolard and P. V. Kroskrity (eds), *Language Ideologies: Practice and Theory*, New York and Oxford: Oxford University Press.
Bolinger, D. (1980) *Language, the Loaded Weapon*, London: Longman.
Borges, J. L. (1941) "Las alarmas del doctor Américo Castro," in *Obras completas*, Barcelona: Emecé, 1989, vol. 2, 31–5.

Bourdieu, P. (1977) *Outline of a Theory of Practice*, trans. R. Nice, Cambridge: Cambridge University Press.
—— (1991) *Language and Symbolic Power*, ed. J. B. Thompson, trans. G. Raymond and M. Adamson, Cambridge, Mass.: Harvard University Press.
Bourricaud, F. (1989) *Poder y sociedad en el Perú*, Lima: Instituto de Estudios Peruanos.
Bunkley, A. W. (1966) *Vida de Sarmiento*, Buenos Aires: EUDEBA.
Caballero Wanguemert, M. M. (1989) "Las polémicas lingüísticas durante el siglo XIX," *Cuadernos Hispanoamericanos* 500: 177–87.
Cabrera Perera, A. (1989) "Unamuno y la Real Academia Española," in D. Gómez Molleda (ed.), *Actas del Congreso Internacional Cincuentenario de Unamuno*, Universidad de Salamanca, 417–19.
Cambours Ocampo, A. (1983) *Lenguaje y nación*, Buenos Aires: Marymar.
Cameron, D. (1995) *Verbal Hygiene*, London and New York: Routledge.
Carilla, E. (1964) *Lengua y estilo en Sarmiento*, La Plata: Facultad de Humanidades y Ciencias de la Educación, Universidad Nacional de La Plata.
Carr, R. (1982) *Spain: 1808–1975*, 2nd edn, Oxford: Clarendon.
Cassullo, C. (1962) "Sarmiento y las lenguas vivas," *Universidad* (Universidad Nacional del Litoral) 52, 149–74.
Castro, A. (1941) *La peculiaridad lingüística rioplatense y su sentido histórico*, Buenos Aires: Losada.
—— (1948) *España en su historia: Cristianos, moros y judíos*, Buenos Aires: Losada.
Castro-Klarén, S. (1977) "Mundo y palabra: hacia una problemática del bilingüismo en Arguedas," *Runa* 6: 8, 9, 10, 39.
Cerrón-Palomino, R. (1987) "Multilingüismo y política idiomática en el Perú," *Allpanchis* 29/30: 17–44.
Chatterjee, P. (1993) *Nationalist Thought and the Colonial World*, Minneapolis: University of Minnesota Press.
Chaves, J. C. (1964) *Unamuno y América*, Madrid: Ediciones Cultura Hispánica.
Contreras, L. (1993) *Historia de las ideas ortográficas en Chile*, Santiago de Chile: Biblioteca Nacional.
Corominas, J. (1983) *Breve diccionario etimológico de la lengua castellana*, 3rd edn, Madrid: Gredos.
Costa Álvarez, A. (1922) *Nuestra lengua*, Buenos Aires: Sociedad Editorial Argentina.
Cotler, J. (1978) *Clases, estado y nación en el Perú*, Lima: Instituto de Estudios Peruanos.
Crowley, T. (1996) *Language in History: Theories and Texts*, London and New York: Routledge.
Cuervo, R. J. (1899) "Prólogo," *Nastasio*, by F. Soto y Calvo, vii–x, Chartres: Durand.
—— (1907) *Apuntaciones críticas sobre el lenguaje bogotano*, 5th edn, Paris: Roger y Chernoviz.
—— (1950) *Disquisiciones sobre filología castellana*, Bogotá: Instituto Caro y Cuervo.
Cúneo, D. (1963) *Sarmiento y Unamuno*, Buenos Aires: Editorial Pleamar.
Darío, R. (1901) "Madrid," in *Obras completas*, Madrid: Afrodisio Aguado, 1950, vol. 3, 41–3.
Deleuze, G. and Guattari, F. (1986) *Kafka Toward a Minor Literature*, trans. D. Polan, Minneapolis: University of Minnesota.
Del Valle, J. (1997) "La historificación de la lingüística histórica: Los 'orígenes' de Menéndez Pidal," *Historiographia Linguistica* 24.1/2: 175–96.

—— (1998) "Andalucismo, poligénesis y koineización: dialectología e ideología," *Hispanic Review* 66: 133–49.

—— (1999a) "La 'doble voz' de la ley fonética en la lingüística histórica española," in M. Fernández Rodríguez, F. García Gondar, and N. Vázquez Veiga (eds), *Actas del I Congreso Internacional de la Sociedad Española de Historiografía Lingüística*. Madrid: Arco Libros, 663–72.

—— (1999b) "Lenguas imaginadas: Menéndez Pidal, la lingüística hispánica y la configuración del estándar," *Bulletin of Hispanic Studies* (University of Liverpool) 76.2: 215–33.

—— (2000) "Monoglossic Policies for a Heteroglossic Culture: Misinterpreted Multilingualism in Modern Galicia," *Language and Communication* 20.1: 105–32.

Derrida, J. (1993) *Spectres de Marx: L'État de la dette, le travail du deuil et la nouvelle Internationale*, Paris: Galilée.

Díaz-Quiñones, A. (1993) *La memoria rota*, 2nd edn, San Juan: Ediciones Huracán.

Díez del Corral, L. (1968) "El joven Ortega y la filología clásica," *Revista de Occidente* 66: 265–96.

Di Tullio, A. (1988) "Precisiones acerca de la actitud de Sarmiento frente a la lengua," *Revista de lengua y literatura* (Universidad Nacional de Comahue) 4: 17–22.

Dobson, A. (1989) *Introduction to the Politics and Philosophy of José Ortega y Gasset*, Cambridge: Cambridge University Press.

Durán Cerda, J. (1957) *El movimiento literario de 1842*, Santiago: Editorial Universitario.

Echeverría, E. (1951) "La situación y el porvenir de la literatura hispanoamericana," in *Obras completas*, Buenos Aires: Antonio Zamora, 509–14.

Escobar, A. (1972) *El reto del multilingüismo en el Perú*, Lima: Instituto de Estudios Peruanos.

—— (1984) *Arguedas o la utopía de la lengua*, Lima: Instituto de Estudios Peruanos.

Fasold, R. (1987) *The Sociology of Society*, Oxford: Blackwell.

—— (1988) "What National Languages Are Good For," in F. Coulmas (ed.), *With Forked Tongues*, Singapore: Karoma, 180–5.

Fell, E. M. (1981–1982) *José María Arguedas et la culture nationale dans le Pérou contemporain (1939–1969)*, diss., L'université de la Sorbonne Nouvelle.

Fernández Larrain, S. (ed.), (1972) *Cartas inéditas de Miguel de Unamuno*, Santiago de Chile: Zig-Zag/Madrid: Rodas.

Fiddian, R.W. (1999) "Miguel de Unamuno y las letras hispanoamericanas: una visión metropolitana," in G. Paolini and C. J. Paolini (eds), *La Chispa '99: Selected Proceedings*, New Orleans: Tulane University, 113–21.

Fogelquist, D. F. (1968) *Españoles de América y americanos de España*, Madrid: Gredos.

Fontanella de Weinberg, M. B. (1988) "Las ideas lingüísticas de Sarmiento," *Filología* 28: 63–76.

Gabriel-Stheeman, L. (2000a) "La etimología como estrategia retórica en los textos políticos de Ortega y Gasset," *Revista de Estudios Orteguianos* 1: 121–33.

—— (2000b) *Función retórica del recurso etimológico en la obra de José Ortega y Gasset*, A. Coruña: Toxosoutos.

García Blanco, M. (1952) *Don Miguel de Unamuno y la lengua española. Discurso inaugural del curso académico 1952–1953*, Universidad de Salamanca.

—— (1964) *América y Unamuno*, Madrid: Gredos.

García de Cortázar, F. and González Vesga, J. M. (1999) *Breve Historia de España*, Madrid: Alianza Editorial.

García del Río, J. and Bello, A. (1823) "Indicaciones sobre la conveniencia de simplificar y uniformar la ortografía de América," in A. Bello, *Obras completas*, Caracas: La Casa de Bello, 1981, vol. 5, 69–87.
Giménez Caballero, E. (1971) *Genio de España*, Madrid: Doncel.
González Prada, M. (1889) "Notas acerca del idioma," in *Obras completas*, Lima: PTCM, 1946, vol. 1, 256–72.
González Stephan, B. (1995) "Las disciplinas escriturarias de la patria: constituciones, gramáticas y manuales, *Estudios* 3.5: 19–46.
Gramsci, A. (1985) *Selections from Cultural Writings*, ed. D. Forgacs and G. Nowell-Smith, trans. W. Boelhower, Cambridge, Mass.: Harvard University Press.
Grijelmo, A. (1998) *Defensa apasionada del idioma español*, Madrid: Taurus.
Guirao Massif, A. (1957) *Memorias de los egresados: Historia de la Facultad de Filosofía y Humanidades*, Santiago de Chile: Universidad de Chile, Facultad de Filosofía y Educación, Instituto Pedagógico, vol. 1.
Guitarte, G.L. (1980/1) "Unamuno y el porvenir del español en América," *Boletín de Filología de la Universidad de Chile* 31: 145–80.
—— (1981) "El origen del pensamiento de Rufino José Cuervo sobre la suerte del español de América," in H. Geckeler *et al.* (eds), *Logos Semantikos: Studia Linguistica in Honorem Eugenio Coseriu*, vol. 1, Madrid: Gredos; Berlin/New York: Walter de Gruyter.
Harris, R. (1980) *The Language Makers*, London: Duckworth.
—— (1981) *The Language Myth*, London: Duckworth.
Hartman, G. H. (1995) "On Traumatic Knowledge and Literary Studies," *New Literary History*, 26: 537–63.
Haugen, E. (1972) *The Ecology of Language*, Stanford, Calif.: Stanford University Press.
Henríquez Ureña, P. (1960) "Seis ensayos en busca de nuestra expresión," in *Obra crítica*, México: Fondo de Cultura Económica.
Hess, S. (1982) *Ramón Menéndez Pidal*, Boston: Twayne Publishers.
Hobsbawm, E. J. (1987) *The Age of Empire 1875–1914*, New York: Pantheon Books.
—— (1992) *Nations and Nationalism since 1780*, Cambridge: Cambridge University Press.
Holguín, A. (1964) "Unamuno y América," in P. Gómez Valderrama *et al.* (eds), *Unamuno en Colombia*, Bogotá: Instituto Colombiano de Cultura Hispánica.
Huarte Morton, F. (1954) "El ideario lingüístico de Miguel de Unamuno," *Cuadernos de la Cátedra Miguel de Unamuno* 5: 5–183.
Huerta, E. (1956) "La prosa de Ortega," *Atenea* 367–68: 48–72.
Instituto Cervantes (2000) *El Español en el Mundo: Anuario del Instituto Cervantes 2000*, Madrid: Círculo de Lectores, Instituto Cervantes y Plaza y Janés.
Iordan, I. and Orr, J. (1970) *An Introduction to Romance Linguistics, Its Schools and Scholars*, rev. by R. Posner, Berkeley and Los Angeles: University of California Press.
Irvine, J. T. and Gal, S. (2000) "Language Ideology and Linguistic Differentiation," in P. V. Kroskrity (ed.), *Regimes of Language: Ideologies, Polities, and Identities*, Santa Fe, NM: School of American Research Press.
Jaksic, I. (1994) "Sarmiento and the Chilean Press, 1841–1851," in T. Halperín Donghi, I. Jaksic *et al.* (eds), *Sarmiento: Author of a Nation*, Berkeley: University of California Press, 31–60.
Jankowski, K. R. (1972) *The Neogrammarians*, The Hague: Mouton.
Jiménez Hernández, A. (1973) *Unamuno y la filosofía del lenguaje*, Río Piedras: Editorial San Juan.

Joseph, J.E. (1989) "Four models of linguistic change," in T. J. Walsh (ed.), *Synchronic and Diachronic Approaches to Linguistic Variation and Change*, Washington, DC: Georgetown University Press.
—— (1995) "Trends in Twentieth-Century Linguistics: An Overview," in E. F. K. Koerner and R. E. Asher (eds), *Concise History of the Language Sciences: From the Sumerians to the Cognitivists*, Cambridge, UK: Pergamon.
Joseph, J. E. and Taylor, T. J. (eds), (1990) *Ideologies of Language*, London and New York: Routledge.
Jover Zamora, J.M. (1991) *La civilización española a mediados del S. XIX*, Madrid: Espasa-Calpe.
Kaplan, R. B. and Baldauf Jr., R. B. (1997) *Language Planning from Practice to Theory*, Clevedon: Multilingual Matters.
Katra, W. (1996) *The Argentine Generation of 1837: Echeverría, Alberdi, Sarmiento, Mitre*, Madison, NJ : Fairleigh Dickinson University Press.
Krauss, W. (1997a) "Falange Española und das spanische Geschichtsbild," in K. Barck (ed.), *Essays zur spanischen und französischen Literatur- und Ideologiegeschichte der Moderne*, Berlin: Walter de Gruyter.
—— (1997b) *Spanien 1900–1965, Beitrag zu einer modernen Ideologiegeschichte*, in K. Barck (ed.), *Essays zur spanischen und französischen Literatur-und Ideologiegeschichte der Moderne*, Berlin: Walter de Gruyter.
Kristal, E. (1993) "Dialogues and Polemics: Sarmiento, Lastarria, and Bello," in J. T. Criscenti (ed.), *Sarmiento and his Argentina*, Boulder, Colo., and London: Lynne Rienner Publishers, 61–70.
Kristeva, J. (1989) *Language: The Unknown*, New York: Columbia University Press.
Kroskrity, P. V. (2000) "Regimenting Languages: Language Ideological Perspectives," in P. V. Kroskrity (ed.), *Regimes of Language: Ideologies, Polities, and Identities*, Santa Fe, NM: School of American Research Press.
Lacy, A. (1967) *Miguel de Unamuno: The Rhetoric of Existence*, The Hague and Paris: Mouton & Co.
Laín, M. (1964) *La palabra en Unamuno*, Caracas: Cuadernos del Instituto de Filología "Andrés Bello," Universidad Central de Venezuela.
Lázaro Carreter, F. (1997) *El dardo en la palabra*, Barcelona: Galaxia Gutenberg: Círculo de lectores.
Linton, R. (1955) *The Tree of Culture*, New York: Alfred A. Knopf.
Lloyd, P. (1970) "The Contribution of Menéndez Pidal to Linguistic Theory," *Hispanic Review* 38: 14–21.
Lodares, J.R. (2000) *El paraíso políglota*, Madrid: Taurus.
Lope Blanch, J.M. (1997) *La lengua española y sus problemas*, México: UNAM.
López García, A. (1985) *El rumor de los desarraigados*, Barcelona: Anagrama.
Lotman, Y. M. and Uspensky, B. A. (1977) "Myth-Name-Culture," in *Soviet Semiotics*, ed. and trans. D. P. Lucid, Baltimore: Johns Hopkins University Press.
Maldonado de Guevara, F. (1957) "El lenguaje de Ortega y Gasset," *Revista de Filosofía* 60–61: 125–39.
Malkiel, Y. (1970) "Era omme esencial . . . ," *Romance Philology* 23: 371–411.
Mannheim, B. (1991) *The Language of the Inka since the European Invasion*, Austin: University of Texas Press.
Mariátegui, J. C. (1979) *Siete ensayos de interpretación de la realidad peruana*, Caracas: Biblioteca Ayacucho.

Mar-Molinero, C. (2000) *The Politics of Language in the Spanish-Speaking World*, London and New York: Routledge.
Martín, F. J. (1999) *La tradición velada: Ortega y el pensamiento humanista*, Madrid: Biblioteca Nueva.
Martínez, F. A. (1954) *Rufino José Cuervo*, with bibliography by R. Torres Quintero, Bogotá: Instituto Caro y Cuervo.
Matos Mar, J. (1974) "El indigenismo en el Perú," in J. Ortega (ed.), *Realidad nacional*, Lima: Retablo de Papel.
Maurín Navarro, J. S. (1952) *La misión de Sarmiento en Chile en 1884 y la democratización de la cultura en Sud América*, Mendoza: Instituto Cultural Sarmiento, Cuaderno no. 1, edición especial.
Menéndez Pidal, R. (1904) *Manual elemental de gramática histórica española*, Madrid: V. Suárez.
—— (1918) "La lengua española," *Hispania* 1: 1–14.
—— (1941) *Manual de gramática histórica española*, 6th edn, Madrid: Espasa-Calpe.
—— (1944) *La unidad de la lengua*, Madrid: Instituto Nacional del Libro Español.
—— (1945) *Castilla, la tradición, el idioma*, Buenos Aires: Espasa-Calpe Argentina.
—— (1950) *Orígenes del español: estado lingüístico de la Península Ibérica hasta el siglo XI*, 3rd edn, Madrid: Espasa-Calpe.
Mermall, T. (1993) "How to Do Things with Rhetoric: The Uses of Argument in Larra, Unamuno, and Ortega," *Siglo XX/20th Century* 11: 155–79.
—— (1994) "Entre epísteme y doxa: El trasfondo retórico de la razón vital," *Revista Hispánica Moderna* 67: 72–85.
—— (1996) "Abstracto/concreto: clave retórica para la comprensión de Ortega," *Revista canadiense de estudios hispánicos* 21: 181–90.
Milroy, J. and Milroy, L. (1999) *Authority in Language*, 3rd edn, London and New York: Routledge.
Morales, L. T. (1971) "José María Arguedas: El lenguaje como perfección humana," *Estudios Filológicos* 7: 133–42.
Morse, R. M. (1989) *New World Soundings: Culture and Ideology in the Americas*, Baltimore: Johns Hopkins University Press.
Mourelle Lema, M. (1968) *La teoría lingüística en la España del siglo XIX*, Madrid: Prensa Española.
Neave, G. and Rhoades, G. (1987) "The Academic Estate in Western Europe," in B. R. Clark (ed.), *The Academic Profession: National, Disciplinary, and Institutional Settings*, Berkeley: University of California Press, 211–70.
Ninyoles, R. L. (1997) *Mare Espanya: Aproximació al nacionalisme espanyol*, València: Tàndem.
Nugent, J. G. (1991) *El conflicto de las sensibilidades. Propuesta para una interpretación y crítica del siglo XX peruano*, Lima: Instituto Bartolomé de las Casas.
Ong, W. (1982) *Orality and Literacy: The Technologizing of the Word*, London and New York: Routledge.
Ortega y Gasset, J. (1908a) "El sobrehombre," in *Obras completas*, Madrid: Revista de Occidente-Alianza, 1962–83, vol. 1, 91–5.
—— (1908b) "Asamblea para el progreso de las ciencias," in *Obras completas*, Madrid: Revista de Occidente-Alianza, 1962–83, vol. 1, 99–110.
—— (1909) "Renan," in *Obras completas*, Madrid: Revista de Occidente-Alianza, 1962–83, vol. 1, 443–67.

—— (1910) "Una primera vista sobre Baroja," in *Obras completas*, Madrid: Revista de Occidente-Alianza, 1962–83, vol. 2, 103–28.
—— (1911) "Problemas culturales," in *Obras completas*, Madrid: Revista de Occidente-Alianza, 1962–83, vol. 1, 546–52.
—— (1915) *Investigaciones psicológicas*, in *Obras completas*, Madrid: Revista de Occidente-Alianza, 1962–83, vol. 12, 331–453.
—— (1918) "Estafeta romántica. Un poeta indo," in *Obras completas*, Madrid: Revista de Occidente-Alianza, 1962–83, vol. 3, 13–24.
—— (1921) *España invertebrada*, in *Obras completas*, Madrid: Revista de Occidente-Alianza, 1962–83, vol. 3, 51–128.
—— (1922) "Ideas políticas," in *Obras completas*, Madrid: Revista de Occidente-Alianza, 1962–83, vol. 11, 14–25.
—— (1924) "Las dos grandes metáforas," in *Obras completas*, Madrid: Revista de Occidente-Alianza, 1962–83, vol. 2, 387–400.
—— (1925) "Para una psicología del hombre interesante," in *Obras completas*, Madrid: Revista de Occidente-Alianza, 1962–83, vol. 4, 467–80.
—— (1926a) "Dislocación y restauración de España," in *Obras completas*, Madrid: Revista de Occidente-Alianza, 1962–83, vol. 11, 92–8.
—— (1926b) "Amor en Stendhal," in *Obras completas*, Madrid: Revista de Occidente-Alianza, 1962–83, vol. 5, 561–96.
—— (1927) "Orígenes del español," in *Obras completas*, Madrid: Revista de Occidente-Alianza, 1962–83, vol. 3, 515–20.
—— (1928) *La redención de las provincias*, in *Obras completas*, Madrid: Revista de Occidente-Alianza, 1962–83, vol. 11, 196–256.
—— (1929) *¿Qué es filosofía?*, in *Obras completas*. Madrid: Revista de Occidente-Alianza, 1962–83, vol. 7, 275–440.
—— (1930) *La rebelión de las masas*, in *Obras completas*, Madrid: Revista de Occidente-Alianza, 1962–83, vol. 4, 143–280.
—— (1931) "Antitópicos," in *Obras completas*, Madrid: Revista de Occidente-Alianza, 1962–83, vol. 11, 147–58.
—— (1932a) *The Revolt of the Masses*, trans. anonymous, New York: Norton.
—— (1932b) "Para el *Archivo de la palabra*," in *Obras completas*, Madrid: Revista de Occidente-Alianza, 1962–83, vol. 4, 366–8.
—— (1932c) "Segunda intervención sobre el Estatuto catalán (Cortes constituyentes)," in *Obras completas*, Madrid: Revista de Occidente-Alianza, 1962–1983, vol. 11, 501–9.
—— (1935) *Misión del bibliotecario*, in *Obras completas*, Madrid: Revista de Occidente-Alianza, 1962–83, vol. 5, 210–34.
—— (1937a) "Prólogo para franceses" [in *La rebelión de las masas*], in *Obras completas*, Madrid: Revista de Occidente-Alianza, 1962–83, vol. 4, 113–39.
—— (1937b) "Miseria y esplendor de la traducción," in *Obras completas*, Madrid: Revista de Occidente-Alianza, 1962–83, vol. 5, 431–52.
—— (1937c) *Invertebrate Spain*, trans. M. Adams, New York: Norton.
—— (1939a) "Meditación de la criolla," in *Obras completas*, Madrid: Revista de Occidente-Alianza, 1962–83, vol. 8, 411–46.
—— (1939b) "Prólogo a un diccionario enciclopédico abreviado," in *Obras completas*, Madrid: Revista de Occidente-Alianza, 1962–83, vol. 6, 358–67.
—— (1943) *Origen y epílogo de la filosofía*, in *Obras completas*, Madrid: Revista de Occidente-Alianza, 1962–83, vol. 9, 347–434.

—— (1946) "Comentario al *Banquete* de Platón," in *Obras completas*, Madrid: Revista de Occidente-Alianza, 1962–83, vol. 9, 751–84.

—— (1947) *La idea de principio en Leibniz y la evolución de la teoría deductiva*, in *Obras completas*, Madrid: Revista de Occidente-Alianza, 1962–83, vol. 8, 61–356.

—— (1948) *Una interpretación de la Historia universal: En torno a Toynbee*, in *Obras completas*, Madrid: Revista de Occidente-Alianza, 1962–83, vol. 9, 11–242.

—— (1949) "De Europa Meditatio Quaedam," in *Obras completas*, Madrid: Revista de Occidente-Alianza, 1962–83, vol. 9, 245–313.

—— (1950a) *El hombre y la gente*, in *Obras completas*, Madrid: Revista de Occidente-Alianza, 1962–83, vol. 7, 73–272.

—— (1950b) *Goya*, in *Obras completas*, Madrid: Revista de Occidente-Alianza, 1962–83, vol. 7, 505–73.

—— (1953a) "Anejo: En torno al 'Coloquio de Darmstadt, 1951,'" in *Obras completas*. Madrid: Revista de Occidente-Alianza, 1962–83, vol. 9, 625–44.

—— (1953b) "Individuo y organización," in *Obras completas*, Madrid: Revista de Occidente-Alianza, 1962–83, vol. 9, 677–90.

—— (1957) *Man and People*, trans. W. R. Trask, New York: Norton.

—— (1960) *What is Philosophy?*, trans. M. Adams, New York: Norton.

—— (1967) *The Origin of Philosophy*, trans. T. Talbot, New York: Norton.

—— (1991) *José Ortega y Gasset: cartas de un joven español*, edición y notas de Soledad Ortega, Madrid: El arquero.

—— (1998) *La rebelión de las masas*, edición, introducción y notas de T. Mermall, Madrid: Castalia.

Osthoff, H. and Brugmann, K. (1967) "Preface to *Morphologische Untersuchungen auf dem Gebiete der indogermanischen Sprachen*," in W. P. Lehmann (ed.), *A Reader in Nineteenth-Century Historical Indo-European Linguistics*, Bloomington, IN: Indiana University Press.

Otero, C. P. (1970) "Lingüística y literatura (A propósito de Unamuno y Ortega)," *Romance Philology* 24.2: 301–28.

Padilla, S. (1916) *Gramática histórico-crítica de la lengua española*, Nueva edición ampliada, Madrid: Saenz de Jubera.

Pascual Rodríguez, J.A. (1985) "Las ideas de Ortega sobre el lenguaje," in R. Senabre (ed.), *El escritor José Ortega y Gasset*, Cáceres: Universidad de Extremadura.

Payne, S.G. (1961) *Falange: A History of Spanish Fascism*, Stanford: Stanford University Press.

Pérez de Mendiola, M. (ed.) (1996) *Bridging the Atlantic*, Albany, NY: State University of New York Press.

Pérez Pascual, J.I. (1998) *Ramón Menéndez Pidal: ciencia y pasión*, Valladolid: Junta de Castilla y León, Consejería de Educación y Cultura.

Pérez Villanueva, J. (1991) *Ramón Menéndez Pidal*, Madrid: Espasa-Calpe.

Pike, F. B. (1971) *Hispanismo, 1898–1936*, Notre Dame and London: University of Notre Dame Press.

Pinker, S. (1995) *The Language Instinct*, New York: HarperPerennial.

Quijano, A. (1978) *Imperialismo, clases sociales y estado en el Perú, 1890–1930*, Lima: Mosca Azul Editores.

Rabanal, M. (1980) "Algo más sobre las ideas lingüísticas de Unamuno," *Senara: Revista de filoloxía* (Vigo, España) 2: 9–24.

Rama, A. (1982) *Transculturación narrativa en América Latina*, México: Siglo Veintiuno.

Rama, C. M. (1982) *Historia de las relaciones culturales entre España y la América Latina. Siglo XIX*, México: Fondo de Cultura Económica.
Ramos, J. (1993) "El don de la lengua," *Casa de las Américas* 34: 13–25.
Real Academia Española (1999) *Ortografía de la Lengua Española*, Madrid: Espasa.
Resina, J. R. (1996) "Hispanism and its discontents", *Siglo XX/20th Century* 14 (1–2): 85–135.
Riva Agüero, J. (1905) *Carácter de la literatura del Perú independiente*, in *Obras completas*, Lima: Pontífica Universidad Católica del Perú, 1962, vol. 1, 63–341.
Robins, P. H. (1990) *A Short History of Linguistics*, 3rd edn, London and New York: Longman.
Roig, M. (1978) *Retrats paral.lels 3*, Montserrat: Publicacions de l'Abadia de Montserrat.
Rosenblat, A. (1940) "Dos observaciones de Sarmiento sobre el seseo," *Revista de filología hispánica* (Buenos Aires) 2.1: 52–4.
—— (1958) *Ortega y Gasset: lengua y estilo*, Caracas: Universidad Central de Venezuela.
—— (1960) "Las generaciones argentinas del siglo XIX ante el problema de la lengua," *Revista de la Universidad de Buenos Aires*, Quinta época, 4.4: 539–84.
—— (1970) *El castellano de España y el castellano de América*, Madrid: Taurus.
—— (1981) "Las ideas ortográficas de Bello," "Prólogo" to A. Bello, *Estudios gramaticales*, in *Obras completas*, Caracas: La Casa de Bello, 1981, vol. 5.
Russell, B. (1972) *A History of Western Philosophy*, New York: Simon & Schuster.
Salas Lavaqui, M. (1876) "La gramática castellana en Chile hasta 1847," *Revista chilena* 4: 453–61.
Salazar Bondy, A. (1965) *Historia de las ideas en el Perú contemporáneo*, Lima: Francisco Moncloa.
Salcedo, E. (1964) *Vida de don Miguel*, Salamanca: Anaya.
Salvador, G. (1987) *Lengua española y lenguas de España*, Barcelona: Ariel.
Sarmiento, D. F. (1842a) *Análisis de las cartillas, silabarios i otros métodos de lectura conocidos i practicados en Chile*, Santiago de Chile: Imp. del Progreso.
—— (1842b) "La cuestión literaria," in J. Durán Cerda (ed.), *El movimiento literario de 1842*, Santiago de Chile: Editorial Universitaria, 1957, vol. 1, 301–4.
—— (1842c) "Ejercicios populares de la lengua castellana," in J. Durán Cerda (ed.), *El movimiento literario de 1842*, Santiago de Chile: Editorial Universitaria, 1957, vol. 1, 225–8.
—— (1842d) "¡Raro descubrimiento!" in J. Durán Cerda (ed.), *El movimiento literario de 1842*, Santiago de Chile: Editorial Universitaria, 1957, vol. 1, 305–7.
—— (1842e) "Segunda contestación a un quidam," in J. Durán Cerda (ed.), *El movimiento literario de 1842*, Santiago de Chile: Editorial Universitaria, 1957, vol. 1, 251–7.
—— (1842f) "Diálogo entre el editor y el escritor," in *Obras completas*, Santiago de Chile: Imprenta Gutenberg, 1885, vol. 1, 323–9.
—— (1843/4) "El Correo de Ultramar i el Observador de Ultramar," in *Obras completas*, Santiago de Chile: Imprenta Gutenberg, 1885, vol. 2, 102–6.
—— (1843a) "Contestación al 'Mercurio,'" in *Obras completas*, Buenos Aires: Luz del Día, 1949, vol. 4, 89–96.
—— (1843b) "Contestación a un profesor de gramática," in *Obras completas*, Buenos Aires: Luz del Día, 1949, vol. 4, 97–114.
—— (1843c) "Memoria sobre ortografía americana," in *Obras completas*, Buenos Aires: Luz del Día, 1949, vol. 4, 1–50.

—— (1843d) "Nueva contestación al 'Mercurio,'" in *Obras completas*, Buenos Aires: Luz del Día, 1949, vol. 4, 114–37.
—— (1843e) "Quinta carta al señor Minvielle," in *Obras completas*, Buenos Aires: Luz del Día, 1949, vol. 4, 71–5.
—— (1843f) "Segunda carta al señor Minvielle," *Obras completas*, Buenos Aires: Luz del Día, 1949, vol. 4, 59–63.
—— (1849) "Biblioteca de autores españoles, publicada por don Manuel Rivadeneyra," in *Obras completas*, Santiago de Chile: Imprenta Gutenberg, 1885, vol. 2, 331–3.
—— (1867) "Una crítica española," in *Obras completas*, Buenos Aires: Mariano Moreno, 1899, vol. 29, 316–25.
—— (1879) "Nuestros trigos," in *Obras completas*, Buenos Aires: Mariano Moreno, 1900, vol. 41, 136–41.
—— (1887) *Artículos críticos y literarios, 1841–1842*, Santiago de Chile: Imprenta Gutenberg.
—— (1899) *Ideas pedagógicas*, Buenos Aires: Mariano Moreno.
—— (1900) *Antonio Aberastain; Vida de Dominguito; Necrologías*, Buenos Aires: Mariano Moreno.
—— (1911) *Sarmiento–Mitre Correspondencia, 1846–1868*, Buenos Aires: Museo Mitre.
—— (1961) *Facundo*, Prólogo y notas del profesor Albert Palcos, Buenos Aires: Ediciones Culturales Argentinas, Ministerio de Educación y Justicia.
—— (1993) *Viajes por Europa, África i América, 1845–1847*, Edición crítica, Javier Fernández, Coordinador, Madrid: CSIC.
Schieffelin, B. B., Woolard, K. A. and Kroskrity, P. V. (eds) (1998) *Language Ideologies: Practice and Theory*, New York and Oxford: Oxford University Press.
Schiffman, H. F. (1996) *Linguistic Culture and Language Policy*, London and New York: Routledge.
Senabre, R. (1964) *Lengua y estilo de Ortega y Gasset*, Salamanca: Acta Salmanticensia.
Serrano, S. (1994) *Universidad y nación: Chile en el siglo XIX*, Santiago: Editorial Universitaria.
Serrano Poncela, S. (1964) *El pensamiento de Unamuno*, 2nd edn, México: Fondo de Cultura Económica.
Silvert, K. H. and Reissman, L. (1976) *Education, Class and Nation: The Experiences of Chile and Venezuela*, New York: Elsevier.
Smith, C. (1992) *Collins Spanish–English Dictionary (Unabridged)*, 3rd edn, New York: HarperCollins.
Solé i Sabaté, J. M. and Villarroya i Font, J. (1990) *L'Exèrcit i Catalunya. 1898–1936*, Barcelona: Edicions de l'Index.
—— (1994) *Cronologia de la repressió de la llengua i la cultura catalanes 1936–1975*, Barcelona: Curial.
Steiner, G. (1971) *Extraterritorial*, New York: Atheneum.
Stern, F. (1965) *The Politics of Cultural Despair: A Study in the Rise of the Germanic Ideology*, New York: Anchor.
Stewart, M. (1999) *The Spanish Language Today*, London and New York: Routledge.
Taylor, T. (1990) "Who's to be Master? The Institutionalization of Authority in the Science of Language," in J. J. Joseph and T. Taylor (eds), *Ideologies of Language*, London and New York: Routledge.
Tönnies, F. (1957) *Community and Society*, trans. C. P. Loomis, East Lansing, MI: Michigan State University Press.

Tuñón de Lara, M. (1980) *La España del siglo XIX*, vol. 2, Barcelona: Laia.
Unamuno, M. (1887) "Espíritu de la raza vasca," in *Obras completas*, Madrid: Escelicer, 1968, vol. 4, 153–74.
—— (1895) "La tradición eterna," in *Obras completas*, Madrid: Escelicer, 1966, vol. 1, 783–98.
—— (1896a) "La crisis del patriotismo," in *Obras completas*, Madrid: Escelicer, 1966, vol. 1, 978–84.
—— (1896b) "Sobre el uso de la lengua catalana," in *Obras completas*, Madrid: Escelicer, 1968, vol. 4, 503–6.
—— (1898) "La vida es sueño. Reflexiones sobre la generación de España," in *Obras completas*, Madrid: Escelicer, 1966, vol. 1, 940–6.
—— (1899a) "De la enseñanza superior en España," in *Obras completas*, Madrid: Escelicer, 1966, vol. 1, 735–72.
—— (1899b) "El pueblo que habla español," in *Obras completas*, Madrid: Escelicer, 1968, vol. 4, 571–3.
—— (1901a) "La reforma del castellano," in *Obras completas*, Madrid: Escelicer, 1966, vol. 1, 998–1003.
—— (1901b) "Sobre la lengua española," in *Obras completas*, Madrid: Escelicer, 1966, vol. 1, 1004–11.
—— (1901c) "Discurso en los Juegos Florales celebrados en Bilbao el día 26 de agosto de 1901," in *Obras completas*, Madrid: Escelicer, 1968, vol. 4, 237–48.
—— (1902a) "La educación. Prólogo a la obra de Bunge, del mismo título," in *Obras completas*, Madrid: Escelicer, 1966, vol. 1, 1012–23.
—— (1902b) "La cuestión del vascuence," in *Obras completas*, Madrid: Escelicer, 1966, vol. 1, 1043–62.
—— (1903a) "Contra el purismo," in *Obras completas*, Madrid: Escelicer, 1966, vol. 1, 1063–73.
—— (1903b) "Sobre el criollismo: A guisa de prólogo," in *Obras completas*, Madrid: Escelicer, 1968, vol. 4, 574–80.
—— (1905a) "Domingo Faustino Sarmiento," in *Obras completas*, Madrid: Escelicer, 1968, vol. 4, 903–6.
—— (1905b) "La crisis actual del patriotismo español," in *Obras completas*, Madrid: Escelicer, 1966, vol. 1, 1286–98.
—— (1906a) "Conferencia en la Sociedad de Ciencias de Málaga, el 23 de agosto de 1906," in *Obras completas*, Madrid: Escelicer, 1971, vol. 9, 204–11.
—— (1906b) "La enseñanza de la gramática," in *Obras completas*, Madrid: Escelicer, 1971, vol. 9, 151–64.
—— (1906c) "Sobre la europeización: Arbitrariedades," in *Obras completas*, Madrid: Escelicer, 1968, vol. 3, 925–38.
—— (1906d) "Sobre la literatura catalana," in *Obras completas*, Madrid: Escelicer, 1968, vol. 3, 1299–303.
—— (1906e) "Solidaridad española: Conferencia dada en el Teatro Novedades, de Barcelona, el 15 de octubre de 1906," in *Obras completas*, Madrid: Escelicer, 1971, vol. 9, 214–31.
—— (1907a) "La civilización es civismo," in *Obras completas*, Madrid: Escelicer, 1968, vol. 3, 303–7.
—— (1907b) "Por la cultura: Las campañas catalanistas," in *Obras completas*, Madrid: Escelicer, 1968, vol. 4, 521–5.

—— (1907c) "La Presidencia de la Academia Española," in *Obras completas*, Madrid: Escelicer, 1968, vol. 4, 369–73.
—— (1907d) "Contra los bárbaros," in *Obras completas*, Madrid: Escelicer, 1968, vol. 4, 513–5.
—— (1907e) "Por la cultura. Las campañas catalanistas," in *Obras completas*, Madrid: Escelicer, 1968, vol. 4, 521–5.
—— (1908a) "El idioma nacional," in *Obras completas*, Madrid: Escelicer, 1968, vol. 4, 584–9.
—— (1908b) "Más sobre el idioma nacional," in *Obras completas*, Madrid: Escelicer, 1968, vol. 4, 590–5.
—— (1908c) "Desde Portugal," in *Obras completas*, Madrid: Escelicer, 1966, vol. 1, 206–11.
—— (1908d) "Su Majestad la lengua española," in *Obras completas*, Madrid: Escelicer, 1968, vol. 4, 374–9.
—— (1909) "Excursión," in *Obras completas*, Madrid: Escelicer, 1966, vol. 1, 281–6.
—— (1910a) "El castellano, idioma universal," in *Obras completas*, Madrid: Escelicer, 1968, vol. 4, 386–91.
—— (1910b) "La sangre del espíritu," in *Obras completas*, Madrid: Escelicer, 1969, vol. 6, 375.
—— (1911a) "Lengua y patria: a propósito de la edición de una obra argentina," in *Obras completas*, Madrid: Escelicer, 1968, vol. 4, 596–9.
—— (1911b) "Sobre el imperialismo catalán," in *Obras completas*, Madrid: Escelicer, 1968, vol. 3, 1304–7.
—— (1911c) "Sobre un 'Diccionario argentino'," in *Obras completas*, Madrid: Escelicer, 1968, vol. 4, 600–5.
—— (1911d) "Lengua y patria," in *Obras completas*, Madrid: Escelicer, 1968, vol. 4, 596–9.
—— (1914a) "Español-Portugués," in *Obras completas*, Madrid: Escelicer, 1968, vol. 4, 526–9.
—— (1914b) "El inglés y el alemán," in *Obras completas*, Madrid: Escelicer, 1968, vol. 4, 530–5.
—— (1915) "Frente a los negrillos," in *Obras completas*, Madrid: Escelicer, 1966, vol. 1, 431–3.
—— (1916) "De Salamanca a Barcelona," in *Obras completas*, Madrid: Escelicer, 1966, vol. 1, 434–40.
—— (1917a) "De nuestra Academia otra vez," in *Obras completas*, Madrid: Escelicer, 1968, vol. 4, 423–6.
—— (1917b) "Vascuence, gallego y catalán," in *Obras completas*, Madrid: Escelicer, 1968, vol. 4, 546–9.
—— (1918) "Cosas de libros," in *Obras completas*, Madrid: Escelicer, 1968, vol. 4, 437–40.
—— (1920a) "Se presta al rico en defensa propia," in *Obras completas*, Madrid: Escelicer, 1966, vol. 8, 435–6.
—— (1920b) "Sobre el dialecto criollo argentino y otras cosas," in *Obras completas*, Madrid: Escelicer, 1968, vol. 4, 635–7.
—— (1923) "La España que permanece. Intermedio lírico," in *Obras completas*, Madrid: Escelicer, 1966, vol. 1, 637–9.
—— (1935) "Comunidad de la lengua hispánica," in *Obras completas*, Madrid: Escelicer, 1968, vol. 4, 651–6.

—— (1970) *Desde el mirador de la guerra (Colaboración al periódico La Nación de Buenos Aires*, Textos nuevos recogidos y presentados por Louis Urrutia, París: Centre de Recherches Hispaniques, Institut d'Études Hispaniques.

—— (1994) *Artículos en "La Nación" de Buenos Aires (1919–1924)*, Recopilación y estudio por Luis Urrutia Salaverri, Ediciones Universidad de Salamanca.

—— (1995) *San Manuel Bueno, Mártir*, ed. M. J. Valdés, Madrid: Cátedra.

—— (1996) *Epistolario americano (1890–1936)*, Edición, introducción y notas de Laureano Robles, Ediciones Universidad de Salamanca.

—— (1997) *De patriotismo espiritual: Artículos en "La Nación" de Buenos Aires, 1901–1914*, Edición y notas de Victor Ouimette, Ediciones Universidad de Salamanca.

—— (n. d.) "Más arabescos," in *Obras completas*, Madrid: Escelicer, 1967, vol. 7, 1374–7.

Urban, G. (1991) "The Semiotics of State-Indian Linguistic Relationships," in G. Urban and J. Sherzer (eds), *Nation-States and Indians in Latin America*, Austin: University of Texas Press.

Valcárcel, L. E. (1981) *Memorias*, Lima: Instituto de Estudios Peruanos.

Valera, J. (1862) "La poesía popular," in *Obras completas*, Madrid: Aguilar, 1958, vol. 3, 1050–64.

—— (1868) "Sobre el concepto que hoy se forma de España," in *Obras completas*, Madrid: Aguilar, 1958, vol. 3, 737–51.

—— (1869) "Sobre la ciencia del lenguage," in *Obras completas*, Madrid: Aguilar, 1958, vol. 3, 1096–115.

—— (1900) "Sobre la duración del habla castellana," in *Obras completas*, Madrid: Aguilar, 1961, vol. 2, 1036–40.

—— (1902) "Prólogo a Reminiscencias Tudescas," in *Obras completas*, Madrid: Aguilar, 1961, vol. 2, 1110–3.

—— (1902a) "Colaboración de "La Tribuna," *La Tribuna*, 31 August 1902, 1–2.

—— (1902b) "Colaboración de "La Tribuna," *La Tribuna*, 2 September 1902, 1–2.

—— (1905) "Gramática histórica," in *Obras completas*, Madrid: Aguilar, 1961, vol. 2, 1176–81.

—— (1958) *Obras completas*, vol. 3, Madrid: Aguilar.

—— (1961) *Obras completas*, vol. 2, Madrid: Aguilar.

Vallejo, C. (1978) *César Vallejo: The Complete Posthumous Poetry*, trans. C. Eshleman and J. R. Rubia Barcia, Berkeley and Los Angeles: University of California Press.

Varela, J. (1999) *La Novela de España*, Madrid: Taurus.

Vargas Llosa, M. (1981) "Arguedas, entre la ideología y la arcadia," *Revista Iberoamericana*, No. 116–17: 33–46.

Vasconcelos, J. (1927) "El nacionalismo en América Latina," *Amauta* 5: 22–4.

Velleman, B. (1987) "The Dynamics of a Literary Standard: The Bello *Gramática*," in G. Paolini (ed.), *La Chispa '87: Selected Proceedings*, New Orleans: Tulane University Press.

Verdevoye, P. (1981) "Don Andrés Bello y Domingo Faustino Sarmiento: Una polémica y una colaboración," in *Bello y Chile: Tercer Congreso del bicentenario*, Caracas: Fundación La Casa de Bello, 1981, vol. 2, 103–24.

Vilar, P. (1985) *Historia de España*, 20th edn, Barcelona: Grijalbo.

Zentella, A. C. (1997) *Growing up Bilingual*, Oxford: Blackwell.

Index

ABC 110
Abeille, Luciano: *Idioma nacional de los argentinos* 32, 72, 73, 97
Abellán, José Luis 81–2
Academia Literaria y Científica de Profesores de Instruccion Primaria 208
accentuation 49, 54
acceptance 7–8, 9, 200, 201
Alancoa, Quispe 181
Alberdi, Juan Bautista 14, 15, 29, 31, 74; 'Reacción contra el españolismo' 15
Alemany, José 69
alfonsí 4
Alfonso X, El Sabio 87
Almodóvar 197
Alvar, Manuel 195, 207–8
América, La 74
American Association of Teachers of Spanish 85
americanismos 67
anachronism 109
Ancien Régime 5
Andalucia 49, 55, 94
Anderson, Benedict 1
Andes 173, 175, 176, 178, 180, 181
anthropology 177
Arabic 68
Aragonese 33, 49
Arana, Sabino 110
Argentina 14, 29, 30
Arguedas, José María 97, 167–85, 194; *Agua* 181–2; 'Método para el caso lingüístico del indo' 174; 'Novela y la expresión literaria en el Perú' 181–5; *Yawar fiesta* 181–2
Aristotle 125
Arthur, King 211

Asociación de Academias de la Lengua Española 210
assimilationism 172–6
Asturias 210
authority 160–1
Aznar, José María 107

Baker 139
Baldauf, Richard 7
ballads 91–2
Banco Santiago 206
Baralt, Rafael M.: *Resumen de la historia de Venezuela* 57
Barcelona 109, 111, 123
Baroja, Pio: *Arbol de la ciencia* 134
Barrès, Maurice 115
Basadre, Jorge: *Multitud, la cuidad y el campo* 175, 176
Basque 5, 10, 68, 78, 110, 113, 114, 116, 117, 124, 127, 154, 202
Bauman, R. 140
Bello, Andrés ('Un Quidam') 9, 17, 19, 21, 22, 24, 25, 71, 75, 93, 94, 194; accentuation 49–50, 54; *Gramática* 32, 42–60; 'Gramática castellana' 57; Imperative 46; 'Indicaciones' 51–2; *Principios de la ortología y métrica* 51, 53, 55; Sarmiento and 28; textual models 56–60; writing and orality 51–6
Benedict, Ruth 177
Benigni 197
Bilbao 110
Bilbao, Francisco 18
Blanch, Juan M. Lope 195
Blommaert, J. 11
Board for the Expansion of Studies and Scientific Research 81
Bopp 68
Bourdieu, Pierre 81, 121

232 *Index*

Brazil 198–9, 210–11
Bréal 141
Briggs, C. L. 140
Brücke 26
Brugmann, Karl 83, 84, 141
Buenos Aires 35, 65, 120, 121
Bühler 141
Bulletin Hispanique 66, 67
Bunkley, A. W. 25

Cameron, Deborah: *Verbal Hygiene* 139, 140, 141, 161
cannibalism 114
capitalism 2, 3
Cardoso, Fernando Henrique 198–9, 210
Carlismo 5
castellana 18
castellanización 172, 173, 174, 176, 178, 180
Castilian 33, 34, 42, 50, 58, 59, 60, 87, 88, 94, 99, 107, 108, 109, 111, 112, 114, 116, 121, 123, 125, 126, 154
Castro, Américo 115
Catalan 5, 10, 33, 70, 78, 107, 108, 109, 110–11, 112, 116, 117, 118, 123, 124, 154, 155, 156, 158, 170, 202
Cavite 119, 120
Cejador y Frauca, Julio: *Cabos Sueltos* 74
Center for Historical Studies, Madrid 81, 110
Cervantes, Miguel de 18, 49, 57, 58, 87; *Don Quixote* 120, 122; *Trabajos* 120, 122
Chatterjee, Partha 179
Chávez, Ignacio 193, 194
Chile 15, 16, 23, 25, 45, 46, 47, 49, 52, 118, 168; Argentine exiles in 18; Banco Santiago 206; education 43; Instituto Nacional 18; Normal School 21
Chile, University of 18, 21, 22, 23–4
Chomsky, Noam 64
civitas 27
codification 7, 9, 95, 200, 201
Coll, José Luis 134
Commelerán 29
convergence 10
COPE 110
Corominas 159
Cristal, Billy 197
Cruz, Juan 197–8
Cuba 1, 123

Cuban War 111
Cuervo, Rufino José 9, 32, 33, 86, 97, 98, 204; *Apuntaciones* 72, 75, 96; 'Castellano en América' 66; pessimism 72; Valera and 64–75, 96
cultural elite 4
cultural empire 6–7
cultural unity 204–5; Spain and Latin America 206–7
Cúneo, D.: *Sarmiento y Unamuno* 26
Curtius 84

Darío, R. 35
Dartmouth College 203
Darwin, Charles 113, 121
del Valle, J. 10
democracy 3
Derrida, Jacques 107, 114; *Specters of Marx* 108
'Desastre', *see* Spanish–American War
dialectal divergence 25
Diario Moderno 111
Díaz Quiñones, Arcadio 209, 210
Díaz, Ramón: *Resumen de la historia de Venezuela* 57
Diccionario de la Real Academia de la Lengua 18, 47, 67, 159
Diccionario del español actual 200
Diez 26
disciplinary texts 3
dissent 96–8
diversity 42
Dobson, Andrew 153
doxa 156
Duvau, Louis 72

Echeverria, Esteban 14, 15, 74
education 43, 45–6
elaboration 7–8, 9, 95, 200, 201
elites 19, 92, 93, 94, 199–200
emythology, *see* etymology
English 23, 74, 108, 203, 204
epísteme 156
erasure 12, 70, 157
error 24, 29, 200
eruditos 30
Escobar, Alberto 180
Escorial 123
Escorial, El 200
Eskamotage 107, 108, 116, 117
España Moderna, La 119
Espasa-Calpe 85
Espinosa, Aurelio 85

etymology 159–60
Euskera 110, 116

Falange Española 107, 121, 122, 124, 125
fascism 122–3, 126
Feijoo, Benito Jerónimo 57
Fell, Eve Maria 172
Ferdinand VII 1
Fernández de Moratín, Leandro 57
Fernández Garfias, Pedro: *Ejercicios populares de lengua* 18
Fiddian, R. W. 35
focalization 10
Fogelquist, Donald F. 73
folk songs 91–2
fragmentation 9, 23, 25, 31–4, 42, 65, 66, 71, 72, 73, 75, 80, 81, 82, 89–90, 92, 98, 167, 194
Franco, Francisco 107, 109, 110
Franks 151
French 14, 17, 23, 26, 57–8, 70, 74, 203
French Revolution 32
functionalism 177
Fundación Principe de Asturias 210

Gaceta del Comercio, La 22
Gal, S. 12, 70, 157
Galdós, Pérez Benito 29
Galician 5, 10, 33, 70, 78, 117, 202
Garcia de Cortázar, F. 4–5
García de la Concha, Victor 194, 195, 199–200, 201, 203, 205, 211
García del Pozo, 54
García del Río, J. 21, 22
García Márquez, Gabriel 202, 208, 210
García–Durán, Manuel 207
Garcilaso 123
Garrido, Antonio 203
Gasco, Carlos 207
Gates, Bill 196
Gauchat 84
Gemeinschaft 119
Generation of 1837 14–18, 32
Generation of 1898 107, 108, 110, 127
geography 153–6
German 74
Gesellschaft 119
Giménez Caballero, Ernesto 124, 126
globalization 98
González Prada, Manuel 97, 169–70, 171, 172, 174

González Stephan, B. 3
González Vesga 4–5
Gramática descriptiva de la lengua española 200
Gramsci, A. 168
Granada, Fray Luis de 57
grandeur of Spanish 195–9
Grijelmo, Alex 203, 204; *Defensa apasionada del idioma español* 199
Grimm 68
Guaman Poma de Avala, Felipe 180, 181
Guarani 118
Güiraldes: *Don Segundo Sombra* 182
Guitarte, G. L. 33, 34
Gutiérrez, Juan Maria 14, 15, 74, 97

Hacker 139
Hamsun, Knut 115
Harris, R. 139
Hartman, Geoffrey 119–20
Hegel, G. W. F. 34, 128
hegemony 6, 12, 81–2, 108, 125
Heidegger, Martin 146, 158
Henriquez Ureña, Pedro 168, 171
Herder, J. G. 15, 26, 32
Hermosilla 20
heterogeneity 84
Hispania 85
hispanidad 68, 114
hispanismo 6, 7, 9, 70, 194
hispanoamericanismo 6, 74
Hobsbawm, E. J. 2, 7, 199
Homer: *Odyssey* 120
homogeneity 7, 10–11, 12, 42, 43, 46, 89, 142–3, 145, 194
Hronzn 141
Humboldt, Wilhelm von 24, 26, 28, 64, 68, 69, 141, 145; *enérgeia/érgon* 143

Ibero-American congresses 74
iconization 12, 157
identity, Spanish 106–28
Ilustración Española y Americana, La 6
Ilustración Ibérica, La 6
imagined community 1
independence movements 1
Indo-European 68
industrialization 5
Inquisition 1, 5, 16, 18
Instituto Cervantes 196, 197, 198, 203, 207, 211
Internet 196, 199, 207

Irvine, J. T. 12, 70, 157
Isabella of Castile 4
Italy 74

Jaksić, I. 18
Jiménez Ilundain, Pedro 35
José, Antonio 124, 125
Juan Carlos, King 211
Juntas Castellanas de Actuación Hispánica 124

Kaplan, Robert 7
Katra, W. 15
Klappenbach, Agustin 26
Krauss, Werner 123, 125
Kristeva, Julia 86
Kulturkampf 113

Langbehn, Julius 115
language: battle 9, 12, 80–1, 198; fragility 199–200; ideologies 11; laws of 91–3; linguistic culture 10; linguistic elite 19, 92, 93, 94, 199–200; linguistic reasoning 11–13, 140–7; mavens 137, 141; national 2, 7–8; planning 7–8, 43; pyramid 200–4; regeneration 30–1; shamans 137; society and 27–8, 30–1; *see also* linguistics
Lapesa, Rafael 141, 195
Larra, Mariano José de 17, 27, 32
Latin 32, 33, 42, 65, 66, 83, 87, 98, 142–3, 145, 148, 152, 157
Latin American Language Academy 204
Lázaro Carreter, Fernando 115, 137, 195, 199; *Dardo en la palabra* 200
Lebensraum 121
legitimacy 11–13
Leipzig 141
León, Fray Luis de 57
Leonese 33
Lerch 141, 147, 148
Levy-Bruhl 175, 176
liberalism 1
linguistics: development of 12, 82
List, Friedrich 2
loanwords 31, 203, 204
Lodares, J. R. 194
Lope de Vega 57, 58
López, Vicente Fidel 15, 35
López García, Angel 195
Lunes de El Imparcial, Los 65

Madrid 17, 66, 93, 204, 206, 208; Center for Historical Studies 81, 110; Pardo 126; School of Philology 75; University 78, 81
Mannheim, B. 172
Maragall, Joan 124
Mariátegui, José Carlos 170–1; *Siete Ensayos* 171
Martín Fierro 33
Martín, Francisco José 130
Martin, Ricky 198
Martínez, Fernando Antonio 72, 73
Martínez de la Rosa, Francisco 57
Marx, Karl 107, 170
Mateo Pumaccahua school, Sicuani 172, 178, 181
Maurras, Charles 115
Meillet 141, 145
Menéndez Pidal, Ramón 26, 35, 69, 70, 72, 73, 75, 78–100, 142, 152, 194, 195; academic texts 86–8; Academy 29; *Castilla* 85; 'Lengua española' 85; *Manual de gramática histórica española* 64, 82–3, 85, 87; *Orígenes del español* 83–5, 88, 141; popular/vulgar 90; popularizing texts 89–91; *Unidad del idioma* 85, 89; 'we' 93
Mercurio, El 18, 19, 23, 24
Mercurio de Valparaiso, El 23
Mermall, Thomas 156, 157
mestizaje 168, 176, 179, 180, 181, 183
metaphor 144, 148
Mexico 29, 67, 174
Microsoft 196
migrations 3
Milroy, James and Leslie 137
Minvielle, Rafael 22, 23
mission civilisatrice 18
Mitre, President 16
modernity of Spanish language 98–100
Molina, Tirso de 57
Mommsen, Theodor 153
monarchy 210–11
monoglossic culture 10–11, 193, 194, 201
Montevideo 15
Montt, Manuel 21
Morales, Leónides 183–4
Müller 26
multilingualism 10

Nación, La 35, 121
nacionalización 154–5

Napoleon 1
National Movement 107
nationalism 1–4, 4–6, 12, 78, 179, 194
Navarro, Maurín 26
neologisms 30, 31
New York City 10
New York Times, The 137
Ninyoles, Rafael 110
Nugent, José Guillermo 171

Observador de Ultramar, El 16
Ollantay 184
Ong, Walter 184–5
Onis, Federico de 79
orality 51–6
Ortega y Gasset, José 124, 134–61, 194, 195, 211; emythology 159–60; *epísteme/doxa* 156; *España invertebrada* 150, 152, 153; *Hombre y la gente* 143, 144; language maven 134–7; metaphor 144, 148; *Rebelión de las masas* 149, 150, 151; *Redencion de las provincias* 155; speak/say 144, 146, 147, 148, 157; 'we' 147
orthographic reform 20–4
Ortiz, Fernando 179
Ortográfia de la lengua española 51, 200, 202, 204, 205, 208
Osthoff, Hermann 83, 84
Oviedo 210

Padilla, Salvador 69
Pais, El 134, 193–211 passim
Palma, Ricardo 9, 80, 98, 204
panhispanismo 6
Paraguay 118
Pastor, Beatriz 203
Paul, Hermann 26, 141
Pellegrini, Carlos 33
Pérez Triana, Santiago: *Reminiscencias Tudescas* 67
Peru 29, 118, 167–8, 194; census (1940) 176; Consejo Nacional de Educación 174; Indians 170; Ministry of Education 174; Quechua 118, 167–85, 194; Reforma de los Planes de Educación Secundaria 174; Spanish 176–9, 180–5; unification 168–72
phonetics 84
Pinker, Steven 137, 138, 139
Poema del Cid 57, 87
Polanco, Jesús de 206, 207

Popular Party 107
press 31
Primer Congreso Internacional de la Lengua Española 201
Primo de Rivera, José Antonio 27, 124
Princeton University 209, 210
Principe de Asturias 210, 211
PRISA 206
Progreso, El 22, 23, 24
Provençal 170
Puerto Rico 1, 209, 210
Puigblanch 96

quality and quantity 12
Quechua 118, 167–85, 194
Querol, Vicente Wenceslao 117
'Quidam, Un', *see* Bello, Andrés

Rajoy, Mariano 205
Rama, Carlos 9
Real Academia Española, *see* Spanish Royal Academy
Reconquest 33
Redondo, Onésimo 124
regeneration 30–1
regionalismos 65
religious intolerance 5
Renan, Ernest 68, 154
Resina, Joan Ramon 69
Restoration 107
Revista Española de Ambos Mundos, La 6, 74
rhetoric 156–60
Ridruejo, Dionisio 109
Riva, Agüero, José de la: *Carácter de la literatura del Perú independiente* 169–71
Rivadeneyra, Manuel 18; *Biblioteca de autores españoles* 17
Rodríguez, Lafuente, Fernando 196, 197, 206, 207
Rodríguez Pinilla, Cándido 25
Rojas, Ricardo 34–5
Roman Empire 145, 148, 153, 157, 167
Romance languages 32, 87, 152, 157, 167
Rosas, Juan Manuel de 15, 27
Rosenblat, Angel 15–16, 204
Rousselot 84
Russell, Bertrand 12

Safire, William 137
Saint–Simon 15
Salamanca 66, 110

236 Index

Salvador, Gregorio 195, 202–3
San Manuel 115
Santa Teresa 57
Santiago 15, 16, 22, 119, 120
Santiago de Cuba 120, 122, 123
Santos Tornero 23
Sarmiento, Domingo Faustino 9, 14–18, 64, 74, 80, 86, 96, 97, 141, 175, 194; Academy 18–20, 28–9; *Análisis* 21; autodidact 26; Bello and 28; Chile 21; conception of the norm 24–5; 'Diálogo entre el editor y el escritor' 18; error 24, 29; Europe and USA 36; *Facundo* 16, 25; 'Memoria' 21, 22, 23, 24; orthographic reform 20–4; Unamuno and 25–7, 28–9; *Viajes* 35
saying and speaking 144, 146, 147, 148, 157
Schiffman, Harold: *Linguistic Culture and Language Policy* 10
Schleicher 64
Schuchardt 84
secessionism 5
Seco, Manuel 200
selection 7, 9, 43–4, 93–5, 200, 201; criteria 44–60; dialectal 47–51; discourse 51–60; semiotic 51–60; socio-cultural 44–6
Semitic 68
Sicuani: Mateo Pumaccahua school 172, 178, 181
Sievers 26, 141
skeptron 82–5, 95
slaves 16
social dimension 147–50
socialism 15
society 150–3
Sociology of Language 43–4
Sol, El 120–1
Solidaritat Catalana 123, 124
Soto y Calvo, Francisco: *Nastasio* 65, 75
Soviet Union 116
Spanglish 203
Spanish Academy of History 81
Spanish Academy of Language 204, 211
Spanish Academy of Natural Science 29
Spanish Association of Book Publishers 85
Spanish Civil War 109, 111, 122, 144
Spanish Royal Academy 18–20, 22, 28–9, 35–6, 81, 167, 196, 199, 200, 202, 204, 205, 207, 208, 209, 211; created (1713) 4; *Diccionario* 18, 47, 67, 159; *Ortográfia* 51, 200, 202, 204, 205, 208
Spanish–American War 5–6, 78, 122, 123, 128
speaking and saying 144, 146, 147, 148, 157
Spencer, Herbert 34
'standard' Spanish 167–8
standardization 7, 200, 201, 204
Steinthal 68
Swadesh, Mauricio 174

Tarradell, Miquel 109–10
Taylor, Talbot 139
Telefónica 196, 206
Telefónica Media 207
Tetuan 4
Third Reich 116
threshold principle 2, 4
Toisón 211
Toledo 47–8
Tönnies, Ferdinand 119
transculturation 176–9, 185
translation 180–5
Tribuna, La 67
tripthongs 49, 50
Trubetzkov 141
turn-of-the-century crisis 78–9

uchronism 109
Unamuno, Miguel de 106–28, 194, 195; Academy 28–9; Hispanic Gospel 115; Latin America 34–5; *Rosario de sonetos líricos* 27; *San Manuel Bueno, mártir* 114; Sarmiento and 25–7 28–9; 'Su majestad la lengua española' 111; 'Vida es sueño' 119
Unión Ibero-Americana 74
unitarios 5
United States of America 7, 74; Spanish in 197, 198, 199, 203; Spanish–American War 5–6, 78, 122, 123, 128; War of Independence 32
unity and uniformity 42–3, 68, 69, 86–8, 89–91, 194, 204
universality of Spanish 195–9, 202
Uruguay 15
utopia of language 180–5

Valencian 33, 108, 118
Valera, Juan 9, 32, 86, 92, 97, 194;
    Cuervo and 64–75, 96; 'Sobre la
    duración del habla castellana' 65
Valladolid 47–8
Vallejo, César 180–1
Varela, Florencio 31–2, 75
Velleman, Barry 80
Vendryès 141
Venezuela 49
Verdevoye, P. 17
Verschueren, J. 11
Veu de Catalunya, La 115

Vilar, Pierre 5
Visigoths 151, 152
Volksgeist 7

War of the Pacific 168
Washington Post, The 206, 207
'we' 93–5, 147
Whitney 26
Wilkins, Lawrence 85
World Wide Web 198, 202
writing and orality 51–6

Zentella, Ana Celia 10

For Product Safety Concerns and Information please contact our EU representative GPSR@taylorandfrancis.com
Taylor & Francis Verlag GmbH, Kaufingerstraße 24, 80331 München, Germany

www.ingramcontent.com/pod-product-compliance
Lightning Source LLC
Chambersburg PA
CBHW070600300426
44113CB00010B/1337